Manchester
www.alkauthar.org
Enriching Lives Through Knowledge

Getting the Best
out of
Al-Hajj
(Pilgrimage)

Second Edition: August 2006

Supervised by:
ABDUL MALIK MUJAHID

© **Maktaba Dar-us-Salam, 2006**
King Fahd National Library Cataloging-in-Publication Data
Davids Ismail
     Getting the best out of Haj./Ismail Davis , - Riyadh, 2006
440p; 21cm
ISBN: 9960-9803-0-8
     1- Al-Hajj   I- Title
     252.5 dc   **1427/4241**
      L.D. no. 1427/4241
      ISBN: 9960-9803-0-8

In the Name of Allah,
the Most Gracious, the Most Merciful.

Getting the Best
out of Hajj

Second Edition

By: Abu Muneer Ismail Davids

DARUSSALAM
GLOBAL LEADER IN ISLAMIC BOOKS
Riyadh, Jeddah, Sharjah, Lahore
London, Houston, New York, Sydney

HEAD OFFICE

P.O. Box: 22743, Riyadh 11416 K.S.A.Tel: 0096 -1-4033962/4043432 Fax: 4021659
E-mail:darussalam@awalnet.net.sa, riyadh@dar-us-salam.com, Website: www.dar-us-salam.com

K.S.A. Darussalam Showrooms:
- **Riyadh**
Olaya branch: Tel 00966-1-4614483 Fax: 4644945
Malaz branch: Tel 00966-1-4735220 Fax: 4735221
- **Jeddah**
Tel: 00966-2-6879254 Fax: 6336270
- **Madinah**
Tel: 00966-503417155 Fax: 04-8151121
- **Al-Khobar**
Tel: 00966-3-8692900 Fax: 8691551
- **Khamis Mushayt**
Tel & Fax: 00966-072207055

U.A.E
- **Darussalam, Sharjah U.A.E**
Tel: 00971-6-5632623 Fax: 5632624
Sharjah@dar-us-salam.com.

PAKISTAN
- **Darussalam, 36 B Lower Mall, Lahore**
Tel: 0092-42-724 0024 Fax: 7354072
- **Rahman Market, Ghazni Street,**Urdu Bazar Lahore
Tel: 0092-42-7120054 Fax: 7320703
- **Karachi,** Tel: 0092-21-4393936 Fax: 4393937
- **Islamabad,** Tel: 0092-51-2500237

U.S.A
- **Darussalam, Houston**
P.O Box: 79194 Tx 77279
Tel: 001-713-722 0419 Fax: 001-713-722 0431
E-mail: houston @dar-us-salam.com
- **Darussalam, New York** 481 Atlantic Ave, Brooklyn
New York-11217, Tel: 001-718-625 5925
Fax: 718-625 1511
E-mail: newyork@dar-us-salam.com.

U.K
- **Darussalam International Publications Ltd.**
Leyton Business Centre
Unit-17, Etloe Road, Leyton, London, E10 7BT
Tel: 0044 20 8539 4885 Fax:0044 20 8539 4889
Website: www.darussalam.com
Email: info@darussalam.com
- **Darussalam International Publications Limited**
Regents Park Mosque, 146 Park Road
London NW8 7RG Tel: 0044- 207 725 2246

AUSTRALIA
- **Darussalam:** 153, Haldon St, Lakemba (Sydney)
NSW 2195, Australia
Tel: 0061-2-97407188 Fax: 0061-2-97407199
Mobile: 0061-414580813 Res: 0061-2-97580190
Email: abumuaaz@hotmail.com

CANADA
- Islmic Books Service
2200 South Sheridan way Mississauga,
Ontario Canada L5K 2C8
Tel: 001-905-403-8406 Ext. 218 Fax: 905-8409

HONG KONG
- **Peacetech**
A2, 4/F Tsim Sha Mansion
83-87 Nathan Road Tsimbatsui
Kowloon, Hong Kong
Tel: 00852 2369 2722 Fax: 00852-23692944
Mobile: 00852 97123624

MALAYSIA
- **Darussalam International Publication Ltd.**
No.109A, Jalan SS 21/1A, Damansara Utama,
47400, Petaling Jaya, Selangor, Darul Ehsan, Malaysia
Tel: 00603 7710 9750 Fax: 7710 0749
E-mail: darussalm@streamyx.com

FRANCE
- **Editions & Librairie Essalam**
135, Bd de Ménilmontant- 75011 Paris
Tél: 0033-01- 43 38 19 56/ 44 83
Fax: 0033-01-43 57 44 31 E-mail: essalam@essalam com-

SINGAPORE
- Muslim Converts Association of Singapore
32 Onan Road The Galaxy
Singapore- 424484
Tel: 0065-440 6924, 348 8344 Fax: 440 6724

SRI LANKA
- Darul Kitab 6, Nimal Road, Colombo-4
Tel: 0094 115 358712 Fax: 115-358713

INDIA
- Islamic Books International Mumbai-India
54 Tandel Street (North)
Dongri, Mumbai 4000 009, India
Tel: 0091-22-23 73 68 75, Fax:23 73 0689
E-mail:sales@irf.net

SOUTH AFRICA
- Islamic Da`wah Movement (IDM)
48009 Qualbert 4078 Durban, South Africa
Tel: 0027-31-304-6883 Fax: 0027-31-305-1292
E-mail: idm@ion.co.za

"And proclaim to mankind

Al-Hajj
(Pilgrimage)

*They will come to you on foot
and on every lean camel,
they will come from every deep and
distant (wide) mountain highway
(to perform Hajj).*

*That they may witness things
that are of benefit to them..."*
Surah Al-Hajj (22:27, 28)

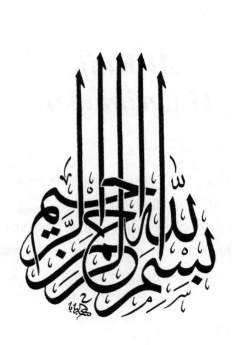

About the Author

Abu Muneer Ismail Davids is and active *Da'ee* (spreader of the faith), conducting classes and giving lectures on various subjects to Muslims and non-Muslims alike. Needless to say that his favourite subject is *Hajj*.

Since performing his *Fard Hajj* in 1989, he has developed a deep desire to share his experiences and knowledge with the "Guests of Allah", in any way he can. In 1990 Allah blessed him with the opportunity to work in Jeddah, Saudi Arabia, where he resided for fifteen years. This great opportunity opened the door for him to enrich his knowledge about all aspects of *Hajj* from the Qur'an and *Sunnah* point of view. Coupled with this he was able to be close to the pilgrims, year after year, to learn about their experiences. All of this allowed him to give the reader a unique account and invaluable advice on all aspects of *Hajj*.

I have reviewed the book and found it to be a serious attempt form and honest and serious *Da'ee*. Through this work he has provided a good and plentiful source of information that helps the pilgrim to do the *Hajj* rites and rituals, from all sides and aspects in a correct way that is solid and established in the Qur'an and *Sunnah*. It fulfils the needs of this everlasting excursion in modern times. It does this in a captivating way with many original ideas. It has enjoyable diversity that attracts the reader to the peaceful cities of Makkah and Madinah especially those from outside the Arabian Peninsula. More importantly, it provides authenticated proof for all *Fiqh* related issues.

We ask Allah (High and Mighty) to reward the author well, give him his due reward and make this book a reserve for him. May Allah benefit all Muslims from this effort and reward everybody who contributed to it. May Allah accept from all pilgrims and visitors to the holy cities, and forgive them and us all. *Aameen.* We pray on the Prophet (ﷺ).

Said Suleiman Al-Mizyen
(Bachelors Degree in Islamic Studies)
Deputy *Imam* and *Khateeb*
Sharbatli Mosque, Jeddah
Saudi Arabia

Chapters at a Glance

Foreword to Second Edition

Praise be to Allah, Lord of the Universe. May peace and blessings be upon Prophet Muhammad, the last of the Prophets and Messengers, and upon his family and esteemed Companions.

Allah, Your help we seek, Your forgiveness we ask, and we seek Your refuge from the evil of our own selves and from our sinful deeds. Whosoever Allah guides, there is none to misguide him. And whosoever He leaves astray, none can guide him. I bear witness that there is no god worthy of worship besides Allah, and I bear witness that Muhammad is His servant and Messenger.

Since the publishing of the first edition in 2000, it has been extremely rewarding and satisfying for me to see how useful and helpful the book has been for the pilgrims. My highest expectations were surpassed. During the last six years, I have experienced so many overwhelming and uplifting moments while delivering *Hajj* lectures and during the actual *Hajj,* when I would come across a pilgrim with the book, where pieces of paper are sticking out from various pages, highlighting of paragraphs, and how protective they would be over the book. So many pilgrims mentioned to me that they have used the book as their complete reference and have guided others with it. They even knew their 'way around the book' better than me. *Alhamdulillah,* I pray that my intentions remain sincere and that all the benefits are written for us all in our book of good deeds, *Aameen*!

Since moving from Saudi Arabia back to Australia in January 2005 (Dhul-Hijjah 1425), I was again blessed with the opportunity to continue being involved in *Hajj* as well as teaching and advising prospective pilgrims, *Alhamdulillah.* Hence, in January 2006 (*Hajj* 1426), I was back 'at home' in Makkah as a guide for a group of Australian pilgrims. This provided me with the golden opportunity to compare my experiences from 1989, arriving as a pilgrim from outside and returning 17 years later. Arriving at the *Hajj* terminal I was anxious to see how and if the processing had improved, but to my dismay, it was no better than in 1989. Fortunately I have learnt to be more patient and now had many years of experience under my belt. So my fellow pilgrims, without a doubt the infrastructure in Mina, Makkah and Madinah, have markedly been improved, but sadly the processing and movement of the pilgrims were still the same. So please 'buy' an extra large bag of patience.

In the first edition, I mentioned that going to Aziziah was not such a good idea, but I have since changed my mind. During the *Hajj* of 2006 (1426), we moved to Aziziah on the 7th of Dhul-Hijjah and used this as our base during and after *Hajj*. I was sceptical in the beginning, but in all honesty I can now vouch that it is one of the best logistical moves for any group, as it provides such easy access to Mina. We were able to walk to and from Mina with ease. We stationed some of the really sick and elderly pilgrims there after stoning the *Jamr'at* and on the 12th and 13th we were able to walk back to Aziziah after stoning and avoiding the long delays in the traffic. In addition departing for the airport was also much easier. So I am 'converted' to the Aziziah concept.

As with so many previous years, in 2006 (1426) there was once again an unfortunate stampede at the *Jamr'at*, and many pilgrims died. As usual the pilgrims' behaviour was to be blamed. Whatever the cause, please heed my suggestions about the *Jamr'at* in chapter 8. Don't enter the bridge if it is overcrowded and don't push. Also don't be in a hurry to get back to Makkah, and don't go at *Zawaal* time on the 12th. Each year the authorities grapple as to what to do about the *Jamr'at*. In 2005 they built new wall shaped *Jamr'at*, which worked wonders, and it did help the stoning, but the problem is still the crowd on their way to the *Jamr'at*. Many proposals including a multi-level bridge have been planned. So whatever picture we publish for the *Jamr'at* could be obsolete in no time, as each year something different comes up. My view and experience is that if the bridge itself is policed properly, these stampedes can possibly be avoided.

My reasoning for this is that after every stampede they apply strict policing (using thousands of army personnel) on and off the bridge (breaking up big crowds, making sure no one pushes, helping older pilgrims, protecting families, etc.), and there is never a repeat stampede in the same year....why? Because this is how it will work best. Maybe one day the authorities will decide to apply these tactics from the beginning of *Hajj* until the completion.

It also became apparent that many pilgrims needed to keep with them certain sections of the book, so with this in mind, and with the Mercy and Blessings of Allah, we published the following pocket guides:

1. Hajj Pocket Guide (fold-out card)

2. Hajj Pocket Guide (32 page)

3. Umrah Pocket Guide (32 page)

4. The demand for chapter 11 (supplications) resulted in a supplication pocket guide, to be published with this second edition, Allah Willing!

With the Blessings of Allah and due to the success and widespread use of the book, meant requests to give lectures and presentations on *Hajj* in various parts of the world and also in Makkah and Mina itself. This opened yet another avenue for me to assist the 'Guests of Allah'. I ask of you, as I ask during my lectures, when pilgrims ask me what they can do for me in return: "Please make *Dua'* for me (by name), my parents, my family, and for all the Muslims when you are on Arafat".

Many people have suggested I get someone famous to write an introduction to the second edition. I have always been reluctant to do that, even with the first edition. To me the most famous and important person is the actual pilgrim. So this is what some of them had to say:

- *Alhamdulillah* your book was very beneficial for *Hajj*, thank you.

- My parents love the book and are trying to get everyone

visiting us to buy one.

- I am feeling quite anxious I have to confess! *Alhamdulillah* your book has been very helpful (my dad is trying to frantically finish reading it but my mum keeps snatching it from him!)

- I'd like to reinforce how helpful the book was and so accurate too. We remembered you in Arafat as promised!

- Anyway, I wanted to thank you for your time on Saturday. What you had to say was invaluable and the way you said it was terrific.

- Once I started reading the book, I could not put it down until I completed it.

- May I thank you on behalf of my wife and myself for giving such a useful and absorbing lecture in London on Saturday.

- We are now reading through your book. Perhaps we should have bought one copy each!

- We cannot thank you enough.

- The book is so easy to read, down to earth and so informative.

- She says to thank you and that you made her *Hajj* much more easy and understanding and memorable.

The first edition was published in full colour with extremely good quality paper, which made its presentation excellent. However it had two drawbacks, one, it was very heavy and two it was quite expensive. Even with this, the first edition sold out, *Alhamdulillah*. With this second edition (revised), I hope it is more affordable and I sincerely hope that it will continue to be of a benefit to the "Guests of Allah".

Abu Muneer Ismail Davids
27 Jumada At-Thani 1427 (23 July 2006)
Sydney, Australia.

Acknowledgments

First and foremost I thank The Almighty Allah for having granted me the health, strength, and time to complete this second edition. Without the Mercy and Blessings of our Sustainer we can achieve nothing.

With a project of this size there are always many people that contribute in various degrees. In the first edition I listed everyone, as their help was a great source of inspiration for me to complete the original work. As with this edition and any subsequent editions I am still indebted to them for their help. The inspiration and need for the second and revised edition is due to the enormous demand for the material. Hence I would like to express my deepest appreciation and thanks to Message of Islam publishing in London who made the first publication and subsequent lectures a reality. Also Darul-Khair publishing in Jeddah who made the pocket guides a reality. Then there are all the brothers and sisters who helped 'advertise', sell and distribute the book as well as those *Hajj* agents who chose to include the book in their *Hajj* packages. Special thanks to my dearest mother and beloved wife for being such great believers and sales ladies for the book, as I was 'useless' with sales, giving away copies most of the time. May Allah bless all of them and write it for them in their book of deeds.

As with the first edition, a very special thanks to Imam Ahmed Al-Jehani, Imam Said Al-Mizyen and Imam Wajdi Hamza Al-Ghazzawi who have been my main sources of reference and instrumental in providing me with the teachings of *Hajj*, according to the Qur'an and *Sunnah*. I am also very grateful for them for having found the time in their busy schedule to review the book and for their research and patience with regards to my continuous questions on *Hajj* and other *Fiqh* related issues.

May Allah grant them all the best rewards in this life and in the Hereafter.

If by chance I failed to thank someone who contributed to this project, please forgive me.

May Allah reward all those who have contributed, directly or indirectly, in all these projects.

Aameen!

Preface of First Edition

Praise be to Allah, Lord of the Universe. May peace and blessings be upon Prophet Muhammad, the last of the Prophets and Messengers, and upon his family and esteemed Companions.

Allah, Your help we seek, Your forgiveness we ask, and we seek Your refuge from the evil of our own selves and from our sinful deeds. Whosoever Allah guides, there is none to misguide him. And whosoever He leaves astray, none can guide him. I bear witness that there is no god worthy of worship besides Allah, and I bear witness that Muhammad is His servant and Messenger.

There are so many books on the subject of *Hajj* in the English language. You may ask, why another one? Well, I have not come across any book on this subject that covers the material, either in content or style, as I have done in this book. This book is a culmination of personal experiences, notes taken over the last twelve years (second edition – seventeen years), research from more than fifteen different books on *Hajj* and various other books about *Salah* and about Islamic behaviour. This book is unique in the sense that it brings together the realities of *Hajj*, as it is today, personal experiences coupled with the related *Fiqh* rulings.

When I started this project, I envisaged that I could put it all together in about six months and have it ready for the *Hajj* of 1415 (1995). Well, here I am almost six years later completing the final layout, *Alhamdulillah*. The project certainly was much larger than I originally envisaged, but I am sure you will agree with me that it was worth the time and effort.

I wanted to maintain a "down to earth" approach to the book, so you may find the style of writing informal and "chatty" in some places.

The wonderful journey of *Hajj* demonstrates the real and

practical unity and brotherhood of the Muslims. People of different languages, colours, levels of society, rich and poor, all meet in one place for one purpose. There is no other event in this entire world that can or will ever match it!

If you have taken the decision to fulfil this obligation you owe unto Allah, then I sincerely hope that this work will assist in making your journey a more pleasant and rewarding one.

﴿فَإِذَا عَزَمْتَ فَتَوَكَّلْ عَلَى اللَّهِ إِنَّ اللَّهَ يُحِبُّ الْمُتَوَكِّلِينَ﴾

"...Then, when you have taken a decision, put your trust in Allah. For Allah loves those who put their trust (in Him)."

Surah Al-Imran (3:159)

Over the course of the last year, I have also embarked on writing an *Umrah* only version of the book. I believe there is a strong need for this, as almost all books on this subject deal with *Hajj* and *Umrah* together. *In Sha Allah*, it will be published soon. (*Published 2006*)

I ask Allah's forgiveness for my own shortcomings and any mistakes I may have made in writing this book. All praise is due to Allah, our Creator and Sustainer, Lord of the Worlds.

Abu Muneer Ismail Davids
Friday, 9th Muharram 1421 (14th April 2000)
Jeddah, Saudi Arabia.

Introduction

The *Hajj* Guide and How to Use it

Preview

- About this Book
- How to use this Book
- Objectives of this Book
- Organisation of Sections
- Organisation of Chapters
- Diagrams and Pictures
- *Hajj* according to Qur'an & *Sunnah*
- The Golden Rule

About this Book

The size of most *Hajj* books is small. This is to allow the pilgrim to carry it in his or her pocket and use it while inside the *Haram*. This book, however, is meant to be used as a work, study and a reference book, hence its size and design. Also the pocket guides that was published to supplement this book, has certainly proved extremely popular and helpful.

The *Fiqh* (Islamic rulings) issues in this book reflect the majority view from: the books (listed on the next page); from various other scholars to whom I had access; and then final confirmation by Imam Ahmed Al-Jehani, Imam Said Al-Mizyen and Imam Wajdi Hamza Al-Ghazzawi.

For the important role and for the special nature of women I have included a separate chapter covering only their related issues. In the bibliography section you will find a list of the other books I used for issues on *Salah* and various other aspects addressed in this book.

I would like to stress that the *Fiqh* rules expressed in this book are not my personal opinions, but those of notable scholars. I would also like to remind my readers that it is acceptable to have a different opinion about an issue. However, one should be prepared to keep an open mind and try to see the other person's point of view, as one may learn something from it. You may even find that the other view may have more authentic proof than the one you ascribe to. One more important point is that there were many changes to the draft version of this book, which meant that not everybody that contributed to it had the chance to review the final version. Hence I believe it to be only fair to mention that it is possible that not all of the contributors mentioned in the acknowledgments, may necessarily agree with all the views expressed in this book.

The books I used as my major source of reference:

1. *The Rites of Hajj & Umrah*
   from Shaikh Muhammad Naasirud-Deen
   Al-Albaanee's book of *Sunnah* and narrations,
   Produced by Jami'at Ihyaa' Minhaj
   Al-Sunnah (U.K.) - 1994

2. *How to perform the rituals of Hajj and Umrah*
   by Shaikh Muhammad As-Salih Al-Uthaimeen,
   Published by the Dawah Centre (Jeddah) - 1992

3. *Hajj, Umrah and Ziyarah*
   by Shaikh Abdul Aziz bin Abdullah bin Baz,
   Published by Maktaba Darussalam (Riyadh) - 1995

4. *Hajj and Umrah according to Sunnah*
   by Maulana Mukhtar Ahmad Nadvi,
   Published by Abul Qasim publishing house
   (Jeddah) - 1995

5. *Hajj and Umrah*
   by Dr. Abu Ameenah Bilal Philips,
   Published by Abul Qasim publishing house
   (Jeddah) - 1993

6. *Sahih Muslim* and *Sahih Al-Bukhari*

This book is designed for easy and comfortable reading. The subjects and style are such, that it is easy to choose topics and points of particular interest for the reader. (See under "Organisation of Sections" for more details.)

Policies and information may change over the course of time, which may mean that some of the information given in this book is not quite accurate or applicable anymore. (i.e., if I had written this a few years earlier, I would have told you that there were many orange coloured containers in the *Haram* filled with *Zamzam* water. Because of a change in the contractor looking after the cleaning of the *Haram*, these containers are now all beige in colour).

Besides the normal practical preparations one has to do for *Hajj*, I believe mental preparation is just as important. This book provides the reader with a realistic view of what to expect and useful information to allow for a better mental preparation.

Apart from that, the rites of *Hajj* are covered in many different ways:

. A comprehensive account of the *Hajj* by rites

. A comprehensive account of the *Hajj* place by place

. A comprehensive account of the *Hajj* day by day

. A detailed diagram of the six days of *Hajj*

. A one-page summary of the *Hajj* days

. A revision section

. An item-by-item checklist of the *Hajj* rites

Certain points are repeated in more than one section for either emphasis or for clarity and completeness of that particular section. It also makes for easier review or if the section is read in isolation.

All suggestions have been fully "tested" and all incidents and points are factual.

How to use this Book

The book has a wealth of information and it may not be possible to remember everything.

Firstly, I suggest you quickly read the book from start to finish in order to give you an idea of its content and its relevance to you.

Secondly, read it again, this time more carefully and make notes and marks for future reference.

Thirdly, revise each section just prior to the actual event (i.e. before you adopt *Ihraam*, revise the rules; before leaving Madinah, read the section on the Journey from Madinah to Makkah, etc.).

Remember, information only becomes knowledge, once it is applied!

Objectives of this Book

1. To provide a realistic view of *Hajj* as it is today, with detailed explanations of all the rites.

2. To provide *Fiqh* related issues about *Hajj*, *Salah* and personal behaviour according to the Qur'an and *Sunnah*, to enable you to obtain the "best value" for your time spent in the holy cities.

3. To provide useful information and suggestions about planning for the journey, what to expect and how to survive, so you can depart with full confidence.

Organisation of Sections

The sections are divided into three parts, where applicable. In the first edition, I used different bullets (symbols) to indicate the three different types of information. I found from the feedback that this was not really necessary, so in this edition, no symbols are used, but the information is still presented in the following order.

Any *Fiqh* (Islamic Rulings) issues are addressed first. The source of the information contained in this section is discussed earlier under "About this book".

This is followed by any GENERAL INFORMATION points and issues. The information contained in this section is common knowledge or is extracted from various books, magazines, maps, etc.

This is then followed by my COMMENTS AND SUGGESTIONS. The information contained in this section is from my own notes and actual experiences compiled over a period of seventeen years.

(This breakdown gives the reader the freedom to choose the sections he or she may wish to read. If for some reason you choose NOT to read the comments and suggestions sections, I challenge you to read it after you return from *Hajj*). This was the challenge I made in the first edition, and I now stand by this challenge even stronger.

The meanings of the Qur'an *Ay'at* and supplications, transliterations, *Ahadith*, and the general text are all in different fonts.

Organisation of Chapters

The chapters are structured in a chronological order, starting from planning for the trip up to the completion of *Hajj*, including a chapter on some historical information. This is followed by a revision chapter and closing with a chapter of useful checklists.

Diagrams and Pictures

The various diagrams were designed and the photographs and pictures were selected to provide the readers with the best graphical view of the rites and actions required during their entire trip.

Hajj* according to Qur'an and *Sunnah

Any form of worship (*Ibadah*) in Islam must be performed according to the Qur'an and *Sunnah* for it to be acceptable to

Allah. One's true intention (*Niyah*) must be for Allah alone and a desire for the Hereafter. It cannot be done with the intention of being seen among men for worldly gain. Strict care should be taken to perform all actions with *Ikhlas* (to perform any act solely for Allah) and *Itiba'a* (adherence to the *Sunnah*). This means performing *Umrah* and *Hajj* as performed by the Prophet (ﷺ) without adding to or deleting from the rituals. Also, the money required for *Hajj* must be earned by lawful (*Halal*) means. One should start on this journey with the exclusive intention of carrying out the commands of Allah and to seek Allah's guidance and pleasure.

The Prophet (ﷺ) said:

$$خُذُوا عَنِّي مَنَاسِكَكُمْ$$

"Take from me your (Hajj) rites."

(Muslim:1297)

The Qur'an explains in detail about *Hajj*. The Prophet Muhammad (ﷺ) performed *Hajj* in the 10th year of *Hijrah*. During this *Hajj*, known as the Farewell Pilgrimage (*Hajjatu-Wadaa'*), the Prophet (ﷺ) practically illustrated how it should be performed.

The Prophet (ﷺ) uttered this ("Take from me your *Hajj* rites") while in Muzdalifah, hence the importance of applying this order during *Hajj*. Thus, there is only one way of performing *Hajj*, and that is according to the Qur'an and *Sunnah*!

$$﴿وَمَا كَانَ لِمُؤْمِنٍ وَلَا مُؤْمِنَةٍ إِذَا قَضَى اللَّهُ وَرَسُولُهُ أَمْرًا أَن يَكُونَ لَهُمُ الْخِيَرَةُ مِنْ أَمْرِهِمْ وَمَن يَعْصِ اللَّهَ وَرَسُولَهُ فَقَدْ ضَلَّ ضَلَالًا مُّبِينًا﴾$$

"It is not for a believer, man or woman, when Allah and His Messenger have decreed a matter that they should have an option in their decision. And whoever disobeys Allah and His Messenger he has indeed strayed in a plain error."

Surah Al-Ahzab (33:36)

The Golden Rule

With so many opinions and interpretations on certain issues it is not uncommon for the pilgrims to find themselves in a state of confusion.

Keep in mind that you CANNOT follow your own desires or make your own rules as you go along.

If there are any disagreements on any issues, always ask yourself the following question:

"What did the Prophet (ﷺ) say, do or didn't do?"

Adopt this simple rule and it will make "your life much easier".

Hajj is not the end; it is just the beginning!

So, fellow Muslims, please "fasten your seat belts", and join me for the journey of a lifetime...

The Fifth Pillar of Islam – *Al-Hajj*

﴿ٱلۡيَوۡمَ أَكۡمَلۡتُ لَكُمۡ دِينَكُمۡ وَأَتۡمَمۡتُ عَلَيۡكُمۡ نِعۡمَتِى وَرَضِيتُ لَكُمُ ٱلۡإِسۡلَٰمَ دِينٗا﴾

"...This day, I have perfected your religion for you, completed My Favour upon you, and have chosen for you Islam as your religion..."

Surah Al-Ma'idah (5:3)

Chapter 1
Hajj as an Obligation,
Types of *Hajj*, Who and When to go

﴿يَـٰٓأَيُّهَا ٱلنَّاسُ ٱتَّقُوا۟ رَبَّكُمْ إِنَّ زَلْزَلَةَ ٱلسَّاعَةِ شَىْءٌ عَظِيمٌ ○ يَوْمَ تَرَوْنَهَا تَذْهَلُ كُلُّ مُرْضِعَةٍ عَمَّآ أَرْضَعَتْ وَتَضَعُ كُلُّ ذَاتِ حَمْلٍ حَمْلَهَا وَتَرَى ٱلنَّاسَ سُكَـٰرَىٰ وَمَا هُم بِسُكَـٰرَىٰ وَلَـٰكِنَّ عَذَابَ ٱللَّهِ شَدِيدٌ ○ وَمِنَ ٱلنَّاسِ مَن يُجَـٰدِلُ فِى ٱللَّهِ بِغَيْرِ عِلْمٍ وَيَتَّبِعُ كُلَّ شَيْطَـٰنٍ مَّرِيدٍ ○﴾

"O Mankind! Fear your Lord and be dutiful to Him! Verily, the earthquake of the Hour (of Judgement) is a terrible thing. The Day you shall see it, every nursing mother will forget her nursling, and every pregnant one will drop her load, and you shall see mankind as in a drunken state, yet they will not be drunken, but severe will be the Torment of Allah. And among mankind is he who disputes concerning Allah, without knowledge, and follows every rebellious devil."

Surah Al-Hajj (22:1-3)

Throughout your journey, reflect on these opening *Ay'at* in *Surah Al-Hajj*. It is a clear reminder of what will happen on the Day of Judgement and also a reminder to those that dispute about Allah. Only from *Ayah* 27 onwards does Allah refer to the *Hajj* itself!

For your convenience I have included the meaning of the entire *Surah* in chapter 14 (taken from *Interpretation of the Meanings of the Noble Qur'an* by Dr. Muhsin Khan). Heed the warnings and take a lesson from it...

The Farewell *Hajj* (*Hajjatul-Wadaa'*) is known as such from the following narration:

«عَنِ ابنِ عُمَرَ رَضِيَ اللهُ عَنْهُما قال: قالَ النَّبِيُّ ﷺ بِمِنًى:

«أَتَدْرُونَ أَيُّ يَوْمٍ هٰذَا؟» قَالُوا: اللهُ وَرَسُولُهُ أَعْلَمُ. فَقَالَ:
«فَإِنَّ هٰذَا يَوْمٌ حَرَامٌ، أَفَتَدْرُونَ أَيُّ بَلَدٍ هٰذَا؟» قَالُوا: اللهُ
وَرَسُولُهُ أَعْلَمُ، قَالَ: «بَلَدٌ حَرَامٌ، أَفَتَدْرُونَ أَيُّ شَهْرٍ هٰذَا؟»
قَالُوا: اللهُ وَرَسُولُهُ أَعْلَمُ، قَالَ: «شَهْرٌ حَرَامٌ»، قَالَ: «فَإِنَّ اللهَ
حَرَّمَ عَلَيْكُمْ دِمَاءَكُمْ وأَمْوَالَكُمْ وَأَعْرَاضَكُمْ كَحُرْمَةِ يَوْمِكُمْ
هٰذَا، فِي شَهْرِكُمْ هٰذَا، فِي بَلَدِكُمْ هٰذَا». وقَالَ هِشَامُ بنُ
الغَازِ: أَخْبَرَنِي نَافِعٌ عَن ابن عُمَرَ رَضِيَ الله عَنْهُما: وَقَفَ
النَّبِيُّ ﷺ يَوْمَ النَّحْرِ بَيْنَ الجَمَرَاتِ فِي الحَجَّةِ الَّتِي حَجَّ بِهٰذَا،
وَقَالَ: «هٰذَا يَوْمُ الحَجِّ الأَكْبَرِ»، فَطَفِقَ النَّبِيُّ ﷺ يَقُولُ:
«اللَّهُمَّ اشْهَدْ». فَوَدَّعَ النَّاسَ فَقَالُوا: هٰذِهِ حَجَّةُ الوَدَاعِ»

Narrated Ibn "Umar: "At Mina, the Prophet (ﷺ) said, 'Do you know what is the day today?' The people replied, 'Allah and His Messenger know it better.' He said, 'It is the forbidden (sacred) day. And do you know what town is this?' They replied, 'Allah and His Messenger know it better.' He said, 'This is the forbidden (sacred) town (Makkah). And do you know which month is this?' The people replied, 'Allah and His Messenger know it better.' He said, 'This is the forbidden (sacred) month.' The Prophet added, 'No doubt, Allah made your blood, your properties, and your honour sacred to one another like the sanctity of this day of yours in this month of yours in this town of yours.' Narrated Ibn 'Umar: On the Day of Nahr (10th of Dhul-Hijjah), the Prophet stood in between the Jamr'at during his Hajj which he performed and said, 'This is the greatest Day (i.e. 10th of Dhul-Hijjah).' The Prophet ﷺ started saying repeatedly, 'O Allah! Be witness (I have conveyed Your Message). 'He then bade the people farewell. The people said, 'This is Hajjatul-Wadaa''.''

(Bukhari:1742)

The Farewell Sermon (*Khutbah*):

The "Farewell *Khutbah*" of our beloved Prophet (ﷺ) as narrated by Jaabir bin 'Abdullah (ﷺ):

حَتَّى إِذَا زَاغَتِ الشَّمْسُ أَمَرَ بِالْقَصْوَاءِ فَرُحِلَتْ لَهُ، فَرَكِبَ حَتَّى أَتَى بَطْنَ الْوَادِي فَخَطَبَ النَّاسَ، فَقَالَ: «إِنَّ دِمَاءَكُم وَأَمْوَالَكُم عَلَيْكُم حَرَامٌ كَحُرْمَةِ يَوْمِكُم هٰذَا فِي شَهْرِكُم هٰذَا فِي بَلَدِكُم هٰذَا أَلَا إِنَّ كُلَّ شَيْءٍ مِنْ أَمْرِ الْجَاهِلِيَّةِ تَحْتَ قَدَمَيَّ مَوْضُوعٌ، وَدِمَاءُ الْجَاهِلِيَّةِ مَوْضُوعَةٌ، وَأَوَّلُ دَمٍ أَضَعُهُ دِمَاؤُنَا. دَمُ» – قَالَ عُثْمَانُ: «دَمُ ابْنِ رَبِيعَةَ». وَقَالَ سُلَيْمَانُ: «دَمُ رَبِيعَةَ بنِ الحَارِثِ بنِ عَبْدِ المُطَّلِبِ». وَقَالَ بَعْضُ هٰؤُلَاءِ: كَانَ مُسْتَرْضَعاً فِي بَنِي سَعْدٍ فَقَتَلَتْهُ هُذَيْلٌ. «وَرِبَا الْجَاهِلِيَّةِ مَوْضُوعٌ، وَأَوَّلُ رِباً أَضَعُ رِبَانَا رِبَا عَبَّاسِ بن عَبْدِ المُطَّلِبِ فَإِنَّهُ مَوْضُوعٌ كُلُّهُ. فَاتَّقُوا اللهَ فِي النِّسَاءِ فَإِنَّكُم أَخَذْتُمُوهُنَّ بِأَمَانَةِ اللهِ، وَاسْتَحْلَلْتُمْ فُرُوجَهُنَّ بِكَلِمَةِ اللهِ، وَإِنَّ لَكُم عَلَيْهِنَّ أَنْ لَا يُوطِئْنَ فُرُشَكُم أَحَداً تَكْرَهُونَهُ، فَإِنْ فَعَلْنَ فَاضْرِبُوهُنَّ ضَرْباً غَيْرَ مُبَرِّحٍ، وَلَهُنَّ عَلَيْكُم رِزْقُهنَّ وَكِسْوَتُهُنَّ بِالمَعْرُوفِ، وَإِنِّي قَدْ تَرَكْتُ فِيكُم مَا لَنْ تَضِلُّوا بَعْدَهُ إِنِ اعْتَصَمْتُم بِهِ كِتَابَ اللهِ وَأَنْتُمْ مَسْؤُولُونَ عَنِّي، فَمَا أَنْتُمْ قَائِلُونَ؟» قَالُوا: نَشْهَدُ أَنَّكَ قَدْ بَلَّغْتَ وَأَدَّيْتَ وَنَصَحْتَ ثُمَّ قَالَ بِإِصْبَعِهِ السَّبَّابَةِ يَرْفَعُهَا إِلَى السَّمَاءِ وَيَنْكُتُهَا إِلَى النَّاسِ «اللَّهُمَّ! اشْهَدْ، اللَّهُمَّ! اشْهَدْ، اللَّهُمَّ! اشْهَدْ». ثُمَّ أَذَّنَ بِلَالٌ، ثُمَّ أَقَامَ فَصَلَّى الظُّهْرَ،

"...When the sun began to incline to the west, he ordered that Qaswaa (his camel) should be saddled for him, and he rode to the bottom of the valley of Uranah where he sat on his camel and addressed the people saying:

Oh People! Shedding of blood and seizing the properties of others in unlawful ways are forbidden to you just as they are forbidden on this day, in this month and in this city. Note well that all customs and practices of the days of ignorance are trampled under my feet; the blood-feuds of the past are abolished, and first of all, I give up our family's claim as regards the son of Rabee'ah bin Al-Haarith bin 'Abdul-Muttalib, who was being suckled by Banoo Sa'd when he was killed by Banoo Hudhail. Abolished also are all the claims of interest (Ribaa) of the past, and first of all I give up the claims in this respect of my uncle, Abbaas ibn 'Abdul-Muttalib.

Oh People! Fear Allah with regard to the rights of your women; you have married them in Allah's Name and they have become lawful to you only by His law. Your special right on them is that they should not entertain anyone whom you dislike in your home; but if they commit an error in this regard, you may punish them lightly. The women's special right on you is that you should clothe and feed them generously according to your means.

Oh people! If you hold fast to what I am leaving behind for you and follow its teachings, you will never go astray. It is the Book of Allah.

Oh people! Listen! Each Muslim is a brother to every other Muslim, and all Muslims are brothers of one another. Therefore, the property of one is unlawful for the other unless given willingly, so do not oppress one another.

On the Day of Resurrection, when you will be asked (about whether I have conveyed fully Allah's Message or not), what will you say?

The whole congregation spoke with one voice: 'We bear witness that you have conveyed to us the whole Divine Guidance in the best way possible and given us the best advice.'

At this the Prophet (ﷺ) raised his forefinger towards the sky and then pointing to the congregation said thrice:

'Oh Allah! May You also be witness! I have conveyed Your Message and Your Commands to Your people, as has been confirmed by them.'

Then Bilaal called the Adhaan and pronounced the Iqaama..."

(Abu Dawud, Muslim:1218:1905)

None of us can dispute the power and clarity of this message. This message is relevant today more than ever, so let us pay heed to it!

Hajj, an Obligation

$$\text{﴿ إِنَّ أَوَّلَ بَيْتٍ وُضِعَ لِلنَّاسِ لَلَّذِى بِبَكَّةَ مُبَارَكًا وَهُدًى لِّلْعَلَمِينَ ۝ فِيهِ ءَايَتٌ بَيِّنَتٌ مَّقَامُ إِبْرَهِيمَ وَمَن دَخَلَهُ كَانَ ءَامِنًا وَلِلَّهِ عَلَى ٱلنَّاسِ حِجُّ ٱلْبَيْتِ مَنِ ٱسْتَطَاعَ إِلَيْهِ سَبِيلًا وَمَن كَفَرَ فَإِنَّ ٱللَّهَ غَنِىٌّ عَنِ ٱلْعَلَمِينَ ۝ ﴾}$$

"Verily, the first House (of worship) appointed for Mankind was that at Bakka (Makkah), full of blessing, and a guidance for Al-Alamin (mankind and jinns). In it are manifest signs (for example) the Maqaam (place) of Ibraheem; whosoever enters it, he attains security. And Hajj (pilgrimage to Makkah) to the House (Ka'bah) is a duty that mankind owes to Allah, those who can afford the expenses (for one's conveyance, provision and residence); and whoever disbelieves (i.e. denies Hajj, then he is a disbeliever of Allah), then Allah stands not in need of any of the Alamin (mankind and jinn)."

Surah Al-Imran (3:96-97)

As we can see from the preceding *Ay'at*, *Hajj* is not only the fifth pillar of Islam, but it is an actual DUTY WE OWE UNTO ALLAH!

Who should go?

Allah does not wish to make things difficult for the Muslims. Apart from the duty being *Fard* (compulsory) only once in a lifetime, there are certain other conditions that have to be met for one to be 'eligible':

1.   To be a Muslim
2.   To have reached puberty
3.   To be of sound mind
4.   To be free (not a slave)
5.   To have the financial means*
6.   To possess the physical means**
7.   To have a *Mahram* (for women)***

* One does not have to be debt free in order to be eligible. As long as arrangements are made for the payment of your debts during your absence, or in the event of your death.

** If your physical disablement is of a permanent nature, and you have the money, then it is advisable to send (deputise) somebody to perform the *Hajj* on your behalf.

*** The issue of *Mahram* is addressed in more detail in chapter three

When should one go?

One should expedite the performance of *Hajj*.

«عَنِ ابْنِ عَبَّاسٍ، عَنِ الْفَضْلِ أَوْ أَحَدِهِمَا عَنِ الآخَرِ قَالَ: قَالَ
رَسُولُ اللهِ ﷺ: «مَنْ أَرَادَ الْحَجَّ فَلْيَتَعَجَّلْ. فَإِنَّهُ قَدْ يَمْرَضُ
الْمَرِيضُ، وَتَضِلُّ الضَّالَّةُ، وَتَعْرِضُ الْحَاجَةُ»

"It is reported on the authority of 'Abdullah bin 'Abbas (ﷺ) that the Prophet (ﷺ) said: 'Expedite the performance of the duty of Hajj. For nobody knows what may obstruct one.' "

(Ibn Maja:2883 & Ahmad:1/214,225)

Once you have met all the listed conditions, it is important to perform your *Fard Hajj* as soon as possible. Many people tend to leave this obligation until much later in their life. It is so much easier and better if one undertakes this journey while one is young and has the health and strength. Believe me, no matter when you go you will regret that you did not go when you were younger. So go as soon as you are able to!

What about those that have been before?

If you have performed *Hajj* before and you feel complacent about it, or if you are not convinced about the benefits of performing *Hajj* again, ponder over the next *Hadith Kudsi*:

«عَنْ أَبِي سَعِيدٍ الْخُدْرِي أَنَّ رَسُولَ اللهِ ﷺ قَالَ: قَالَ اللهُ: إِنَّ عَبْدًا صَحَّحْتُ لَهُ جِسْمَهُ، وَوَسَّعْتُ عَلَيْهِ فِي الْمَعِيشَةِ يَمْضِي عَلَيْهِ خَمْسَةُ أَعْوَامٍ لاَيَغِدُ إِلَيَّ لَمَحْرُومٌ»،

"Narrated Abu Said Al-Khudrie, the Prophet (ﷺ) said, Allah said: 'Any of My slaves who is healthy and are by the means and for five years did not visit My house, he is Mahroum.'"*

(Ibn Hiban & Musnad Abu Ya'laa: 3703:1031)

Mahroum: The direct translation of the word is 'deprive', meaning that a person who is able and does not do so, has certainly deprived himself of something good. It is like a very rich person who does not spend or use his money. He deprives himself of the benefit of having that money. Also, for example, if a person lives away from his parents, and he is able to visit them, but chooses not to, he has certainly deprived himself of great benefits. Now when Allah uses the word *Mahroum* we can be certain that it means that we are depriving ourselves of benefits that we cannot imagine and we will regret it on the Day of Judgement.

Umrah and *Hajj* in the same year

Hajj months:

Shawaal (10th month of the *Hijrah* calendar);

Dhul-Qadah (11th month) and Dhul-Hijjah (12th month).

There appears to be a great deal of confusion on this issue.

Some COMMON MISCONCEPTIONS:

☒ If you perform *Umrah* in the *Hajj* months, you must

perform *Hajj* in the same year.

☒ If you perform *Umrah*, you must perform *Hajj* in the same year.

☒ You are not allowed to perform *Umrah* in the *Hajj* months if you are not going to perform *Hajj* also.

☒ You are not allowed to perform *Umrah* in the *Hajj* months.

There is no instruction from the Qur'an or the *Sunnah* that one MUST perform *Umrah* and *Hajj* in the same year. There is also nothing to substantiate that you cannot perform *Umrah* in the *Hajj* months. This is a belief from the days of polytheism and there is plenty of evidence to the contrary.

If a person performs *Umrah* in the *Hajj* months followed by performing *Hajj* the pilgrim automatically opts for the *Tamattu* method of *Hajj* (and without coming out of *Ihraam*, the *Qiran* method). This means that the *Hady* (a sacrifice to THANK Allah for being able to perform *Umrah* and *Hajj*) becomes compulsory. See *Surah Al-Baqarah*, *Ayah* 196 for more details.

The Prophet (ﷺ) performed four *Umrahs* in Dhul-Qadah without performing *Hajj* also!

«حَدَّثَنَا قَتَادَةُ أَنَّ أَنَسًا [رَضِيَ اللهُ عَنْهُ] أَخْبَرَهُ أَنَّ رَسُولَ اللهِ ﷺ اعْتَمَرَ أَرْبَعَ عُمَرٍ، كُلُّهُنَّ فِي ذِي الْقَعْدَةِ إِلَّا الَّتِي مَعَ حَجَّتِهِ: عُمْرَةً مِنَ الْحُدَيْبِيَةِ، أَوْ زَمَنَ الْحُدَيْبِيَةِ، فِي ذِي الْقَعْدَةِ، وَعُمْرَةً مِنَ الْعَامِ الْمُقْبِلِ، فِي ذِي الْقَعْدَةِ، وَعُمْرَةً مِنْ جِعْرَانَةَ، حَيْثُ قَسَمَ غَنَائِمَ حُنَيْنٍ، فِي ذِي الْقَعْدَةِ، وَعُمْرَةً مَعَ حَجَّتِهِ»

"Qatadah said that Anas (ﷺ) had informed him that the Prophet (ﷺ) performed four Umrahs, all during the month of Dhul-Qadah including the one he performed along with Hajj (and these are): The Umrah that he performed from Al-Hudaibiyah or during the time of (the truce of) Hudaibiyah in the month of Dhul-Qadah, then the Umrah of the next year in the month of Dhul-Qadah, then the Umrah for which he had

*started from Jiranah, the place where he distributed the spoils
of (the battle of) Hunain in the month of Dhul-Qadah, and
then the Umrah that he performed along with his Hajj (on the
occasion of the Farewell Pilgrimage)."*

(Muslim:1253)

Methods (types of *Hajj*)

There are three types or methods of performing *Hajj*. The type
you choose will depend upon, whether you live in Makkah
(*Ifrad*); you wish to perform *Umrah* and then *Hajj* (*Tamattu*); or
you wish to perform *Umrah* and *Hajj* together in one Niyah
and also take with you your animal for sacrifice (*Qiran*). All
three methods fulfill all the Islamic requirements of *Hajj*.

Do you know?

1.   What method the Prophet (ﷺ) performed?

2.   What method the Prophet (ﷺ) recommended?

Answers:

1.   *Qiran*

2.   *Tamattu*

So fellow Muslims, the best method is *Tamattu* as
recommended (instructed) by the Prophet (ﷺ), as narrated
in *Sahih Muslim*:

«خَرَجْنَا مَعَ رَسُولِ اللهِ ﷺ نَصْرُخُ بِالْحَجِّ صُرَاخًا، فَلَمَّا قَدِمْنَا
مَكَّةَ أَمَرَنَا أَنْ نَجْعَلَهَا عُمْرَةً، إِلَّا مَنْ سَاقَ الْهَدْيَ، فَلَمَّا كَانَ
يَوْمُ التَّرْوِيَةِ، وَرُحْنَا إِلَى مِنًى، أَهْلَلْنَا بِالْحَجِّ»

*"When the Prophet (ﷺ) performed Tawaaf and Sa'ee during
the year of the Farewell Hajj with his Companions, he ﷺ
ordered all those who hadn't brought sacrificial animals to
change their niyah for Hajj to Niyah for Umrah, cut their hair
and disengage from Ihraam until Hajj. He said: 'If I had not
brought the sacrificial animal, I would have done what I've
ordered you to do.'"*

Even after reading the preceding *Hadith*, some people still argue that *Qiran* is the preferred method. For most pilgrims coming from overseas, *Tamattu* is the only method they can perform, because for *Qiran* or *Ifrad*, they will not be able to stay in *Ihraam* for that long apart from not being able to bring the sacrificial animal with them.

There are also some minor differences of opinion in the matter of when a pilgrim performs *Umrah* during the *Hajj* months and then leaves the *Haram* area. As an example: a pilgrim comes to Makkah and performs *Umrah* and then leaves for Jeddah or Riyadh or back overseas. The pilgrim returns to Makkah for *Hajj*. Can he or she now perform the *Ifrad* or *Qiran* method or is the *Tamattu* still valid? Some scholars rule that once the pilgrim leaves the *Meqaat* area, the *Tamattu* is "cancelled" and the pilgrim can now do *Ifrad* or *Qiran*, and has to do *Umrah* again in order to do satisfy the *Tamattu* rule. Another ruling is that it does not matter, as long as the *Umrah* was done in the *Hajj* months, the pilgrim remains a *Mutamatti*. In any case as mentioned earlier this should not affect most of the pilgrims. If you are unsure (or worried), after taking a trip to Jeddah, then just do *Umrah* again, if that will make your mind settled.

The Three Methods of *Hajj*

1. *Hajj Tamattu*

- *Hajj* combined with *Umrah* with two *Niy'at*, one for *Umrah*, and then one for *Hajj*.
- Pilgrim is called a *Mutammati*.

Regulations:

- Enter into *Ihraam* at the *Meqaat* with the *Niyah* for *Umrah*.
- Complete the *Umrah* during the *Hajj* months of the same year, and this must be completed before beginning the rites of *Hajj*.
- The first *Tawaaf* made is that of *Umrah* and the welcome *Tawaaf* (*Qudoom*) is not required.

- The performance of *Sa'ee* is a must. This is *Sa'ee* for *Umrah* and not for *Hajj*. The Sa'ee for *Hajj* must be performed with *Tawaaful-Ifadah*.

- The *Mutamatti* should clip his hair after *Umrah* instead of shaving it to come out of the state of *Ihraam* after the *Sa'ee* for *Umrah*. For males, if he has time before *Hajj* to re-grow his hair, then he should shave it (as it has more reward) after completing his *Umrah*.

- The *Mutamatti* MUST come out of the state of *Ihraam* after *Umrah* (all the *Ihraam* restrictions are lifted for the *Mutamatti*).

- Animal sacrifice is compulsory for the *Mutamatti*. If one cannot afford it, then one is required to fast for ten days. This applies to the *Qaarin* also.

$$\text{﴿فَمَا ٱسْتَيْسَرَ مِنَ ٱلْهَدْيِ فَمَن لَّمْ يَجِدْ فَصِيَامُ ثَلَٰثَةِ أَيَّامٍ فِى ٱلْحَجِّ وَسَبْعَةٍ إِذَا رَجَعْتُمْ تِلْكَ عَشَرَةٌ كَامِلَةٌ﴾}$$

"....But if someone cannot afford a sacrifice, he can fast three days during Hajj and seven days after returning home. That is ten days in all..."

Surah Al-Baqarah (2:196)

- The *Mutamatti* enters back into the state of *Ihraam* with the *Niyah* for *Hajj* (second *Niyah*), from where he is on the 8th of Dhul-Hijjah, before departing for Mina.

- Those living in Makkah cannot perform this method of *Hajj*.

$$\text{﴿ذَٰلِكَ لِمَن لَّمْ يَكُنْ أَهْلُهُ حَاضِرِى ٱلْمَسْجِدِ ٱلْحَرَامِ وَٱتَّقُوا۟ ٱللَّهَ وَٱعْلَمُوٓا۟ أَنَّ ٱللَّهَ شَدِيدُ ٱلْعِقَابِ﴾}$$

"...This is for him whose family is not present at Al-Masjid-al-Haram (i.e. non-resident of Makkah)..."

Surah Al-Baqarah (2:196)

2. *Hajj Qiran*

- *Hajj* combined with *Umrah* (one *Niyah*) without coming out of *Ihraam*.
- Person is called a *Qaarin*.

Regulations:

- Enter into *Ihraam* at the *Meqaat* with *Niyah* for *Umrah* and *Hajj*.
- Animal sacrifice is compulsory (see under *Tamattu*).
- Some scholars rule that it is a prerequisite for the pilgrim to have the sacrificial animal with him. Meaning that if he did not have the animal with him he must perform the *Tamattu* method instead. Hence, the pilgrim who has the animal with him cannot change his *Niyah*. However, the *Qaarin* who did not bring the animal with him SHOULD change his *Niyah* to *Tamattu*. Some scholars rule it is a must! Changing one's *Niyah* is covered in chapter 9.
- On arrival in Makkah the pilgrim performs *Tawaaf-ul-Qudoom* (welcome *Tawaaf*). This is optional, as the pilgrim may go directly to Mina on the 8th of Dhul-Hijjah from the *Meqaat*.
- The *Sa'ee* for *Hajj* may also be performed with this *Tawaaf* (recommended).
- The *Qaarin* must remain in *Ihraam* no matter how long the period between his arrival in Makkah and *Hajj* may be.
- Those living in Makkah cannot perform this method of *Hajj* (see under *Tamattu*).

3. *Ifrad*

- *Hajj* only (without *Umrah*)
- Person is called a *Mufrid*

Regulations:

- Enter into *Ihraam* at the *Meqaat* with *Niyah* for *Hajj* (only).

- Animal sacrifice is optional.

- Not to perform *Umrah* during the *Hajj* months of the same year.

- On arrival in Makkah the pilgrim performs *Tawaaful-Qudoom* (welcome *Tawaaf*). This is optional, as the pilgrim may go directly to Mina on the 8th of Dhul-Hijjah from the *Meqaat*.

- The *Sa'ee* for *Hajj* may also be performed with this *Tawaaf*. If it is done here, it places the pilgrim in the same position as the *Qaarin*, with regards to the order of changing his *Niyah* to *Tamattu* (except for the residents of Makkah).

- The *Mufrid* must remain in the state of *Ihraam* no matter how long the period between his arrival in Makkah and *Hajj* may be.

- This method of *Hajj* is for those living in Makkah or those within the *Meqaat* area (see *Surah* 2:196).

- If circumstances permit (time and one chooses to sacrifice), the *Mufrid* can change his *Niyah* from *Ifrad* to *Qiran* or *Tamattu*. If he does this, then he should follow the rules accordingly, as described previously. Residents of Makkah cannot change their *Niyah*.

- Changing one's *Niyah* is covered in chapter 9.

Confused? Do not worry, you are not alone. Let me stress again, the *Tamattu* method is the one the Prophet (ﷺ) instructed us to perform (if all the requirements are met), so concentrate on understanding that method.

In all three methods, the pilgrim is allowed to change his/her *Ihraam* clothes with clean ones (not into normal clothes for men, but another *Ihraam*).

Hajj Tamattu at a glance

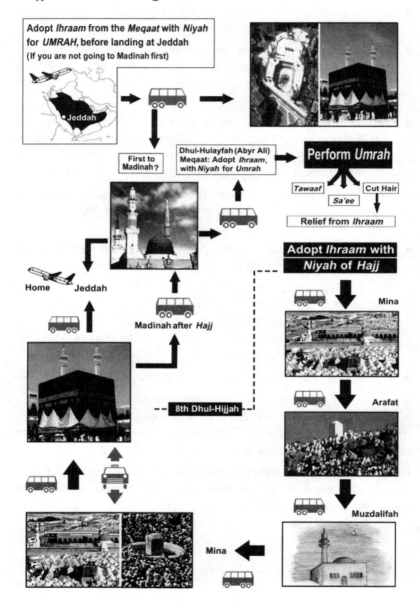

Below I have listed the actions as the Prophet (ﷺ) performed them or advised us to do. I have called them the "best actions".

There are various allowable deviations or options open to the pilgrim, depending on his or her condition and circumstances. If you are able to perform the *Hajj* by abiding as close as possible to these actions listed, then you should.

The "Best Actions" are:

√ Perform *Hajj Tamattu*.

√ Prepare for *Ihraam* (cut nails, pubic hair, under arm hair, etc., if needed. Remember as per the *Sunnah*, one should not exceed 40 days without trimming one's nails and pubic hair).

√ Perform *Ghusl*.

√ Men perfume themselves.

√ Adopt *Ihraam* at the *Meqaat* with the *Niyah* for *Umrah*.

√ Perform *Umrah* upon reaching Makkah.

√ Cut your hair (out of *Ihraam*).

√ 8th of Dhul-Hijjah:

  o Prepare for *Ihraam* (cut nails, pubic hair, under arm hair, etc., if needed);

  o Perform *Ghusl*;

  o Men perfume themselves;

  o Adopt *Ihraam* from where you are, with the *Niyah* for *Hajj*;

  o Proceed to Mina before *Salatul-Zuhr*;

  o Perform 5 *Salawaat* in Mina (*Zuhr, 'Asr, Maghrib, 'Eshaa & Fajr*);

  o Shorten your *Salah* (*Zuhr, 'Asr* and *'Eshaa*), but do not join them while in Mina.

√ Always perform the two *Sunnah Rak'at Salah* before *Salatul-Fajr*.

√ Always perform *Salatul-Witr*.

√ Enter Arafat after the sun has declined from its zenith (*Zawaal*) on the 9th of Dhul-Hijjah.

√ Listen to the *Khutbah*.

√ Join the congregation to perform *Salatul-Zuhr* and *Salatul-'Asr* shortened (2 each) and joined at the time of *Zuhr* (one *Adhaan* and two *Iqaama't*).

√ Spend the time from *Zuhr* until *Maghrib* in supplication.

√ Leave Arafat for Muzdalifah immediately after sunset.

√ Perform *Salatul-Maghrib* (3) and *Salatul-'Eshaa* (2) joined upon arrival in Muzdalifah, or where you are if you have not reached Muzdalifah by midnight.

√ Perform *Salatul-Witr*.

√ Spend the night in rest and sleep.

√ Perform two *Rak'at Sunnah* for *Salatul-Fajr*.

√ Perform *Salatul-Fajr*.

√ Supplicate.

√ Proceed to Mina just before sunrise.

√ Collect 7 pebbles in Muzdalifah or on the way to the *Jamrah*.

√ Stone the big *Jamrah* (*Aqaba*) only (7 stones, casting one at a time).

√ Perform the animal sacrifice yourself.

√ Have your head shaved (men), starting from the right side.

√ Women cut about one inch of hair from one place only.

√ Proceed to Makkah.

√ Perform *Tawaaful-Ifadah*.

√ Perform *Sa'ee* for *Hajj*.

√ Return to Mina to spend the night (10th).

√ Spend the next 3 days and 2 nights in Mina (11th, 12th and 13th).

√ Stone all three *Jamr'at* after *Zawaal* on all 3 days (collect 21 pebbles daily).

√ Stone, starting at the small *Jamrah* and finishing at the big *Jamrah*.

√ Turn to face *Qiblah* and make a long supplication after stoning the small and middle *Jamr'at* (all 3 days).

√ Leave for Makkah on the 13th after stoning the *Jamr'at* (after *Zawaal*).

√ Perform *Tawaaful-Wadaa'* as the last rite before going home.

In my experience, I have found the following to be some of the most common actions many pilgrims opt to do, which do not conform to the *Sunnah*:

× Passing the *Meqaat* without adopting *Ihraam*.

× Adopting the *Ihraam* in Jeddah and refusing to perform the expiation.

× Women wearing turbans or hats on their head, to avoid the veil touching their faces.

× Men wearing an *Ihraam* with studs to keep it closed.

× Performing a special prayer (*Salah*) after putting on the *Ihraam*.

× Keeping the right shoulder uncovered all the time.

× Women refusing to enter into *Ihraam* while in their menses.

× Women insisting on wearing white clothes for *Ihraam*.

× Pilgrims not keeping themselves clean by refusing to bath, shower, or change their clothes while in *Ihraam*.

× Uttering a special *Niyah* to perform *Tawaaf* and *Sa'ee*.

× Reciting loudly (or behind a group) during *Tawaaf* and *Sa'ee*.

× Performing *Tawaaf* and *Sa'ee* in large groups.

✗ Kissing the *Rukn-Yamani* Corner.

✗ Kissing and touching/rubbing the *Maqaam Ebraheem*.

✗ Stopping at the starting place and repeating "*Allahu-Akbar*" many times.

✗ Adhering to special booklets that contain specific *Dua'* for each circuit.

✗ Adding to the *Sunnah Dua'* read between the *Yamani* Corner and the Black Stone.

✗ Hiring a special guide for *Tawaaf* to read aloud for you to follow.

✗ Reciting the Verse: "*Inna Safaa Wal-Marwatta...*" at the beginning of each round in *Sa'ee*.

✗ Men cutting only a few strands of hair.

✗ Performing multiple *Umrahs* and missing the *Fard Salah* due to tiredness.

✗ Performing *Salah* outside the *Haram* even though there is space inside.

✗ Men and women standing next to each other while performing *Salah*.

✗ Women standing in front of men during *Salah*.

✗ Pushing and hurting fellow pilgrims, in order to kiss the black stone.

✗ Insisting on entering the *Haram* from *Baabus-Salaam*.

✗ Fasting instead of paying for the *Hady*, even though they can afford it.

✗ Performing their *Hady* (sacrifice) before the 10th.

✗ Having the *Hady* slaughtered in their home country.

✗ *Tamattu* pilgrims performing two sacrifices, believing one is a penalty (for performing *Umrah*) and one is the *Hady*.

✗ Pilgrims entering Makkah (early) without performing

Umrah, and then perform it after *Hajj* in order to avoid performing the *Hady*.

✗ *Tamattu* pilgrims performing *Nafl Tawaaf* and then *Sa'ee* for *Hajj* on the 8th.

✗ Not stopping or staying at least a part of the night in Muzdalifah.

✗ Insisting on collecting the pebbles in Muzdalifah.

✗ Washing the pebbles.

✗ Not performing *Salatul-Witr* in Muzdalifah.

✗ Not performing the two *Sunnah Rak'at* for *Salatul-Fajr* in Muzdalifah.

✗ Pelting the *Jamr'at* before *Zawaal* (11th, 12th & 13th).

✗ Deputising the pelting due to fear of the crowds.

✗ Staying in Makkah during the days/nights of *Tashreek*.

✗ Refusing to shorten their *Salah* while in Mina.

✗ Refusing to join *Salatul-Zuhr* and *'Asr* on *Arafat*.

✗ Intentionally omitting an action and performing the expiation instead.

✗ Omitting *Tawaaful-Wadaa'*.

Let us look at the following analogy:

One person enters the mosque before the *Adhaan* and performs *Tahiyatul-Masjid Salah*. After the *Adhaan* he performs *Sunnah Salah*. He is with the *Imam* for *Takbir-Tahrimah*. He is in the first row. Another person enters after the first *Rak'at*. Another person enters during the last *Rak'at*. Although all of them are regarded as having performed the required *Fard Salah*, can we say that they all have the same reward? The same applies to *Hajj*. We certainly cannot expect the same reward if we choose to leave out many of the recommended actions, even though we would have fulfilled the duty of having performed *Hajj*.

The Prize

One may wonder why so many people tend to deviate from the "best actions" even though the rules are so clear.

The way I look at is as follows:

If a very rich man were to offer you one million dollars, if you were to do, say 10 actions for him. However, the condition is that you must follow the rules exactly as stated, unless you have a valid reason not to. Say for example that one of the actions is that you must visit his office at 8.00am everyday for 3 days. Now, I am sure that you will do exactly that, be at his office at 8:00am for the 3 days, even though a very close friend or you may read somewhere, or your spiritual leader may tell you that it is ok to go at 8:30am. Why? Because you are focused on the prize and you would do everything as requested in order to secure the prize. The prize is much too valuable!

The reason so many Muslims tend to deviate and take the easy way out during *Hajj* is that they are not focused on the prize. And what is that prize...?

... and there is no reward for an accepted Hajj except Paradise!

So my fellow Muslims, focus on the prize and let that help you guide your decision making with regards to the rites of *Hajj*.

Chapter 2
Planning and Preparation

Like any other trip be it business or vacation, *Hajj* requires lots of planning and preparation; tickets, visas, money, accommodation, etc. Let us begin with a reminder of the best provision Allah instructs us to "take with us" on this journey:

﴿ٱلْحَجُّ أَشْهُرٌ مَّعْلُومَٰتٌ فَمَن فَرَضَ فِيهِنَّ ٱلْحَجَّ فَلَا رَفَثَ وَلَا فُسُوقَ وَلَا جِدَالَ فِي ٱلْحَجِّ وَمَا تَفْعَلُوا مِنْ خَيْرٍ يَعْلَمْهُ ٱللَّهُ وَتَزَوَّدُوا فَإِنَّ خَيْرَ ٱلزَّادِ ٱلتَّقْوَىٰ وَٱتَّقُونِ يَٰأُولِي ٱلْأَلْبَٰبِ﴾

"The Hajj (pilgrimage) is (in) the well-known (lunar year) months. So whosoever intends to perform Hajj therein by assuming Ihraam, then he should not have sexual relations (with his wife), nor commit sin, nor dispute unjustly during Hajj. And whatever good you do, (be sure) Allah knows it. And take a provision (with you) for the journey, but the best provision is At-Taqwa (piety, righteousness, etc.). So fear Me, O men of understanding!"

Surah Al-Baqarah (2:197)

Debts

Pay all your outstanding debts if possible.

If you are not able to, make arrangements for their payment during your absence, or in the event of your death.

Being debt free is not a precondition for performing *Hajj*.

Ensure that family members are aware of any outstanding debts. Money owed to someone is something many people tend to treat very lightly, even though it is a very serious matter in Islam. It may keep you from entering *Jannah*.

Have a will drawn up. Ensure that it conforms to the Islamic rules.

Dates/Bookings/Passport/Visas

Visiting Madinah is not a part of *Hajj*. However it is commendable to visit the Prophet's (ﷺ) mosque if you are able to.

There is no *Sunnah* requirement to spend a minimum of 8 days in Madinah. See chapter 12 on Madinah for more details about this misconception.

Tawaaful-Ifadah is a compulsory act of *Hajj* and cannot be omitted by anyone. Plan accordingly for your departure from Makkah (for women, keeping in mind your menstrual cycle).

* The Islamic Months are:
  (each month has a maximum number of 30 days)

1.   Muharram

2.   Safar

3.   Rabial-Awal

4.   Rabiat-Thaani (Rabi-ul-Akhir)

5.   Jumada-al-Awal (Jumada I)

6.   Jumadaat-Thaania (Jumadal-Akhara; Jumada II)

7.   Rajab

8.   Sha'ban

9.   Ramadan

10.   Shawaal

11.   Dhul-Qadah

12.   Dhul-Hijjah

The *Hajj* months are from the 1st Shawaal until the 13th Dhul-Hijjah.

The actual days of *Hajj* are from the 8th until the 13th Dhul-Hijjah.

  o Arafat is on the 9th;

  o *Eid* day is on the 10th ("no *Eid*" for the pilgrims).

According to the current regulations in Saudi Arabia, all pilgrims coming by air must be in the country by the 5th of Dhul-Hijjah.

Do NOT leave home without a visa. You will be sent back!

The Saudi Arabian Embassy may have some special requirements before issuing you with a *Hajj* visa. This may vary from country to country:

- o Marriage certificate (if applicable);
- o Birth certificates for accompanying children;
- o Letter from your local Islamic society stating that you are a Muslim;
- o Copy of airline tickets & itinerary;
- o Proof of money (copy of travellers cheques);
- o Copy of the two cheques (drafts) needed for landing in Saudi Arabia;
- o Proof of vaccinations (meningitis, cholera, etc.);
- o Proof of *Mahram* for female pilgrims. Women over the age of 45 that have no *Mahram* may obtain a visa if they are travelling with an organised *Hajj* group.

Send the passport and 2 photographs for each applicant.

The visa rules and requirements may change from year to year.

The visa issuing time is normally from Shawaal onwards.

Check the site www.mofa.gov.sa for more details.

Your *Hajj* or travel agent will process and obtain your visa for you.

Dates

Determine the dates of *Hajj* in the Gregorian calendar and make the necessary arrangements for the children (if applicable), vacation from work, etc.

In most western countries it may be difficult to find out about the exact dates for *Hajj*. Use the following method to give you an approximate date:

Assuming you know when it is Ramadan and *Eidul-Fitr* in your country. Calculate as follows: Add 29 days (Shawaal) + 30 days (Dhul-Qadah) + 8 days (Dhul-Hijjah).

Example: *Eidul-Fitr* is on 8th February; add 29 days which takes it to the 9th of March; add 30 days which takes it to the 8th of April; add 8 days which makes Arafat day on 16th April, *Eid* on 17th and the days of *Tashreek* the 18th, 19th and 20th April.

The above calculation will be accurate within a 3-day range, as the months may only be 29 days, and the new moon will be different, depending on your locality. However this should give you a good enough date for the purpose of planning your flights and vacations.

Another place to find the dates is on the Internet or the *Hajj* brochures.

Don't forget to plan for Madinah, either before or after *Hajj*, if time and money permit.

Let me state again: Plan your departure from Makkah very carefully taking into consideration the menstrual cycle of the ladies accompanying you (*Tawaaful-Ifadah* is compulsory for all pilgrims). Year after year, pilgrims have return airline bookings one or two days after *Hajj* (14th, 15th Dhul-Hijjah). Some even have it for the 13th. This can become a major problem if one of the ladies is unable to complete her *Tawaaful-Ifadah* due to her menses. Remember that the *Ihraam* restriction of no sexual relations applies to all pilgrims until this *Tawaaf* is completed. Gentlemen, if you are doing the planning, this is a serious matter. This is a compulsory act of *Hajj* and cannot be omitted and there is no expiation. If your wife leaves Makkah without completing this *Tawaaf*, she is sexually illegal to you until she performs it.

You may wonder why I keep stressing on the above point

throughout the book. Because every year without fail, there are couples that face this problem. Even many who have read my book, but did not take the ruling seriously, until they got to Makkah and attended some lectures. Then it is too late as it is almost impossible to change flight dates.

Many packages cost the same whether you arrive in Makkah one month or one week before *Hajj*. So, if time permits, go early and stay longer.

There are many benefits in arriving early for *Hajj* (at least 3 weeks before). By the last week before *Hajj*, there are about one million people in Makkah. Being early allows you to enjoy Makkah when it is less crowded.

Bookings

Make your bookings with a reputable travel agent. This is another point I cannot stress enough. Get references from the agent and call or visit pilgrims that used the agent previously.

Avoid special deals with friends or relatives who are in the travel business. Of course, an exception should be made if you are getting a free trip.

Ensure that you have a confirmed booking out of Saudi Arabia. If your outbound flight is only waitlisted, you will not be allowed to board the aeroplane for Jeddah. If your agent is unable to get confirmation prior to your departure, ask him to obtain the first available confirmed date for you as well as keeping you waitlisted for the requested date.

Waitlisted means that your selected bookings (dates) are not confirmed, and will automatically be confirmed once seats become available on that particular flight.

A word of caution: Do not depend on or plan on waitlisted bookings, in and out of Jeddah. Take your confirmed dates and use them for your planning. These are not "normal" flights and there are very few passengers who do not turn up (no-show) or cancel during the *Hajj* period.

Do not assume that your travel agent knows everything. Double-check everything to avoid conflict later. It is extremely difficult (almost impossible) to change your flights once you are in Saudi Arabia due to the overwhelming number of passengers trying to do the same thing.

Select your flights carefully and keep to the itinerary.

If you plan to go to Madinah by aeroplane, purchase your Madinah tickets separately from your *Hajj* tickets. Ask your agent not to include it in your *Hajj* ticket itinerary. It is much easier to obtain a refund if the tickets are separate. (The cost of the Madinah tickets are fixed, so there will be no discount on them. There is a small possibility that you may not be able to utilise these tickets as you may need to go to Madinah by bus instead, due to the flight over-bookings and crowds.)

Also have a separate booking made for the Madinah sector. If you do end up going to Madinah by bus, the rest of your itinerary will not be cancelled. (Example: Kuala Lumpur-Jeddah; Jeddah-Madinah; Madinah-Jeddah; Jeddah-Kuala Lumpur. If for some reason you do not show up for the Jeddah-Madinah leg, the rest of your itinerary will automatically be cancelled.)

In summary: Separate tickets and bookings for Madinah! And give yourself at least 6 hours transit time in Jeddah.

When you receive your tickets, verify that the dates and times are the ones you have requested. Also check that the names on the tickets are spelt correctly. Many airlines now use e-tickets, so you will only receive a piece of paper.

If the dates are not the ones you requested and your travel agent tells you that he or she will fix it in Saudi Arabia, don't believe them!

Obtain from your agent your booking computer reference number. By using this number reconfirmation is much easier.

It is normally a 6-digit alphanumeric number. Write it down on the cover of your ticket, so it is easily accessible.

Use this number during any communication with the airline regarding your booking. The airline refers to this number as your PNR (Passenger Name Record).

Also obtain a computer printout of your booking if possible. See the example on the next page.

Request special food, depending on the airline you will be flying with (i.e., Muslim or vegetarian meals). Certain airlines such as Malaysian Airlines and Saudi Arabian Airlines serve only *Halal* food. If you are travelling on an airline that does not serve all *Halal* meals, and you have children travelling with you, request special meals for them also. On most airlines, the adult meals will be the requested ones, but the children get the child meal served to all other children and it is not *Halal*.

If applicable, request a bassinet for the baby on the aeroplane at booking time, and don't forget to reconfirm it prior to your flight.

Review the details of your booking very carefully. Other than the information listed in the example, there are two other items of special importance:

1. If for example your flight departure time is 0230 on Monday the 16th. This means you need to go to the airport on the Sunday night the 15th (or the morning of the 16th), and not on the Monday night. Many pilgrims mistakenly turn up 24 hours late for their flight.

2. '+1' next to the arrival time means you arrive at that time the following day.

See the next page for an example of a booking printout which contains the Passenger Name Record (PNR) or Computer Reference (locator) Number.

Passport and Visas

Determine all the necessary visas required for en route stopovers.

Make sure your passport expiry date is at least six months
after your planned returned date. Visa regulations for some
countries require even longer validity dates. Also ensure that

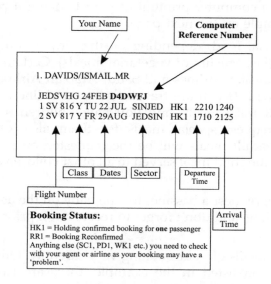

there are enough blank pages in your passport.

All female pilgrims whose passport contains a photo without
a head covering, should try to have it changed prior to the
issuing of a visa. The visa will be issued, but this is to avoid
embarrassment during the journey. It is a good time to start
correcting everything in your life.

Your agent will arrange your *Hajj* visa. The rules and
requirements may change from year to year. If you have
limited time in which to arrange all this, then I suggest you
call the embassy to obtain their requirements.

It may seem that I do not place much faith in the travel agent.
On the contrary, they do an excellent job. However, they are
very busy people and you are not their only customer. I
suggest that you double-check everything.

Before leaving home:

○ Place a unique identifying mark on your passport so that it is easily recognisable within a pile of passports. (A distinct, bright coloured tape on the edge of your passport will do the trick.)

○ Make photocopies of your passport and keep them separate from the passport.

○ Keep some extra passport-size photographs with you (at least 4).

○ Obtain the Jeddah, Makkah and Madinah (where applicable) telephone numbers and addresses of the airline (or agent) you are departing from Saudi Arabia with. This is important information, as you may need to call them or visit their offices.

Baggage

Your ticket will show (in the last column on the right side) your baggage allowance. The standard weight is 20kg (44lb) per ticket. Some airlines allow more during *Hajj*. In the USA it is the number of bags and not weight.

During *Hajj* the airlines are very strict about overweight (excess) baggage. Excess baggage charges at airports, including Saudi Arabia, are extremely high. Check this with your agent or airline if you have any doubts. The normal rule for overweight charges is 1% of the 1st class fare, for each kilo. Do your sums and you will be very surprised.

There are facilities and agents in Makkah who handle cargo. Many pilgrims send their heavy bags as cargo prior to their departure from Makkah.

Most airlines allow only one piece of hand luggage, and it should weigh no more than 5kg (11lb). This is excluding a handbag or a briefcase.

Keep the size of your suitcase in the normal size range (max. 28in/70cm). It is very difficult to travel with very large suitcases, and you will definitely be overweight.

Do not take your very expensive and favourite suitcases. Ensure that your luggage is sturdy as it will be "well travelled and knocked around" by the time you return.

Sometimes during check-in the airline may allow you 5 to 7kg (11-15lb) more, depending on the person checking you in. Do not depend on this.

If you are leaving home with your bags already weighing 20kg (44lb), then you will most likely be overweight coming back, unless you do not plan to buy anything, or you have plenty of gifts/parcels for people in Saudi Arabia.

Mark all your luggage clearly, inside and outside. Mark the outside with a unique identifying mark so that it is easily recognisable. Remember there are many bags that look alike. A bright coloured ribbon attached to the carrying handle is a good trick. (Hopefully, not everyone reading this will use the same colour ribbon).

Upon your return you will most likely bring back *Zamzam* water. Check with your customs authorities prior to leaving home the maximum number of litres of water you are allowed to bring back with you. There is no sense in carrying 10 litres of water when the customs in your country will only allow 1 litre per passenger.

In the past some airlines allowed *Zamzam* containers as hand luggage. This is no more the case. All *Zamzam* has to be checked in (and most airlines count it as part of your weight allowance). So 20 litres of *Zamzam*, and you have already reached your 20kg weight allowance. Check with your airline.

Do not pack the *Zamzam* container inside your suitcase.

Lost Luggage

One of the more unpleasant aspects of travelling is when the airline "loses" your luggage. This happens on the best of airlines.

Most airlines have a very good lost baggage tracking system.

If your bags have not been stolen (which is unlikely), then in most cases the bags are found and returned to you within a few days.

Always keep the luggage tags (stickers) that you received during check-in with you, as you will need them in the event of your bags being lost.

You must have one tag (sticker) for each piece of checked luggage.

If you did not receive all your luggage, ALWAYS report, and complete any paperwork, at the first point of arrival. The forms have a field where you have to put your residential telephone number and this is used as the contact number. Most pilgrims make the mistake of not adding their local numbers (hotel in Makkah or Madinah). Once you get checked into the hotel, call the airline to provide them with your room number.

Obtain the required file and telephone numbers that you will need for follow-up.

Under normal circumstances the procedures are that the airline will endeavour to get your luggage to you (to your hotel). With *Hajj* I found that in most cases, the pilgrim needs to do the "running around" and you may have to go to the airport a few times to search for your bags. This can sometimes be very difficult, as you may be in Madinah and your bags are in Jeddah.

On numerous occasions the pilgrims only received their bags after *Hajj*.

I have been to numerous "lost baggage" warehouses around the world. Not because I enjoy going to them; no, I have experienced the agony of lost luggage. I am amazed at the amount of bags in these warehouses. This highlights that in most instances that if you are prepared to do some "running around", you will find your bags.

One more reason why you MUST mark your bags inside and

outside with your name and contact details.

Also for this reason you should never pack perishable food items in your luggage.

Remember or note down the following before you travel:

- The size of your bags;
- The colour of your bags;
- The make (brand name) of your bags;
- Any other special identification (i.e. black stripes, broken handle, etc.).

This information is very important when you have to complete the required paperwork at the "lost baggage" counter.

If you check in very late (30 minutes before departure), don't be surprised if your bags don't arrive on the same flight as you.

This is when the group leader or the travel agent (assuming they are with you) should be of great assistance to you.

Taking all the above into consideration, I strongly suggest you keep some spare clothes (and underwear) in your overnight bag.

If you have not been reunited with your luggage prior to your departure for home, make sure you obtain a claim form (file number, contact numbers, procedure to follow, etc.) from the airline, in order to pursue the case further once you reach home.

Accommodation

All pilgrims stay in tents in Mina. Mina now has permanent fire-proof tents with air-conditioning and electricity. They are quite comfortable compared to the previous tents. For most the bed is either a carpet or a thin foam mattress. The tents are designed so it can be sub-divided, depending on the size of your group. So don't be surprised if you are in a tent with 300 other people. (I am not exaggerating). Men and women are in separate tents.

All pilgrims are housed in large canvass tents in Arafat. They are not as comfortable as the Mina tents. Then again, you do not need comfort in Arafat.

Your night stay in Muzdalifah will certainly make up for anything that you may have complained about. If the 5 star accommodation you were promised did not eventuate, or even the 2 star place, in Muzdalifah you will have as many stars as you like, when you lay on the ground looking towards the sky and counting the stars. Yes, all pilgrims spend the night in the open in Muzdalifah.

Accommodation problems cause so many disputes and frustration for the pilgrims. This is due to many reasons. One of the most common reasons is that the agents make too many promises they cannot keep. Another reason is that the pilgrims' expectations are sometimes too high and unrealistic. One cannot compare this trip (in accommodation, transport facilities, etc.) to any other trip. *Hajj* is unique!

Even though there are 5 star hotels (at 10 star prices), most accommodation in Makkah is geared to be functional rather than fashionable. Most of the rooms/apartments are sparsely furnished with the bare minimum, yet clean, neat and tidy. Do not expect the same standard 5 or 4 stars, as most are about 2 stars, if not less. Some are minus 2 stars, so be prepared. How you rate the accommodation will depend on what you are used to. Those that are used to luxury may be in for a shock. Try to always think of those that are worse off than you.

You must clarify with your agent exactly what you are paying for.

There are various types of packages with a varying range of accommodation. Let your agent explain to you in detail what type of accommodation they provide. If you are told your accommodation is close to the *Haram* (mosque), ask how high up. There are plenty of hilly streets, and although you may be "close", the hills can be very tiring and strenuous. This is especially important for those with leg or back ailments as well as the not-so-young pilgrims.

There are some packages that move the pilgrims from Makkah to Aziziah (a suburb in Makkah, near Mina) about ten days before the actual *Hajj*. Other packages move the pilgrims after the *Hajj* (12th). These packages normally cost less as the building in Makkah is rented out again. This is a good option if you are on a low budget. The drawback is that you will not be near the *Haram* as it is not within walking distance. Transport by bus is normally provided.

Like most things, the more you pay the better the accommodation. If you prefer en suite type rooms, or only two persons per room, then it will cost you much more. Most accommodation has separate quarters for men and women. It is not uncommon for up to ten people to be sharing a single room.

Don't let the name of the accommodation (Makkah Palace) fool you.

Many pilgrims have a sort of comradeship attitude when planning and making their bookings. They are all very keen to live in the same building or to share rooms. Once in Makkah, it is another story. Take what is convenient for you and your partner and avoid making decisions based on others requirements. Trust me, even if it is with close family!

If you are able to choose the floor you can be on, choose the lower floors as the elevators get extremely busy. This way you can use the stairs when needed. One drawback though: if the hotel is located in a busy street, the noise of the cars can be very disturbing at night when you are trying to sleep.

If the package has an option to include food, I suggest you take it. If you choose not to, at least choose to include food for the *Hajj* days.

If the package has an option to include the sacrifice, I suggest you take it. If not, see under the preparation section for more details about the sacrifice. (Sacrifice is compulsory for pilgrims performing the *Tamattu* and *Qiran* method.)

Do not take anything for granted; ask questions so you know what you are paying for.

Most of the accommodation facilities (Makkah, Mina, Arafat) have the "Eastern toilets". If you have been reared in the West and are not familiar with these "flat toilets", the trick is to sit and lean (rest) slightly more on your left leg.

Ask your agent or any person recommending accommodation at least the following questions. These questions are applicable to both Makkah and Madinah:

- How far is it from the mosque (by time)?
- Are there any hills or hilly streets on the way?
- Are there any stairs to climb to get to the building?
- How many persons will share a room?
- Are the men and women separate?
- How many bathrooms are there per room?
- How many elevators are there?
- On which floor will you be and how many rooms per floor are there?
- Is the hotel located in a busy or a main street?
- Do the rooms have telephones, refrigerators, air-conditioning, etc.?
- Do the people (receptionists) who manage the hotel speak English?
- Do they provide a room cleaning service?
- Do they provide laundry facilities?
- Is food included? If yes, what type of food is provided? (If I choose not take the food option, is food provided for the *Hajj* days?)

- Are there kitchen/cooking facilities in the rooms?
- Who will represent the agent during the trip?
- Will you be moved to Aziziah prior to *Hajj*?
- Will the rooms be available during the *Hajj* days?
- Will the rooms be available after *Hajj*?

These questions are repeated in a checklist format for your convenience. See chapter 15.

Let me give you some reasons why these questions are important. Many smaller hotels only have one phone line, so the chance of anyone calling you from home getting through to you is zero, as the line will always be busy; most of the receptionists don't speak a word of English, so the chances of getting anything done or getting any telephone message are pretty low.

Most of the big 5 star hotels, are rented in the following manner for *Hajj*:

Up to 1st Dhul-Hijjah - Group 1 (country 1)

1st to 7th Dhul-Hijjah - Group 2 (country 2)

8th to 13th Dhul-Hijjah - Group 3 (country 3)

14th onwards - Group 4 (country 4)

So if you wondered why the facilities in these hotels are in such a bad shape, you now know why.

Once you have decided about your Makkah and Madinah accommodation, don't forget to ask:

- What the format of the actual *Hajj* package is:

  6 days - 8th to Mina until the 13th

  5 days - 8th to Mina until the 12th

  5 days - 9th to Arafat until the 13th in Mina

  4 days - 9th to Arafat until the 12th in Mina

- How many will share a tent in Mina?
- Are the buses air-conditioned?

- How far is your tent from the Namira mosque in Arafat?
- How far are you from "Jabal-Rahmah" (Mount of Mercy) in Arafat?
- How far are you from the *Jamr'at* in Mina?
- Will the group spend the night in Muzdalifah?
- Will food be provided in Muzdalifah?
- On which day will the group return to Makkah to perform *Tawaaful-Ifadah*? Is transport provided?

The agent in your country may not have all the answers, but they should be able to give you a fair idea of what to expect. Keep in mind that there are many things that are beyond the control of the agent, so always try to see the issue from both sides. I would like to relate some stories to illustrate that many things are beyond the control of the agent. The best of plans can go wrong...

During the 1415H (1995) *Hajj* year an agent was canvassing and selling his Makkah accommodation at a particular price. This price was somewhat higher than the normal price for this agent, due to the fact that they had a new building very close to the *Haram*. Unfortunately the agent was unable to attract many customers, so he lowered his prices. In the meantime, the agents' partner in Makkah changed the building to one further away from the *Haram* due to the cost reduction without informing the selling agent about the change. You can imagine what happened when the pilgrims did not get what they were promised. It was not totally the fault of the selling agent; neither can he do much about it once you are in Makkah. So take it easy on them and say *"Alhamdulillah"* instead of fighting with your agent. Avoid arguing and shouting, especially while you are in the state of *Ihraam*.

In the same year many agents sold packages that included building accommodation in Mina, instead of tents. What the agents did not know was that the *Jamr'at* bridges in Mina was being widened and about 200 buildings around the *Jamr'at* were demolished due to the expansion. The agents had no choice but to accommodate their people in tents as their normal buildings were now non-existent. The pilgrims were in an uproar and demanded their money back. Be realistic, the agents were unaware of this expansion and there was not much they could do, other than provide tent accommodation as the remaining building accommodation prices increased tenfold.

During the 1416H (1996) *Hajj* year the group were told that they were very close to the *Jamr'at* in Mina. In actual fact they were told that they could see the *Jamr'at* from their camp. Both these statements were correct. However, the pilgrims had to negotiate 300 stairs to get down to the *Jamr'at* street and then the same 300 stairs to get back!

In the same year it was agreed that the buses would stop for the night in Muzdalifah. After leaving Arafat at about 9.00pm (this is normal due to the crowd), the journey to Muzdalifah took 6 hours. At 2.30am was the first time the bus was able to stop at an open area to allow the group to perform *Maghrib* and *'Eshaa Salah*. This was still outside Muzdalifah. At 3.30am the bus crossed into the boundary of Muzdalifah. At this point the group leader decided to go straight ahead to Mina. About 500 metres from the Mina boundary the bus broke down. The group stayed and performed *Salatul-Fajr* in Muzdalifah. At 5.00am the bus was fixed and the group was on their way to Mina. By 8.00am the bus had moved only 5 metres from where it started. The traffic was at a standstill. The group decided to walk to Mina. After a harrowing and crushing walk through a maze of buses and people going in all directions, the group reached the *Jamr'at* at 10.00am. After stoning the big *Jamrah* they returned to their camp. Fortunately they knew the location of their camp in Mina. How could we forget the 300 stairs. By 10.30am we were all back in the camp. The bus finally arrived at 11.00am.

During the 1417H *Hajj*, there was a group of 6 buses travelling together. Within one hour of departing Jeddah on the 8th, two buses were "lost" in the traffic pandemonium in Aziziah (suburb of Makkah), due to the fire in Mina. While waiting in Aziziah, we "lost" one group member, as he went wandering off. On the 10th morning the bus was once again "stuck" in the traffic in Muzdalifah and believe it or not, the exact same scenario as in as the previous year (point 4) ensued.

On the other hand, during the same year (1417) some other groups had no such problems. They reached Muzdalifah in 40 minutes, spent the night and reached Mina in one hour. By 8.00am they were in Makkah performing *Tawaaful-Ifadah*, while we were still sweating it out in the bus in Muzdalifah.

I can relate so many more stories of bus delays, lost pilgrims, food not getting to the camps on time, but I think I've made my point. I may also add that during the *Hajj* of 1424 (2004), we lost no one, had no bus delays, only food was a problem in Mina, and in 1426 (2006) everything went according to plan, *Alhamdulillah*.

What these stories illustrate is that many things can happen that are totally outside the control of the organisers. So be prepared for some surprises.

This is when you will need some of that valuable patience you saved up.

There are many roads and it all depends on which road you take, what time you leave, where your camp is located, etc.

Another important point to keep in mind: the owners of the hotels, buildings, tents and the agents are not necessarily in the same "spiritual state" as you are. This is their business and livelihood, so do not expect them to be very compassionate or to lose money on the deal. If they do not make sufficient money, then the service you get will suffer. (Maybe you believe they make too much money. Well, that's another story!)

If you are not too fussed about things and have a tight budget, I suggest you take the package that costs the least. This way you will not worry and complain about how much things cost you. Even if you pay a lot, say "*Alhamdulillah*" to whatever comes your way.

In the checklist section there is also a table that will help you to evaluate different packages. I have listed some criteria as a guide. It is up to you to add your own criteria and decide which ones are more important, and rate them accordingly. As an example, if cost is very important, rate it as H (high). Then score each package out of five, the cheapest being five; the best accommodation being five and the worst being one. You may wish to score with a larger range (10 to 1). You then add up all the scores (high, medium and low), which will give you a better idea of the value of each package.

The example on the next page shows that the package from Orient is the best value based on the listed requirements.

One final note: after all the precautions, preparations and planning that you may have done, still be prepared not to get what you paid for or have been promised. The later (closer to *Hajj*) you arrive the more likely it is that this will happen.

Package evaluation example:

Example		Packages:				
		Orient	*Hajji*	*Trilite*	*Hasans*	*Ocean*
Overall Scores:		20	14	14	12	19
Total for High:	H	8	2	4	2	9
Total for Medium:	M	7	11	8	9	7
Total for Low:	L	5	1	2	1	3
Criteria:		Scores:				
Agent Reputation	*m*	5	1	2	1	3
Agent – other factors	*l*	5	1	2	1	3
Cost:						
Airfare	*h*	5	1	2	1	3
Accommodation	*h*	3	1	2	1	3
Other	*h*	-	-	-	-	3
Accommodation:						
Location (Makkah)	*m*	1	5	3	5	2
Location (Madinah)	*m*	1	5	3	3	2

Personal Behaviour

$$﴿ٱلْحَجُّ أَشْهُرٌ مَّعْلُومَٰتٌ فَمَن فَرَضَ فِيهِنَّ ٱلْحَجَّ فَلَا رَفَثَ وَلَا فُسُوقَ وَلَا جِدَالَ فِي ٱلْحَجِّ وَمَا تَفْعَلُوا۟ مِنْ خَيْرٍ يَعْلَمْهُ ٱللَّهُ وَتَزَوَّدُوا۟ فَإِنَّ خَيْرَ ٱلزَّادِ ٱلتَّقْوَىٰ وَٱتَّقُونِ يَـٰٓأُو۟لِى ٱلْأَلْبَـٰبِ﴾$$

*"The Hajj (pilgrimage) is (in) the well-known (lunar year)
months. So whosoever intends to perform Hajj therein by
assuming Ihraam, then he should not have sexual relations
(with his wife), nor commit sin, nor dispute unjustly during
Hajj. And whatever good you do, (be sure) Allah knows it.
And take a provision (with you) for the journey, but the best
provision is At-Taqwa (piety, righteousness, etc.). So fear Me,
O men of understanding!"*

Surah Al-Baqarah (2:197)

It is essential that you adopt good behaviour at all times
during *Hajj*. Always act and behave in a manner that will
please Allah. The above ayah gives you six instructions, so
abide by it!

Abu Hurrairah (ﷺ) related that the Prophet (ﷺ) said:

$$«مَنْ حَجَّ هَذَا البَيْتَ فَلَمْ يَرْفُثْ ولَمْ يَفْسُقْ رَجَعَ كَمَا وَلَدَتْهُ أُمُّهُ»$$

*"One who performs Hajj without having marital relations or
committing any sin returns from Hajj as pure as he was on
the day he was born."*

(Bukhari & Muslim: 1819:1350)

Remember Allah at all times (below are a few of the basics):

When:	Say:	Translite-ration:	Meaning:
Starting to do something	بِسْمِ اللهِ	"Bismillah"	In the Name of Allah
Intending to do something	إِنْ شَاءَ اللهُ	"In Sha Allah"	If Allah wills
Something is being praised	سُبْحَانَ اللهِ	"Subhan-Allah"	How perfect Allah is
Expressing appreciation	مَا شَاءَ اللهُ	"Maa Sha Allah"	By the will of Allah
Thanking someone	جَزَاكَ اللهُ خَيْرًا	"Jazak-Allahu-Khairan"	May Allah reward you with good
Thanking Allah	الْحَمْدُ للهِ	"Alhamdu-lillah"	All praise is for Allah
Sneezing	الْحَمْدُ للهِ	"Alhamdu-lillah"	All praise is for Allah
Repenting of a sin	أَسْتَغْفِرُ اللهَ	"Astaghfir-ullah"	I seek Allah's forgiveness
A death message is received	إِنَّا للهِ وَإِنَّا إِلَيْهِ رَاجِعُونَ	"Inna-Lillahi-Wa Inna Ilayhi Raji'un"	We belong to Allah and to Allah we return
Someone sneezes (and he says "Alham-du-lillah")	يَرْحَمُكَ اللهُ	Yar hamuk-Allah"	May Allah have mercy upon you

It is very common for people to perform certain "good deeds" that have no basis in the *Sunnah* and also they have no proof of its origin. "They are merely following traditions and cultures. They also say, "There's nothing wrong with doing so and so..."

Aishah (🌸) narrated that the Prophet (ﷺ) said:

«مَنْ أَحْدَثَ فِي أَمْرِنا هذَا ما لَيْسَ فِيهِ فَهُوَ رَدٌّ»

"If somebody innovates something which is not in harmony with the principles of our religion, that thing is rejected."

(Bukhari:2697)

Make peace with those with whom you have a dispute and pay or make arrangements for your debts.

When I was preparing for *Hajj*, a friend told me that for every dollar I save for *Hajj*, I should save ten bags of patience. He was half right. I suggest that you save about "twenty bags of patience". Meaning that if you are generally an impatient person, train yourself to be more patient. You will need it on this trip.

Mentally prepare yourself:

- o To maintain a positive attitude;
- o To say "*Alhamdulillah*" for everything, be it good or bad;
- o To think of those who are possibly in a worse situation, when your situation is not to your liking;
- o To make *Dhikr* and make *Istighfaar* (seek Allah's pleasure and forgiveness) when you get impatient with people or situations;
- o To cope with crowds.

It is quite natural for a person to be upset when he does not get what he has paid for (e.g., the accommodation does not meet his or her expectations etc.). Avoid making a big fuss when you feel that you are being short-changed. Ask yourself instead, am I getting my money's worth of *Ibadah*? Don't short-change yourself by not fulfilling all the duties of *Umrah* and *Hajj*, by being too lazy to go to the mosque, or by taking all sorts of shortcuts and making all types of excuses during *Hajj*. This is the real tragedy of money wasted!

Get your money's worth of *Ibadah* and try not to fret too much over the material things! I am not saying don't do anything if you are blatantly being cheated. I am saying, try not to argue and fight over petty differences. Evaluate the situation and ask yourself, if arguing will make any difference to the outcome.

Make this journey a reformation for yourself by ensuring that the entire trip is an act of *Ibadah* and not only a mere performance of the *Hajj* rituals.

There are people from varied backgrounds, some of which may never have seen an escalator before. Try to always smile, be polite, and show patience.

Try to greet first when you meet or see fellow Muslims, even if you don't know them. Always return a greeting with equal or better (i.e. if your fellow Muslim greeted you with "*Asalamu Alaykum*", return his greeting with "*Wa-alaykum-Salaam wa-Rahmatullahi wa-Barakaatuhu*". This is his right!). Observe the surprise yet warm response when you greet people you don't know. And best of all, you are rewarded for it.

Money and Banking

To have the financial means is one of the preconditions for the performance of *Hajj*. However it is acceptable to accept a free trip as a 'gift', as *Sadaqah*, or as a 'worker'.

The money used for *Hajj* MUST be earned or obtained by *Halal* (lawful by Allah) means.

The Saudi Arabian monetary unit is the riyal, which is divided into 100 halalahs. Notes are in 1,5,10, 20, 50, 100, 200 and 500 riyal denominations. The coins are in 10, 25, 50 halalahs and 1 riyal denominations.

The riyal is quoted in US dollars but is based on Special Drawing Rights (SDR). As the SDR/dollar rate varies, so the official riyal/dollar rate is revalued at intervals to keep within a narrow band around the dollar (dollar = SR3.75). This fixed rate has been in place for many years, but may change in future.

The rate of exchange (for US dollars) you will obtain in Saudi Arabia will vary between 3.70 and 3.75, depending on where you change your money (bank or money changers). It also depends on whether you have cash or traveller's cheques.

There are many banks and money exchangers in Makkah, Madinah and Jeddah. They both give about the same rate of exchange. The banks do not deal with all currencies. They deal mainly with the mainstream currencies (i.e. American dollar, British pound, French franc, Dutch guilder).

Saudi Arabia has an excellent ATM (Automatic Teller Machine) network called SPAN. If your bank subscribes to Cirrus or Maestro you should be able to withdraw money from the ATM using your debit card. (I say should, as there is no guarantee that it will work, so do not depend on it.)

All major credit cards are widely accepted in the larger stores, and you can obtain a cash advance at certain banks on your card.

To exchange some of the less commonly used currencies you need to go to a money exchanger. (How does one know if the bank will change it or not? Well, it's a kind of "trial and error" situation.)

The banks require a lot of proof in order to change your traveller's cheques. They need a copy of your passport and proof of purchase of the cheques (the receipt showing the serial numbers).

The queues in the bank are also normally very long. The money exchangers normally don't require a lot of details (proof), and their queues are generally shorter.

You should budget about 900 Saudi riyals for the two drafts you need when landing at Jeddah. One draft is for the buses and the other is for the *Hajj* services in Arafat and Mina. These drafts are sometimes referred to by some agents and pilgrims as the landing tax. You may need a copy of these drafts to obtain your visa.

As you read this, check the expiry dates on all your cards and make sure they do not expire during the duration of your trip. (A friend was unable to withdraw cash from the Cirrus ATM at a critical time, as his card had expired the previous day.)

It is much easier to change your money at the money exchanger, so avoid the banks wherever possible.

The "best" currency to take with you is American dollars, traveller's cheques as well as some cash notes. It is much easier to change notes than it is traveller's cheques during the busy period of *Hajj*. Some shops will accept cash dollars.

Take some small denominations of US dollars. These are useful if you need to change a small amount of money for food or departure tax at an airport.

Also take a small amount of money in the currencies of countries you will be visiting or passing through. Transit delays are common, and you may need to buy something to eat or drink or for trolley services.

Budget for any departure taxes that you need to pay. Most countries now include the departure tax in the price of the airline ticket. Since 1/6/99 a SR50.00 per passenger departure tax was introduced in Saudi Arabia. However passengers with *Hajj* or *Umrah* visas are exempted. This may change in future, so check with your agent.

Do not make all the traveller's cheques in your name. Make some in your partner's name.

Sometimes the bank will insist on seeing your passport when cashing your traveller's cheques, even though they are fully aware that none of the pilgrims have their passports with them. Don't argue, go to another bank instead. This is one more reason why I suggest you change most of your money at the airport.

For *Hajj Tammattu* and *Qiran* there is only one compulsory sacrifice (*Hady*). You may find that some pilgrims are confused and understand that there are two *Dumms, Dumm-*

Shukr and the *Hady*. There is only ONE! So budget about SR300 - SR550 for your sacrifice (*Hady*). Also keep in mind that if you miss any of the *Wajib* (obligatory) acts, you need to make a sacrifice (e.g., sheep, goat, etc.) as expiation (*Dumm*). So keep these expenses in mind when budgeting. There are more details about the sacrifices in chapter 6 under "Sacrifices" and in chapter 8, under "*Hady* (Sacrifice)".

Budget some money for *Sadaqah* (voluntary charity).

Make a list of all the people for whom you plan to buy a gift. Estimate the amount you plan to spend on each person. Budget, and put the money aside. This is essential as the shopping in Makkah and Madinah is very enticing, and you do not want to run out of money. (See the checklists in chapter 15.)

If you plan to do plenty of shopping, budget for excess baggage charges and possibly customs duties.

Be ready when you arrive in Jeddah to change your money at the airport. Calculate how much you require and change as much as you can. Queuing in banks later on is not much fun and the time could be better spent in *Ibadah*.

Do not carry all your money with you all the time. Give some to your partner to keep (spend) and keep some in some other safe place. This way you are covered if you happen to lose your wallet.

Write down in a small pocket-size notebook all your traveller's cheque numbers and their respective values. Also photocopy and make a note of the bank drafts in your possession. Alternatively you may note down all the above details in the checklists provided in chapter 15 of this book.

Take enough money so you do not have to resort to borrowing during the trip.

Unfortunately and sadly I need to mention that there are pickpockets during *Hajj*. As with any other trip, you need to take care of your money. Do not be careless because you are on *Hajj*. Buy yourself a good money belt. Good belts (canvas type) are available in Makkah and Madinah.

Health and Medicine

There are many general and specialised hospitals in the Kingdom, as well as clinics, infirmaries and private clinics offering their services.

Medicines and drugs are easily obtainable without prescription in pharmacies, but sometimes prescriptions with generic names are needed, since brand names in the Kingdom may differ from elsewhere.

Basic hospital and clinic facilities are provided free of charge for the pilgrims (see in chapter 8 in the "Makkah" section of this book under Medical Facilities for more details).

There are wheelchair facilities available (see in chapter 8 in the "Makkah" section of this book under Wheelchair Facilities for more details).

There are also hospital facilities in Arafat and Mina.

You will notice that the doctor or pharmacist, making pen stripes on the box of your prescribed medicine. Three stripes, means take three times a day, two stripes means take twice a day etc.

There is a very high probability that during this trip you may catch a cold or the flu due to being in and out of the sun and air-conditioned rooms.

It is also very likely that you will be coming home with a cough, affectionately known as the "Hajji cough".

Take all the required vaccinations. Meningitis jab is always recommended.

Obtain a certificate or a doctor's note of proof of the vaccinations you've taken. The Saudi Arabian Embassy may need this before issuing you with a visa. Details can be obtained from the embassy as to which vaccinations are required.

If you are allergic to certain antibiotics, get your doctor to prescribe an antibiotic for flu and throat infections and have it dispensed in order to take with you.

If you are carrying any medicine with you, also keep a doctor's letter regarding it.

Take some or all of the following with you. These things are all available in Saudi Arabia however; it is much easier to go prepared:

- Headache tablets;
- Salt tablets (especially if you sweat a lot);
- Muscle cramp ointment;
- Vitamin C tablets (take one of these daily);
- Throat lozenges & Cough syrup;
- Cream for skin irritation (Remember, you (men) will be wearing no underwear and pants while in *Ihraam*, and the friction can become painful);
- Moisturising cream (for your dry skin and heels);
- Plasters (band aids) and some bandages;
- Antibiotics;
- Diarrhoea tablets.

Sun block or some sun protection cream may also be very handy. Do not use it while you are in *Ihraam*.

Take a pair of sunglasses, especially if you have sensitive eyes.

Take a dust mask if you are allergic to dust. This also helps reducing the hazards of the car fumes.

There is a checklist in chapter 15 of this book listing all these items.

Ensure that all the medicine taken along with you is clearly labelled to avoid problems at customs.

A fellow pilgrim once asked me why I recommended that he bring all these medicines, when he did not use any of them.

(This was during the first week of Dhul-Hijjah.) I told him to say "*Alhamdulillah*" and use the medicine for fellow pilgrims. After *Hajj* he had the flu and was then very appreciative of the suggestions. Don't be over confident. As I said, the probability of getting a cold is very high! If you don't get sick, thank Allah.

To make an analogy: When you study for an exam you need to revise everything, just in case it comes up in the exam. Many times you study an entire book and only one small part is contained in the exam. Similarly you need to take all the possible medicines with you, just in case...

One final note: Do not be in a hurry to give away any of your medicine, as many pilgrims get sick a few days after *Hajj*.

Clothes and Toiletries

Ihraam: For men it is two clean, unfitted pieces of cloth, preferably white, while women are free to wear what they please except clothes that are attractive to or imitating men. (More details about *Ihraam* conditions and restrictions are covered in chapter 6 of this book.)

Women must not wear perfume when going to the mosque or in the company of strange (non-*Mahram*) men (this rule applies at all times and not only during *Hajj*).

Many Muslims are confused about the issue of stitched clothes and shoes while in *Ihraam*. It is not a matter of stitches, rather it should not be fitted clothes, such as a shirt or trousers, and the shoes or sandals must not cover the ankles.

Some accommodation packages provide washing facilities for clothes (i.e. washing machines).

There are dry-cleaning services available at a very reasonable cost.

Clothes: Take comfortable, loose-fitting clothes.

If possible take another set of *Ihraam* clothes with you. You are in *Ihraam* for 3 days and 2 nights during *Hajj*. It is nice to be able to change or in case you accidentally dirty your *Ihraam*. (The *Ihraam* cloths (men) can be used as towels, shades, blankets, etc., later on.)

You do not need lots of clothes. Take clothes that are acceptable to wear to the mosque, and are easily washed and ironed.

Take clothes with material that require little or no ironing.

Take dark-coloured towels.

Keep packets of hand tissues (for the toilet, sweating, etc.). Some tissues are perfumed, so avoid using them while in *Ihraam*.

Washing powder is available in the supermarkets if you plan to do washing. A bar of washing soap is also very handy. (Do not panic, your towels and white garments will regain their white splendour as soon as you get back home and you put them in the washing machine.)

Take appropriate clothes with you. Tight jeans and T-shirts with fancy slogans or photos on them are not appropriate for this trip or any trip for that matter.

Take a comfortable pair of sandals to wear with your *Ihraam* and for going to and from the mosque. Take a flat, soft pair if possible, as these are much easier to carry in your hand when you are in the *Haram*. Leave the expensive slippers for another trip, as you may lose them in the *Haram*.

Carry a small plastic bag or a small cloth string bag with you, to place your sandals/shoes in when you are inside the mosque.

Take a pair of sand shoes (runners, joggers, tennis shoes). "What for?" you may ask. You will need them in Mina. They are the ideal shoes for going to the *Jamrah* as they provide you with grip and balance. Remember you are only in *Ihraam* on the first day of stoning the *Jamrah*. Thereafter you are out of *Ihraam*, meaning you can now wear your joggers. Avoid going to the mosque with them, as they are normally bulky. This applies to women as well.

Take socks, as you will need these to wear with your shoes.

Do not buy new pairs of slippers or shoes for *Hajj*, if you don't have to. Instead, use the tried and tested ones. Most of the time, new shoes tend to hurt one's feet when you initially wear them.

Toiletries

Toiletries to take with you: (these items are available in Makkah. However, as with the medicines, it is good to go well prepared):

- Shampoo (if perfumed, do not use it while in *Ihraam*)
- Non- perfumed soap (for while you are in *Ihraam*)
- Liquid soap (shower hair and body wash)*
- Toothpaste (use a *Miswak* instead while you are in *Ihraam*)
- Perfume (men only)
- Underarm deodorant (perfume-free for the women)
- Sanitary pads.

* I suggest you buy the liquid soap instead of a soap bar. Take the ones that can be used as shampoo as well. Also, try to get the ones in a container with either a hook or a tube shape with a flat back. This will make your trips to the shower in Mina much easier.

Is this your FIRST trip overseas?

I am assuming that you will be travelling by plane. The requirements are different if you are travelling by bus or by ship.

- Wear loose-fitting clothes and a comfortable pair of shoes.
- Swollen feet are a common complaint when flying. To avoid this discomfort, try the following:

- While travelling take off your shoes and wear socks (preferably made of a natural fibre).

- Also ensure the shoes you wear while travelling are a good fit and preferably lace-ups so the lacing system can be loosened if your feet swell.

- Use a pillow to rest your feet on. By raising your feet a little it will help the circulation.

- Drink plenty of water.

Do not sit throughout the journey. Get up and walk around a little bit to allow proper blood circulation.

You may suffer from some earache or your ears may "close-up" during the landing of the aeroplane. Chew on some gum or a sweet or "force" a yawn. This will "open" your ears.

If you are suffering from a cold, then your earache may be very severe. Carry some pain tablets with you and take them at least ten minutes prior to the landing.

Most travellers suffer from jetlag after arriving at their destination. This is when your biological clock is out of synch with the local time, meaning you either travelled forward or back in time. There are various methods proposed to overcome jetlag. Each person is different, so there is no clear, uniform method that I know of.

Do not take many heavy items of hand luggage. It can become a burden on the aeroplane and many airlines do not allow more than one bag.

Drink plenty of liquids while travelling to avoid dehydration. The drawback is that you may need to frequent the toilet.

Try to use the toilets as early as possible during the flight, while they are still clean.

Perform *Wudu* before travelling and put on your socks. This way you can wipe over your socks if you need to perform *Wudu* again in the aeroplane.

Other essential items you should take with you

√ In the checklist section of this book (chapter 15) all the suggested items to take with you are summarised. Some items are obvious ones that a person normally takes on a trip. However, I have listed them for the less experienced travellers.

√ A small pocket-size Qur'an. There are many Qur'ans available in the mosque. However, it is much easier to have your own. Also you won't have to get up to get it or take it back, as you may lose your valuable spot in the mosque. (Remember not to enter the toilet with the Qur'an in your pocket.)

√ The book of *Hajj* from Sahih Muslim or Sahih Bukhari. This is a handy authentic reference in case you are unsure about a particular issue.

√ Your *Hajj* reference books that you studied from (including this one).

√ Prayer mat. You may need it when "caught" outside the *Haram* or when on the road due to traffic or crowds. It can also be used as a sun shield when required and can be very useful during travelling.

√ Compass for *Qiblah*. This will be needed while travelling.

√ A Pen. This is always a handy item. Be prepared to share it with other pilgrims, therefore do not take an expensive pen.

√ Paper or a small notebook. If you have a pen, you will need something to write on. Use an A4 paper and divide it into small (business card size) pieces.

√ A small bag (backpack/knapsack) that you can carry on your back. This is very useful for your trip to Arafat as well as for moving between Mina and Makkah.

√ Shaving machine, blades and scissors. This is not for the beard but for preparing yourself for *Ihraam* and to shave/cut your hair on the 10th of Dhul-Hijjah.

√ Scissors (to cut the hair of the female pilgrims).

√ Hairbrush or comb.

√ Small mirror.

√ Toothbrush.

√ Nail clippers.

√ Alarm clock.

√ Money belt.

√ Umbrella (avoid a black one, as it draws the heat).

√ A hat/cap/*Koefia* or scarf to protect your head from the sun if you plan to shave it (men) on the 10th of Dhul-Hijjah.

√ A straw *Hajji* mat. (If you do not have one, you can buy it in Makkah. It is a woven straw or plastic mat with a plastic blow-up pillow. Essential for your night stay in Muzdalifah.)

What is useful to take with you

√ Shoe bag for your shoes while you are in the mosque.

√ Stone bag to keep your stones for the stoning (*Ramy*) of the *Jamr'at* in Mina.

√ Sun block (do not use it while you are in *Ihraam*).

√ Small water spray bottle. This is most refreshing, but can give you a cold.

√ An address book, E-mail addresses and business cards.

√ A small pocket knife. You should pack this in your suitcase and not in your carry-on luggage, as it will be confiscated (the camping type that contains a scissors, can-opener, etc.).

√ Some string. (This is useful to hang clothes or to tie a damaged suitcase.)

√ Some clothes pegs for hanging your washing.

√ An inflatable air mattress. This is very useful in Mina and Muzdalifah. The plastic pool ones will do the trick.

√ A blow-up travelling neck-pillow. This is very useful during the long journeys (plane or bus).

√ A small radio. You can listen to the *Khutbah* on Arafat.

What NOT to take with you

✗ Taking photos and video taping is discouraged in Makkah and Madinah near or around the *Haram* areas. You may have trouble (delays) with the video camera at customs upon entry. Then again, some years they don't seem to bother as you see pilgrim's videoing right outside the *Haram* itself. So there is no guarantee.

✗ Lots of clothes.

✗ Expensive jewelry.

✗ Any political books or fashion magazines.

✗ Any video cassettes. This may delay you considerably at customs upon arrival.

✗ Lots of toys, if you have accompanying children.

What you should study

Apply the golden rule to every aspect of *Umrah* and *Hajj*:

"What did the Prophet (ﷺ)
say, do or didn't do?"

Needless to say, you should understand all the rites of *Umrah* and *Hajj*.

There is absolutely no need to memorise any of the long and short *Dua's* you find in many *Hajj* books, for the different rounds of *Tawaaf* and *Sa'ee*. Most of these *Dua's* have no basis in the teachings of our beloved Prophet (ﷺ).

There is no special *Dua'* except between the *Yamani* and Black Stone Corner.

Learn the *Dua's* from the Qur'an and *Sunnah*. For a list of some of these *Dua's* see in chapter 11 in this book entitled "Supplications from Qur'an and the *Sunnah*".

Also in chapter 14 ("Revision") I have listed the few supplications I suggest you memorise. This will make your *Tawaaf* and *Sa'ee* much easier as you won't need to keep any books in your hand.

Read the meaning and try to understand the *Ay'at* in the Qur'an about *Hajj*. The spirit and meaning of *Hajj* cannot be understood without its historical background.

Read the detailed description of the Farewell *Hajj* as related by Jabir (ﷺ) in Sahih Muslim, Volume 2, page 611.

Memorise the *Talbiyah* and its meaning:

«لَبَّيْكَ اللَّهُمَّ لَبَّيْكَ، لَبَّيْكَ لَا شَرِيكَ لَكَ لَبَّيْكَ، إِنَّ الْحَمْدَ وَالنِّعْمَةَ لَكَ وَالْمُلْكَ، لَا شَرِيكَ لَكَ» .

"Labbayk Allahumma labbayk. Labbayka laa shareeka laka labbayk. Innal-hamda wan-ni'mata laka wal mulk. Laa shareeka lak."

(Here I am, O Allah, Here I am. Here I am, You have no partner, here I am. Surely all praise, grace and dominion are Yours, and You have no partner.)

For more details, rules and rites of *Hajj*, I recommend the following material:

1. The book of *Hajj* in *Sahih Muslim*.

2. The book of *Hajj* in *Sahih Al-Bukhari*.

3. Any of the five books mentioned in the introduction section of this book.

4. *Fiqhus-Sunnah,* volume 5.

Study authentic references and discuss any unclear issues with a learned scholar.

Discuss with those who have performed *Hajj* so you may learn about any difficulties they may have faced.

Wudu: Learn the *Fard* and *Sunnah* requirements for *Wudu*. Learn how to perform *Tayammum*.

Salah: As you will be performing many prayers in the *Haram* in Makkah (where the reward is 100,000 times for each *Salah*) and in the *Haram* in Madinah, (where the reward is 1,000 times for each *Salah*), it is imperative that you perform the prayers correctly in order to obtain the highest reward.

Learn about: What is *Fard*, what is *Sunnah* and what is *Bidah* (innovation).

Learn about the rewards of using a *Miswak* (tooth-stick) before every *Salah*. (The *Miswak* is sold around the *Haram* areas in Makkah and Madinah.)

I recommend the following reading:

1. The book of Salah in *Sahih Muslim*
2. The book of Salah in *Sahih Al-Bukhari*
3. *The Prophet's Prayer* by Shaikh Muhammad Naasir-ud-Deen Al-Albaani
4. *A Guide to Prayer in Islam* by M.A.K. Saqib
5. About Wudu, a book entitled, *Sifat Wudu-in-Nabee* by Fahd bin Abdur-Rahman Ash-Shuwaib

Janazah Salah: During *Hajj* it is more than likely that there will be a *Janazah Salah* (*Salah* for the deceased), after the *Fard Salah*.

It is normally announced over the loud speakers in the *Haram*. The announcement will also indicate whether it is for a male, female or a child, also if it is for more than one person.

A few important points I would like to mention:

1. Learn how to perform* the *Janazah Salah*.

2. There are many rewards* for performing *Janazah Salah*.

3. Do not be in a hurry after the *Fard Salah* to perform your *Sunnah Salah*. As a *Musafir* (traveller) you are not required to perform any *Sunnah Salah*, except that of *Salatul-Fajr* and *Salatul-Witr*.

4. Obey the *Sunnah* by sitting for a while after *Salah*, making *Istighfaar* and *Dhikr*. This way you will not miss the *Janazah Salah* if it is being performed.

5. Women should not miss this opportunity to perform the *Janazah Salah*, as they are equally rewarded.

(* for more details see chapter 8, under "*Janazah Salah*", in this book).

As you will be performing many prayers while en route to Makkah, acquaint yourself with the rules and laws governing the *Salah* for the traveller (*Musafir*).

Learn about the rules of wiping over your socks/shoes/*Khufs* during *Wudu*, as it is very useful while you are in the aircraft.

If you plan to visit Madinah, learn:

o About the history of Madinah;

o What and where is Raudah-tul-Jannah, Quba Mosque, Al-Baqee cemetery, mountain of Uhud, etc.;

o The etiquette of visiting graves and the grave of the Prophet (ﷺ).

Learn some basic Arabic words, i.e. thank you; please; the numbers (this will help during shopping); hotel; where; clean my room; hospital; water; etc.

Sometimes only the slang Arabic words are used in shops, so if the shopkeepers do not understand you, try the slang instead of the colloquial Arabic. If they still don't get it, then maybe it is your accent or the way you are pronouncing the words. Do not despair, it is not easy!

If all else fails, speak English. You will be surprised to find that most of the shopkeepers can speak a variety of languages such as English, Urdu, and Malaysian.

Special attention items

Following, is a short list of items I suggest you spend some extra time to understand, the reason being that some or all of these points seem to generate arguments and confusion. This is due to the various opinions on the same point and also sometimes due to a lack of understanding.

The list is definitely not exhaustive; these are merely the ones that I have experienced to be "sticky" points.

As a reminder, the answers given here represent once again the most common view taken from my primary reference materials, in addition to the *Imams* and scholars I had access to at the time of writing this book.

I urge you to make the effort to try and fully grasp and understand these issues, as I can assure you that these items will be a source of arguments and heated debates during your trip. By the way, give the arguments a miss!

More details about the answers provided here are covered in this book under its respective headings.

Topic	Done?	Remarks
Niyah: Should one pronounce one's *Niyah* aloud for *Salah, Tawaaf, Sa'ee,* etc.?	Some *Hajj* books teach the pilgrim many *Niy'at* to be read aloud. (i.e.: I intend to make my *Tawaaf* seven times..........).	According to the *Sunnah* one's *Niyah* should be made by the heart and not the tongue. The only exception being the *Niyah* one makes for *Umrah* or *Hajj*. (Even with this *Niyah* certain books teach a *Niyah* that has no authentic basis in the *Sunnah*).
Dua's: Is it necessary to memorize the long *Dua's* for each round of *Tawaaf* and *Sa'ee*? (In chapter 11 of this book is a list of some of the *Dua's* from the Qur'an and the *Sunnah*).	Some books have many long and beautiful *Dua's* for each circuit of *Tawaaf* and *Sa'ee*. Many pilgrims insist on memorising and reading only these *Dua's*.	Just looking at all these *Dua's* to prepare for *Hajj*, can make one reluctant to study at all. There are no specific *Dua's* to be read for each circuit, except for the *Dua'* between the *Rukn-Yamani* Corner and the *Hajrul-Aswad* (Black stone). Most of these *Dua's* have no authentic basis in the *Sunnah*.
Ihraam: What are the rules and restrictions of the *Ihraam*? (In chapter 6 of this book all the *Ihraam* rules and restrictions are addressed in detail).	1. When should the right shoulder be open (men)? 2. Can one use perfume while in *Ihraam*? 3. Can one smoke while in *Ihraam*? 4. Should a woman's *Ihraam* clothes be white in colour?	1. Only during *Tawaaf* 2. No. (It is *Sunnah* for the men to apply perfume to the body prior to making *Niyah* and going into the state of *Ihraam*). 3. No. 4. They can be of any colour.
Sacrifice: What are the rules for each type of *Hajj*? (In chapter 10 in this book, under sacrifice, the details are discussed).	How many sacrifices and for whom is it compulsory. Some pilgrims believe that the *Tamattu Hajj* has to make two sacrifices. (*Dumm-Shukr* and *Hady*). The timing of the sacrifices. Some pilgrims perform their *Hady* before the 10th Dhul-Hijjah. Rules for *Fidyah* (expiation).	*Hajj Tamattu*:- Compulsory to do one sacrifice; *Hajj Qiran*: - Compulsory to do one sacrifice. *Hajj Ifrad*:- Optional to do a sacrifice; The rules for fasting if you cannot afford the sacrifice, see Qur'an (2:196). The *Hady* MUST be done from the 10th Dhul-Hijjah onwards and not before. The *Fidyah* (expiation), if required, can be done before. (If for example you violated

		the *Meqaat* rule or *Ihraam* restrictions during your *Umrah*). Missing an obligatory (*Wajib*) act:-One sacrifice. Violation of an *Ihraam* rule (such as cutting your nails): - Fast for 3 days or feed 6 poor persons or one sacrifice.
Meqaat: Is it acceptable to pass the *Meqaat* without being in *Ihraam*? (If you are going directly to Makkah) (In chapter 7 of this book the *Meqaat* rules are addressed in detail).	Some pilgrims believe that it is acceptable to enter into *Ihraam* in *Jeddah*, after arriving from outside the *Meqaat*.	This is not acceptable and the pilgrim should either return to the nearest *Meqaat* or perform expiation (sacrifice). Jeddah is not a *Meqaat*, except for those residing in it.
Salah: What is the *Sunnah* regarding *Salah* during the *Hajj* days?	1. Some pilgrims insist on performing 4 *Rak'at* for *Salatul-Zuhr*/'*Asr*/'*Eshaa* during the days of *Hajj* in Mina (8th, 10th -13th).	1. The *Sunnah* is to shorten the *Salah* from 4 to 2 *Rak'at* during these days. Although many will argue that Uthman (⬥) performed 4 *Rak'at*, it is agreed by almost all scholars that the correct action is to shorten the *Salah*.
	2. Some books teach that *Salatul-Zuhr* and *Al-'Asr* is not to be joined if you are NOT in the mosque in Arafat.	2. The *Sunnah* is to join *Salatul-Zuhr* and *Al-'Asr*, at the time of *Zuhr*, wherever you are located on the plain of Arafat.
	3. Some pilgrims perform *Salatul-Maghrib* in Arafat.	3. *Salatul-Maghrib* is to be joined with *Salatul-'Eshaa* upon arrival in Muzdalifah or before midnight wherever you are.
	4. Do I perform *Salatul-Witr* and the *Sunnah* before *Fajr*?	4. Yes.
	5. What about performing the other *Sunnah-Muakkadah salah*?	5. It was not the practice of the Prophet (⬥) to perform any *Sunnah Salah*, except that of *Fajr*, and *Witr*, during his stay in Mina.

	6. What about performing other Nafl *Salah*, such as *Salatul-Duha* or *Salatul-Tahajjud*?	6. Even though it is not required to perform any of the *Sunnah Salah*, it is acceptable to perform other *Nafl Salah*, as part of your *Ibadah* and *Dhikr* while staying in Mina.
Muzdalifah: After leaving Arafat, what is the *Sunnah* regarding the night in Muzdalifah and which group of people are allowed to leave prior to *Salatul-Fajr*?	1. In my experience, I have found that many pilgrims believe that it is not necessary for them to spend the night in Muzdalifah.	1. The *Sunnah* is to spend the night here (*Mash'ar-il-Haram*) and to leave for Mina just before sunrise after *Salatul-Fajr* and having made *dua* (also see *Surah Al-Baqarah, Ayah* 198). According to the *Hadith* in *Sahih Bukhari*, the weak, ladies and children are allowed to leave after moonset. Some books relate the time to be after midnight.
	2. Many pilgrims leave early and then continue to perform the other rites ahead of its prescribed time (*Ramy* and *Tawaaful-Ifadah*).	2. If you leave early, you should still wait for the correct time before continuing with the rest of the *Hajj* rites.
	3. Many pilgrims rush to get to Makkah to 'catch' *Eid Salah*.	3. There is no requirement for the pilgrim to perform *Eid Salah*.
	4. Many pilgrims insist on collecting pebbles for the stoning here.	4. There is no *Sunnah* requirement to collect the stones here as the *Hadith* regarding this relates that the Prophet (ﷺ) collected the stones on his way to the *Jamrah* (not indicating any specific place). It is therefore acceptable to collect the stones anywhere, including Mina.
	5. Many pilgrims wash the pebbles.	5. There is no authentic basis for this practice in the *Sunnah*.
	6. Some books teach that this night is to be spent in supplication.	6. The pilgrim is to rest and sleep as per the *Sunnah*.

Mina: Which days are the pilgrims supposed to spend in Mina?	Is it a requirement to spend the nights of the 10th, 11th and possibly the 12th in Mina?	As per the *Sunnah* the best action is to spend the nights in Mina. This is a *Wajib* act and omitting it incurs expiation (sacrifice).
Jamr'at: What is the correct time for the stoning (*Ramy*) of the *Jamr'at*? (One narration has it that the Prophet (ﷺ) stood and made *Dua'* for a very long time – the time it takes to read the entire *Surah Al-Baqarah*).	1. Some pilgrims throw in the morning due to the crowds on all three/four days.	1. As per the *Sunnah* the starting time is after sunrise on the 10th and after *Zawaal* (when the sun moves from its zenith) for the 11th, 12th and 13th. It is better to delay the *Ramy*, even until midnight or the next day, due to crowds, instead of doing an act of *Ibadah* before its prescribed time.
	2. What is the order on each day and action after the *Ramy*?	2. On the 10th of Dhul-Hijjah only the big *Jamrah* (*Aqaba*) is to be pelted, from after sunrise. On the 11th, 12th and 13th, all three *Jamr'at* are to be pelted starting from the small one and finishing at the big one. After the small and middle *Jamr'at*, it is *Sunnah* to move to one side, face *Qiblah* and make *Dua*.
	3. Is it acceptable to stone after *Fajr* on the 13th?	3. No, it is not, even though some scholars say that it is acceptable. Ask yourself: " What did the Prophet (ﷺ) do?" Also, you chose to stay the extra day, so why not a few extra hours?
Tawaaful-Wadaa' (Farewell *Tawaaf*)	Many pilgrims confuse this *Tawaaf* with *Tawaaf-Al-Ifadah*. Many also dispute whether those living in Jeddah or pilgrims going for shopping in Jeddah after *Hajj*, need to perform *Tawaaful-Wadaa'* or not, prior to leaving Makkah. It is worth noting that not all scholars agree on this subject, but my suggestion is to be 'safe'.	*Tawaaful-Wadaa'* is the last act to be performed by the pilgrim prior to leaving Makkah. Menstruating or post-natal bleeding women can omit *Tawaaful-Wadaa'*. If the pilgrim plans to go to Jeddah (leaving the *Haram* area) and plans to return to Makkah, or for those who

		live in Jeddah, it is important to note that *Tawaaful-Wadaa'* should be performed either as the last rite or prior to leaving the *Haram* area. Meaning that if you go to Jeddah for shopping or visiting then you should perform *Tawaaful-Wadaa'*, even though you plan to return to Makkah. Look at it as the last rite to complete the *Hajj* rites, before you leave the *Haram* area. *Tawaaful-Ifadah* also referred to as *Tawaafus-Ziyarah* in some books or *Tawaaful-Hajj*, is a pillar of *Hajj* and cannot be omitted by any pilgrim. If *Tawaaful-Ifadah* is the last act to be done by the pilgrim prior to leaving Makkah, then *Tawaaful-Wadaa'* is 'joined' with it. Meaning only one set of *Tawaaf* is required. The *Niyah* has to be for *Tawaaful-Ifadah*. *Sa'ee* for *Hajj* must be done also for *Tamattu* and for *Qiran* and *Ifrad* if it was not done before.

﴿مَّن يُطِعِ ٱلرَّسُولَ فَقَدْ أَطَاعَ ٱللَّهَ﴾

"He who obeys the Messenger (Muhammad), has indeed obeyed Allah..."

Surah An-Nisaa' (4:80)

In addition to these issues being addressed in this book, I suggest for more detailed information, refer to the books of *Hajj* of Sahih Muslim and Sahih Bukhari. By using these books as a reference, you will get the actual *Hadith* of what is required to do: no explanation or interpretation. This will tell you what the Prophet (ﷺ) did. Now before you say, "I'm only a layman, how will I understand these *Ahadith*", try it, you will be pleasantly surprised. The English is very simple and clear to understand, e.g., what further explanation or interpretation or commentary do you need, when a *Hadith* clearly tells you, that the Prophet (ﷺ) spent the night in Muzdalifah or that he stoned the *Jamr'at* (11ᵗʰ, 12ᵗʰ & 13ᵗʰ) after *Zawaal*?

The *Ahadith* are clear as to what the best actions are. If you have a special condition or circumstances, I suggest you consult a reputable scholar to guide you.

You should now know the best actions to follow!

Try to keep an open mind if you do not agree with the views expressed in this book. Do not follow anything or anybody blindly, as YOU will be answerable for your actions on the Day of Judgement. It is important that for any act of *Ibadah* you should have authentic proof from the Qur'an and *Sunnah*.

عَنْ أَبِي هُرَيْرَةَ ﷺ أَنَّ رَسُولَ اللهِ ﷺ قَالَ: «كُلُّ أُمَّتِي يَدْخُلُونَ الجَنَّةَ إِلَّا مَنْ أَبِىٰ»، قَالُوا: يَا رَسُولَ اللهِ، وَمَنْ يَأْبِىٰ؟ قَالَ: «مَنْ أَطَاعَنِي دَخَلَ الْجَنَّةَ، وَمَنْ عَصَانِي فَقَدْ أَبِىٰ»

"Abu Hurrairah (ﷺ) related that the Prophet (ﷺ) said: "All my followers will enter Paradise except those who refuse.' They said, 'O Allah's Messenger! Who will refuse?'He said, 'Whoever obeys me will enter Paradise, and whoever disobeys me is the one who refuses (to enter it)'."

(Bukhari:7280)

Chapter 3
About Women

Some of the most disputable points in relation to *Hajj* are, not surprisingly, regarding women:

1. The issue of *Mahram*
2. Covering of the face while in *Ihraam*
3. Visiting of graves

At this point I would like to remind the readers about a *Hadith* regarding doubtful things. Although this *Hadith* is a reminder to us all, I find it pertinent to mention it in this chapter as some of the serious disputable issues are regarding women.

Narrated An-Nu'man bin Bashir (ﷺ): I heard Allah's Messenger (ﷺ) saying:

«الْحَلَالُ بَيِّنٌ وَالْحَرَامُ بَيِّنٌ، وَبَيْنَهُمَا مُشَبَّهَاتٌ لَا يَعْلَمُهَا كَثِيرٌ مِنَ النَّاسِ، فَمَنِ اتَّقَى الْمُشَبَّهَاتِ اسْتَبْرَأَ لِدِينِهِ وَعِرْضِهِ، وَمَنْ وَقَعَ فِي الشُّبُهَاتِ كَرَاعٍ يَرْعَى حَوْلَ الْحِمَى، يُوشِكُ أَنْ يُوَاقِعَهُ، أَلَا وَإِنَّ لِكُلِّ مَلِكٍ حِمًى، أَلَا إِنَّ حِمَى اللهِ مَحَارِمُهُ، أَلَا وَإِنَّ فِي الْجَسَدِ مُضْغَةً إِذَا صَلَحَتْ صَلَحَ الْجَسَدُ كُلُّهُ، وَإِذَا فَسَدَتْ فَسَدَ الْجَسَدُ كُلُّهُ، أَلَا وَهِيَ الْقَلْبُ»

"Both legal and illegal things are evident but in between them there are doubtful (unclear) things, and most people have no knowledge about them. So whoever saves himself from those doubtful (unclear) things, he saves his religion and his honour. And whoever indulges in these doubtful (unclear) things, is like a shepherd who grazes (his animals) near the Hima (private pasture) of someone else, and at any moment he is liable to get in it. (O people!) Beware! Every king has a Hima and the Hima of Allah on the earth is His illegal

(forbidden) things. Beware! There is a piece of flesh in the body, if it becomes good (reformed), the whole body becomes good but if it gets spoilt the whole body gets spoilt and that is the heart."

(Bukhari:52)

Mahram

It is essential that you be accompanied by your husband or some other *Mahram* on the journey for *Hajj*.

Mahram: Apart from your husband, a male relative whom you cannot legally marry (at any time in your life), such as your brother, father, son, husband's father.

Abu Hurrairah (ﷺ) reported that the Prophet (ﷺ) said:

$$\text{«لا يَحِلُّ لامْرَأَةٍ تُؤْمِنُ بالله واليَوْمِ الآخِرِ أَنْ تُسافِرَ مَسِيرَةَ يَوْمٍ وَلَيْلَةٍ لَيْسَ مَعَها حُرْمَةٌ»}$$

"It is forbidden for any woman who has faith in Allah and the Day of Judgement to undertake the distance of a day or more without being accompanied by a Mahram."

(Bukhari, Muslim and Ahmad: 1088:1339:10401)

Your sister's husband cannot be your *Mahram*, even if your sister is present. Although you cannot marry him, while he is married to your sister, you can actually marry him if they are divorced or she dies.

Below are a few points, which are common practice today. Are they acceptable? NO!

✗ A man making an agreement with a married woman who is about to make *Hajj* and has no *Mahram*, that he will be her *Mahram*.

✗ A woman taking a non-related man as her brother so that he can be a *Mahram* for her and then treating him as a *Mahram*.

✗ A woman travelling together with a group of women. Not

all scholars agree on this point.*

✗ Also, similarly travelling along with a man who is a *Mahram* for one of them claiming that he is *Mahram* for all of them.

The immediate questions that arise are:

-   What about women doing their *Fard Hajj*?
-   What about unmarried women?
-   What about women without sons or brothers?

One additional condition for eligibility to perform *Hajj* for a female, is that she should have a *Mahram*.

If a women has no *Mahram* (and this situation is permanent), and she has the money, then she should send somebody to perform the *Hajj* on her behalf.

* There are many books that ascribe to the view that for a woman's *Fard Hajj*, she can travel with a group of other women. None of the major references I used for this book ascribe to this view.

The Prophet (ﷺ) said:

«لا يَخْلُوَنَّ رَجُلٌ بامْرَأةٍ إلَّا مَعَ ذي مَحْرَم»، فَقامَ رَجُلٌ فَقالَ: يا رَسُولَ اللهِ، امْرَأتي خَرَجَتْ حاجَّةً واكْتُتِبْتُ في غَزْوَةِ كَذَا وَكَذَا، قالَ: «ارْجِعْ فَحُجَّ مَعَ امْرَأتِكَ»

"No man should be in the company of a woman alone. Unless the woman is accompanied by a Mahram or her husband, she should not undertake a journey."

"A man told the Prophet (ﷺ) that his wife had gone for Hajj while he had enrolled himself for a particular battle. The Prophet (ﷺ) told the man to accompany his wife on Hajj instead."

(Bukhari and Muslim: 5233:1341)

In general, the Saudi Arabian Embassy will not issue Hajj visas for women without a *Mahram*. However, women over the age of 45 that have no *Mahram*, may obtain a visa if they are travelling with an organised *Hajj* group.

I'ddah (Waiting Period)

If a woman is in her *I'ddah* period (her husband died), she MUST complete her *I'ddah* period first, even though she may meet all the other requirements of *Hajj* (*Mahram*, money, health, etc.) before she can embark on her journey. The *I'ddah* period is 4 months and 10 days as per the Qur'an. See *Surah Al-Baqarah Ayah* 234. If her husband dies while they are on *Hajj*, then she may complete her *Hajj* rites.

Preparation

All pilgrims MUST perform *Tawaaful-Ifadah*. *Tawaaful-Wadaa'* (Farewell *Tawaaf*) can be omitted by menstruating or post-natal bleeding women.

If your passport contains a photo of you without a head covering, you should have it changed. It is *Haraam* (forbidden) to display such photos, apart from it causing you embarrassment during the trip.

Ensure that your departure dates from Makkah allow you enough time to complete *Tawaaful-Ifadah*, in the event of your menstruation starting prior to you having completed it.

Check what the accommodation packages offer. Shared rooms; couple rooms; en suites; food included, etc. Prepare yourself physically and mentally.

Ensure that you have all the necessary medicines and toiletries. The clothes, toiletries and other items to take with you are covered in chapter two of this book.

Take some of the traveller's cheques in your name. Also keep some of the cash money with you. Avoid keeping all your money in one place.

Mentally prepare yourself for the toilet, bathroom and sleeping facilities in Mina, Arafat and Muzdalifah.

Personal Behaviour

No attractive clothes, perfume or make-up should be worn while going to the mosque or in the company of non-*Mahram* men.

Other points regarding the clothes:

- It must be thick enough to be completely opaque (non see-through).
- It must be loose enough as not to make clear the shape of the body.
- The material itself must not be decorative.
- It must not resemble the dress of men.
- It must not resemble the dress of disbelieving women.
- It must not be ostentatious.

Keep the following *Hadith* in mind whenever you feel the difficulties of *Hajj*:

«عَنْ عَائِشَةَ أُمِّ الْمُؤْمِنِينَ رَضِيَ اللهُ عَنْهَا أَنَّهَا قَالَتْ: يَا رَسُولَ اللهِ! نَرَى الْجِهَادَ أَفْضَلَ الْعَمَلِ، [أَفَلَا نُجَاهِدُ]» قَالَ: [لَا] «لَكُنَّ أَفْضَلُ الْجِهَادِ حَجٌّ مَبْرُورٌ»

"Narrated 'Aishah, the Mother of the Believers (﷐) that she said: 'O Allāh's Messenger! We consider Jihād as the best deed." He said: "(No!) But the best Jihād (for women) is Hajj Mabrūr."

(Bukhari and Ahmad and Ibn Majah: 1520:2442)

Ihraam

The clothes for *Ihraam* can be of any colour.

Some women refuse to enter into the state of *Ihraam* at the *Meqaat* as they are in their menses. They argue that they should first become clean. However, a woman in menses can and should get into the state of *Ihraam* at the prescribed place and can perform every religious rite, except *Tawaaf* and *Salah*.

See under menstruation in this chapter for more details.

«عَنْ عَائِشَةَ [رَضِيَ اللهُ عَنْهَا] قَالَتْ: خَرَجْنَا مَعَ النَّبِيِّ ﷺ عَامَ
حَجَّةِ الْوَدَاعِ، فَأَهْلَلْتُ بِعُمْرَةٍ، وَلَمْ أَكُنْ سُقْتُ الْهَدْيَ، فَقَالَ
النَّبِيُّ ﷺ: «مَنْ كَانَ مَعَهُ هَدْيٌ، فَلْيُهْلِلْ بِالْحَجِّ مَعَ عُمْرَتِهِ،
[ثُمَّ] لَا يَحِلَّ حَتَّىْ يَحِلَّ مِنْهُمَا جَمِيعًا» قَالَتْ: فَحِضْتُ،
فَلَمَّا دَخَلَتْ لَيْلَةُ عَرَفَةَ، قُلْتُ: يَا رَسُولَ اللهِ! إِنِّي كُنْتُ أَهْلَلْتُ
بِعُمْرَةٍ، فَكَيْفَ أَصْنَعُ بِحَجَّتِي؟ قَالَ «انْقُضِي رَأْسَكِ،
وَامْتَشِطِي، وَأَمْسِكِي عَنِ الْعُمْرَةِ، وَأَهِلِّي بِالْحَجِّ» قَالَتْ: فَلَمَّا
قَضَيْتُ حَجَّتِي أَمَرَ عَبْدَ الرَّحْمَٰنِ بْنَ أَبِي بَكْرٍ، فَأَرْدَفَنِي،
فَأَعْمَرَنِي مِنَ التَّنْعِيمِ، مَكَانَ عُمْرَتِيَ الَّتِي أَمْسَكْتُ عَنْهَا.»

*"Aishah (ﷺ) reported: We went with the Messenger of Allah
(ﷺ) during the year of the Farewell Pilgrimage...'Aishah said:
'The monthly period began. When it was the night of Arafat, I
said to the Messenger of Allah (ﷺ): 'I entered into the state of
Ihraam for Umrah, but now how should I perform the Hajj?'
Thereupon he said: 'Undo your hair and comb them, and
desist from performing Umrah, and put on Ihraam for Hajj.'
She ('Aishah) said: 'When I had completed my Hajj he
commanded 'Abd ur-Rahman bin Abu Bakr (her brother) to
carry me behind him (on horseback) in order to enable me to
resume the rituals of Umrah from Tana'ym, the place where I
abandoned its rituals'."*

(Muslim:1211)

Covering the face and hands while in *Ihraam*

The *Hadith* related in Bukhari states that a woman should not
cover her face with a *Niqaab* (sewn face cover) or cover her
hands with gloves.

Some people use this *Hadith* to "prove" that women are not
supposed to cover their face and hands while in the state of
Ihraam. The Prophet (ﷺ) told the men that they should not

wear fitted clothes (shirts or trousers), but that did not mean that they should go naked. Similarly the women are instructed not to wear gloves and a *Niqaab*. This does not mean that their face and hands should not be covered.

The *Hadith* narrated by 'Aishah ( ) proves that they did cover their faces while in the presence of non-*Mahram* men:

«عَنْ عَائِشَةَ رَضِيَ اللهُ عَنْهَا قَالَتْ : كَانَ الرُّكْبَانُ يَمُرُّونَ بِنَا وَنحْنُ مَعَ رَسُولِ اللهِ ﷺ مُحْرِمَاتٌ فَإِذَا حَاذَوْا بِنَا سَدَلَتْ إحْدَانَا جِلْبَابَها مِنْ رَأْسِها عَلَىٰ وَجْهِها ، فَإِذَا جَاوَزُوْنَا كَشَفْنَاهُ»

"Aishah ( ) said: 'The riders had been passing by us while we were with the Messenger. When they came opposite to us or parallel to us we (the women) would let our veils down on our faces and heads, and when they had passed away we unveiled our faces.'"

(Abu Dawud:1833)

So if you normally cover your face then it is acceptable to do so while in *Ihraam*, as long as you don't do it with a *Niqaab*. There is also no need to wear a baseball type hat to avoid your scarf from touching your face as many sisters do, as there is no basis for this.

Women should cover their feet (with socks or otherwise), especially during *Salah*. For some unknown reason many women do not cover their feet. It is a requirement as instructed by Allah that their *Aurah* must be covered and the feet are part of a women's *Aurah*.

While in *Ihraam* it is permissible to remove the socks or change one's clothes.

About Menstruation

The subject of *Tahaarah* (purification, etc.) is a very large subject and has many viewpoints from many renowned scholars, each having substantial support for his point of view. This makes the rulings on this topic all the more difficult. This is especially true for the critical rite of *Tawaaful-Ifadah*, where many scholars agree that it is acceptable for a menstruating woman to perform this *Tawaaf* if she is unable to delay her departure and that she will not be able to return. On the other hand many scholars disagree and rule that she MUST wait or leave and return later, and she will be "sexually illegal" to her husband until this *Tawaaf* is performed, no matter how long it takes.

While I was gathering the information for this topic, I realised how complicated this matter can be. At one stage I wanted to leave it out, but then I thought, if it is so hard for me to gather the right rulings, and I have plenty of time, what about the pilgrim, if she needs to find a ruling for her situation, while she is on *Hajj*, with very limited time? Hence, I spent a great deal of time, researching and checking with my references that I used for the rest of the *Fiqh* related issues in this book, in order to compile the following data. Allah knows best.

A woman MUST adopt *Ihraam* at the *Meqaat*, even though she is menstruating. This applies for *Umrah* as well as for *Hajj*.

If she fails to do so intentionally, and adopts her *Ihraam* only in Makkah once she has completed her menstruation, then she should pay an expiation (sacrificing one sheep) for violating the *Meqaat* rule.

Hence, a woman can and should adopt *Ihraam* and perform all the *Hajj* rites except *Tawaaf* and *Salah* while she is menstruating or during post-natal bleeding. (She is not allowed to enter the mosque.)

She MUST complete *Tawaaful-Ifadah* and *Sa'ee* for *Hajj* once her menstruation is completed.

If she is unable to remain in Makkah and will not be able to return, and did not complete *Tawaaful-Ifadah* and *Sa'ee* for *Hajj*, she must pad herself really well and proceed to perform the *Tawaaf* and *Sa'ee*. (This must be done as a last resort and not merely for convenience.) This rite of *Hajj* CANNOT be omitted and there is no expiation for it. Remember, no sexual marital relations are allowed until you have completed this rite of *Hajj*, regardless of the length of time it takes before you perform it. Some scholars say that she should make *Wudu* first, but others disagree as the *Wudu* or *Ghusl* has no "value" for her in this state.

Some scholars agree that it is permissible for a woman to use pills which prevent or delay the menstruation during *Hajj*, after she has confirmed the safety of their usage from a doctor.

- The comment I have received from many pilgrims is that they discourage the use of these pills, as it has caused them more problems instead of having helped them.

- Another point they asked me to mention: if you do decide to use these pills, then you should start taking them at least two months before travelling and not for the *Hajj* period only.

Menstruating women and post-natal bleeding women may omit the farewell *Tawaaf* (*Tawaaful-Wadaa'*).

«عَنْ ابنِ عَبَّاسٍ رَضِيَ اللهُ عَنْهُما قَالَ: أُمِرَ النَّاسُ أَنْ يَكُونَ آخِرُ عَهْدِهِمْ بِالبَيْتِ إِلَّا أَنَّهُ خُفِّفَ عَنِ الحَائِضِ»

"Narrated by Ibn Abbas: 'The people were ordered to perform the Tawaaf of the Ka'bah (Tawaaful-Wadaa') as the lastly thing, before leaving (Makkah), except the menstruating women who were excused.'"

(Bukhari:1755)

«عَنْ طَاوُسٍ قَالَ: كُنْتُ مَعَ ابْنِ عَبَّاسٍ، إِذْ قَالَ زَيْدُ بْنُ ثَابِتٍ: تُفْتِي أَنْ تَصْدُرَ الْحَائِضُ قَبْلَ أَنْ يَكُونَ آخِرَ عَهْدِهَا بِالْبَيْتِ؟ فَقَالَ لَهُ ابْنُ عَبَّاسٍ: إِمَّا لَا! فَسَلْ فُلَانَةَ الْأَنْصَارِيَّةَ؟ هَلْ أَمَرَهَا بِذَلِكَ رَسُولُ اللهِ ﷺ؟ قَالَ: فَرَجَعَ زَيْدُ بْنُ ثَابِتٍ إِلَى ابْنِ عَبَّاسٍ يَضْحَكُ، وَهُوَ يَقُولُ: مَا أَرَاكَ إِلَّا قَدْ صَدَقْتَ»

"Narrated by Abdullah bin Abbas: Tawus reported: I was in

the company of Ibn Abbas (﷠) when Zayd bin Thabit said:
'Do you give religious verdict that the woman who is in
menses is allowed to go without performing the last
circumambulation (Tawaaf) of the House?' Ibn Abbas (﷠)
said to him: 'Ask such and such woman of the Ansar, if you
do not (believe my religious verdict) whether Allah's
Messenger (ﷺ) had commanded her this.' Zayd bin Thabit
(went to that lady and after getting this verdict attested by
her) came back to Ibn Abbas (Allah be pleased with them)
smilingly and said: 'I did not find you but telling the truth'.''

(Muslim:1328)

Sometimes women get upset when their menses start while
they are in Makkah, as they cannot attend prayer in the
Haram. Try not to be too upset, as this is a natural process
from Allah. Allah in His Mercy will certainly not give you any
less reward than what you would have obtained if you did
not have your menses.

Use this time to indulge in other forms of *Ibadah*, such as
Dhikr, *Dua'*, and reading. Read books that will help you
increase your knowledge about Islam or books on *Tafseer* in
order to increase your understanding of the Qur'an.

«حَدَّثَنَا أَفْلَحُ بنُ حُمَيْدٍ قَالَ: سَمِعْتُ القَاسِمَ بنَ مُحَمَّدٍ، عَنْ
عَائِشَةَ رَضِيَ اللهُ عَنْهَا قَالَتْ: فَدَخَلَ عَلَيَّ رَسُولُ اللهِ ﷺ وأنا
أَبْكِي فَقَالَ: «ما يُبْكِيكِ يا هَنْتَاهُ؟» قُلْتُ: سَمِعْتُ قَوْلَكَ
لأَصْحَابِكَ فَمُنِعْتُ العُمْرَةَ. قَالَ: «وَما شَأْنُكِ؟» قُلْتُ: لا
أُصَلِّي، قال: «فَلا يَضُرُّكِ إِنَّمَا أَنْتِ امْرَأَةٌ مِنْ بَنَاتِ آدَمَ كَتَبَ
اللهُ عَلَيْكِ ما كَتَبَ عَلَيْهِنَّ، فكُوني في حَجَّتِكِ فَعَسَى اللهُ أَنْ
يَرْزُقَكِيها». قالَتْ: فَخَرَجْنا في حَجَّتِهِ حتَّى قَدِمْنا مِنًى،
فطَهَرْتُ ثُمَّ خَرَجْتُ مِنْ مِنًى فأَفَضْتُ بالبَيْتِ»

"Narrated by Al Qasim bin Muhammad:... 'Aishah added,
'Allah's Messenger came to me and saw me weeping and said,

'What makes you weep, O Hantah?' I replied, 'I have heard your conversation with your companions and I cannot perform the Umrah.' He asked, 'What is wrong with you?' I replied, 'I do not offer the prayers (i.e. I have my menses).' He said, 'It will not harm you for you are one of the daughters of Adam, and Allah has written for you (this state) as He has written it for them. Keep on with your intentions for Hajj and Allah may reward you that.' 'Aishah further added, 'Then we proceeded for Hajj till we reached Mina and I became clean from my menses. Then I went out from Mina and performed Tawaaf round the Ka'bah'."

(Bukhari:1560)

Menstruating women are not allowed to enter a mosque, including the *Haram* in Makkah and Madinah (the only exception being as explained earlier).

On many occasions it happens where the menstruation "comes early", by even up to two weeks. Possibly due to excessive walking, stress, anxiety, lack of sleep, etc. So be prepared, and take the necessary toiletry items to Mina and Arafat. If this happens, your plans for *Tawaaful-Ifadah* will also have to change.

Let us look at some examples

I hope that I have managed to cover most of the cases. If your condition is not covered, then review the general principles of the examples and I am sure that you will be able to formulate what you are supposed to do.

Case 1:

You arrived for *Hajj* and went to Madinah first. Prior to departing for Makkah (with plenty of time before *Hajj*) your menstruation starts:

- √ You must adopt your *Ihraam* at the *Meqaat* (Dhul-Hulaifah) and proceed to Makkah.
- √ You remain in *Ihraam* for the duration of your menstruation.

✓ Once your menstruation is completed, you perform *Ghusl*.

✓ Proceed to the *Haram* to perform *Umrah*.

✓ Cut your hair and you are relieved from *Ihraam*.

✓ The above is for the *Mutamatti*. The *Qaarin*, will do the same, but will perform *Tawaaful-Qudoom* (welcome *Tawaaf*) and *Sa'ee* for *Hajj*, instead of *Umrah*. They must not cut their hair and they remain in *Ihraam* until *Hajj*.

Case 2:

You arrived for *Hajj* and went to Madinah first or you are coming from within Saudi Arabia (e.g. Riyadh). Prior to you reaching the *Meqaat*, your menstruation starts, and it is on the 8th or 9th of Dhul-Hijjah. (You are not in the state of *Ihraam* yet.):

✓ If you had intention to perform *Hajj-Tamattu* then you are forced to change your *Niyah* to *Qiran* or *Ifrad*.

✓ If your *Niyah* is to perform *Hajj-Ifrad*, then the same steps as below apply, except for the sacrifice.

✓ You must adopt your *Ihraam* at the *Meqaat* and proceed to Mina/Arafat. If the group goes to Makkah for *Umrah* or *Tawaaful-Qudoom* (welcome *Tawaaf*), you should wait for them without performing any rite or entering the mosque.

✓ You continue by performing all the *Hajj* rites except salah. (Staying and supplicating in Arafat; leaving Arafat after *Maghrib*; staying in Muzdalifah; stoning of the *Jamr'at*, etc.).

✓ After you have stoned *Jamrah Aqaba* on the 10th and your sacrifice has been done, you may cut your hair and you are relieved from *Ihraam* restrictions, and obviously except sexual relations.

✓ If your menstruation is completed while in Mina, then

you perform *Ghusl* and may proceed to Makkah to perform *Tawaaful-Ifadah* and *Sa'ee* for *Hajj*.

√ If your menstruation is not completed after the 12th or 13th of Dhul-Hijjah, you can proceed back to Makkah, but you still cannot perform *Tawaaful-Ifadah* or *Sa'ee* for *Hajj*.

√ Once your menstruation is completed, you perform *Ghusl*.

√ Proceed to the *Haram* to perform *Tawaaful-Ifadah* and *Sa'ee* for *Hajj*.

√ All *Ihraam* restrictions are now lifted.

Case 3:

You arrived for *Hajj* and went to Madinah first or you are coming from within Saudi Arabia (e.g. Riyadh), with the intention of performing *Hajj-Tamattu*. Prior to you starting or completing your *Umrah*, your menstruation starts, and it is on the 8th or 9th of Dhul-Hijjah. (You are already in the state of *Ihraam*):

√ You are now forced to change your *Niyah* to *Qiran*. There is no need to utter the new *Niyah*.

√ All the same steps, from continuing with *Hajj* rites, as in case 2 apply.

For both cases 2 & 3:

There is no requirement to perform *Umrah* after *Hajj* for the *Qaarin* (or for *Ifrad* and *Tamattu*). However, if you wish to do so, (as what 'Aishah did), then this will be an "extra" *Umrah* and not part of *Hajj*:

√ Adopt your *Ihraam* clothes again and proceed to Tana'ym (*Meqaat*), where you will make your *Niyah* for *Umrah*.

√ Proceed to the *Haram* to perform *Umrah*.

√ Cut your hair and you are relieved from *Ihraam*.

√ It is still *Hajj-Qiran* (and not *Tamattu*).

Case 4:

On your way to Saudi Arabia your menstruation starts. You are planning to proceed directly to Makkah from Jeddah:

√ If you have plenty of time before *Hajj*, then the same steps as that for case 1 apply.

√ If there is not enough time to perform *Umrah*, then the steps for case 2 apply.

Case 5:

You have completed your *Umrah* and you are staying in Makkah. Prior to, or on the 8th of Dhul-Hijja, your menstruation starts or it's not completed:

√ You must adopt your *Ihraam* and proceed to Mina.

√ All the same steps, from continuing with *Hajj* rites, as in case 2 apply.

Case 6:

It is the 9th of Dhul-Hijjah and your menstruation is due at any time. Your departure from Makkah is soon after *Hajj*:

√ On the 10th you may go directly to Makkah to perform *Tawaaful-Ifadah* and *Sa'ee* for *Hajj*, prior to performing any other rite (stoning, sacrifice or cutting of your hair). You may also leave Muzdalifah early and go directly to Makkah if required.

√ Return to Mina and perform all the other rites of *Hajj* even if your menstruation has started (except *Salah*).

√ You need not perform *Tawaaful-Wadaa'*, if you have to leave for home, before your menstruation has completed.

√ You do not need to perform any expiation.

Case 7:

Your menstruation is not completed and you have not

performed *Tawaaful-Ifadah* and *Sa'ee* for *Hajj*, and you are about to depart for home:

- √ Delay your departure, until you are "clean". This is the BEST thing to do!
  - ○ Once your menstruation is completed, you perform *Ghusl*.
  - ○ Proceed to the *Haram* to perform *Tawaaful-Ifadah* and *Sa'ee* for *Hajj*.
  - ○ All *Ihraam* restrictions are now lifted.
  - ○ Perform *Tawaaful-Wadaa'* before proceeding for home. If *Tawaaful-Ifadah* was the last rite before going home, then you need not do a separate *Wadaa'*.
- √ If you cannot delay your depature (and you are not able to return to Makkah):
  - ○ You should pad yourself really well and proceed to perform *Tawaaful-Ifadah* and *Sa'ee* for *Hajj*.
  - ○ Do not perform any *Salah*, including the two *Rak'at* after *Tawaaf*.
  - ○ Do not perform a separate *Tawaaful-Wadaa'*.
  - ○ You do not need to perform any expiation.
- √ You may proceed home.

Case 8:

You have completed all your *Hajj* rites and you are about to depart for home, then your menstruation starts:

- √ You are exempted from performing the Farewell *Tawaaf* (*Tawaaful-Wadaa'*).
- √ You do not need to perform any expiation.
- √ You may proceed home.

Case 9:

Your menstruation starts:

1. While you are performing *Tawaaf* for *Umrah*:

   √ You cannot continue.

   √ If there is time before *Hajj*, then you follow the steps as in case 1.

   √ If there is no time before *Hajj*, then follow the steps as in case 3.

2. While you are performing *Tawaaf* for *Hajj* (*Tawaaful-Ifadah*):

   √ Follow the steps as in case 7.

   √ If you take the second option in case 7: If you are sure that you will not "soil" the mosque then you may continue. If you have to leave to pad yourself, and there is only a short time lapse, then you need not start the *Tawaaf* from the 1st round again. However you must redo the incomplete circuit, if applicable.

3. While you are performing the farewell *Tawaaf* (*Tawaaful-Wadaa'*):

   √ You cannot continue.

   √ Follow the steps as in case 8.

4. While you are performing *Sa'ee* for *Umrah* (*Hajj-Tamattu*) or *Sa'ee* for *Hajj*:

   √ You may continue, as you do not need to be *Taahir* (on *Wudu*, etc.) to perform *Sa'ee*. However you must ensure that you will not "soil" the mosque. If you have to leave to pad yourself, and there is only a short time lapse, then you need not start the *Sa'ee* from the 1st lap again. However you must redo the incomplete lap, if applicable.

In all cases you must start the *Tawaaf* or *Sa'ee* from the beginning again, once there is a large time lapse (e.g.: day) between the time you stop and the time you restart.

Please do not treat this issue lightly, as *Tawaaful-Ifadah*

CANNOT be omitted.

Pregnancy

A pregnant woman can be considered unable to perform *Hajj*, due to health reasons. However she cannot send (deputise) somebody else to do it on her behalf, as her condition is not permanent.

There are a few considerations pregnant women should take into account before embarking on this journey. As with everything else, each person knows his or her own strengths and weaknesses. Therefore, the information given below is only a general guide and should not be used as definite rules.

In the early stages (first 3 months) of pregnancy it is more risky as the rituals of *Hajj* can be very strenuous.

In the last stages of pregnancy it can also be risky and uncomfortable apart from the bus journeys being very long.

Pregnant women should not take any vaccinations, especially for meningitis.

Pregnant women should take extra care during *Tawaaful-Ifadah* and at the *Jamr'at* as it can be very crowded and there is a lot of pushing. It is advisable to deputise someone to perform the *Ramy* on their behalf.

Most airlines will not allow a woman who is more than seven months pregnant to fly.

If you happen to give birth in Saudi Arabia, do not forget to obtain all the proper paperwork (birth registration, etc.) prior to departing.

Ensure that you budget for the possible additional cost.

Children

I am adding this section in this chapter as I have found that in most cases it is the women that take care of, or are most concerned about issues regarding children.

Apologies to all my male readers who disagree.

When one thinks of children, you automatically think of younger ones, however keep in mind that if you have children that have reached the age of puberty, you should seriously consider taking them with you for *Hajj* if you are able to do so. This fulfils their duty of performing their *Fard Hajj*, and you will be rewarded for having provided them with this opportunity.

«عَنِ ابْنِ عَبَّاسٍ قَالَ: رَفَعَتِ امْرَأَةٌ صَبِيًّا لَهَا، فَقَالَتْ: يَا رَسُولَ اللهِ! أَلِهَٰذَا حَجٌّ؟ قَالَ: «نَعَمْ، وَلَكِ أَجْرٌ»

"Abdullah bin Abbas (ﷺ) reported: During the Farewell Pilgrimage journey a lady brought her child before the Prophet (ﷺ) and inquired whether the child's Hajj was valid. The Prophet (ﷺ) replied, 'Yes, and you will get a reward as well.'"

(Muslim:1336)

Hajj is not compulsory for a child. When he/she reaches puberty it is still obligatory upon him/her, even if he/she has already performed it as a child.

The child should wear *Ihraam* and the *Niyah* can be made by the parent.

It is acceptable to carry the child on your shoulders during *Tawaaf* and *Sa'ee*.

It is commendable if the child is able to complete all the rites. However, there is no penalty if certain rites or pillars are missed. The parent can also complete the rites on behalf of the child, such as the *Ramy* of the *Jamr'at*. (The parents should pelt their 7 pebbles first, followed by the 7 for the child.)

Many pilgrims take children and infants with them on *Hajj*. The children can either be a pleasure or a very big distraction for you during *Hajj*.

Many pilgrims do not have a choice and this is understandable. There is reward in taking care of them. However, if you have a choice, I suggest you leave them with some family members, especially if it is your *Fard Hajj*.

It can be very hot and infants and children get restless. You may end up spending a lot of time taking care of them and you will not be able to concentrate on your *Ibadah*.

Never take small children or infants with you to stone the *Jamr'at*.

Following are some more points to keep in mind for the different categories of children:

Teenagers:

Same rules as those of adults apply in relation to acts of *Ibadah*.

Assist them to prepare for the journey, keeping in mind that the needs and interests of teenagers are different from adults.

A companion, such as a sibling or a friend will be of great value if they can also accompany them.

Save some of that patience for them. Many times you may get upset and annoyed that they do not find this journey as exciting and spiritual as you, and they may even complain about being bored. You may even feel that you have wasted your money. Don't, the results may not show immediately as you would hope, but believe me, it is a good lesson for them. Don't stress out, this is part of teenage hood.

Ages 7-12:

Don't take too many clothes, as it is easy to wash and dry your clothes in Makkah.

Despite the heat, it is advisable to dress them modestly, especially when going to the mosque.

Encourage the girls to wear *Hijab*, even though they may not have reached puberty yet. This is a good chance for you to get them use to it.

The Prophet (ﷺ) advised us that we should encourage our children to perform *Salah* from the age of 7 and start disciplining/punishing them at the age of 10 if they do not perform *Salah*. So heed this advice and don't let the children be an excuse for not going to the mosque, instead let them frequent the mosque.

Most airlines have special meals for children. If you are not flying with an airline that normally serves all *Halal* food, and you have booked *Halal* meals for yourself, then double-check with the airline if the children's meals are also *Halal*. Most of the time the children's meals are not *Halal*, hence you may have to take your own food. Take some potato chips, biscuits and some sandwiches for the children, just in case.

Also take some sweets or chewing gum for them to chew on, during take-off and landing, to minimise earache.

Ages 0-6:

Diapers are readily available, but take enough for the journey and for at least a few extra days. I suggest you take more than what you would normally use in a day, as babies are prone to diarrhoea when travelling.

Take baby food, bottles, milk, and medicine (especially for pain and fever). Do not rely on getting baby food on the plane as it is not always *Halal*.

Take enough clothes for the baby. Keep at least two sets of clothes for the baby in your hand luggage.

Also a change of clothes for the toddlers in your hand luggage is a good idea. Pack some bright coloured clothes.

For infants it is best to give them some painkiller medicine about half an hour before take-off and landing.

If you are breastfeeding, wear appropriate clothes that will facilitate easy breastfeeding on the plane.

Take a stroller, but not a bulky one. Although the stroller can get in the way sometimes in the crowds, most times it is of great value.

Take toys and books to keep them occupied during the journey. Do not take too many toys, as there are plenty of cheap toys to buy in Makkah. The little ones get bored very quickly on the plane and your nerves will be tested, so be patient.

Let the children use the bathroom in the plane prior to landing, to avoid toilet trips while queuing at immigration or customs.

Children also tend to fall asleep at the "worst" possible times, so you may have to carry them. Meaning you should try to minimise hand luggage.

Book a bassinet for the baby on the plane, and don't forget to reconfirm it prior to your flight. During check-in make sure that you are allocated the bassinet seats. So check-in early.

In Makkah:

Once you are in Makkah, I suggest you rest yourself and the children before performing *Umrah*. Remember children also suffer from jetlag, and will make your *Umrah* very stressful if they are tired and miserable. So let them sleep and eat first. There is no rush. The *Umrah* will take in excess of two hours and the distance of *Sa'ee* alone is about 3.5km.

You can go to the *Haram* with your stroller, but you will have to leave it outside. Put the stroller behind or on top of the shoe racks outside the *Haram* doors.

You are allowed to rest during *Tawaaf* and *Sa'ee*, and it is acceptable to carry the children on your shoulders.

You may consider getting a wheelchair, see chapter 8, to push the children in.

Once you have completed your *Tawaaf*, you and your partner can take turns in performing the two *Rak'at Salah*, while the other minds the children.

The mosque gets very crowded, so you should take care of toddlers and babies in the crowds. Babies that crawl, should either be watched by a toddler or tied to you, during *Salah*. You may use a harness like belt or just a normal scarf to ensure baby does not crawl too far. Give them some room to move around, otherwise they will cry and cause a bigger distraction.

Warn toddlers not to wander off during *Salah.*

If you do plan to take them to the *Haram* often, dress them in their bright coloured clothes so they are easily recognisable in a crowd.

Always pin an identification tag on them.

The business card of your hotel is also useful to keep in their pocket.

Explain to them the procedure they should follow if they are lost and show them the lost children's section at door no 13.

Alternatively, teach them to stay (wait) in one place in the event they get lost.

General

When you are in Makkah and you wish to perform *Tawaaf,* keep track of the *Salah* times to avoid starting your *Tawaaf* very close to *Iqaamah* time. If you do not watch the times, it will result in you getting "caught" among the men during the *Fard Salah.* It is unacceptable for women to perform their *Salah* in front of men, even though you may see it happen in the *Haram.* You may argue that the *Haram* is exempted due to the crowds. This is definitely not so. Plan your *Tawaaf* times to avoid inconvenience to yourself, and the rest of the pilgrims. If for some reason you are caught up in this situation, then it is best for you to stand in one place without performing your *Salah,* and to perform the *Salah* later.

Avoid walking in front of a person performing their *Sunnah Salah.* The *Harams* are not exempted from the prohibition of walking in between a person and his *Sutrah* (wall or item directly in front of a person performing *Salah*). Sometimes it is almost impossible to avoid this. However, do your best.

It is also more relevant for women NOT to pass in front of

men performing their *Salah*. As per the *Hadith*, this action invalidates the *Salah* of the man (except congregational *Salah*). There is a difference of opinion on this point, but be aware of it and do try to avoid walking in front of the men.

Women should also perform the *Janazah Salah*, as they are equally rewarded. Don't miss this opportunity!

Visiting of Graves

The strongest view as per my sources of reference is that it is not recommended for a woman to visit graves.

The Prophet (ﷺ) said:

«لَعَنَ رَسُولُ اللهِ ﷺ زُوَّارَاتِ الْقُبُورِ»

"May Allah curse the women who are frequent visitors of the graves."

(Ahmad, Ibn Majah and Tirmidhi: 8449:1576:320)

This is another controversial issue. Also the book most commonly used by many people (*Fiqh-us-Sunnah*) contradicts this view.

Keep in mind your objective – to perform a perfect *Hajj*. The visiting of various graves is neither a requirement nor a rite of *Hajj*. My suggestion is to err on the side of caution: meaning that, if there is uncertainty or disagreement on a particular issue, "stay on the safe side".

Take heed of the instruction given to us by our beloved Prophet (ﷺ) as related in the *Hadith*:

«الْحَلَالُ بَيِّنٌ وَالْحَرَامُ بَيِّنٌ، وَبَيْنَهُمَا مُشَبَّهَاتٌ لَا يَعْلَمُهَا كَثِيرٌ مِنَ النَّاسِ، فَمَنِ اتَّقَى الْمُشَبَّهَاتِ اسْتَبْرَأَ لِدِينِهِ وَعِرْضِهِ، وَمَنْ وَقَعَ فِي الشُّبُهَاتِ كَرَاعٍ يَرْعَى حَوْلَ الْحِمَى، يُوشِكُ أَنْ يُوَاقِعَهُ، أَلَا وَإِنَّ لِكُلِّ مَلِكٍ حِمًى، أَلَا إِنَّ حِمَى اللهِ مَحَارِمُهُ، أَلَا وَإِنَّ فِي الْجَسَدِ مُضْغَةً إِذَا صَلَحَتْ صَلَحَ الْجَسَدُ كُلُّهُ، وَإِذا

فَسَدَتْ فَسَدَ الْجَسَدُ كُلُّهُ، أَلَا وَهِيَ الْقَلْبُ»

*"Both legal and illegal things are evident but in between them
there are doubtful (unclear) things, and most people have no
knowledge about them. So whoever saves himself from those
doubtful (unclear) things, he saves his religion and his
honour. And whoever indulges in these doubtful (unclear)
things, is like a shepherd who grazes (his animals) near the
Hima (private pasture) of someone else, and at any moment
he is liable to get in it.*

*(O people!) Beware! Every king has a Hima and the Hima of
Allah (Azawajal) on the earth is His illegal (forbidden) things.
Beware! There is a piece of flesh in the body, if it becomes good
(reformed), the whole body becomes good but if it gets spoilt
the whole body gets spoilt and that is the heart."*

(Bukhari:52)

Chapter 4
What to Expect

More details about what to expect in Makkah (i.e. medical, access to the *Haram*, accommodation, etc.) and about Mina, Arafat, and Muzdalifah are covered in chapters 8 and 10 respectively. Madinah is covered in chapter 12.

Food

There are various kinds of food available in Makkah and Madinah. You will find food and fruit from just about every country you can think of. Some of the more common ones are: Indonesian, Pakistani, and Turkish.

There are also many "brand name" foods to enjoy: Pizza-Hut, Kentucky Fried Chicken, Burger King, Hardees, etc. That's if you are not boycotting certain products.

Cappuccinos, doughnuts, cream cakes, burgers and chips (French fries) are all readily available.

Hungry yet? I guess the diet will have to wait a little bit longer!

If your package has an option to include food, I advise you take it if it does not cost too much extra. In most packages the food cost is minimal. You can always buy your favourite burger when you get tired of the hotel food.

If you plan to do your own cooking, don't forget to check whether your accommodation provides cooking facilities.

I hope you like chicken as you will have plenty of it during your trip. Remember this point!

You can also eat at the restaurants located in certain hotels. These are relatively more expensive.

Try the grilled chicken from 'Taza' located in the Makkah Towers (Hilton) building. It is unique and delicious. (A personal note from one of the contributors to this book, "The tahina (white sauce) you get with the chicken may give you gas, making *Salah* a difficult affair for the rest of the day."). Many people have asked me if I get discount at Taza for advertising it. The answer is, no, though it would be nice if I could.

There are many small shops that also sell groceries including essential toiletries and household items, such as detergents and toilet paper. Each shop has different stock. In some cases you can buy milk, cereals, tin foods, fruit, vegetables, cheese etc., from one small shop.

Diet and Diabetic food

Diet drinks are available in most shops. They are sometimes called Pepsi/Coke light and not "diet".

In the bigger supermarkets, such as Bin Dawood in the Makkah Towers (Hilton) building, you will find a small variety of diet and diabetic food items.

Artificial sweeteners are also available in most shops.

There are many juice shops selling freshly squeezed juice.

Before you get into the habit of having a fresh mango or strawberry juice every morning, a word of caution. These juices are made with fresh fruit, but they add at least one cup of sugar as well as a small tin of condensed milk. This is to make it sweeter. The only true fresh juice is the orange juice. Do not be disappointed, the supermarkets do stock 100% real fruit juices.

Take a break from the diet and enjoy the trip.

Diabetic pilgrims should take special care as most things, including most bread, contain sugar.

Food during the *Hajj* days

Not all packages provide food during the days of *Hajj*. Check with your agent, as it may cost extra. The most common food provided is meat and rice.

Normally there is no food provided in Muzdalifah. See under "Food" in chapter 10 to avoid going hungry.

If you can, try a water, date and fruit diet for the *Hajj* days. This will reduce your need to visit the toilets.

During my presentations I often ask: "What time is lunch time in Mina?"; "What time is dinner time in Mina?" The answer is: "When the food arrives." We have had lunch at 5pm and dinner at 2am on numerous occasions. And guess what? On some occasions the food did not make it...

Believe me, when you are done with *Hajj*, you will never ever complain again at home about: cold meals; your old mattress, your small toilet or the leaky shower.

Shopping

Please remember that you have come for *Hajj* and that you should try and gain as much reward as possible. Spend your time in the mosque and try to minimise the time spent shopping.

If you are one of those who "shop until you drop" then take lots of money. There are so many things that you can buy. You name it, you will find it.

If you plan to shop for small children, do not take their clothes or shoe sizes, instead measure them and draw the size of their feet on a piece of paper. This will make it easier to buy by measurement instead of size. Do not forget to take the measuring tape with you.

If you plan to buy jewelry such as rings, then measure their finger size with a piece of cotton or string. Cater for growth if you will be away from home for a while (children grow fast).

Use your gift list and tick the name of the list as you buy. This will alleviate the stress and worry. Most pilgrims spend most of their money on buying gifts for family and friends. It costs them even more for excess baggage and customs duties.

Shop wisely and keep an eye on the suitcase weight and your

financial budget. See under checklists (chapter 15) for the tables provided especially for gift shopping.

If you see something that you like, buy it. Chances are you will not be able to find the same shop again or the item will be sold. Sometimes even the shop is changed within the space of a few days.

If you bought an item and you find it cheaper at another shop, do not feel cheated or accuse the shopkeeper of cheating. Just return the item and ask the shopkeeper to give it to you at that price. Most times they are obliging.

Do not necessarily accept the first price they quote you. Bargaining is the name of the game.

The closer you get to *Hajj* the less bargaining power you will have ("supply and demand"). So if you are in Makkah or Madinah early, buy your things early as the prices of the goods go up a great deal during the very busy periods.

After *Salah* you may find many street 'vendors' selling all sorts of things, from clothes, toys, electrical items, and watches to pyjamas. You will see them along the street displaying their goods on a bed sheet, while he is holding on to the ends of the sheet and his eyes are ever watchful. The reason for this is that they are illegal traders and plain-clothes police are constantly chasing and arresting them. Many times you will be standing with goods in your hand and the seller will have run away. This is to your advantage, but once I was waiting for my change, when the police came and the vendor ran off breaking the 100 meters world record. Another time I had to run after him to pay him. They do have some good bargains though.

If you are buying any electrical items, check the voltage for 110v or 220v.

Do not depend on the shopkeeper to give you the right sizes (e.g., "Will this fit my 5-year-old?" Chances are, he will say yes).

Having the right change (one and five riyals) to buy small

items (e.g., drinks, fruit, etc.) is a great help.

Sometimes you will find the shops extremely busy, so it helps to have the right amount of money available. This way, you will not have to wait for change.

You will be amazed to see how the shopkeepers deal with so many customers at the same time.

You may experience the shopkeeper "throwing" your change at you. Do not become flustered and think that he is rude. This is normal, so don't take it personally.

Most shopkeepers are reputable, but do not be surprised when you get some bad service.

Some pilgrims debate whether it is better to buy things (gifts, etc.) in Makkah or Madinah. I suggest you buy whenever and wherever it is convenient. The prices are generally the same.

Shopping in Jeddah is marginally more expensive. You also don't get all the same things that you get in Makkah or Madinah. On the other hand, you can get many other things, cheap to very expensive. All types of fashion clothes and perfumes are available: many varieties of shoes, suites, watches, materials and all the latest toys.

You can also find the latest electrical gadgets (games, radios, and kitchen utilities, etc.).

Computer software and hardware are also reasonably cheap in Jeddah. Ask the taxi to take you to Khalid bin Walid Street, Baroom Centre or City Centre (this is not the centre of the city, but a complex called City Centre).

Gold (jewelry), well, what can I say? There are gold markets everywhere (Makkah, Madinah and Jeddah) just waiting for you...

Before you buy your favourite perfume, t-shirt, shoe or watch, make sure that the name (label) is authentic (i.e. Charlie and not Charly, Lacoste and not Locaste, Panasonic and not Pensonic, Citizen and not Citazen).

Most groups take a day trip to Jeddah for sightseeing and shopping. If you do visit Jeddah, don't miss visiting the mosque on the water (built partially into the Red Sea).

If you are not able to visit Jeddah, there are other shopping areas around Makkah City: Mansour Street, Sitteen Street and Aziziah. Ask the taxi driver.

Do not lose sight of the purpose of your journey, so avoid getting into arguments with any shopkeepers.

Signs

Most of the street and shop signs are in both Arabic and English.

Some of the street and location names vary from sign to sign (e.g., one sign may show Mina and the next one may show Muna; Arafat is spelt Arafah on some signs).

You will have some fun with the English spelling on some of the shop signs.

Telephones

The telephone system is fully automatic and you can dial almost all long-distance calls without operator assistance.

There are public telephones from which you can phone.

There are a few shops that have public telephone facilities.

There are also "International Telephone Cabins", where you can make your calls.

There are coin as well as phone card phones. The minimum cost is SR50.00 for the phone card. Some years these phones disappear and reappear (different shape) the following year. So if you don't see any, you know why.

There are also pre-paid access-number phone cards available. The minimum cost is SR25.00 per card. These cards are useful as you can use any telephone to make an international call, by simply calling the access number on the card.

Mobile (cell) phones are widely used. If you wish to take your mobile phone with you, I suggest you check with your local supplier whether the service will work in Saudi Arabia. Since 2004 they have distributed a special *Hajj* mobile card, with special numbers, and the validity is for the *Hajj* period only. The minimum cost is SR100.00. If you plan to be in touch with family, this is highly recommended as the hotel phone service is very bad. Once it took me three days to locate a pilgrim (by phone) in a 5 star hotel. Even if you have the room number, they tend to move pilgrims around. Now imagine the cost for a family member on an international call.

Some hotels provide facsimile facilities.

The city codes are:

Jeddah	-	02
Makkah	-	02 (yes, the same as Jeddah)
Madinah	-	04
Riyadh	-	01

The code for Makkah and Jeddah is the same, so you must dial 02 to call Jeddah from Makkah and vice versa.

The country code is 966, so in order to dial to Makkah from outside the country: 9662+hotel number; 9664+ (for Madinah) and 966+mobile number without the leading zero.

You need at least a 25 halalah coin to make a local (Makkah to Makkah) call or a 50 halalah coin to make an inter-city (Makkah to Jeddah) call.

Some emergency telephone numbers are:

Fire	- 998
Ambulance	- 997
Police	- 999
Road accidents	- 993
Telephone dir.	- 905

Avoid using the hotel telephones for international calls, as it can be very expensive due to the hotel service charges.

Obtaining coins or a phone card can be difficult; so if you plan to phone often, buy them at the first opportunity you get.

The telephone cabins are useful as their charges are based on the exact length of the call (seconds).

The "menace" of the mobile phone has reached its peak as you notice some people talking on the phone while performing *Tawaaf*.

Internet and E-mail

Internet has been available in Saudi Arabia since 1998. For the e-mail junkies, there are Internet Cafés springing up all over the place. There are also some hotels in Makkah and Madinah that provide this service.

Postal

There are post offices available, though not easy to find, if you wish to post a letter.

Posting parcels can be a bit more complicated. Big items will have to be sent via cargo. See under the "baggage" section in chapter 2 of this book.

Electricity supply

The electricity supply varies:

-       Most of the hotels in Jeddah provide outlets for both 110v and 220v.

-       Makkah and Madinah are mainly 220v.

The wall plug holes are mainly the small two-point, round-holed ones.

Buy an international plug adapter if you plan to use any electrical item.

If your electrical items are 110v, be very careful when using them in Makkah or Madinah. You may not be able to use them at all, if the hotel does not provide 110v outlets.

If the item is dual voltage, 110v and 220v, it is best to keep the switch set at 220v. This will save your item if you plug it into the wrong voltage socket.

There are frequent power fluctuations. I suggest you leave any expensive electrical items at home.

Transport

Your transport for *Hajj* is paid for by the one draft cheque you had to give at the airport upon arrival. You will receive a bus coupon book. It is stapled inside your passport. Remove it prior to giving in your passport to obtain your *Hajj* identity card.

So you do not have to worry about finding a bus or taxi. I have listed the following information, in the event you need to find your own transport for some reason (like looking for a lost bag or ticket changes).

There are air-conditioned buses and taxis at reasonably cheap prices.

Saudi Arabian Public Transport Company (SAPTCO) operates a very efficient bus service. All their buses are air-conditioned and provide an hourly service between Jeddah and Makkah. They also operate between Jeddah and Madinah and Makkah and Madinah, but on a less frequent interval.

SAPTCO also have offices at the airport where they provide a service to Makkah and Madinah. The service to Madinah is sometimes from airport to airport, and not to the bus terminal. These offices are not open 24 hours a day, so if you arrive late at night, you will need to go to the bus terminal downtown.

The locations for the arrival and departure of the SAPTCO buses are:

Jeddah

Downtown - it is opposite the "Corniche Commercial Centre" in the city. (This area is known as the Balad or downtown Jeddah.)

Saudi Arabian Airlines Terminal - The office location is the second last office to the extreme right of the exit doors at the airport.

Foreign Airlines Terminal - It is at the last section to your left of the care hire and the hotel reservation desk, right in front of the arrival area.

If you have trouble finding it, simply ask someone.

Makkah

Next to the Makkah Towers (Hilton) building. This area is known as Shubaika. Facing the front of the building, to the right side: If you exit from the King Fahd Door (no 79) it will be directly in front of you. At the time of writing (first edition) a new building is been constructed right next to this area, so over time the location may move. The building is complete but the station is still there.

Madinah

It is further away from the Haram. It is in between the areas called Baabul-Khuma and Baabus-Shami (these are referring to areas and not doors). If you are inside the *Haram* near the *Mihrab* (front), stand with your back towards it (*Mimbar*) and walk straight ahead, past the two open areas and exit by the big new door right at the end. You should now be in the new open courtyard area with many new hotels in front of you. Turn to your left and walk until you cross the street where there is a traffic light and a tunnel. You should find the buses in this area. Also, as with Makkah the location may change over time, so please ask somebody before you walk too far.

There are also non-air-conditioned buses and taxis, at almost the same prices.

The yellow coloured taxis are referred to as taxis, whereas the white coloured taxis are referred to as limousines. Their prices may vary somewhat, with the yellow taxis being marginally cheaper, as they are not always air-conditioned. The condition of the yellow taxis leaves a lot to be desired, let alone the way they drive. If you are a nervous passenger, never sit in front in the taxi.

Distances between places:

Jeddah	to	Makkah	72km	45miles
Jeddah	to	Madinah	424km	264miles
Makkah	to	Madinah	447km	278miles
Makkah (*Haram*)	to	Mina	8km	5miles
Makkah	to	Arafat	22km	14miles
Arafat	to	Muzdalifah	9km	6miles
Muzdalifah	to	Mina	6km	4miles

The distances given are approximate distances from Muzdalifah to the *Jamr'at*, and from Mina to the *Haram*. The boundaries of Mina and Makkah are right next to each other.

The actual layout is as follows:

Makkah ⇨ Mina ⇨ Valley of Muhassir ⇨ Muzdalifah ⇨ Vally of Uranah ⇨ Arafat

According to Saudi law, one must have a valid Saudi driver's licence to drive in Saudi Arabia. It is therefore not advisable to even chance it as you will be breaking the law, although there are many car rental places around that will rent you a car. You may "get away" with an international driver's licence for a short time.

If you plan to drive, keep in mind that driving is on the right side of the road and not on the left as in the United Kingdom and some other places.

Your agent/group normally arranges your transport for you (except on the 10th of Dhul-Hijjah, when you need to go from Mina to Makkah to perform *Tawaaful-Ifadah*). All packages include transport, as it is the government assigned buses. Some packages have private buses, and this may cost you extra. The agent or the *Hajj* office may hold on to all the coupons for you.

You can get a refund for all unused coupons. This can be done at the airport upon your departure. There is normally a desk outside the *Hajj* office where you need to complete some forms and in turn collect your money from the bank at the airport. You have to do it in person, as it requires your signature.

Various bus systems have been tried to expedite the flow of traffic. The most recent being a rotation of the same buses; meaning that instead of sending two buses to take 100 people to Arafat, one bus will make two trips. This means longer waiting time, but less time in traffic.

Most taxis do not "go by the meter". You have to negotiate the price. So before you venture off, get an idea from somebody about the approximate distances and cost. These prices are negotiable with the driver. However, at the airports the taxis are more controlled and they have fixed prices, and you may have to pay first.

If you need an English speaking driver, you have a better chance with the limousines (white taxis). The Saudi government has introduced a law that will 'force' all taxi companies to ensure that all drivers to be Saudi only. So, you may be stuck with a non-English speaking driver who does not know where he is going and you can't explain where to go. Whatever you do, don't pay upfront.

You can get a taxi for as low as SR10 per person from Makkah to Jeddah. The bus costs about SR10-15. Then again, if you take a limousine from Makkah to Jeddah by yourself, it could cost you as much as SR150 and up to SR250 during peak time. A taxi from Jeddah to Madinah could cost you from about 50 to SR400, depending on the type of car and the number of passengers. As you can see there is a big variation, so be careful!

If you are a small group of six to eight people, you can also hire a big car (GMC), referred to as a "Jimms". The prices vary a great deal, so you need to do some skilful negotiating with the driver.

Be prepared for a big hike in taxi charges during the busy periods of *Hajj*. A trip that normally costs about SR10 may now cost you as much as 30 to SR50. I once paid SR200 for a trip that normally cost SR10. I was desperate and the driver knew that. Believe me, during *Hajj*, there may be times when you will be that desperate.

If you are travelling by taxi from one place to another during *Hajj*, agree on the price up-front and do not pay the driver until he has reached the agreed destination. If the driver insists on being paid first, then get another taxi. Believe me, if you pay first, chances are you could get dropped at the first traffic jam.

News

There are three English daily newspapers available: the 'Arab News', the 'Saudi Gazette' and the 'Riyadh Daily'. They are generally sold in the bookstores, which can be found in the general market areas.

There are also Saudi English radio channels and one English TV channel. Most 5 star hotels now have satellite channels, so you can get your daily 'feed' of CNN or BBC.

Now if there is a great time-waster and possibly causing one to be involved in sin, then it is the television. Many pilgrims waste precious time watching television while in Makkah.

Use this opportunity to take time out from the worldly issues. It is a great feeling. Besides, your time can be better spent in *Ibadah*.

Meeting people

Hajj is a great meeting place for Muslims; it provides a unique opportunity to get to know each other, and love each other, to help each other and solve each other's problems, and to witness that which is of benefit to you in the religion and your worldly affairs.

You will make life-long friends with some of the people you meet during *Hajj*.

You will meet some extraordinary people, and you will also meet some real nasty people. *Hajj* brings out the true nature of people so you will be surprised, astonished and sometimes very disappointed.

Make a small paper/card with your name and address on it, for easy exchange when meeting new and old friends.

This is when that pen and paper becomes very handy.

One of the more astonishing things I experienced during *Hajj* was that I met many old friends in the most unlikely places. The other uncanny thing is that I also met and was introduced to some "long lost" family. Some I knew, and many I didn't know existed. Once I met a friend (we have been trying to meet throughout his trip, without luck) amongst the millions at the *Jamrah*.

This was a very rewarding experience for me for two reasons:

1. It was wonderful to meet family and old school friends in Makkah.

2. It was good to see that I was not the only one getting older.

Many other pilgrims have had similar experiences. I have witnessed brothers meeting each other during *Hajj*, after many years apart (as they live in different countries). What an emotional experience!

Crowds

Another question I often ask during my presentations in Makkah is: "How many pilgrims are there on *Hajj* this year?" Always the answers range from 3 million to 5 million. And each year the same rumour goes around, about that year being the highest ever.

There are on average ONLY 2 million people performing *Hajj* each year. Believe me, with about 2 million people in the same place, it will feel like 10 million anyway.

If you find difficulty being in big crowds, try to prepare yourself mentally.

Recognise that you are going on a spiritual trip that necessitates hardship and sacrifice. It demands from you to be patient. Expect the least relaxation and the maximum rewards from Allah.

Expect less sleeping, less comfort, less eating, and lots of walking because of the crowds.

Expect too many people that overcrowd the streets, the hotels, the tents, and every other place you can imagine.

Prepare yourself, so you can transcend all these barriers and remember the Day of Judgement when every human being is to be assembled and to be judged by Allah. The crowd during *Hajj* is but a fraction of what it will be like on that Day.

Climate

Seasons:

- June onwards it is summer.
- It gets extremely hot.
- The temperatures can go as high as 55°Celsius (131°F).
- December onwards it is winter.
- The weather during winter is very pleasant.
- In Madinah the temperature sometimes falls below zero (32°F).
- The marble tiles on the floor in both *Harams* can be very cold, so take socks with you (ever wondered what to do with those socks you received on the aeroplane?).

Average temperatures:

Makkah:

May to October	32°- 40°C	90°- 104°F

November to April	28°- 33°C	82°- 92°F
Madinah:		
May to October	32°- 48°C	90°- 118°F
November to April	10°- 30°C	50°- 86°F

Take appropriate clothes, depending on the time that you will be in Saudi Arabia. With all the world temperatures changing it is hard to predict the weather though.

I have experienced very cold weather in Madinah during the month of December.

Time and Working hours

Jeddah, Makkah and Madinah are all in the same time zone, 3 hours ahead of Greenwich Mean Time (GMT).

The *Salah* times may vary by about 5 to 10 minutes between these cities.

The shop hours vary a great deal during the *Hajj* period. In Makkah and Madinah shops are open almost all the time. There are some supermarkets that are open 24 hours, except during *Salah* times.

In Saudi Arabia everything (shops, banks, petrol stations) are all closed during *Salah* times.

The weekend in Saudi Arabia is on Thursday and Friday and not on Saturday and Sunday.

Most government offices and banks are closed over the weekend. Some banks and offices provide services until *Salatul-Zuhr* on Thursdays.

Official public holidays are one week at *Eidul-Fitr*, and ten days at *Eidul-Adha*. Most shops are open after about the second day of *Eid*.

If you plan to visit Jeddah for shopping or for official business, the working hours for shops are normally from 10.00am - 1.00pm and from 5.00pm -10.30pm.

As with all other expensive items, I suggest you leave any

expensive watches at home and travel with a less expensive one. (This way you will not be too upset if by chance you lose or forget your watch somewhere.)

Banking

As mentioned in chapter two, there are many banks and money exchangers where you can change your cash or traveller's cheques. They deal in most currencies.

Automatic teller machines for debit and credit card withdrawals are widely available.

WARNING!

Trafficking in drugs whether smuggling, supplying or receiving incurs capital punishment in the Kingdom of Saudi Arabia.

Preparation Review

Ready to go?

- √ Check passport validity
- √ Obtain necessary visas
- √ Speak to your doctor about any particular medical problems
- √ Arrange extra medication, prescriptions or glasses
- √ Take vaccinations
- √ Arrange traveller's cheques, foreign cash, etc.
- √ Write or update your will
- √ Arrange for someone to look after your house, car, pets, pot plants, mail, etc.
- √ Check if you need adapter plugs for the trip
- √ Revise your study notes
- √ Cancel newspapers, milk, mail etc.
- √ Reconfirm your airline reservations, special food, and

baby bassinet seat (if applicable)

√ Recheck your travel documents

√ Leave a copy of your itinerary with your family/friends

√ Leave a copy of your travel documents, traveller's cheque numbers, etc.

√ Label all luggage clearly (inside and outside)

√ Finalise security arrangements for the house, locks, timers, etc.

√ If you are taking any children with you on the trip, ensure that you have taken all the necessary items as listed in chapter 3

√ If you are taking an infant, don't forget the stroller, diapers and baby food.

Out by the door?

√ Passport

√ Tickets

√ Money

√ Contact telephone numbers

√ Keys for suitcase locks

√ Medicine

√ Lockup house

√ Oh yes, and all that patience that you saved up...

Chapter 5

What about those staying behind?

Visitors

Making *Adhaan* at the departure of pilgrims has no authentic basis from the Qur'an or *Sunnah*. It is an innovation, do not do it!

Naturally, before you leave and upon your return, you will have many family members and friends visiting you. Take this opportunity to "spread the word". On most occasions the visitors discuss worldly matters and indulge in idle talk. Use the opportunity and talk to them about *Hajj*.

Remind them of the duty they owe unto Allah (to perform their *Hajj*).

As you can see there are many good things to talk about, instead of idle discussion.

Upon your return from *Hajj*, stick to the positive points in order to encourage others to undertake the journey.

Apply the same rules as you did before you left. No idle talk. Now you can talk and encourage them with your personal experiences.

First 10 days of Dhul-Hijjah

Remind your family and friends of the virtues of the first 10 days of Dhul-Hijjah.

These days can be viewed in a similar light as the last 10 nights of Ramadan.

So, if any of your family or friends says: "Is there anything I can do to help?" say: "Sure there is. Do as many if not all of the following recommendations in the first ten days of Dhul-Hijjah."

Virtues

The Prophet (ﷺ) said:

«مَا العَمَلُ فِي أَيَّامٍ [العَشْرِ] أَفْضَلُ مِنْهَا فِي هذِهِ». قالوا:
ولا الجِهادُ؟ قالَ: «ولا الجِهادُ، إلَّا رَجُلٌ خَرَجَ يُخاطِرُ بِنَفْسِهِ
ومالِهِ فَلَمْ يَرْجِعْ بِشَيْءٍ»

'There are no days better in which to perform righteous deeds than these days (the first 10 days of Dhul-Hijjah'). The companions said: 'Oh! Prophet of Allah, not even Jihad in the cause of Allah?' The Prophet (ﷺ) said: 'Not even Jihad in the cause of Allah except for one who sacrificed his life and wealth'."

(Bukhari:969)

«مَامِنْ أَيَّامٍ أَعْظَمَ عِنْدَ اللهِ، وَلَا أَحَبَّ إِلَيْهِ مِنَ ٱلْعَمَلِ فِيهِنَّ،
مِنْ هَذِهِ ٱلأَيَّامِ ٱلْعَشْرِ، فَأَكْثِرُوا فِيهِنَّ مِنَ التَّهْلِيلِ وَالتَّكْبِيرِ
وَالتَّحْمِيدِ»

"There are no days in which the good deeds are greater or more beloved by Allah than these 10 days, therefore praise and glorify Allah abundantly in these days."

(Ahmad:5446, 2/75)

«أَفْضَلُ الأَيَّامِ يَوْمُ عَرَفَةَ»

"The best of days is that of Arafat."

(Ibn Hibban)

Recommended deeds

Performing **Hajj** and **Umrah** are the best deeds as is supported by numerous *Ahadith*. The Prophet (ﷺ) reminded us that sins committed between two *Umrahs* are forgiven...

Ibn Mas'ud (ؓ) related that the Prophet (ﷺ) said:

«تابِعُوا بَيْنَ الحَجِّ والعُمْرَةِ فَإِنَّهُما يَنْفِيانِ الفَقْرَ والذُّنُوبَ كَمَا
يَنْفِي الكِيرُ خَبَثَ الْحَدِيدِ والذَّهَبِ والفِضَّةِ ولَيْسَ لِلْحَجَّةِ
المَبْرُورَةِ ثَوَابٌ إِلَّا الجَنَّةُ»

"Perform Hajj and Umrah one after the other, because both remove poverty and sins, just as a blacksmith's bellows remove impurities from iron, gold and silver, and there is no reward for an accepted Hajj except Paradise."

(Ahmad, Nasa'i & Tirmidhi: 3669:2631:810)

Fasting as many of these days as possible, particularly the day of Arafat (9th Dhul–Hijjah - for those that are not performing *Hajj*). Fasting is among the best deeds that can be performed as Allah in the *Qudsi Hadith* says:

«وَسُئِلَ عَنْ صَوْمِ يَوْمِ عَرَفَةَ؟ فَقَالَ: «يُكَفِّرُ السَّنَةَ الْمَاضِيَةَ
وَالْبَاقِيَةَ»

"The reward for fasting the day of Arafat would cancel the sins committed in the year before and the year after that day."

(Muslim:197)

«إِلَّاالصَّومَ فَإِنَّهُ لِي وَأَنَا أَجْزِي بِهِ، يَدَعُ شَهْوَتَهُ وَطَعَامَهُ مِنْ
أَجْلِي»

"Fasting is performed for My sake and I Myself shall decide its reward (for each person) for he (the servant) has abstained from his desire, eating and drinking for My sake."

(Muslim:1151)

Nafl fasting may be extremely difficult for many people. The following *Ahadith* should provide some encouragement to fast as many of the first nine days as possible. (The tenth day is *Eid* day and it is not allowed to fast on this day.)

The Prophet (ﷺ) said:

«مَنْ صَامَ يَومًا في سَبِيلِ اللهِ بَعَّدَ اللهُ وَجْهَه عَنِ النَّارِ سَبْعِينَ
خَرِيفًا»

"Anyone who fasts a day for the sake of Allah (seeking His pleasure), Allah would distance his face (him) by seventy seasons (years) away from the Hellfire."

(Bukhari & Muslim: 2840:1153)

Takbir (saying *"Allahu Akbar"*) and to praise and glorify Allah in those days, as Allah says in the Qur'an:

﴿وَيَذْكُرُواْ ٱسْمَ ٱللَّهِ فِى أَيَّامٍ مَّعْلُومَتٍ﴾

"...And celebrate the Name of Allah through the days Appointed..."

Surah Al-Hajj (22:28)

The scholars recommend praising and glorifying Allah by saying: *"Laa Ilaha illallah, Allahu Akbar, Alhamdu Lillah"*. Al-Bukhari mentioned that when Ibn Umar and Abu Hurrairah (&) went out to the markets they used to say aloud *"Allahu Akbar, Allahu Akbar"* and the people would emulate them. It is also reported that the people in the early days of Islam (known as *At-Tabieen*), in the first ten days of the month of Dhul-Hijjah, used to say aloud: *"Allahu Akbar, Allahu Akbar, Walillahil-hamd"*. It is recommended to raise one's voice with *"Takbir"* when one is out in the markets, streets, mosques and other places. It is also possible to praise and glorify Allah by various forms of *"Takbir"*, *"Tahmeed"*, *"Tasbeeh"* and other supplications.

Takbir in general is allowed and recommended in these ten days, during all hours of the day and night up to the time of *Eid Salah*. After the *Eid Salah Takbir* is recommended for non-pilgrims after each congregational prayer starting from *Salatul-Fajr* on the day of Arafat (9th) and for pilgrims starting from noon time on the tenth. *Takbir* for both groups can continue up to the time of *Salatul-'Asr* on the 13th of Dhul-

Hijjah.

Repentance and refraining from sins and ill deeds, so that one's deeds might gain Allah's forgiveness and mercy.

The Prophet (ﷺ) said:

$$\text{«إِنَّ اللهَ يَغَارُ، وَإِنَّ الْمُؤْمِنَ يَغَارُ، وَغَيْرَةُ اللهِ أَنْ يَأْتِيَ الْمُؤْمِنُ مَا حَرَّمَ عَلَيْهِ»}$$

"Allah can be displeased and the believers can be displeased and His displeasure is in one who commits what Allah forbids."

(Muslim:2761)

Performing extra optional acts of worship (*Nawaafil*) like *Salah*, charity, *Jihad*, reciting the Qur'an, promotion of virtue and prevention of vice, and other acts of worship, as their reward is multiplied in these 10 days.

Udhiyah (sacrifice): It is recommended to offer animals for slaughter on the days of 10th - 13th Dhul-Hijjah as this is very strongly recommended in the *Sunnah*; also in commemoration of the very act by Prophet *Ibraheem* (ﷺ). This is sometimes referred to as *Qurbani*.

This *Sunnah* (*Udhiyah*) is so strong that the Prophet (ﷺ) said that those who have the financial means and do not do it, are not "entitled" to perform the *Eid Salah* with them.

Abu Hurrairah (ﷺ) reported that the Prophet (ﷺ) said:

$$\text{«مَنْ كَانَ لَهُ سَعَةٌ، وَلَمْ يُضَحِّ، فَلَا يَقْرَبَنَّ مُصَلَّانَا»}$$

"The one who is by the means and does not perform the Udhiyah (sacrifice), should not approach the place of Eid Salah."

(Ahmad & Ibn Majah: 8273:3123)

Note: A Muslim who plans to offer an animal for sacrifice (UDHIYAH) during the 10th-13th of Dhul-Hijjah should refrain from cutting any of his or her hair and nails, starting from the sighting of the crescent of the month of Dhul-Hijjah (i.e. the 1ˢᵗ of the month) until the actual slaughtering of the animal. This is in accordance with the *Hadith* reported by Muslim. This applies to the person who will be slaughtering or wishes to sacrifice, but the spouse or children are not asked to refrain from doing so unless one of them in particular wishes to sacrifice.

Endeavour to perform *Eid Salah* and attend the *Khutbah*. Understand the wisdom behind the *Eid*: that it is a day of expressing gratitude to Allah and of righteousness. Thus, one should not make it a day of ill deeds and sin through forbidden practices.

Hajj on behalf of someone else

Any person who can afford (financially) *Hajj* but due to a permanent illness or old age cannot perform it should send someone else to perform it on his or her behalf.

One can perform *Hajj* on behalf of a deceased relative or friend.

The pre-conditions to perform *Hajj* on behalf of someone else are:

    1.   You must have performed your *Fard Hajj* already.

    2.   It must be that person's *Fard Hajj*.

The method for performing *Hajj* on behalf of someone else is very simple; everything is the same as if you would do it for yourself except at the time of uttering the *Niyah*. The method and details are in the next chapter.

Travel Supplications

Before you leave, supplicate for your family and friends and ask them to supplicate for you. The supplications listed below are not only for pilgrims, but for all travellers.

Supplication of the traveller for those remaining behind:

«أَسْتَوْدِعُكَ اللهَ الَّذِي لَا تَضِيعُ وَدَائِعُهُ»

"As-tawdi'uk-Allah alladhee laa tadhee'u wadaa'i'uhu."

(I entrust you to Allah, whose trust is never lost.)

(Ahmad 2/403 & Ibn Majah 2825)

Those who come to see off the pilgrims should supplicate for them. Supplication of those seeing off the traveller:

«أَسْتَوْدِعُ اللهَ دِينَكَ وَأَمَانَتَكَ وَخَوَاتِمَ عَمَلِكَ»

"As-tawdi u'allah deenaka wa amaanataka wa khowaatima a'malika."

(I entrust your faith, your trust (i.e., family and property), and your final deeds to Allah.)

(Abu Dawud 2600, Tirmidhi 3442 & Ahmad 2/7)

When the pilgrims actually leave, those wishing them farewell should supplicate the following:

«اللَّهُمَّ اطْوِلَهُ الْبُعْدَ وَهَوِّنْ عَلَيْهِ السَّفَرَ»

"Allahumma-at-wilahul-bu'da wa howwin a'layhis-safara."

(Oh Allah, shorten the distance for him and make the journey easy for him.)

(Tirmidhi:3445)

See in chapter 7 for more supplications for the journey.

Chapter 6

About the *Ihraam*

General Guidelines:

The rites of *Umrah* and *Hajj* begin by entering into the state of *Ihraam*.

For men it is very apparent as they have a specific garment to wear.

It is two clean preferably white unfitted pieces of cloth. The lower part of the *Ihraam* is referred to as *Izar* and the top part as *Rida*.

The shoes/sandals must not cover the ankles (it does not have to be plastic, as stitched leather or other material, sandals or shoes are acceptable).

Women are free to wear what they please. Needless to mention, it should conform to the Islamic code of dress. It can be of any colour. Some women insist on wearing white or green. There is no authentic basis in the *Sunnah* for this action.

Wearing the *Ihraam* garments does not mean that you are in the state of *Ihraam*. The state of *Ihraam* means to be in a state of ritual consecration. This is normally done at a specific area called the *Meqaat* (discussed in chapter 7 of this book).

A pilgrim is in the state of *Ihraam* ONLY once the *Niyah* has been uttered.

Adopting the *Ihraam*

1. Preparation

- Trim your finger and toe nails if needed
- Shave under your arms if needed
- Shave your pubic hair if needed

«قَالَ أَنَسٌ: وُقِّتَ لَنَا فِي قَصِّ الشَّارِبِ، وَتَقْلِيمِ الْأَظْفَارِ،
وَنَتْفِ الإِبطِ، وَحَلْقِ الْعَانَةِ، أَنْ لَا نَتْرُكَ أَكْثَرَ مِنْ أَرْبَعِينَ لَيْلَةً. »

*"As narrated by Anas (ﷺ) that the Prophet (ﷺ) set a period
during which the moustaches and nails be trimmed, hair
under the armpit be removed and those below the navel be cut.
He asked us not to leave them unattended for more than forty
days."*

(Muslim:258)

√ Trim the moustache (leave the beard as it is)

√ To perform *Ghusl* (shower) is *Sunnah*

√ Apply perfume to your head and beard (men only), and
   not to the garments. Women are strictly forbidden to wear
   perfume in *Ihraam* or while in the presence of men who are
   not their *Mahram*.

The Prophet (ﷺ) said:

«الْفِطْرَةُ خَمْسٌ: الاخْتِتانُ، وَالاسْتِحْدَادُ، وَقَصُّ الشَّارِبِ،
وَتَقْلِيمُ الْأَظْفَارِ، وَنَتْفُ الإِبطِ» .

*"Five things are part of nature: to get circumcised, to remove
the hair below one's navel, to trim moustaches and nails and
remove the hair under the armpit."*

(Bukhari:5891 & Muslim:257)

If possible avoid buying the very thin cotton *Ihraam*. It sticks
to you if you sweat. The toweling or the thicker cotton ones
are much better. They can be used as towels, blankets, for
shading, etc., later on. One may imagine that it will be hot
using a towelling cloth; however, this is not normally the case.

The one piece is wrapped around your waist like you would
normally do with a towel when coming out from the bath.
(This is very easy for those people who are used to wearing a
"lungi/sarong"). The other piece is thrown over your
shoulders covering the upper part of your body. Your right

shoulder is open only during *Tawaaf* for *Umrah* and the welcome *Tawaaf* (*Tawaaful-Qudoom*). It should be covered at all other times, especially while performing *Salah*. Do not be concerned when you notice that so many of the male pilgrims are walking around with their right shoulder exposed.

If you are not used to it, it may be a good idea to practise walking with it, making sure it does not fall off and also that you can move your legs. Remember, you will be in this gear for about 2 to 3 days (8, 9 & 10th of Dhul-Hijjah).

There appears to be a new fashion from some countries. The bottom of the *Ihraam* has the name of the travel agent printed in big bold colours. One of the purposes of the two pieces of cloth and no head gear is so that there is no distinction among the people. Advertising where you are from on your *Ihraam* is taking marketing concepts too far, in my opinion.

As the pilgrim is preparing for the journey and for the state of *Ihraam*, it is natural that most men have a haircut and some men clean-shave their beards. I guess this is to be "neat and tidy" for the trip.

As mentioned earlier, only the moustache should be trimmed and the beard should not be shaved:

The Prophet (ﷺ) said:

«خالِفُوا المُشرِكِينَ، وَوَفِّرُوا اللِّحَى، وأحْفُوا الشَّوَارِبَ»

"Oppose the polytheists. Let your beards grow and trim your moustaches.'"

(Bukhari & Muslim: 5892:259)

About the haircut. Save your money, as you will be cutting your hair after having completed your *Umrah*!

2. Put on your *Ihraam* clothes

Men wear the lower part by wrapping it around their waist.

The top part is thrown over, covering both shoulders. The right shoulder is only open during *Tawaaf* for *Umrah* and

Tawaaful-Qudoom.

It is acceptable to wear a money belt to assist in "keeping up" the lower part. A safety pin is also very useful to keep the top part from falling off or constantly opening up.

Watches, hearing aids, eye-glasses, contact lenses, sunglasses, etc. are all acceptable to wear while in *Ihraam.*

No head gear (men only).

No underwear (men only).

Slippers/shoes must not cover the ankles.

Women should cover their feet. They can wear socks.

Covering of the face and hands for women (see chapter 3 in this book).

It is acceptable to adopt the *Ihraam* clothes prior to reaching the *Meqaat* if it's more convenient.

Though unlikely in this day and age, there are exceptions allowed for those who do not have the recommended garments or shoes:

The Prophet (ﷺ) said:

«مَنْ لَمْ يَجِدْ إِزَارًا فَلْيَلْبَسْ سَرَاوِيلَ، وَمَنْ لَمْ يَجِدْ نَعْلَينِ فَلْيَلْبَسْ خُفَّينِ»

"Some who cannot get Izar (wrap) may put on trousers and who cannot get shoes may put on the leather socks.'"

(Bukhari & Muslim: 5804:1178)

3. Recite your *Niyah* out loud

The *Niyah* should be uttered at the *Meqaat* or close to it after your transport has started moving towards it.

This is the only instance where one's *Niyah* is made aloud. All other times any *Niyah* is to be done by heart only, and not the tongue.

To enter the state of *Ihraam* one must make *Niyah* for *Umrah* or

Hajj by saying:

For *Umrah* (*Hajj Tamattu*
- the *Niyah* for *Hajj* is to be made later):

«لَبَّيْكَ اللَّهُمَّ عُمْرَةً»

"Labbayk Allahumma Umratan."

(Oh Allah here I am performing *Umrah*.)

For *Hajj* only (*Hajj Ifrad* and for Tamattu later):

«لَبَّيْكَ اللَّهُمَّ حَجًّا»

"Labbayk Allahumma Hajjan."

(Oh Allah here I am performing *Hajj*.)

For *Umrah* & *Hajj* together (*Hajj Qiran*):

«لَبَّيْكَ اللَّهُمَّ عُمْرَةً وَحَجًّا»

"Labbayk Allahumma Umratan wa Hajjan."

(Oh Allah here I am performing *Umrah* and *Hajj*.)

It is preferred that this is done after a *Salah*. (The Prophet (ﷺ) pronounced his *Niyah* after having performed *Salatul-Zuhr*.)

There is no *Salatul-Ihraam* as some books teach (to perform two *Rak'at Salah* after adopting *Ihraam*).

There are also no other *Niy'at* to recite (i.e., "*Allahumma Innee Ureedu Hajj...*"). Both these actions have not been established in the *Sunnah* whereas the listed method has.

Menstruating or post-natal bleeding women MUST also enter into the state of *Ihraam*. They should follow the steps as listed and proceed to Makkah, Mina or Arafat (as appropriate). They should complete all the rites of *Hajj* except for *Tawaaf* while in the state of menstruation or post-natal bleeding. (See chapter 3 for more details and case examples.)

If you are performing *Hajj* for someone else (e.g., your mother or father), the only place where you mention the name of that

person is in the *Niyah*. The rest of the *Hajj* rites are the same as
if you were doing it for yourself.

Niyah for *Hajj* on behalf of someone else:

«لَبَّيْكَ اللَّهُمَّ حَجًّا عَنْ فَلَانٍ بنِ فُلانٍ»

"Labbayk Allahumma Hajjan 'an; name of the person."

(Oh Allah here I am performing *Hajj* for ....)

Niyah with a stipulation (*Ishtirat*)

If one, while entering the state of *Ihraam*, fears one is likely to
be subjected to illness or anything else that might obstruct
one's *Umrah* or *Hajj*, then one can recite a clause of stipulation
to Allah by saying:

«فَإِنْ حَبَسَنِي حَابِسٌ، فَمَحِلِّي حَيْثُ حَبَسْتَنِي»

"Fa in habasani haabisun, fa mahilli haithu habastani."

(Thus, if I am hindered by any obstacle, then my place
of conclusion is where You have held me.)

This is based upon the Prophet's (ﷺ) order to Dhuba'ah bint
Al-Zubair (﵂) to pronounce the statement of the *Ishtirat*
(stipulation) when she complained of being ill. This *Hadith* is
related by Bukhari and Muslim. The advantage of this is that
if one is faced with an obstacle that prevents one from
completing *Umrah*, then it is permissible for one to make
Tahallul, i.e. to conclude *Umrah* early without offering *Fidyah*
(expiation). Shaving (men) the head or cutting the hair
(women) must still be done, in order to be released from the
state of *Ihraam*.

Men should recite the *Talbiyah* loudly once they are in the state
of *Ihraam* as often as possible. A woman raises her voice only
to the extent of being heard by the person next to her.

«لَبَّيْكَ اللَّهُمَّ لَبَّيْكَ ، لَبَّيْكَ لَاشَرِيكَ لَكَ لَبَّيْكَ ، إِنَّ الْحَمْدَ
وَالنِّعْمَةَ لَكَ وَالْمُلكَ، لَا شَرِيكَ لَكَ»

"Labbayk Allahumma labbayk. Labbayka laa shareeka laka labbayk. Innal-hamda wan-ni'mata laka wal mulk. Laa shareeka lak."

(Here I am O Allah, Here I am. Here I am, You have no partner, here I am. Surely all praise, grace and dominion are Yours, and You have no partner.')

(Muslim:1184)

You are now in the state of *Ihraam*! A person in the state of *Ihraam* is a *Muhrim*.

Conditions of the *Muhrim*

Before uttering the *Niyah*, one is not considered a *Muhrim* (in the state of *Ihraam*) even if one wears the clothes of *Ihraam*. Only after uttering the *Niyah* does one become a *Muhrim* and thus the following prohibitions apply. Expiation (*Fidyah*) is due if any of the prohibitions are violated intentionally:

☒ Men must not wear clothes that are tailored to fit parts of the human body, for example trousers, jackets, shirts, etc. Meaning fitted clothes. There is a common misconception that one may not wear stitched clothes or sandals. However, this has no basis in the *Sunnah*, as it as an issue of fitted and not stitches. Hence, the *Ihraam* tops with studs should be avoided as it forms a fitted garment. Also, any sandal or shoe must not cover the ankle.

☒ Men MUST NOT wear any underwear or headgear. Men are not allowed to cover their heads. Note that the face is a part of the head and thus it must not be covered.

☒ Though women can wear normal clothes, they must NOT wear gloves or a face cover that has openings for their eyes (*Niqaab*). Instead, they can fully cover their faces and hands in the presence of men who are not their *Mahram* (see chapter 3 for more details).

☒ Must not apply perfume, wear perfumed clothes, nor use any perfumed substances (shampoo, soap, etc.). Caution, some tissues are perfumed.

☒ Must not trim his/her nails.

☒ Must not cut his/her hair.

☒ Must neither marry, give anyone else in marriage, nor propose marriage.

☒ Must not perform any act likely to arouse sexual passion or indulge in any intimate marital relations.

☒ Must not hunt or participate in hunting (fishing is allowed).

☒ Must not commit an act of disobedience to Allah, such as smoking.

☒ Must not get involved in idle talk or disputes, i.e. fights, arguments and quarrels.

Permissible actions while you are in the state of *Ihraam*:

☑ Wearing a wristwatch, eyeglasses, money belt, rings, sunglasses, hearing or speech aid, etc.

☑ Cleansing oneself (including having a bath or shower) with unscented soap and to wash and gently scratch one's head and body, even if hair may fall out.

☑ Changing one's *Ihraam* garments. Removing the *Ihraam* clothes does not nullify the state of *Ihraam*. One's *Niyah* places one in the state of *Ihraam* and cutting of one's hair removes one from this state.

☑ Having a shelter over one's head, whether in a car, under an umbrella, or in a tent or building.

☑ Men may also cover their feet (but not their head) while sleeping, with their *Ihraam* or a blanket.

If a person does not complete his *Umrah* or *Hajj* after entering into the state of *Ihraam* or commits an act which is prohibited (while in the state of *Ihraam*), then a sacrifice (expiation/ *Dumm*) is due upon him or her. See chapter 3, for more details about menstruation being the cause for not allowing a woman to complete her *Umrah*.

Etiquette for men, while in *Ihraam*:

- Avoid walking around with only the bottom part of your *Ihraam*.

- Keep your right shoulder covered (except during *Tawaaf*).

- Avoid throwing the 'lose' end of your *Ihraam* over your shoulder, as you may 'hit' the person behind you in the face.

- Keep your *Ihraam* clean and do not use it as a cloth to wipe your hands.

- Take extra care as to how you sit, especially on stairs, to avoid exposing yourself. As it is unusual for you to be without underwear, you can easily expose your private parts. This is very common while sitting on the stairs inside the mosque.

Sacrifices

As you will see from the data that follows, there are various rules depending on the actions. These sacrifices should not be viewed as penalties, rather as expiation. As this is a very serious matter, I urge you to review the tables carefully. The data in these tables was compiled from the following books (Arabic) and was verified by many scholars:

1.   *Tafsir Ibn Kathir*
     Ibn Kathir

2.   *Hajj & Umrah Rulings (Fatwas)*
     Sheikh bin Baz

3.   *The Umrah & Hajj Guide*
     Imam Saud As-Shreem

4.   *Hajj & Umrah and Visiting*
     Dr. Abdullah At-Tayyar

5.   *Hajj & Umrah Rulings – Comparison study for the Four Madhabs*
     Dr. Abu Saree'ah M. Abdulhadi

6.   *Al-Mughnee*
          Ibn Qudama

The general rule is that if a person committed an act in ignorance of the rule then there is no sacrifice required.

There are 3 types of sacrifices. The best way to remember them and what they are for is to remember the Arabic names.

1. *Hady*

﴿فَإِذَآ أَمِنتُمْ فَمَن تَمَتَّعَ بِالْعُمْرَةِ إِلَى الْحَجِّ فَمَا اسْتَيْسَرَ مِنَ الْهَدْيِ فَمَن لَّمْ يَجِدْ فَصِيَامُ ثَلَاثَةِ أَيَّامٍ فِي الْحَجِّ وَسَبْعَةٍ إِذَا رَجَعْتُمْ تِلْكَ عَشَرَةٌ كَامِلَةٌ ﴾

"...Then if you are in safety and whosoever performs the Umrah in the months of Hajj, before (performing) the Hajj, (i.e. Tamattu and Qiran), he must slaughter a Hady such as he can afford, but if he cannot afford it, he should fast three days during Hajj and seven days after his return (to his home), making ten days in all..."

Surah Al-Baqarah (2:196)

This sacrifice is performed by the *Tamattu* and *Qiran* pilgrims. It is only one sacrifice, and not two like many pilgrims believe.

This is neither a penalty nor expiation.

Sacrifices for *Hady* CANNOT be performed in your home country. This sacrifice must be done on the 10th of Dhul-Hijjah or during the 3 days of *Tashreek* (11th, 12th, and 13th). It cannot be done before the 10th.

It is one sheep or goat, or you can share with 6 others (7 in total) in a camel or a cow.

The animal sacrifices must be performed in the Makkah/ Mina/ Muzdalifah area only.

If one cannot afford the sacrifice? See previous *Ayah*. Fasting (3 days) should be done prior to the 8th of Dhul-Hijjah if possible otherwise it should be the 3 days of *Tashreek*. Pilgrims should not fast on the 9th (day of Arafat) or *Eid* day (10th). Do not forget to do the rest (7) of the days once you are home.

2. *Udhiya*

The *Udhiyah* is the sacrifice normally performed by those not performing *Hajj*. The *Udhiya* is also referred to as *Qurbani* (see chapter 5 for more details). The pilgrim (if one can afford it) may also perform *Udhiya*h (as *Sadaqah*) in addition to the *Hady*. Remember this is not a requirement for the pilgrim.

3. *Fidyah*

The *Fidyah* (expiation) is a means of compensation (Mercy from Allah) for a missed action or for transgressing a *Hajj* related law. It is a means of 'fixing' a shortcoming in your *Hajj*, so do not look at it as a penalty. It is commonly referred to as *Dumm*.

It is important to keep in mind that the expiation is for the purpose mentioned above and should not be used (as many pilgrims do) to intentionally omit an action and opt to sacrifice instead.

To make an analogy: During *Salah*, if we unintentionally omit or add a required (*Wajib*) act, we perform *Sujudus-Sahu* at the end to compensate for the mistake. We cannot intentionally leave out a *Tashahud* and make *Sujudus-Sahu* at the end. Similarly we cannot decide to intentionally (without a valid reason) omit a required (*Wajib*) act of *Hajj* (e.g., leaving Arafat before sunset; not staying/passing in Muzdalifah; not spending the nights in Mina) and plan to perform a sacrifice instead.

A novel way to remember the three different types of sacrifices (HUF):

Hady - Hajj sacrifice (for me)

Udhiya - Uthers (others) sacrifice (for those at home)

Fidyah - Fixing or (*Dumm* for being dumb)

You will notice in the table that for any sexual relations there is no expiation and this does constitute an actual penalty (invalid *Hajj*). Maybe the separate (men and women) accommodation option is not so bad after all. Nevertheless, almost all the packages provide separate accommodation for men and women for the *Hajj* days, even though you may have private accommodation in Makkah.

In chapter 15 of this book there is a table where you can note down any sacrifices (expiations) that you may need to perform.

Action	Expiation/Options/ Location	Remarks/References
If you are prevented from completing your *Hajj*:		*"... But if you are prevented (from completing the Hajj and Umrah) sacrifice a Hady such as you can afford, and do not shave your heads until the Hady reaches the place of sacrifice..."* (Al-Baqarah:196)
1). Made *Niyah* with the stipulation (*Ishtirat*).	1). Nil	1). Cut your hair and you are relieved from the *Ihraam*.
2). Made *Niyah* without the stipulation.	2). 1 x sheep or goat or Share with 6 others in a camel or a cow or Fast for 10 days.	2). Perform the sacrifice and cut your hair and you are relieved from the *Ihraam*. or Cut your hair followed by fasting.
	Sacrifice can be performed at any location (the best place is where you are stopped or where you cut your hair).	

Violating the *Ihraam* restrictions (e.g., cutting your hair or nails, men: applying perfume, wearing fitted clothes, covering their heads): 1) Unintentionally or due to ignorance of the rules. 2) Intentionally (ailment in your scalp; need to remove a nail due to injury).	Nil Fast for 3 days or feed 6 poor persons or 1 x sheep or goat. Animal sacrifice to be performed in the Makkah/ Mina/ Muzdalifah area or at the place where the violation occurred.	"...And whosoever of you is ill or has an ailment in his scalp (necessitating shaving), he must pay a Fidyah of either observing Saum (fast three days) or giving Sadaqah (feeding six poor persons) or offering a sacrifice (one sheep)..." (Surah Al-Baqarah:196)
Hunting while in the state of *Ihraam*	There are different penalties: Sacrifice a* (animal) or feed* poor persons or fasting for* days. *= The number and also the animal to be sacrificed is to be determined by 2 just men. The animal sacrifices are to be performed in the Makkah / Mina area only.	"O you who believe! Kill not game while you are in a state of Ihraam for Hajj or Umrah (pilgrimage), and whosoever of you kills it intentionally, the penalty is an offering, brought to the Ka'bah, of an eatable animal (i.e., sheep, goat, cow) equivalent to the one he killed, as adjudged by two just men among you; for expiation, he should feed Masakin (poor persons), or its equivalent in Saum (fasting), that he may taste the heaviness (punishment) of his deed..." (Surah Al-Mai'dah:95) Fishing is allowed.
Killing a Bird (pigeon) in or around the *Haram* area: Intentional	1 x sheep or goat or fast for 10 days or feed 10 poor persons.	This rule applies at all times and not only when you are on *Hajj* or in *Ihraam*.
Getting Married	Nil	The marriage is INVALID

Kissing, Hugging Caressing your partner:		
1. No sexual discharge	One ruling is:- 1 x sheep or goat. Another ruling is:- No sacrifice, just seek Allah's forgiveness.	*Hajj* remains valid
2. Sexual discharge	One ruling is:- 1 x sheep or goat. Another ruling is:- 1 x camel or cow. Animal sacrifice to be performed in the Makkah/ Mina/ Muzdalifah area only.	*Hajj* remains valid
Sexual Intercourse:		
1. Before completing any of the following 3 rites: 1 - *Ramy Aqabah* 2 - *Cutting the hair (1st Tahallul)* 3 -*Tawaaful-Ifadah (2nd Tahallul)*	*Hajj* is null and void and The pilgrim Must complete the rest of the rites of *Hajj* and Slaughter a camel or a cow (some rule that this can be done when the *Hajj* is repeated) and The pilgrim Must repeat the *Hajj* (some rule that even if it was a *Nafl Hajj*).	*Hajj* is INVALID
2. After any one rite (out of the three as above) is completed.	Some scholars rule that only one action is required to be completed.	*Hajj* is Valid
3. After any two rites (out of the three as above) are completed.	Some scholars rule that two actions are required to be completed. One ruling is:- 1 x sheep or goat. Another ruling is:- 1 x camel or cow Animal sacrifice to be performed in the Makkah/ Mina/ Muzdalifah area only.	*Hajj* is Valid If the pilgrim committed these actions in ignorance (did not know about the rule), then the *Hajj* remains valid and there is no sacrifice required. Repentance (*Tauba*) is also required.

Not completing the Wajib acts of *Hajj*:		
1. Passing the *Meqaat* without *Ihraam*	1 x sheep or goat	
2. Not staying in Arafat until sunset	1 x sheep or goat	
3. Not staying/ stopping in Muzdalifah	1 x sheep or goat	
4. Not spending the nights in Mina	1 x sheep or goat	
5. Not pelting the *Jamr'at*	1 x sheep or goat	
6. Not shaving or cutting your hair	1 x sheep or goat	
7. Omitting *Tawaaful-Wadaa'*	1 x sheep or goat The options for each expiation: Share with 6 others in a camel or a cow. Animal sacrifice to be performed in the Makkah/ Mina/ Muzdalifah area only.	Menstruating women are exempted.

Smoking

﴿وَيُحِلُّ لَهُمُ ٱلطَّيِّبَٰتِ وَيُحَرِّمُ عَلَيْهِمُ ٱلْخَبَٰٓئِثَ﴾

"...He will make lawful for them all good things and prohibit for them as unlawful Al-Khaba'ith (i.e. all evil and unlawful as regards things, deeds, beliefs, persons and foods)..."

Surah Al-A'raf (7:157)

There is absolutely no doubt that smoking is harmful to the human body. Hence smoking is *Haraam* (forbidden).

It is therefore, a sin to smoke and even worse so while one is in *Ihraam*.

Remember that one is promised an accepted *Hajj* only if it is performed according to the Qur'an and *Sunnah*. Intentionally committing a sin may deprive you of this special reward.

You will find so many pilgrims in *Ihraam* smoking it will make you wonder whether it is allowed to smoke a cigarette while you are in the state of *Ihraam*.

I am sure that it is not easy for smokers to give it up for 3 days. However, during Ramadan they seem to cope without a cigarette during the day. I suggest that if you are a smoker, try sincerely try to refrain from doing so while you are in the state of *Ihraam,* and also make the intention to give it up permanently (for the sake of Allah).

You are now a "Guest of Allah" and you should behave accordingly.

Chapter 7

The Journey from Home to Makkah

Travelling (*Musafir*) *Salah*:

Do not neglect your *Salah* while travelling.

Yes, it is possible to perform your *Salah* while in the aircraft.

This is a 'big' subject with many viewpoints, and I do not plan to delve into all these views and rulings. Based on my resources, below is the preferred method as per the *Sunnah* for travellers:

√ For *Salah* one must stand and face *Qiblah*. (If the direction of the aircraft changes during the *Salah*, this is ok.)

√ For *Nafl Salah* one can sit.

√ Only sit in your seat to make your *Fardh Salah* if it is absolutely impossible to do otherwise.

√ While you are travelling you can shorten your *Salah*.

√ Joining of the *Salah* is not part of travelling only, but rather as per one's need at anytime. However, during travelling it is acceptable to join and shorten while on the journey, and to shorten (not join) once you have reached your destination.

√ *Fajr* = 2 *Sunnah Rak'at* and 2 *Fard Rak'at*. The Prophet (ﷺ) never omitted the *Sunnah* for *Fajr*, even while travelling.

√ *Zuhr* = 2 *Rak'at* and *'Asr* = 2 *Rak'at*. You can join the *Salah* at any time from the start of *Zuhr* until the end of *'Asr*.

√ *Maghrib* = 3 *Rak'at* and *'Eshaa* = 2 *Rak'at* + *Witr*. You can join the *Salah* at any time from the start of *Maghrib* until the end of *'Eshaa* (no later than midnight).

√ *Witr*. This is another *Salah* the Prophet (ﷺ) never omitted, even while travelling.

There appears to be great deal of confusion on how to perform or join *Salah* while travelling. On many occasions you will enter a mosque, on your way to Madinah or Makkah, where you may find more than one congregation performing *Salah*. One group performing *Salatul-Maghrib* and another group performing *Salatul-'Eshaa*. This is incorrect, as there should only be one *Imam* (congregation) at any given time in the same mosque or prayer area. This phenomenon stems from the fact that those performing *Maghrib* believe that they cannot join the group performing *'Eshaa*. Many times you will actually find someone standing there stopping people (coming in late for *Maghrib*) from joining the group performing *'Eshaa*. My fellow Muslims, it is so easy. If you enter the mosque to perform *Maghrib*, and the congregation is performing *'Eshaa* (2 *Rak'at*), join them and complete three *Rak'at* as you would have normally when they complete the two. If you enter and there are two groups, join the group that started first (they will generally be to the front of the mosque).

Meqaat

The *Meqaat* boundaries were defined by the Prophet (ﷺ), and anybody (with the intention of performing *Umrah* or *Hajj*) who passes through them without *Ihraam* is liable for an expiation (sacrifice).

The Prophet (ﷺ) said:

«هُنَّ لَهُمْ وَلِمَنْ أَتَى عَلَيْهِنَّ، مِنْ غَيرِهِنَّ، مِمَّنْ أَرَادَ الحَجَّ وَالعُمْرَةَ»

"They (i.e. the Mawaqit) are for those who come from them and those coming from beyond them who intend Hajj or Umrah."

(Bukhari & Muslim: 1524:1181)

Jeddah is not a *Meqaat*. Many pilgrims adopt their *Ihraam* at Jeddah airport. This is a violation of the *Meqaat* rules. The pilgrims should return to their respective *Meqaat* or the nearest one, or perform an animal sacrifice as expiation.

Only the people who reside in Jeddah can adopt their *Ihraams* from their homes in Jeddah.

Pilgrims intending to proceed to Madinah upon arrival in Jeddah, should adopt *Ihraam* at Dhul-Hulaifah in Madinah, before going to Makkah.

«عَنِ ابْنِ عَبَّاسٍ قَالَ: وَقَّتَ رَسُولُ اللهِ ﷺ لِأَهْلِ الْمَدِينَةِ ذَا الْحُلَيْفَةِ، وَلِأَهْلِ الشَّامِ الْجُحْفَةَ وَلِأَهْلِ نَجْدٍ قَرْنَ الْمَنَازِلِ، وَلِأَهْلِ الْيَمَنِ يَلَمْلَمَ، فَهُنَّ لَهُنَّ وَلِمَنْ أَتَى عَلَيْهِنَّ مِنْ غَيْرِ أَهْلِهِنَّ لِمَنْ كَانَ يُرِيدُ الْحَجَّ وَالْعُمْرَةَ، فَمَنْ كَانَ دُونَهُنَّ فَمُهَلُّهُ مِنْ أَهْلِهِ، وَكَذَاكَ وَكَذَاكَ حَتَّى أَهْلُ مَكَّةَ يُهِلُّونَ مِنْهَا.»

"Narrated Ibn Abbas (ﷺ) that the Prophet (ﷺ) fixed Dhul-Hulaifah as the Meqaat for the people of Al-Madinah, Al-Juhfah for the people of Sham, Qarnul-Manazil for the people of Najd, and Yalamlam for the people of Yemen; and these Mawaqit are for those living at those very places, and besides them for all those who come through them with the intention of performing Hajj and Umrah; and whoever is living within these Mawaqit should assume Ihraam from where he starts, and the people of Makkah can assume Ihraam (for Hajj only) from Makkah."

(Bukhari:1526)

Some airlines such as Saudi Arabian Airlines, Malaysian Airlines, Emirates Airlines, Kuwait Air and Pakistan International Airlines make an announcement in the aircraft prior to it reaching the respective *Meqaat* boundary. Some display a message on the screen about 10 to 20 minutes before the *Meqaat*.

Meqaat names and locations

1.   *Zul-Hulaifah*, is also now known as Abyar Ali or Abaar

Ali (the wells of Ali). It is situated about 10 kilometres (6 miles) outside Madinah. It is for the pilgrims of Madinah and those coming from the North.

2.   Dhat-Irq is for the pilgrims coming from the direction of Iraq. It is about 67 kilometres (42 miles) from Makkah.

3.   *Qarn Al-Manazil*, now known as As-Sayl. This is for the pilgrims coming from the Najd and the East. It is situated near the city of Taif.

4.   *Yalamlam*, also known as As-Sadiah. This is for the pilgrims coming from Yemen and its direction (South). It is about 48 kilometres (30 miles) from Makkah.

5.   *Al-Juhfah* is today an abandoned village north west of Makkah near the town of Rabigh. Pilgrims coming from Syria and its direction adopt their *Ihraam* from Rabigh.

As there are many pilgrims and the aircraft facilities are limited, it is advisable to prepare oneself (*Ghusl*, trim nails, etc.) and to put on one's *Ihraam* clothes, prior to boarding the aircraft, and only utter the *Niyah* at the *Meqaat* boundary.

On the next page is a very general diagram to give you an idea of the boundaries.

Some examples (of pilgrims arriving by air direct to Jeddah):

◆ People coming from the United Kingdom will adopt *Ihraam* at or over Rabigh ❺

◆ People coming from Australia, Malaysia, Singapore, etc. will adopt *Ihraam* at As-Sayl ❸ (assuming that the flight is direct and not via Riyadh).

◆ People coming from America and Canada will adopt *Ihraam* at Rabigh ❺

◆ People coming from South-Africa and Nigeria will adopt Ihraam at As-Sadiah ❹

◆ People from Egypt will adopt *Ihraam* at Rabigh ❺

◆ People coming from Pakistan will adopt *Ihraam* at As-Sayl❸

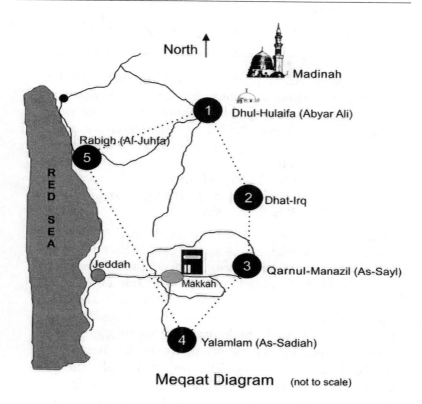

North ↑

Madinah

1 Dhul-Hulaifa (Abyar Ali)

Rabigh (Al-Juhfa)

5

R
E
D

S
E
A

2 Dhat-Irq

Jeddah

Makkah

3 Qarnul-Manazil (As-Sayl)

4 Yalamlam (As-Sadiah)

Meqaat Diagram   (not to scale)

The Journey

Once you have boarded your means of transport, supplicate
the following:

«اللهُ أَكْبَرُ اللهُ أَكْبَرُ اللهُ أَكْبَرُ سُبْحَانَ الَّذِي سَخَّرَ لَنَا هَٰذَا وَمَا كُنَّا
لَهُ مُقْرِنِينَ، وَإِنَّا إِلَىٰ رَبِّنَا لَمُنْقَلِبُونَ، اللَّهُمَّ! [إِنَّا] نَسْأَلُكَ فِي
سَفَرِنَا هَٰذَا الْبِرَّ وَالتَّقْوَىٰ، وَمِنَ الْعَمَلِ مَا تَرْضَىٰ، اللَّهُمَّ! هَوِّنْ
عَلَيْنَا سَفَرَنَا هَٰذَا، وَاطْوِ عَنَّا بُعْدَهُ، اللَّهُمَّ أَنْتَ الصَّاحِبُ فِي

السَّفَرِ، وَالْخَلِيفَةُ فِي الْأَهْلِ، اللَّهُمَّ! إِنِّي أَعُوذُ بِكَ مِنْ وَعْثَاءِ السَّفَرِ، وَكَآبَةِ الْمَنْظَرِ، وَسُوءِ الْمُنْقَلَبِ فِي الْمَالِ وَالْأَهْلِ»

"Allahu Akbar Allahu Akbar Allahu Akbar. Subhanaladhee sakh-khar-ra-lana hadhaa wamaa kunnaa lahu muqrineen wa innaa ilaa rabbanaa lamunqaliboon, Allahumma innaa nasaluka fee safarinaa hadhal-bir wa-taqwaa wa minal a'malimaa tarthaa. Allahumma howwin a'laynaa safaranaa hadhaa wa-tawe'annaa bu'dahu. Allahumma anta saahibu fissafari walkhalifatu fil-ahli. Allahumma inni a'uoodhubika min wa'thaa'issafari wa kaabatil manthari wa soo'almunqalabi filmaali wal ahli"

(Allah is the Greatest, Allah is the Greatest, Allah is the Greatest. How perfect He is, the One Who has placed this (transport) at our service, and we ourselves would not have been capable of that, and to our Lord is our final destiny. O Allah we ask You for *Birr* and *Taqwaa* in this journey of ours, and we ask You for deeds which please You. O Allah, make easy for us this journey of ours and fold up (i.e., shorten) for us its distance. O Allah, You are the companion in travel and the caretaker of the family. O Allah, I seek refuge in You from the hardship of travel and from (finding) a distressing sight or an unhappy return in regard to (my) property and family.)

(Muslim:1342)

(*Birr* & *Taqwaa* = Two comprehensive terms which individually, refer to all good actions and obedience).

One advantage of choosing to fly with Saudi Arabian Airlines is that this *Dua'* is read prior to the take-off. Apart from the food also being *Halal*, it is good practice to try and support the Muslim countries and airlines, whenever possible.

Supplications during the journey:

➢   Upon ascending and elevation —

Allahu Akbar الله أَكْبَرُ

(Allah is the Greatest.)

➢ Upon descending —

Subahanallah سُبْحَانَ الله

(Glorified is Allah.)

➢ Upon approaching a town during a journey:

«اللَّهُمَّ رَبَّ السَّمَاوَاتِ السَّبْعِ وَ مَا أَظْلَلْنَ، وَرَبَّ الأَرَضِينَ السَّبْعِ وَمَا أَقْلَلْنَ، وَرَبَّ الشَّيَاطِينِ وَمَا أَضْلَلْنَ، وَرَبَّ الرِّيَاح وَمَا ذَرَيْنَ، أَسْأَلُكَ خَيْرَ هَذِهِ الْقَرْيَةِ، وَخَيْرَ أَهْلِهَا وَخَيْرَ مَا فِيهَا، وَأَعُوذُ بِكَ مِنْ شَرِّهَا وَشَر أَهْلِهَا وَشَرِّ مَا فِيهَا»

"Allahumma rabbas-samaawaatissab'i wa maa athlalna, wa rabbal-ardhainis-sat'i wa maa aqlalna wa rabbash, shayaateeni wa maa adhlalnaa, wa rabbar-riyaahi wa maa dharayna. Asaluka khayra haadhihil qaryati, wa khayra ahlihaa wa khayra maa feehaa, wa a'uoodhu bika min sharri haa wa sharri ahlihaa wa sharri maa feehaa."

(O Allah, Lord of the seven heavens and that which they cover, Lord of the seven earths and that which they carry, Lord of the devils and those they lead astray, and Lord of the winds and that which they scatter, I ask of You the good of this town and the good of its people and the good of that within it. And I seek refuge in You from its evil and from the evil of its people and from the evil of that within it.)

(Nasa'i:5/256 and Ibn Hibban:2709)

When you stop for the night during your journey, supplicate the following:

«أَعُوذُ بِكَلِمَاتِ اللهِ التَّامَّاتِ مِنْ شَرِّ مَا خَلَقَ»

"A'uoodhu bikalimaatillahit-taammaati min sharri maa khalaqa."

(I seek refuge in the perfect Words of Allah and from the evil of that which He created.)

(Muslim:2708)

Do not neglect your *Salah* while en route to Saudi Arabia. If you are travelling during sunset, you will notice that on the one side, looking out of the aircraft, the sun will still be shining, whereas on the other side it will be dark. This makes it difficult to determine the time of *Salatul-Maghrib*. If you will be disembarking prior to 11.30pm, then you can delay and join *Salatul-Maghrib* and *Salatul-'Eshaa*. If not, then perform *Salatul-Maghrib* when the sun has set on the side of the aircraft where you are sitting.

If you are going directly to Makkah (not to Madinah first), ensure that you enter into *Ihraam* at the *Meqaat* points (see the *Meqaat* diagram).

Do not forget to remove your underwear (men only). This may sound funny, but there are many male pilgrims who forget to remove their underwear while in *Ihraam*.

Do not forget to remove any headgear you may be wearing (men only).

Make your *Niyah* as described in chapter 6.

Once you are in the state of *Ihraam*, recite the *Talbiyah* as often as possible.

Leave home for the airport as early as possible. The *Hajj* flights are extremely busy. Even though you may hold a confirmed seat, you may find no seats available if you are late (1 hour before departure) to check-in.

Most airlines operate on an overbooking procedure- meaning if everybody that has a confirmed booking turns up, there will not be enough seats. So be early.

During check-in, reconfirm any special food or seating you

may have requested.

The flight attendant or pilot (depending on the airline) will announce the *Meqaat* point prior to you reaching it.

As you depart "cash in one bag" of patience.

Carry your small Qur'an and your *Hajj* notes/books with you. Utilise every minute of your time, to seek Allah's pleasure and reward.

Give the movie (film) on the aeroplane a miss and read Qur'an instead. Start your journey the right way.

Most airlines provide the passengers with socks and eye-covers. Take these with you, as the socks are useful to wear if the *Haram* floor is too cold or too hot. The eye-covers are useful, if you will be sharing rooms, and the lights are still on while you are trying to sleep.

It may be more practical to adopt your *Ihraam* clothes prior to boarding the aircraft for Jeddah. This means that you only have to make your *Niyah* at the *Meqaat* point. (The toilets in the aircraft are extremely small and you might get tangled in your *Ihraam* and get stuck in the toilet. Now wouldn't that be a sight?)

If you do choose to adopt your *Ihraam* in the aircraft, try to use the toilet that provides facilities for baby diaper change. They are normally bigger in size and you can use the table to place your clothes on.

Men, don't forget your shoes under your seat when disembarking. Sound silly? Ok this is what happens...You decide to adopt *Ihraam*; you take out your garments as well as your slippers to wear while in *Ihraam*. You take of your shoes as it is easier to go to the toilet with the slippers. You return with your *Ihraam* on and slippers. You put your clothes in your overnight bag, and very likely forget about your shoes......Just recently a friend called me from Makkah and asked how he can go about getting his shoes back that he left under his seat on the plane. He was surprised when I did not ask him how he managed to leave his shoes on the plane.

Once you are in the state of *Ihraam*, you may experience that suddenly very minor things and issues start to annoy or affect you. Remember, *Shaytaan* will be doing his best to make you violate the rules of *Ihraam*. Be aware and alert!

Now is the time to "cash in" another few bags of patience.

Remember, this is a spiritual journey. Don't concern yourself too much with what you see wrong around you. Concern yourself only about whether Allah will accept your *Hajj* performance or not.

The journey is to perform *Hajj* and the *Eid* is called "*Eidul-Adha*" - Feast of Sacrifice. Try to sacrifice your time, your effort, your knowledge, your behaviour and your money in helping fellow Muslims during this auspicious journey.

The time has come...!

Arrival at Jeddah

The procedures below are for those pilgrims that will be arriving by air into Jeddah. Many pilgrims arrive by ship or some pilgrims go directly to Madinah. The procedures for them are marginally different (not addressed in this book).

Jeddah IS NOT a *Meqaat*.

Only the residents of Jeddah can adopt their *Ihraams* from their homes in Jeddah.

There is no air transport between Jeddah and Makkah. Madinah has its own airport and you are able to go there by aeroplane. Over the last few years some flights go directly to Madinah. If you can be on one of these flights, that will be great as you can save plenty of bags of patience not mentioning time.

Jeddah's King Abdul Aziz International Airport has three terminals:

1. Saudi Arabian Airlines *Terminal;*

2. Foreign Airlines Terminal (about 15min by car from the Saudia *Terminal*);

3. *Hajj* Terminal (located next to the Foreign Airlines Terminal).

The *Hajj Terminal* is known as "Tent City". It is constructed with huge tent-like structures (pictured below).

The customs at all three terminals are extremely strict and thorough. Be prepared to have all your bags unpacked and checked with a fine tooth comb. (Unlock all your suitcases before you arrive at the customs desk.)

This is where you need to produce the two cheques you were required to have to obtain your visa. One is for the *Mutawwif* (see under *Mutawwif* in this chapter) office and one is for the United Agents Office (bus coupons).

All three terminals have restaurants (expensive), bathrooms, showers, toilets, telephones and *Salah* facilities.

Processing

Now is the time to "cash in" the rest of your patience that you have "saved".

When you arrive, you may be tired and exhausted and in a

hurry to get to Makkah. Keep in mind that the authorities have to process visas for thousands of pilgrims like you in one day. It will take time as you may expect.

Meanwhile, sit, relax, read Qur'an, and make *Dhikr, Tasbeeh, Istighfaar,* and recite the *Talbiyah.* There is no hurry.

Also, try to extend your help to others.

There are delays of all kinds. There is no specified time as to how long it will take from the time you land until the time you depart for either Makkah or Madinah. It could take from 1 to 12 hours or more.

If you are fortunate to arrive as early as Shawaal then you may not be processed at the Hajj Terminal. After about the first week into Dhul-Qadah, all pilgrims are processed via the Hajj Terminal, even if you arrive on a non-*Hajj* scheduled flight. All pilgrims will be requested to stay on board the aircraft after landing at the appropriate terminal. All other passengers will disembark and you will then be taken to the Hajj Terminal.

Money

Change your money into riyals at the airport. Calculate how much you require and change as much as you can. Queuing in banks later on is not much fun and the time could be better spent in *Ibadah.*

Unfortunately and sadly, I need to mention that there are pickpockets during *Hajj*. So, like any other trip you need to take care of your money. Do not be careless because you are on *Hajj*. Buy yourself a good money belt. Good belts (canvas type) are available in Makkah and Madinah.

When you change your money, obtain some small denominations (e.g., 1 & 5 riyals). These are extremely useful when buying small items (such as drinks) when the shops are very crowded. This way you do not have to wait for change.

Facilities

Take your luggage and settle down in a good spot. The Hajj Terminal is huge and comfortable in its own way.

There are also banks for cashing your cheques and obtaining sacrificial vouchers. Check with your agent if they provide the sacrificial service and compare their price to that of the banks. The bank's price is normally higher as it includes the slaughtering, cleaning, packaging and the transportation of the meat to the Muslim countries in need.

If you are going to Madinah first, the bus will depart from this terminal once it is full. You should use your bus coupons for this journey.

If you plan to go by aeroplane then you will have to go to the Saudia Terminal. The authorities will make the transfer arrangements for you.

Other

Some pilgrims plan to travel to other countries after or before *Hajj* and thus may have two passports (different countries/ nationalities) with them. Be aware that to enter Saudi Arabia with two valid passports in your possession is illegal.

If you are at the Hajj Terminal, normally, no friends or family will be able to meet you, as they are not allowed to enter this terminal.

If you have friends or family in Saudi Arabia, it is best if they meet you in Makkah or Madinah.

If you plan to call them, and they are not expecting you, please take a moment to check the local time. (It is not very polite to wake a person at 3.00am, especially if it's just a social call.)

If you arrive a few days (5 or less) before *Hajj*, there is a very high probability that the authorities will not allow you to go to Madinah first. This is regardless of what bookings or tickets you hold. Normally all pilgrims from abroad must be in the

Kingdom before the 5th of Dhul-Hijjah. So plan carefully.

If you arrive during the peak arrival time (1 to 2 weeks before *Hajj*), there is a high probability that you will not be able to leave the Hajj Terminal to go to Madinah by aeroplane, even if you have the tickets. They will put you on a bus, which in actual fact is easier and more practical.

This is another reason why I suggest that you purchase your Madinah air tickets separate from all your other tickets. This way you can get it refunded if you do not use it. If the ticket is part of an excursion or special fare ticket, you may have difficulty in obtaining a refund.

Mutawwifs

There are persons assigned by the Saudi Arabian government known as *Mutawwifs*, who are responsible for the needs of the pilgrims, such as transportation, tents in Mina and Arafat.

Mutawwifs are assigned to the pilgrims. Pilgrims are divided according to nationality.

The *Mutawwifs* office is also named, Experimental National Establishment for Pilgrims of...(country or area, e.g., African, European, Asian).

They are an official division of the Ministry of *Hajj*.

They will take your passport upon your arrival and return it to you on your departure.

On arrival, the pilgrim pays a fixed amount (one of the two cheques you are supposed to have with you) to the *Mutawwif*. The Saudi Arabian Embassy in your country will inform you of the amount and may wish to see the draft/cheques prior to issuing you with a *Hajj* visa.

Some of the other services they provide

√ Furnish you with an ID card in lieu of your passport.

√ Their offices are open 24 hours and provide assistance with accommodation too.

√ As mentioned earlier they arrange your transportation, and provide the tents in Mina and Arafat.

√ Inspectors who visit all *Hajj* accommodations to check their conditions (clean, water available, room occupancy, etc.). The owner of a hotel can be fined if he does not provide adequate provisions for the pilgrims.

√ Deal with disputes (between pilgrims and the agent/hotel).

√ You can lodge any complaint you may have about your accommodation and they will assist you.

√ Assist during illnesses and emergencies with ambulance and hospital facilities. In the event of a death, they will arrange for the necessary documentation and funeral.

√ They have offices in Makkah, Mina and Arafat that take care of pilgrims who are lost. If you lose someone or you are lost, try to find one of these offices.

√ Provide an Islamic service, books, guides, etc. They can also arrange a visit to various places in and around Makkah, Madinah and Jeddah.

√ Their offices are normally staffed with individuals who can speak the appropriate language of the countries they represent.

In order to go to Mina on the 8th, if you are a group of more than 50, the buses will be sent to your accommodation. However if you are only a few, you may have to go the Muassasah office to get the bus. Your agent should arrange all this for you.

The ID card they provide for you is in lieu of your passport. Keep it safe as you will need this card to cash money and to obtain your passport prior to your departure from Makkah or Madinah. If you lose this card, report it to this office.

It is a good idea to familiarise yourself with the location of the appropriate office that serves your country. Your agent or hotel receptionist will normally be able to direct you to the appropriate office in Makkah or Madinah.

The trip to Makkah

Before you leave the terminal for Makkah or Madinah, use the toilet, and refresh your *Wudu*. You will not see such good toilet facilities again for a while. So make the best of them.

Keep some biscuits and a small bottle of water with you on the bus.

Once the bus on which you have boarded is filled to capacity, the driver will proceed. This may take a few hours.

You will stop at several checkpoints where all the passports will be checked.

The bus driver will take your passport from you and keep them with him. The next time you will see your passport is when you depart for home after *Hajj*. He will hand it in at the *Mutawwifs* office where they will give you an ID card. If you are going to Madinah first, the procedure is slightly different.

Jeddah to Madinah

The distance is 424km (265 miles).

Most of the buses are air-conditioned.

This journey can take from 4 to 12 hours or longer.

The driver will stop at a few places for food and rest. (Do not be surprised if your driver disappears to have a short rest.)

The driver will hand in all the passports at the relevant office in Madinah (different countries, different offices). You will not be provided with an ID card at this stage. Sometimes they issue a temporary card. The cards are normally issued from the Makkah offices.

A representative from the *Mutawwifs* office will be with you all the time, even if you go by plane.

If you are going by aeroplane:

- You will depart from the Saudi Arabian Airlines

Terminal.

- The flight is about 45 minutes.

- Once in Madinah, the *Mutawwifs* office will make the arrangements for you to get to your hotel.

Sometimes (actually most of the time) the bus driver is not familiar with all the locations of the various offices, so you may get lost for a while, while the driver tries to find the right office. Be patient! (It happened in 1989, and as you may have guessed it was still the same in 2006).

If you are a big group, all residents or nationals from the same counry, then it is much easier as you will need to stop only at one office. However, if there are people from different countries on the bus, the driver will have to stop at many different offices. The authorities at the airport will instruct the driver as to which offices he needs to go to. Hence it is better to try and fill the bus or taxi with only one group.

Try to remember where the office (for your country) is, as you may need to go there yourself, or direct the taxi or bus to collect your passport. There are no formal addresses as such. There are street names. However, it is best to try and remember the place, by using landmarks (i.e., how far it is from the mosque, what the building next to it is, etc.).

Madinah details - see chapter 12 in this book.

Madinah to Makkah

The distance is 447km (278 miles).

If you plan to use the *Muassasah* buses, you should make arrangements with them at least a few days beforehand.

If you are going to Makkah by bus or by plane (via Jeddah), the procedures are the same.

You will not be allowed to hire a private taxi at this stage.

A representative from the *Mutawwifs* office will be with you all the time, even if you are going by plane.

If you do not have the two unfitted pieces of cloth for your

Ihraam (men), you should purchase them in Madinah.

Prior to your departure for Makkah, prepare yourself for the state of *Ihraam*, i.e. *Ghusl*, trim your nails etc.

Attire yourself with your *Ihraam clothes.*

Do not forget to collect your passport prior to leaving Madinah for Makkah. (The authorities at these offices will only give the passport to the bus or taxi driver or to your agent.)

The bus or taxi will stop at the *Meqaat* on its way to either Makkah or to the airport.

The *Meqaat* is at Abyar-Ali (Dhul-Hulaifah) which is situated about 10km (6 miles) outside Madinah. (The mosque at this *Meqaat* has showers and good *Wudu* and toilet facilities.)

If you have not put on your *Ihraam*, you need to do so at this stage and make your *Niyah* for *Umrah* (*Tamattu*). (*Niyah*, see chapter 6.)

Recite the *Talbiyah* as often as possible. (See chapter 6, for the *Talbiyah*).

Before you leave the *Meqaat* for Makkah, use the toilet if required and "refresh" your *Wudu*. You will not see such good toilet facilities again for a while, so make the best of them.

Keep some biscuits and a small bottle of water with you on the bus.

This journey can take 6 to 18 hours or longer, depending on what time of the *Hajj* period it is.

If you are travelling by plane from Madinah, you will need to take a bus from Jeddah airport to Makkah. The *Mutawwifs* office at Jeddah airport will arrange this for you.

Jeddah to Makkah

You should be in *Ihraam*.

If you had planned to go to Madinah first and for some reason you are unable to go, and you are now going to Makkah first, than adopt your *Ihraam* immediately. You are not liable for expiation for violating the *Meqaat* rule, as it was outside your control.

Recite the *Talbiyah* as often as possible (see chapter 6, for the *Talbiyah*).

The distance is 72km (45 miles).

This journey can take 1 to 8 hours or longer. Most of the buses are air-conditioned, so the journey should be quite pleasant but tiring.

Checkpoints

You will stop at the major *Hajj* checkpoint just before entering Makkah. This could be quick or very long, so be patient.

At this checkpoint all your passports will be handed in to the relevant office.

At this checkpoint and at the one in Madinah, a person will count the people on the bus to match it with the number of passports. On many occasions this could take a while as you will notice that they cannot seem to match the numbers. Be prepared to be counted a number of times.

The most common reason for this is when there are children on the bus and they are included in their mother's passport. The quickest solution (if they will listen to you) is to take each passport and call the person's name, after which you will be able to identify who was not called or you may have an extra passport which belongs to another group.

They will provide you with a card in lieu of your passport, sometimes at a later stage. You will need to provide them with a passport-size photo of yourself to be put on the card. Keep it as safe as you would your passport.

You need this card to get your passport back and also as a form of identification when changing money.

Remember where the office (for your country) is as you may

need to go there yourself, or direct the taxi or bus to collect your passport or obtain assistance. There are no formal addresses as such. There are street names. However, it is best to try and remember the place by using landmarks. (i.e., how far it is from the *Haram*, what the building next to it is, etc.).

Prepare yourself, for the great moment...entering the *Haram* in Makkah and seeing the Ka'bah...

Chapter 8
Makkah Al-Mukarramah

﴿إِنَّ أَوَّلَ بَيْتٍ وُضِعَ لِلنَّاسِ لَلَّذِى بِبَكَّةَ مُبَارَكًا وَهُدًى لِّلْعَٰلَمِينَ ○ فِيهِ
ءَايَٰتٌ بَيِّنَٰتٌ مَّقَامُ إِبْرَٰهِيمَ وَمَن دَخَلَهُ كَانَ ءَامِنًا﴾

"Verily, the first House (of worship) appointed for mankind was that at Bakkah (Makkah), full of blessing, and a guidance for Al-Alamin (the mankind and the jinn). In it are manifest signs (for example), the Maqaam (place) of Ibraheem; whosoever enters it, he attains security..."

Surah Al-Imran (3:96-97)

It is desirable to have a bath (*Ghusl*) before entering Makkah. Once the pilgrims enter Makkah, their first duty is to perform

Umrah (*Tamattu*).

For those performing the *Ifrad* or *Qiran* method, they should perform *Tawaaful-Qudoom* (the welcome *Tawaaf*). *Sa'ee* for *Hajj* may also be performed (recommended for the *Qaarin*).

There is no particular supplication prescribed by the *Sunnah* upon entering Makkah and also for upon entering the boundaries of *Al-Haram*.

It is reported by Muslim that Abdullah bin Umar (ﷺ) used to recite the following upon entering the boundaries of *Al-Haram*:

«لَا إِلَهَ إِلَّا الله وَحْدَهُ لَا شَرِيكَ لَهُ لَهُ الْمُلْكُ وَلَهُ الْحَمْدُ وهُو
عَلَى كُلِّ شَيْءٍ قَدِيرٌ»

"Laa ilaha illallahu wahdahu laa shareekalahu lahulmulk wa lahulhamdu wahuwa alaa kulli shay'in qadeer."

(None has the right to be worshipped except Allah, alone, without partner. And to Him belongs all praise and sovereignty and He is over all things omnipotent.)

(Ahmad:1/440,2/10,21 & Tirmidhi:950,3534)

Most pilgrims are very anxious to complete their *Umrah*. However, before you go rushing off to the *Haram*, first settle yourself into your accommodation.

Have something to eat or drink, if you feel hungry or thirsty, and have a rest if you are tired.

If you have children with you, please see chapter 3 under "Children / In Makkah" for very important advice.

Keep track of the time. It is not a good idea to perform *Tawaaf* when it is very hot. If you are not used to extreme heat, as is the case in the middle of the day during summer, delay your *Umrah* until later in the day when the weather is a little cooler. Do not be brave; there is no rush. You will need your strength and energy later.

Before you leave to go to the *Haram*, ensure that you are

familiar with your surroundings and that you know how to get back to your accommodation. Use certain landmarks as a means of directions and locations.

As in any hotel, check and familiarise yourself with the emergency exits.

Take an address card of the hotel with you and keep it in your pocket, in addition to your identity card. If you do not have your *Hajj* card at this stage, keep some other form of identity with you (e.g., driver's licence, medical card, etc.).

Before discussing the *Umrah* and *Hajj* in detail, there are many other aspects related to Makkah, which I would like to address first.

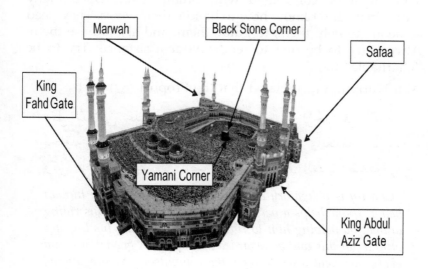

General Diagram of the *Haram*

There are more diagrams to follow. Each diagram contains a little more detail. (This way you can familiarise yourself with the various important landmarks step by step.)

The *Hajrul-Aswad* (Black Stone) corner is where the *Tawaaf* starts and ends.

The *Rukn-Yamani* corner is also referred to as the South Corner. It is between this corner and the next one (*Hajrul-Aswad*) that one recites: "Rabbanaa aatina fidunya..."

As-Safaa is where you start your *Sa'ee* finishing at Al-Marwah.

More details about the door/gate (*Baab*) names and numbers are covered later in this chapter.

Personal Behaviour

As Allah has instructed us that the best provision we can take with us on *Hajj*, is good conduct, I would like to start with a reminder about our personal behaviour. Also, you should be on your best behaviour as you are now a Guest of Allah!

You might be confronted with situations in which many individuals don't know how to handle themselves. They need someone to help them, to guide them, and also advise them. Always try to be first to render your assistance. Try to be "charitable" in all your actions.

Abu Hurrairah (رضي الله عنه) related that the Prophet (ﷺ) said:

«كُلُّ سُلَامَىٰ عَلَيْهِ صَدَقَةٌ كُلَّ يَوْمٍ، يُعِينُ الرَّجُلَ فِي دَابَّتِهِ، يُحامِلُهُ [عَلَيْها] أَوْ يَرْفَعُ عَلَيْها مَتَاعَهُ صَدَقَةٌ، والكَلِمَةُ الطَّيِّبَةُ، وكُلُّ خَطْوَةٍ يَمْشِيها إلى الصَّلاةِ صَدَقَةٌ، ودَلُّ الطَّرِيقِ صَدَقَةٌ»

"Charity is obligatory every day on every joint of a human being. If one helps a person in matters concerning his riding animal by helping him to ride on it or by lifting his luggage onto it, all this will be regarded as charity. A good word, and every step one takes to offer the compulsory congregational prayer are regarded as charity; and guiding somebody on the road is regarded as charity."

(Bukhari & Muslim: 2891:1009)

√ Avoid idle talk, arguments and disagreements.

Abu Hurrairah (رضي الله عنه) related that the Prophet (ﷺ) said:

«لَيْسَ الشَّديدُ بالصُّرَعَة، إنَّمَا الشَّديدُ الَّذي يَمْلِكُ نَفْسَهُ عِنْدَ
الغَضَب»

"The strong is not the one who overcomes the people by his strength, but the strong is the one who controls himself while in anger."

(Bukhari:6114)

√ Take utmost care when quoting *Ahadith* to prove your point. You must be 100% sure that the *Ahadith* are authentic. Do not claim you read or heard from so and so. The responsibility is on you.

Abdullah bin Amr bin Al-'Aas (ﷺ) related that the Prophet (ﷺ) said:

«بَلِّغُوا عَنِّي ولَوْ آيَةً، وحَدِّثُوا عَنْ بَني إسْرَائِيلَ ولا حَرَجَ،
ومَنْ كَذَبَ عَلَيَّ مُتَعَمِّدًا فَلْيَتَبَوَّأْ مَقْعَدَهُ مِنَ النَّارِ»

"Convey from me to the people though it may be only one Verse; and you may narrate events from the accounts of Bani Israil, there is no harm in doing so. But a person who deliberately attributes to me something which is not true, shall find his abode in Hell."

(Bukhari:3461)

√ Avoid asking too many questions.

Abu Hurrairah (ﷺ) said that the Prophet (ﷺ) once delivered a sermon and addressing us said:

«إنَّ اللهَ عَزَّ وجَلَّ قَدْ فَرَضَ عَلَيْكُمُ الْحَجَّ» فَقَالَ رَجُلٌ: فِي كُلِّ
عَامٍ؟ فَسَكَتَ عَنْهُ حَتَّى أَعَادَهُ ثَلاثًا فَقَالَ: «لَوْ قُلْتُ: نَعَمْ،
لَوَجَبَتْ، وَلَوْ وَجَبَتْ مَا قُمْتُمْ بِهَا»

"O people, Allah have made it obligatory for you to perform Hajj, and as such you should perform it. A man asked: 'O Messenger of Allah, should we perform Hajj every year?' The

Prophet (ﷺ) kept quiet, till the man repeated his question thrice. Then the Prophet (ﷺ) said: 'Had I said yes then this Hajj would have become a yearly obligatory duty, and this you could not have afforded.' "

(Nasai:2620)

The Prophet (ﷺ) further said:

«ذَرُونِي مَا تَرَكْتُكُمْ، فَإِنَّمَا هَلَكَ مَنْ كَانَ قَبْلَكُمْ بِكَثْرَةِ سُؤَالِهِمْ وَاخْتِلَافِهِمْ عَلَىٰ أَنْبِيَائِهِمْ، فَإِذَا أَمَرْتُكُمْ بِشَيْءٍ فَأْتُوا مِنْهُ مَا اسْتَطَعْتُمْ، وَإِذَا نَهَيْتُكُمْ عَنْ شَيْءٍ فَدَعُوهُ»

" 'Leave me when I omit something for you (i.e. don't pester me with such questions, when I am not imposing anything on you). Some people who lived before you, used to ask too many unnecessary questions, and would disagree with their prophets. On this account they were destroyed. As such when I call upon you to do something, you must obey and carry out my direction as far as it may be within your capacity, and when I forbid you to refrain from anything then avoid it'."

(Muslim:1337)

√ **Avoid backbiting**

Abu Hurrairah (ﷺ) relates that the Prophet (ﷺ) asked the companions:

«أَتَدْرُونَ مَا الْغِيبَةُ؟» قَالُوا: اللهُ وَرَسُولُهُ أَعْلَمُ، قَالَ: «ذِكْرُكَ أَخَاكَ بِمَا يَكْرَهُ» قِيلَ: أَفَرَأَيْتَ إِنْ كَانَ فِي أَخِي مَا أَقُولُ؟ قَالَ: «إِنْ كَانَ فِيهِ مَا تَقُولُ، فَقَدِ اغْتَبْتَهُ، وَإِنْ لَمْ يَكُنْ فِيهِ، فَقَدْ بَهَتَّهُ»

"Do you know what is meant by backbiting?' They answered, 'Allah and His Messenger know better.' He said: 'To narrate such things about your brother which he dislikes.' One of the audience asked: 'Even if my brother may be like that?' He

*said: 'If such defects as you say, be present in him, then you
have backbitten and if he does not have what you say, then
you are committing a slander'."*

(Muslim:2589)

√ Refrain from indulging in **backbiting** at all levels,
including at nationality or group level. It is very common
among many pilgrims to talk "bad" about different
nationalities and their behaviour.

﴿يَـٰٓأَيُّهَا ٱلَّذِينَ ءَامَنُوا۟ لَا يَسْخَرْ قَوْمٌ مِّن قَوْمٍ عَسَىٰٓ أَن يَكُونُوا۟ خَيْرًا مِّنْهُمْ
وَلَا نِسَآءٌ مِّن نِّسَآءٍ عَسَىٰٓ أَن يَكُنَّ خَيْرًا مِّنْهُنَّ وَلَا تَلْمِزُوٓا۟ أَنفُسَكُمْ وَلَا
نَابَزُوا۟ بِٱلْأَلْقَـٰبِ﴾

*"Oh you who believe! Let not a group scoff at another group;
it may be that the latter are better than the former; nor let
(some) women scoff at other women; it may be that the latter
are better than the former; nor defame one another; nor insult
one another by nicknames..."*

Surah Al-Hujurât (49:11)

√ There are only three places at the Ka'bah that you can and
should touch, if at all possible:

1.   The *Hajrul-Aswad* (Black Stone) -
      Kiss it if possible, otherwise touch or gesture.

2.   The *Rukn Yamani* (South Corner) -
      Touch it, but do not kiss or rub it.

3.   The area from the Black Stone Corner to the end of the
      Ka'bah door (*Multazam*) –
      The pilgrims normally hang on to this area as the
      companions did, but it is not to be kissed.

There is absolutely no reward and it is contrary to the *Sunnah*
to touch, rub or hang on to the *Maqaam Ibraheem*, the doors,
the Ka'bah cloth, etc. Furthermore, refrain from kissing it.

√ Lower your gaze...! We are instructed in the Qur'an and
Sunnah to do so:

﴿قُل لِّلْمُؤْمِنِينَ يَغُضُّوا مِنْ أَبْصَـٰرِهِمْ﴾

"Tell the believing men to lower their gaze..."

Surah An-Nur (24:30)

﴿وَقُل لِّلْمُؤْمِنَـٰتِ يَغْضُضْنَ مِنْ أَبْصَـٰرِهِنَّ﴾

"And tell the believing women to lower their gaze.."

Surah An-Nur (24:31)

«عَنْ جَرِيرِ بْنِ عَبْدِ اللهِ، قَالَ: سَأَلْتُ رَسُولَ اللهِ ﷺ عَنْ نَظْرَةِ الْفُجَاءَةِ، فَأَمَرَنِي أَنْ أَصْرِفَ بَصَرِي.»

"Jarir (رضي الله عنه) says: 'I asked the Prophet (ﷺ) as to what should be done when our glance accidentally falls (upon somebody forbidden) to look at.' He said: 'Turn your eyes'."

(Muslim:2159)

√ Reflect on the meaning of the following *Ayah*:

﴿إِنَّ ٱلَّذِينَ كَفَرُوا وَيَصُدُّونَ عَن سَبِيلِ ٱللَّهِ وَٱلْمَسْجِدِ ٱلْحَرَامِ ٱلَّذِى جَعَلْنَـٰهُ لِلنَّاسِ سَوَآءً ٱلْعَـٰكِفُ فِيهِ وَٱلْبَادِ وَمَن يُرِدْ فِيهِ بِإِلْحَادٍ بِظُلْمٍ نُّذِقْهُ مِنْ عَذَابٍ أَلِيمٍ﴾

Verily, those who disbelieved and hinder (men) from the Path of Allah, and from Al-Masjidul-Haram (at Makkah) which We have made (open) to (all) men, the dweller in it and the visitor from the country are equal there (as regards its sanctity and pilgrimage (Hajj and 'Umrah)) – and whoever inclines to evil actions therein or to do wrong (i.e. practice polytheism and leave Islamic Monotheism), him We shall cause to taste a painful torment.

Surah Al-Hajj (22:25)

√ Maintain a positive attitude and always say *"Alhamdulillah"* for everything, be it good or bad.

√ When the situation is not to your liking, always think of

those who are possibly in a worse situation than you:

- If your bed is too hard for your liking or the air-conditioner is making too much noise, think of the people sleeping in the street.

- If the food has too much salt, think of those who have no food.

- If the bus journey is too long, think of those who are walking.

- If you feel sick, think of those who have died.

- If your legs hurt and you are tired of walking, think of those without legs.

√ If you get impatient with people or situations, make *Dhikr* and make *Istighfaar* (seek Allah's pleasure and forgiveness).

√ Share with your fellow pilgrims. Be it time, guidance, advice, medicine, food, etc.

√ Help and assist the sick, elderly and those in need. Be cooperative and patient with your fellow pilgrims.

√ If you see older persons carrying something heavy, ask them if they need assistance. Do not wait to be asked to help.

Assisting people who are lost is also very rewarding. You do not have to know where they have to go, but you can comfort them and maybe help them to find somebody who can assist them further.

Cleanliness is very important in Islam. With such a large number of people this becomes even more important. Do not spit or throw litter in the street.

When you arrive early at the *Haram* for prayer you may find lots of space to sit and perform *Salah* comfortably. Within no time you will find that this "space of yours" gets eroded bit by bit as the *Haram* starts filling up. Now you can do one of two things. You can "fight" with every person that tries to sit too close to you, or you can try and accommodate them. From experience, I can guarantee you that you will not be able to hold on to "your territory" for very long. So avoid stress and adopt an attitude of: "This mosque does not belong to me; we are all guests of Allah, therefore we are all entitled to be in it." This is especially true for the *Jumu'ah* prayer.

However, when you are late, try not to push in and walk over the top of people. Your rightful place for being late is at the back. You may ask, but why should I adhere to the rules when nobody else does? Simple, Allah knows!

﴿وَلَا فُسُوقَ وَلَا جِدَالَ فِى ٱلْحَجِّ وَمَا تَفْعَلُوا۟ مِنْ خَيْرٍ يَعْلَمْهُ ٱللَّهُ﴾

"... nor commit sin, nor dispute unjustly during Hajj. And whatever good you do, (be sure) Allah knows it..."

Surah Al-Baqarah (2:197)

If you lose your shoes, or if someone "takes" them, do not take somebody else's shoes. Rather make *Dua'* and believe that the person who took them may need them more than you. Buy yourself another pair. They sell for as little as five Saudi riyals.

It is almost inevitable that there will be some religious arguments about various points of view on *Hajj* rites or any other *Fiqh* related matters in your group. I suggest you excuse yourself from the discussion or go for a walk. Never attend any group meeting, which is called to resolve some *Fiqh* related issue.

Some people rush violently in order to touch and kiss the Black Stone. Such behaviour is wrong. Besides exerting effort to the level of fatigue, rushing and pushing in a mixed crowd of males and females may cause harm to someone. It is lawful (*Sunnah*) to touch and kiss the Black Stone when possible. It is sufficient for a pilgrim to merely point at it, whereas causing others harm or inconvenience is sinful.

It is natural that with so many people in one place some confusion, impatience, pushing, etc. will occur, especially with people from such varied backgrounds.

Try your best to perform your activities and movements in a calm and quite way. Do not push, harm or rush anybody, especially in the crowded areas such as during *Tawaaf, Sa'ee,* at the *Maqaam Ibraheem,* at the *Jamrah,* etc.

You must expect that many people may come from very primitive areas, where there are possibly no escalators, proper toilets, technology, etc. Respect their backgrounds and do not look down upon them or make fun of them.

Do not harm people even with words or behave impolitely. Remember that the mouth can be a serious weapon of harm. Always think first before you speak, and ask yourself if what you are about to say will be hurtful or not.

Abu Hurrairah (ﷺ) reported that the Prophet (ﷺ) said:

«إنَّ العَبْدَ لَيَتَكَلَّمُ بالكَلِمَةِ ما يَتَبَيَّنُ فيها يَزِلُّ بها في النَّارِ أبْعَدَ مَا بَيْنَ المَشْرِقِ والمغرب»

> *"Often a person says something without realizing its implications or importance. This causes him to enter the fire of Hell to a depth equal to the distance between the east and the west."*
>
> (Bukhari & Muslim: 6477:2988)

Always consider the feelings of your fellow Muslims.

Ibn Mas'ud (ﷺ) says that the Prophet (ﷺ) said:

«إذَا كُنْتمْ ثَلاثَةً فَلا يَتَناجَى رَجُلانِ دُونَ الآخَرِ حتَّى تَخْتَلِطوا بِالنَّاسِ، أجَلَ أنَّ ذٰلِكَ يُحْزِنَهُ»

> *"Where there are three of you in company, two should not hold confidential talks together till the number increases, lest the third man might feel annoyed."*
>
> (Bukhari & Muslim: 6290:2184)

Always smile, be polite and greet the people you know as well as people you do not know. Always return a greeting.

$$﴿وَإِذَا حُيِّيتُم بِتَحِيَّةٍ فَحَيُّواْ بِأَحْسَنَ مِنْهَآ أَوْ رُدُّوهَآ إِنَّ ٱللَّهَ كَانَ عَلَى كُلِّ شَىْءٍ حَسِيبًا﴾$$

*"When you are greeted with a greeting, greet in return with
what is better than it, or (at least) return it equally. Certainly
Allah is Ever a Careful Account Taker of all things."*

Surah An-Nisâ (4:86)

Narrated Abdullah bin 'Amr (☻): A man asked the
Prophet (ﷺ) "What sort of deeds or traits of Islam are
good?" The Prophet (ﷺ) said:

$$«تُطْعِمُ الطَّعَامَ وَتَقْرَأُ السَّلامَ، عَلى مِنْ عَرَفْتَ وعَلى مَنْ لَمْ تَعْرِفْ» .$$

*"To feed others, and to greet those whom you know and those
whom you do not know."*

(Bukhari:6236)

One of the strangest things I found was that no matter where
you are in the *Haram* or during the *Hajj* days, there is always
somebody trying to go in the opposite direction of the general
flow of the people. Avoid walking in the opposing direction of
the *Tawaaf.* Rather walk all the way around to the starting
point.

Do not perform *Salah* close to the *Maqaam Ibraheem* if it's
crowded. If you insist, be forewarned that you may get
trampled on and somebody may step on your head. Do not
even think of standing in front of your wife as protection for
her to make *Salah* in this area. You are asking for trouble! It is
acceptable to perform your two *Rak'at Salah* after *Tawaaf*
anywhere in the mosque. (During the *Hajj* of 1416, while
performing *Tawaaful-Ifadah* a female pilgrim was performing
Salah in this area with her husband trying to "protect" her. A
male pilgrim tripped over her and fell with his knees into her

side, badly hurting her.)

Try not to constantly throw the top part of your *Ihraam* (men) over your shoulder as you may hit the person behind you in the face.

To avoid fraying tempers, do not wait in the hotel reception or outside the hotel for the group bus (to go to Mina or elsewhere). Most of the time the buses are delayed, sometimes for hours. Rather wait and relax in your room and do not move until somebody tells you that the bus has arrived. Do not even move if they tell you: "The bus is coming now!" Remember that with the new bus rotation scheme the chances are that the wait could be quite long.

Your behaviour is of the utmost importance at all times. Do not let bad behaviour ruin your good deeds. It is your deeds that you will take with you to your grave.

Perform as many good deeds as possible.

Narrated Ibn Abbas (ﷺ) that the Prophet (ﷺ) narrating about his Lord said:

«إِنَّ اللهَ عَزَّ وجَلَّ كَتَبَ الحَسَنَاتِ والسَّيِّئَاتِ ثُمَّ بَيَّنَ ذلكَ، فمَنْ هَمَّ بِحَسَنَةٍ فَلَمْ يَعْمَلْها كَتَبَها اللهُ لَهُ عِنْدَهُ حَسَنَةً كَامِلَةً، فإنْ هَمَّ بِها وعَمِلَها كَتَبَها اللهُ لَهُ عِنْدَهُ عَشْرَ حَسَنَاتٍ إلى سَبْعِمائَةِ ضِعْفٍ إلى أَضْعافٍ كَثِيرَةٍ، ومَنْ هَمَّ بِسَيِّئَةٍ فَلَمْ يَعْمَلْها كَتَبَها اللهُ لَهُ عِنْدَهُ حَسَنَةً كَامِلَةً، فإنْ هُوَ هَمَّ بِها فَعَمِلَها كَتَبَها اللهُ لَهُ سَيِّئَةً واحِدَةً».

"Allah ordered (the appointed angels over you) that the good and bad deeds be written, and He then showed (the way) how (to write). If somebody intends to do a good deed and he does not do it, then Allah will write for him a full good deed (in his account) with Him; and if he intends to do a good deed and actually did it, then Allah will write for him (in his account) with Him (its reward equal) from ten to seven hundred times,

to many more times; and if somebody intended to do a bad deed and he does not do it, then Allah will write a full good deed (in his account) with Him, and if he intended to do it (a bad deed) and actually did it, then Allah will write one bad deed (in his account)."

(Bukhari:6491)

Health

If you are sick, be patient and try not to complain too much.

«حَدَّثَنَا جَابِرُ بْنُ عَبْدِ اللهِ أَنَّ رَسُولَ اللهِ ﷺ دَخَلَ عَلَىٰ أُمِّ السَّائِبِ، أَوْ أُمِّ الْمُسَيَّبِ، فَقَالَ: «مَا لَكِ؟ يَا أُمَّ السَّائِبِ! أَوْ يَا أُمَّ الْمُسَيَّبِ! تُزَفْزِفِينَ؟» قَالَتِ: الْحُمَّىٰ، لَا بَارَكَ اللهُ فِيهَا، فَقَالَ: «لَا تَسُبِّي الْحُمَّىٰ، فَإِنَّهَا تُذْهِبُ خَطَايَا بَنِي آدَمَ، كَمَا يُذْهِبُ الْكِيرُ خَبَثَ الْحَدِيدِ».

Jabir (ﷺ) relates that the Prophet (ﷺ) visited Umm Sa'ib or Ummul-Musaiyab and asked her: "What has happened to you, O Umm Sa'ib or Ummul-Musaiyab? Why are you shivering?" She answered: "It is a fever; may Allah not bless it." He (ﷺ) said to her: "Do not abuse the fever, because it cleans the sins of the children of Adam as a furnace cleans the dirt of iron."

(Muslim:2575)

Drink plenty of fluids to avoid dehydration. Drinking very cold drinks after being in the hot sun is NOT very good for your throat. It may cause you to develop a sore throat or cough. (However, there are times when nothing but an ice cold drink will quench your thirst.)

Drinking yogurt or *laban* (milky drink) helps in providing the salt your body needs.

Avoid standing in front of an air-conditioner to cool down.

Do not sleep with the air-conditioner blowing directly on top of you.

The days of *Hajj* require 100% of your health and strength. Try to avoid doing strenuous things, such as climbing mountains, which will reduce your energy and health capacity.

Heat exhaustion and heat stroke are two of the most common clinical disorders pilgrims face during *Hajj*.

Stay out of direct sunlight as much as possible. However, do not use this as an excuse to miss *Zuhr* or *'Asr Salah* in the *Haram*. Remember that the reward for *Salah* in the *Haram* is worth 100,000 times that of a *Salah* in another mosque except the *Haram* in Madinah (1,000) and *Masjidul-Aqsa* (500).

Some other common complaints

Food poisoning: Take care of your personal hygiene and be careful of what and where you eat. In most hotels the tap water is not potable (drinkable water). You will need to buy bottled water or bring *Zamzam* from the *Haram*.

Diarrhoea: Some steps you should take if you have diarrhoea – only eat fruit with a thick skin (i.e. that must be peeled); boil water before you drink it or only drink bottled beverages; don't eat cold meats, shell fish, raw seafood or reheated food; don't drink tap water; don't use ice cubes unless you know they've been made with purified water; don't eat fried or fatty foods, dairy products, spicy foods or acidic fruits or vegetables (e.g. oranges, tomatoes); try to eat bland food (boiled rice or potatoes), toast (without butter or margarine but with jam or honey) or plain biscuits; drink plenty of fluids (no fruit juices or milk); drink a liquid that will help replace the salt in your body.

Upper respiratory tract infections (sore throat, coughing): This is usually caused by viruses. Minimise the risk of infection by unnecessary exhaustion, taking proper bed rest and using a face mask when required. Also don't share the same drinks, eating utensils or water flasks with fellow pilgrims, especially if they are sick.

Use sunglasses if you have sensitive eyes. Around the *Haram* areas and inside at the *Tawaaf* areas are marble tiles which create a very strong glare in the sun. This can be harmful to your eyes. Try the following: instead of putting your hand on your forehead to cover your eyes from the glare, put your hand on your nose directly under your eyes. This will stop the glare, which is reflecting upwards.

Use an umbrella. This can be purchased in Makkah. Buy one without the sharp point as this can be harmful to other pilgrims when you are in a crowd. Also buy a white or green coloured one, instead of a black one (the black draws the heat).

Keep a water flask (container) with you. It is sometimes very difficult to buy or obtain cold water.

You will notice that the doctor or pharmacist, making pen stripes on the box of your prescribed medicine. Three stripes means take three times a day, two stripes means take twice a day etc.

Medical Facilities

There are clinics and hospitals which provide basic services free of charge to the pilgrims.

There are emergency clinics inside the *Haram*. See under "Access to the *Haram*" in this chapter for the locations of these clinics.

There is also a specialist hospital in one of the suburbs. There is also a hospital in Makkah very near to the *Haram* in the Ajyad area:

- It is a four-storey building, with arch-like windows.
- The signs on the hospital are both in English and in Arabic.
- It has a black and beige fluorescent sign in Arabic and a green and white English sign.
- There are no signs directing you to the hospital.
- There is no hospital (red crescent) sign.

- There are trees in front of the building.
- The Arabic word for hospital is:

Mustashfa مستشفى

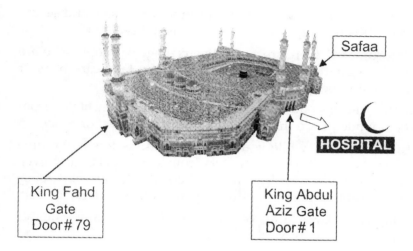

The above listed guidelines have been the same for at least the last fourteen years. However, that does not mean it may not change in the future. Recently there was a 'rumour' that this hospital will be demolished to make place for a hotel.

Death of a Pilgrim

Ibn Abbas (🙼) reported that a person fell down from his camel (in the state of *Ihraam*) and his neck was broken and he died. Thereupon the Prophet (🙼) said:

«اغْسِلُوهُ بِمَاءٍ وَسِدْرٍ، وَكَفِّنُوهُ فِي ثَوْبَيْهِ، وَلَا تُخَمِّرُوا رَأْسَهُ، فَإِنَّ اللهَ يَبْعَثُهُ يَوْمَ الْقِيَامَةِ مُلَبِّيًا».

"Bathe him with water mixed with the leaves of the lote tree and shroud him in his two (pieces of) cloth (Ihraam), and do not cover his head for Allah will raise him on the Day of

Resurrection pronouncing Talbiyah."

(Muslim:1206)

Money and Safety

As with any other trip, keep your money in a safe and secure place. (Keeping it in the refrigerator is not secure.)

Unfortunately there are a small percentage of people who are not here for the same reason you are. So take care of your money and belongings.

Many pilgrims had their bags, wallets and money stolen from them while inside the *Haram*, performing *Tawaaf* or *Salah*.

Take extra care while you are in crowds, as this is the time when they tend to steal wallets from your pocket and even from your money belt. Some of these thieves are experts as they are able to cut right through your clothes and money belt.

Don't carry large sums of money with you or any valuable documents in your wallet.

Shopping

Jabir (ﷺ) says that the Prophet (ﷺ) said:

«رَحِمَ اللهُ رَجُلًا سَمْحًا إِذَا بَاعَ، وإِذَا اشْتَرَى، وإِذَا اقْتَضَى».

"May Allah have mercy on a person who is easy and courteous when he sells, buys or asks for the payment of his dues."

(Bukhari:2076)

Always keep some small denomination notes with you. (one and five riyal notes). This is very helpful when the shops are very crowded and all you need is a drink. This way you will not need to wait for change.

You will find the shopkeeper dealing with many customers at the same time. He may give you the wrong change by mistake or even forget totally about you. You may need to give him a gentle reminder that you are waiting. Sometimes you may need to be a bit more forceful.

Sometimes you may find the shopkeeper "throwing" your change at you instead of giving it to you in your hand. Please do not feel insulted. This practice is normal and it is definitely not a form of disrespect.

Hady (sacrifice)

You need to make arrangements for the sacrifice (*Hady*) for *Hajj Tamattu* and *Qiran* and possibly for other expiation's (*Fidyah*). See chapter 6 under "Sacrifices" for more details.

This sacrifice CANNOT be done in your home country!

If this is not part of your package, arrange it before the *Hajj* days.

The Hady is a form of *Ibadah* and a major ritual of *Hajj*, therefore it should not be treated lightly by merely buying a coupon or asking someone else to perform it. It is recommended that you do it yourself. This may be difficult due to the sheer number of people. However, one should at least try to arrange it.

Do not treat it as a burden.

One may eat of the *Hady* meat.

The expiation for omitting a *Wajib* (necessary) action is a sacrifice of a sheep or goat (*Fidyah*). This is normally not included in the *Hajj* packages.

Both for the *Hady* and *Fidyah* you have a few options:

1. You can arrange it through the Islamic Development Bank programme. You buy a coupon (normally from the Al-Rajhi Bank) indicating the purpose (*Hady*, *Fidyah* or *Udhiya*) of the sacrifice in addition to giving them your name. There are also cubicles around Makkah and Mina where you can purchase these coupons.

2. Arrange it with your agent if it can be included in the *Hajj* package.

3. Your group or *Mutawwif* may provide this facility in Makkah.

4. You can go to the slaughter-house in Mina during your stay there. This is very difficult and not for the faint hearted.

5. You can share in a camel or cow with six other pilgrims (7 in total).

6. If you are unable to afford the cost:

$$\text{﴿فَإِذَآ أَمِنتُمْ فَمَن تَمَتَّعَ بِٱلْعُمْرَةِ إِلَى ٱلْحَجِّ فَمَا ٱسْتَيْسَرَ مِنَ ٱلْهَدْيِ فَمَن لَّمْ يَجِدْ فَصِيَامُ ثَلَٰثَةِ أَيَّامٍ فِى ٱلْحَجِّ وَسَبْعَةٍ إِذَا رَجَعْتُمْ تِلْكَ عَشَرَةٌ كَامِلَةٌ﴾}$$

"...Then if you are in safety and whosoever performs the Umrah in the months of Hajj, before (performing) the Hajj (i.e. Hajjat-Tamattu and Al-Qiran), he must slaughter a Hady such as he can afford, but if he cannot afford it, he should observe Saum (fasts) three days during Hajj and seven days after his return (to his home), making ten days in all..."

Surah Al-Baqarah (2:196)

Beggars

There are various types of beggars in and around the *Haram*. There are:

- the poor
- the children
- the physically deformed

- the "not so sure"
- the professionals

The first three categories are easily recognisable, and you can decide on whether you would like to give them any money or not.

The "not so sure" category is those who do not appear to be poor. Once again this is your call.

The last category is the most skilful ones. Be aware of them and do not part with your money unless you are 200% sure the beggar with his "sad story" is authentic. Do not be fooled by the tears or the medical papers. Remember they are professionals and this is an art for them. Many of them are in Ihraam or are very "well dressed". Be careful!

Hajj video

You will find video cassettes being sold in many shops after the *Hajj*, labelled "This year's *Hajj*." A word of caution. Firstly this video is merely a recording from the Saudi Arabian television. It mainly covers the 9th (Arafat day), and does not show the full *Hajj* as one would hope it would. Secondly, it is recorded using the "Secam" frequency, meaning that if your VCR signal in your country is PAL or NTSC, the video will replay in black and white with no sound.

Even though the shopkeeper will try to convince you that it will work and that it contains all 5 days of *Hajj*, from experience, it doesn't.

If you really want one, then get the shopkeeper to play the video for you.

There are some other good videos available, such as the Ramadan *Taraawih* prayers (check the recording frequency).

Sharing Accommodation

If you are sharing accommodation, there are a few basic rules you can apply to make life much more pleasant for everybody.

Accommodate all the cigarette smokers together.

Agree with your fellow pilgrims on the following (on friendly terms):

- "Lights out" time at night (any person who wishes to continue to read should do so outside the room).
- No visitors in the room after a specified time at night or any agreed resting time during the day.
- No loud talking in the room at night after an agreed time or during any agreed resting time during the day.
- No smoking in the room.
- No eating in the room (or clean up after eating).
- Suitcases and clothes to be kept tidy and in agreed areas of the room.

If you have a snorer in the room, the earplugs from the airlines are very useful (for your ears).

If you wish to sleep before "lights out" time, use the eye covers from the airlines.

Check the bathroom ensuring that everybody cleans it after using it. If the person entering it finds it dirty, request the previous occupant to clean it (assuming it was clean prior to that). The first clean-up can be done by the group.

The same clean-up rule can be applied if there are any kitchen facilities involved.

Ban jumping the bathroom queue. String a line, where people can hang their towels as a means of queuing, instead of waiting outside the bathroom all the time. One way of avoiding the rush is to wake up 15 minutes before everyone else.

The group may be annoyed with you at first for setting these rules, but I can assure you that within a few days everybody will appreciate your efforts.

Conserve water. You may notice trucks pumping water into

the buildings in Makkah and Madinah. If the water runs out it could take a few hours to refill.

Keep some bottles of water in your room for emergencies (*Wudu*, *Istinja*). Mark them, "for *Wudu*". This is in case the building runs out of water at a critical time. It happens!

If you go to the toilet, ensure first that there is water available.

One of the first things you need to do when you enter your rooms is to turn on the hot water heater. This is if you like to take hot water showers. During the summer months, the cold water tap is sufficient, as the water is quite hot.

If you wish to take a bath and the bath-tub does not have a rubber plug, some aluminium foil folded as a plug will do the trick.

General

Makkah is a very lively and busy city. There are always plenty of activities, cars and taxis blowing their horns, people shopping, people going to and from the *Haram*, day and night. This city does not sleep!

Cameras and tape recorders are not allowed inside the *Haram*. Do not risk it!

Keep a business card of the hotel where you are staying with you at all times. In the event of you getting lost, you can show it to the police or taxi driver. It is also useful in case you fall ill or end up in hospital.

Most of the smaller hotels only have one telephone line, which means that it is sometimes impossible to receive any calls, as the line is always busy. This is especially a problem for any family members or friends that are trying to call you from home. Also don't expect to always receive your telephone messages from the reception. If the hotel you live in suffers from this, inform your family, as many times they give up as they think they have the wrong number or they leave messages and may wait for you to return their call. Also give them your room number, as the receptionists do not always have the list of names with them.

You will notice many stray cats around Makkah. They are all very skinny. If you have a little food left over, don't throw it in the garbage bin, feed it to the cats instead.

Public Toilet Facilities

There are good toilet and *Wudu* facilities close to the *Haram*. There are none inside the mosque, with the exception of the roof area where there are some *Wudu* facilities. Although you may notice many pilgrims performing *Wudu* at the other *Zamzam* taps, they are not there for this purpose.

If you exit by Marwah (end of *Sa'ee* area) turn to your right; you will be near the big toilet and *Wudu* facilities, for both men and women. It is a large marbled structure, light brown in colour.

Also exiting from door no. 1, facing the clock tower, to the right of the tower are toilets for men and to the left are toilets for women.

If you exit from door no. 62 (Baabul-Umrah), turn to your right and underneath the road (bridge) there are stairs leading to the road level. Inside to the right of this small tunnel there are toilets, for men only.

See the diagram under "Access to the *Haram*" later in this chapter for the approximate locations.

Lost and Found

There is a lost and found area near to the Baabus-Safaa Door (no. 11). It is actually at doors no. 12 & 13. This is for lost pilgrims as well as for lost children and lost articles and documents.

If you are lost, go to this office. If you lose an article or your wallet, this office will assist you.

In the event of loss of identification cards or wallets, certain paperwork needs to be completed at this office. (It helps a great deal if you can take an Arabic speaking person with you.)

If you have children with you, take them to this area and show it to them. Teach them to wait there (and not to panic) in the event of you "losing" them.

Put the hotel business card in your children's pockets, as well as yours.

Dress the children in bright coloured clothes, which make it easier to see them in crowds. See chapter 3 for more details about children.

The police in the *Haram* will take all lost articles and persons to this office.

From my experience the police looking after the lost children are not trained for this task.

See the diagram under "Access to the *Haram*" later in this chapter for the location.

Hairdressers/Barbers

There are many barbers in Makkah. You can pay from between 5 to 50 Saudi riyals for a haircut, depending on where you go or what you like.

To have your head shaved will cost only 5 riyals, and maybe up to 15 riyals during the peak season.

A haircut will cost you about 10 riyals at most barbers. If you choose the hairdresser inside the Hilton shopping complex, it will cost you 20 riyals, and if you choose the hairdresser inside one of the 5 star hotels it will cost you 50 riyals or more. The choice is yours.

There are over a dozen barbers located right outside the Marwah door. If you exit on the ground floor at Marwah, you will find them immediately to your left. If you exit from the middle floor, you will have to turn right, and walk down the road as the barbers are located under the bridge.

Shoes

Use a soft pair of slippers (instead of shoes) as these are easier to carry with you.

There are shoe racks inside and outside the *Haram*. You may leave them in these racks and for the most part they will be there when you return. On the odd occasion you may find that someone has "taken" them. It is not always the case of someone taking shoes. If you leave your shoes in the wrong place, the cleaners will sweep them away. Outside some of the big doors of the *Haram*, you will find a mountain of lost or unclaimed slippers and shoes. You may find a pair that fits you or you could use some as a temporary pair until you get to a shop. You may even find your own shoes.

It is best to keep your shoes/slippers with you (in a plastic bag, if possible). This is useful as you may "lose" them or forget where you placed them. Sometimes you may not leave from the same door you entered.

If you are keeping them with you, be considerate as to where you place them while performing *Salah*, so that they do not cause any inconvenience to other pilgrims.

Do not place your shoes on the ground with the soles facing upwards. Instead, place it on its side.

If you have to leave your shoes in one of the racks, and you are afraid of losing them, then you may consider the following: place your shoes apart from each other, meaning one shoe in one place and the other shoe somewhere else. Now do remember where you put them.

There are many times when you may have to perform *Salah* in the street due to the crowds. During the *Hajj* days you may have to perform *Salah* wherever you find a "suitable" place, in the street or in the sand. Also in Muzdalifah you may need to keep your shoes on while performing *Salah*.

It is acceptable to perform *Salah* with your shoes on.

Abu Hurrairah (☙) reported Allah's Messenger (ﷺ) saying:

«إِذَا صَلَّى أَحَدُكُم فَلَا يَضَعْ نَعْلَيْهِ عن يَمِينِهِ وَلَا عن يَسَارِهِ
فَتَكُونَ عن يَمِينِ غَيْرِهِ إِلَّا أَنْ لَا يَكُونَ عن يَسَارِهِ أَحَدٌ
وَلْيَضَعْهُمَا بَيْنَ رِجْلَيْهِ»

"When any of you prays he should not place his sandals at his right or left, but should place them between his feet." Another version has, "or pray with them on".

(Abu Dawud:654,655)

Where to meet

It is important that you agree beforehand with your partner or group where to meet after *Salah* or in the event of you losing each other.

If your accommodation is not far from the *Haram* then it may be better to meet back in the room.

If you plan to meet somewhere inside the *Haram*, avoid the green light area as this is a very common meeting place and is therefore always very crowded.

The clock tower outside some of the main doors (i.e., King Abdul Aziz Door) is also a very common meeting place. One disadvantage of making this a meeting place is that the clock tower has four sides and you may spend your time waiting on one side while the other person is waiting on the opposite side (experience talking).

There are really no good meeting places (other than your hotel) that I can suggest. It all depends on your routine and location. Once you have established a good place, stick to it and try not to change it from day to day.

Flight reconfirmation

Reconfirm your flights prior to the actual *Hajj* days. Do not wait until the last minute.

Obtain a printout of your reconfirmation from the airline, if possible.

Once again I need to stress that you plan your departure based on your confirmed bookings and not any waitlisted bookings. See chapter 10 for more details.

Arrange to ship any cargo you may have well ahead of your departure date, ideally also before the actual *Hajj* days.

Access to the *Haram*

It is neither a *Fard* nor a *Sunnah* requirement to enter from Baabus-Salaam.

There are about 100 doors around the *Haram*.

All the doors are numbered. The numbers are inscribed near the door, on the wall tiles on the inside and on the outside of the *Haram*.

The door numbers go in an anti-clockwise direction.

Most of the doors also have a name, in addition to the number. The names and numbers are written in Arabic and in English. The doors are referred (named) to as gates on the signs.

Some of the door names and numbers are:

Name of the door	Arabic	Number
King Abdul Aziz Gate	باب ملك عبدالعزيز	1
Ismail Gate	باب اسماعيل	10
Safaa Gate	باب صفا	11
Salaam Gate	باب سلام	24
Qarrarah Gate	باب قراره	43
Fath Gate	باب فتح	45
Shamiah Gate	باب شامية	52
Umrah Gate	باب عمرة	62
King Fahd Gate	باب الملك فهد	79

I have listed the location and door number of **Baab-us-Salaam** only because I have experienced so many times that some pilgrims insist on entering from this door. On occasions this door is actually closed as it causes disruption to those performing *Sa'ee*. You will then have to enter at Baab-us-Salaam flyover (Door no. 25). These flyovers are bridges across the *Sa'ee* area. If this door is far from where you are, please be aware that there is no evidence from the Qur'an or the *Sunnah* to indicate or instruct pilgrims to enter from this door or any other specific door.

Both Baabus-Salaam and the flyover have stairs, so the elderly and people with wheelchairs should definitely avoid them.

The following picture should give you a general idea of some of the door locations, general direction of the toilets, lost & found section and door no. 12 is the office where you notify and obtain information if you lose any of your identification papers.

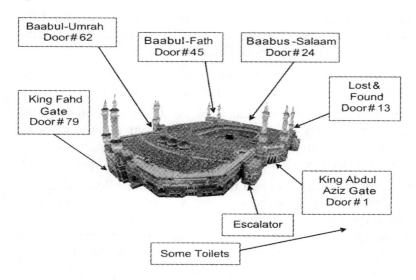

Floors

For *Salah* there are 4 floor levels inside the mosque:

- Basement level
- Ground floor level
- Middle floor level
- Roof level

Tawaaf and *Sa'ee* can also be performed on the middle floor as well as the roof.

The roof area is normally only for males. During the very busy days of *Hajj* the roof is also open for females for *Salah, Tawaaf* and *Sa'ee*.

The middle floor and basement are for both males and females.

There is a huge basement area in the *Haram* which is not very well known to all.

Escalators, Stairs and Bridges

There are escalators and stairs at various locations around the *Haram*, which can either be accessed from outside, the middle floor or from the basement inside the *Haram*.

The roof is accessible via the escalators. There is also stair access to the roof area, but it is not always open.

You can get to the middle floor or the basement from the doors, the stairs or escalators, either from outside or from inside the mosque. There are stairs directly inside (to your right and left) of all the major doors (mentioned previously).

Some of the escalators and most of the middle floor stairs also go down to the basement. There are also some other stairs inside the *Haram* that have white metal gates at the entrance. These gates are open during the busy periods and provide direct access to the basement area from inside the *Haram*.

The stairs immediately to the right of door no. 1 (there is a sign showing basement); door nos. 75, 76, 77, 81, 82, 83 and 85 are among the doors that provide access to the basement.

The middle floor for *Sa'ee* can also be accessed from the street level at Marwah.

The escalator entrances are also part of the door number sequence (i.e. the escalator to the right of door no. 1 is called the Ajyad Escalator - door nos. 5 & 6; the one to the right of door no 79, Baab-ul-Malik Fahd is named Malik Fahd Escalator, door nos. 91 & 92; Al-Shubaika Escalator, nos. 65 & 66).

At the Shamiah side of the *Haram* (near Baab-ul-Umrah, door no. 62), you can access the middle floor directly, as it is the same level as the street. The entrances are bridge-like structures. Some of the names and numbers are:

- Al-Nadwa Bridge   No. 50
- Al-Madinah Bridge   No. 57
- Al-Mahdi Bridge   No. 61

To get to the middle floor for the *Sa'ee* area there are elevators at door no. 11 in addition to stairs. The stairs are located (standing at Safaa, facing Marwah) to your left, next to the wheelchair ramp.

In the *Sa'ee* area on the ground floor you will find aluminium stairs. These stairs are not for access to the middle floor. They are the stairs to the flyover, which leads to outside the mosque.

Try the roof area in the evening and for *Salatul-Fajr*. It is very comfortable and peaceful. If you get the chance, try to view the *Haram* from the roof. In my opinion the view of the *Haram* and the Ka'bah is spectacular from up there. It also gives you the opportunity to see, how NOT to behave during *Tawaaf*.

Wheelchair Access

There are various doors around the *Haram* that provide access for wheelchairs. It is important that you are familiar with them as most of the other doors have plenty of stairs. Door no. 11 is the designated area for wheelchair access. Some other entrances that provide wheelchair access are door nos. 1, 10, 64, 94.

Another special door for wheelchairs is at door no. 43, Baabul-Qarrarah.

You can obtain a wheelchair from either outside the *Haram* near door number one, or from inside the *Haram*. At Safaa Door (no. 11), to your right are the elevators and to your left you will find the place where you can obtain a wheelchair. If you wish to push it yourself, they are free of charge. You need to leave some form of identification.

If you require a chair and somebody to push it, it will cost you about 100 Saudi riyals (if not more) and you can obtain these chairs also from outside door no. 13.

If you do not find any wheelchairs on the bottom floor, go to the middle floor directly above (the location as described in a previous point); you may find one there.

If you have your own wheelchair you will need to obtain a permit allowing you to enter the *Haram* with it. This you can obtain from the office at door no. 12.

During the busy periods they may not allow wheelchairs in the *Tawaaf* area. You will need to hire a "Shubriah" or sometimes referred to as a *"Kursi"*. This is a stretcher like chair, which you sit in and is carried by four persons. The cost of this service is in excess of 300 Saudi riyals. The cost includes the carriers. You are not allowed to carry it yourself. Some years these chairs (facility) 'disappear', only to 'appear' again. Not sure why, and if they are not available then you will be allowed with the wheelchair.

For *Sa'ee* the wheelchairs are allowed on the ground floor (there is a designated area) and also on the middle floor and roof. The middle floor and roof has no designated walking areas for the wheelchairs, so do watch the heels of the pilgrims in front of you, as it is extremely painful to knock someone with the wheelchair.

If you are lost

If you are lost, go to door no. 13 (lost & found section) where you will be provided with assistance.

If you hire a "Shubriah" for one of the pilgrims in your company, make arrangements where to meet again, as the people carrying the 'Shubriah" will finish the *Tawaaf* long before you.

If you have a card of your accommodation, ask any of the policemen for directions. Sometimes the best way is to ask at the reception of another hotel for directions to your accommodation.

If you come out from the "wrong" door, do not walk around the *Haram* to try and find your way, instead go back inside the *Haram* and try to find the "right" door from inside. This method has some distinct advantages:

- You may find someone you know inside.
- It is much cooler inside the *Haram*.
- Find the side of the Ka'bah you entered from.
- Look for the colour-coordinated doors (the colours are addressed later in this chapter).

If all else fails, stay inside the *Haram* until the next *Salah* instead of wandering around outside in the heat or darkness. Move towards the area where you normally perform your *Salah* as you may find some fellow pilgrims there.

If you cannot remember the door numbers or names and you are lost, try to remember at least the following one. If you cannot remember the number, think of the name of the author of this book. This door is close to the lost and found; the elevators; the wheelchair access; the medical facilities; the hospital; the roof and basement access and also the toilets: Ismail Door (Baab-ul-Ismail, No. 10)

Entering the *Haram*

As with any *Masjid* enter the *Haram* with your right foot and it is Sunnah to say:

«بِسْمِ اللهِ وَالصَّلَاةُ وَالسَّلَامُ عَلَى رَسُولِ اللهِ، أَعُوذُ بِاللهِ الْعَظِيمِ
وَبِوَجْهِهِ الْكَرِيمِ وَسُلْطَانِهِ الْقَدِيمِ مِنَ الشَّيْطَانِ الرَّجِيمِ. اللَّهُمَّ
افْتَحْ لِي أَبْوَابَ رَحْمَتِكَ»

"Bismillah wassalatu wassalamu ala Rasoolillah. A'oudhu billahil-'Azeem, wa be waj'hihil-Kareem, wa sultanihil-qadeem, minash-shaytanir-rajeem. Allahumma iftahly abwaaba rahmatik."

(In the Name of Allah and blessings and peace be upon the Messenger of Allah. I seek refuge in Allah the Great, and His Honourable face and His ancient authority from the accursed *Shaytaan*. Oh Allah open for me the doors of Your mercy.)

(Abu Dawud:465,466)

All bags including ladies handbags will be searched.

You will not be able to take any food or dangerous items inside with you. A simple pocketknife will be confiscated.

Large (1 litre) water bottles to fill with *Zamzam* are not allowed inside the mosque.

You will not be allowed to take any shopping bags inside with you. So if you did lots of expensive shopping, make sure you have enough time to take it back to your accommodation prior to *Salah*.

Sometimes you may not be able to take even your umbrella inside with you.

Inside the *Haram*

Inside the *Haram* the names of the main doors are indicated by big signs placed across the pillars leading towards these doors. To make it even easier, these signs have different colours. (The big doors are underneath the minarets. There are 9 minarets in case you wondered).

Name of door:	No:	Colour of sign:
King Abdul Aziz Door (Baab-ul-Malik Abdul Aziz)	1	Turquoise (light bluish).
Umrah Door (Baab-ul-Umrah)	62	Dark Gray
Fath Door (Baab-ul-Fath)	45	Dark Blue
King Fahd Door (Baab-ul-Malik Fahd)	79	Gold/Yellow
* Some other Door numbers are:		
Safaa Door (Baab-us-Safaa)	11	White
Salaam Door (Baabus-Salaam)	24	No coloured sign

If you are entering the *Haram* for the first time, I suggest you spend a few moments to orientate yourself with the surroundings and landmarks. As you should be performing *Tawaaf* as your first rite, you need to proceed directly towards the Ka'bah. (Do not sit down unless you perform *Tawaaf* or two *Rak'at Tahiyatul-Masjid Salah* first.)

Make a mental note of the name and number (and colour, if applicable) of the door from which you entered. Also observe from which side of the Ka'bah you entered. These signs should help you in finding your way out. (I have heard stories of older people being lost inside the *Haram* for many hours, even days.)

The sides of the Ka'bah are:

1. The side of *Maqaam Ibraheem*.

2. The side of the *Hijr* (and water spout).

3. The side where the *Rukn Yamani* Corner is to the right and the *Hijr* is to your left (facing the Ka'bah).

4. The side where you start your *Tawaaf* (*Hajrul-*

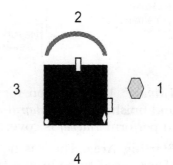

Aswad) is to your right, and the *Rukn Yamani* Corner is to your left (facing the Ka'bah).

These landmarks are a mere guideline. You may find other and easier means of remembering where to enter and exit from.

Remove or turn your photo badge around so that the picture is not visible while you are in the *Haram*.

A closer look at the Ka'bah area

In relation to the following diagram:

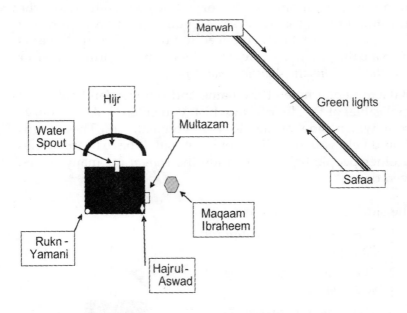

Tawaaf: The direction for *Tawaaf* is anti-clockwise, starting and finishing at the *Hajrul-Aswad*. (A detailed account of how to perform *Tawaaf* is covered later in this chapter.)

Starting Area: There is no need to stop at the starting area. (There used to be brown tiled line, but it has been removed due to the congestion it caused.) There is also a green light on the wall at the end of the starting area. The middle floor and the roof both have a green light (with a sign indicating "Beginning and Completion of *Tawaaf'*) for this purpose.

Multazam: This is the area from the *Hajrul-Aswad* up to the door of the *Ka'bah*. It is reported that the Companions (☙) of the Prophet (ﷺ) used to make Dua' here.

Maqaam Ibraheem: This is where the pilgrim performs two *Rak'at Salah* after *Tawaaf*. This is the station of Ibraheem referred to in the Qur'an.

Al-Hijr: It is part of the Ka'bah therefore the pilgrim should walk around it during *Tawaaf*. Try to perform some *Sunnah/ Nafl Salah* in this area. Many books refer to this area as the *Hijr-Ismail*. Some go as far as to say that Prophet Ismail and his mother Hagar (ﷺ) are buried here, hence the name. There is no authentic proof for this or the name. The fact that we are allowed to make *Salah* in this area is proof enough that this cannot be true, as we are not allowed to make *Salah* on graves. Also the Prophet (ﷺ) referred to this area as *Al-Hijr.*

Water Spout: This is located on the roof of the Ka'bah in the middle of the *Hijr*. Its purpose is to allow any water on the roof to drain down. It has no spiritual or historical significance. Why mention it? Well, some pilgrims believe it has certain spiritual significance and fight to perform *Salah* directly beneath it. Also, it is a new addition to the Ka'bah, and did not exist in the time of the Prophet (ﷺ).

South Corner: This is also known as *Rukn Yamani.* During *Tawaaf* the pilgrim touches this corner without kissing it.

Safaa: The *Sa'ee* starts at Safaa and the direction is towards Marwah. (A detailed account of how to perform *Sa'ee* is covered later in this chapter.)

Green Lights: Between these green lights the male pilgrims "run" during *Sa'ee.*

Marwah: The *Sa'ee* ends at Marwah.

For a more historical view of these landmarks, see chapter 13,

"A Touch of History".

Air-conditioned section

The newer section of the *Haram* is air-conditioned (including the basement), whereas the older sections only have roof fans as a means of cooling.

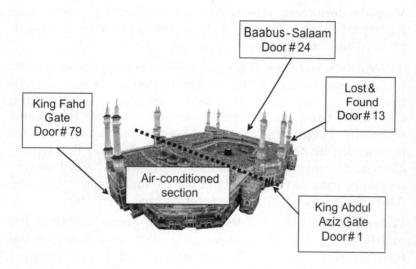

Qiblah

Needless to say that it is a condition of *Salah* that one faces *Qiblah* (direction of the Ka'bah) while performing *Salah*.

The marble tiles (in the newer areas) and the ones immediately around the Ka'bah are positioned facing *Qiblah*.

There is also a thin strip of darker coloured tiles (in a line format) to indicate the *Qiblah*.

The entire courtyard area (outside the *Haram*) has the tiles laid facing the *Qiblah*.

The following diagram illustrates what I mean.

In the older areas of the *Haram* where the tiles are laid straight

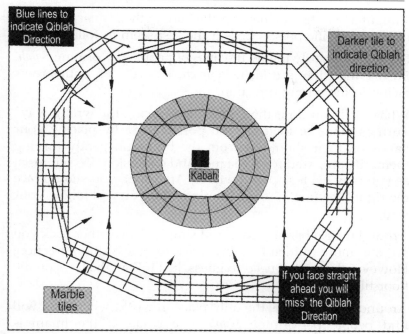

there are two blue lines carved into the marble floor tiles of the *Haram*. This is to indicate the direction of *Qiblah* (also in the *Sa'ee* area).

One of the more amazing things in the *Haram* is that the closer you are to the Ka'bah the more likely you are to "miss" the direction.

The arrows clearly indicate that the person will be 'missing' *Qiblah*, if he does not follow the lines carved into the floor which guide the person towards *Qiblah*.

It is almost impossible not to face *Qiblah* when standing closer to the Ka'bah in the circled area. In the courtyard areas the direction is indicated by the tiles and also by a thin strip of a darker coloured tile, serving as a line (guide).

You will find many people (especially in the women's areas) facing in the wrong direction while performing *Salah* (*sunnah* and *Fard*). This is because most people assume that facing straight ahead from wherever they are in the *Haram* is correct. (As soon as one person does it the rest seem to follow.)

Do not necessarily follow the lines of people performing *Salah*. Ensure that they are facing *Qiblah*. I have seen entire rows facing in the wrong direction.

What shall you do if the entire line is facing the wrong way? Turn as many of them as you possibly can by placing your hands on their shoulders from the back and gently turning them. (Be prepared for resistance and confusion. Do not insist as you may get a slap in the face.) After that, you should face the right direction, as those coming after you will follow your lead.

Around the Ka'bah it is easy and simple. The further back you go the more difficult it becomes to guess the direction. However there is no need to guess, just follow the lines on the floor tiles.

Around the Ka'bah is the only place in world where you will find people performing *Salah* in a circle. If the Imam is standing further back under the covered area (as he sometimes does), where is the first line you may ask? Well, that's another topic all together.

Zamzam

The Prophet (ﷺ) said:

«مَاءُ زَمْزَمَ لِمَا شُرِبَ لَهُ»

"Zamzam water is for whatever (purpose) it is drunk for."

(Ahmad & Ibn Majah: 14849:3062)

«مَاءُ زَمْزَمَ فِيةِ طَعَامٌ مِنَ الطَّعْمِ وَشِفَاءٌ مِنَ السُّقْمِ»

"It satisfies as food and cures illness."

(*As-Sahihan*:1056)

There is no particular supplication established in the *Sunnah* when drinking *Zamzam*. However, Abdullah bin Abbas (ﷺ)

used to recite the following after drinking *Zamzam* water:

«اللَّهُمَّ إِنِّي أَسْأَلُكَ عِلْمَانَافِعَاوَرِزْقًاوَاسِعَّاوَشِفَاءً مِنْ كُلِّ دَا ءٍ»

*"Allahumma innee asaluka 'ilman naafi'an wa rizqan
waasi'an wa shifaa 'an min-kulli daa'in"*

(Oh Allah, I ask of You beneficial knowledge, abundant provision, and a cure from all disease.)

There is no requirement to stand while drinking *Zamzam*.

There is also no evidence from the Qur'an or the *Sunnah* about soaking one's *Ihraam* clothes or any other shroud in *Zamzam* water to be later used for one's burial, as a means of salvation.

The *Zamzam* well entrance used to be located diagonally behind the *Maqaam Ibraheem* towards Safaa. Since 2004, the entrance has been closed to make more places for *Salah*. *Zamzam* taps are now located against the wall (near the same area)

There are sufficient taps and drums (beige in colour) all around the *Haram*, with cold *Zamzam* for your enjoyment.

Facing the drum the cups in the holder on the right side of the drum are the clean cups and the used ones are in the left cup holder.

During the busy periods of *Hajj* the drums are removed in order to provide the much-needed space.

Most of the time the water is cold. However, there are a few drums with room temperature water, marked with writing "*Zamzam* water not cold".

If you wish to fill your own bottles, there are some taps available inside the *Haram*. The guards will normally allow you to enter the mosque with small bottles. If you wish to fill larger containers, there are taps outside door number 45. It is located under the ramp leading to the street.

There are people selling containers of *Zamzam* outside the *Haram* area. They charge about 5-10 Saudi riyals for about ten litres. Alternatively you may take a small water bottle or flask inside the *Haram* with you and fill it up at the taps or drums. (Contrary to what many people believe, it is quite acceptable to make tea or coffee, etc., with *Zamzam* water.)

Copies of the Qur'an

It is good to keep your own small Qur'an with you all the time. Many times people lose their place due to fetching or taking Qur'an from the stands. Keep in mind that the person has the right to claim his place back, if for some reason you are in his place. (Remove the Qur'an from your pocket, when going to the toilet.)

There are many copies of the Qur'an (on stands) inside the *Haram* area. During the busy periods of *Hajj* some of them are moved closer to the walls, to provide *Salah* space.

The benefits of reading Qur'an are covered later in this chapter.

Sometimes you will find people selling copies of the Qur'an outside the *Haram* area, asking you to buy them in order to place them inside the *Haram*. It sounds very attractive as you will provide more copies of the Holy Book for the pilgrims to read inside the *Haram*. However, this is not the case. You will notice that all the copies of the Qur'an in the *Haram* have the same design on the cover (different colours). They are all printed at the King Fahd Holy Qur'an Printing Complex in Madinah and are the only ones officially allowed to be placed on the stands inside the *Haram*. All other copies will be removed from the stands.

There are two "print styles" of Qur'an in the stands. The most common one is "print style 1" as shown in the two examples. These are the green covered copies as well as the big blue ones. The second example (print style 2) is used in the blue covered (not the big size) Qur'an. There are normally not many of these on the stands, so if this is your preferred style you have to be quick, or carry your own.

I have on occasions found that there are also some green

covered copies in this style (print style 2). Anyway, as long as you are aware that they are available. There are also a few copies with the translated meanings, in various languages, such as English, Turkish, French and Albanian.

Style 1 **Style 2**

First Aid: Emergency and medical facilities

At various locations inside the *Haram* there are emergency medical facilities.

They are located close to certain doors. Some of the clinics can be found:

- Next to door no. 5 (Ajyad Door) and also in the same location on the middle floor;
- Next to door no. 64 (has no name);
- Next to door no. 94 (has no name).

The clinics are identified by a white sign with a red crescent.

There is also an emergency medical station outside door no. 45, Baabul-Fath.

See earlier in this chapter for details on other medical facilities and health related issues.

Where to sit

During the very busy periods of *Hajj*, it is important to choose a good place to sit. The best is to be early.

Avoid sitting near the doors or walkways. When the mosque gets very crowded people will trample all over you in these areas.

Try to sit in the middle or front areas. Directly in front of the Qur'an stands is also a good place.

Sitting near the *Zamzam* drums or taps is not such a good idea as this is always busy with people drinking water and the area can sometimes get very wet. However, this might be the only available place, especially when you are on the roof.

If you are sitting in the *Tawaaf* area, move immediately after *Salah* has completed to allow people to perform *Tawaaf* comfortably.

Tips:

- If you are early, try to keep a small space where at least one more person can squeeze in. When the mosque starts to get full you will find people arguing and fighting over small spaces. What you do with this small space is to offer it to somebody who's been looking for a space for a while. He will be very grateful and from that point onwards you will not need to fend off people from sitting in front of you, as your new-found "friend" will be so grateful to you and he will be doing all the "protection" of the spaces. Sneaky, but it works.

- Avoid keeping a place for friends. This will be difficult and you will spend your time protecting this space, instead of making *Ibadah*.

- If you are forced to sit near a walkway or door, move immediately after the *Salah* is complete. If you attempt to perform your *Sunnah Salah* here, you may get hurt as people will be walking over you.

- Beware of the ones offering water. As soon as you accept, you are now obliged to make some space. If you are thirsty, you may not have a choice. If you get up to get water, your place may be gone when you return.

- Please keep in mind, that everybody has the right to be inside the mosque, so try to accommodate your fellow pilgrims wherever possible. Do not try to keep a big and comfortable space for yourself. You will not be able to do so for very long and you will be stressed and creating unnecessary arguments.

Even after taking all precautions, don't be surprised when you find somebody coming to sit directly in front of you, leaving you no space to make salah properly.

Some pilgrims also give their shoes (space) a higher priority, rather than giving you space to sit. Be patient!

Where to sit (position yourself) in Mina and Arafat is covered in chapter 10.

Behaviour

As with everything else, your behaviour inside the *Haram* is of the utmost importance.

Do not walk backwards out of the *Haram*. This is dangerous, as you could fall and hurt somebody or even yourself. Many people believe that it is showing disrespect to the Ka'bah to turn one's back towards it. The Prophet (ﷺ) was the best of teachers and he did not do this (walk backwards) nor instruct us to do so.

Avoid shouting and walking in big groups during *Tawaaf* and *Sa'ee*.

Do not push your hands or fingers into the back of the person in front of you while in crowds or during *Tawaaf*. If somebody else does this to you, politely move their hands from your back.

Try not to push when the doors are congested. Keep in mind that there are many elderly people and that you could push somebody down the stairs.

Do not stop or perform *Salah* at the starting area. If you need to determine the starting place, look at the people (3 or so levels) in front of you. This way you can tell where the starting place is as they will be raising their hands.

You will notice that there are always people going in the opposite direction, no matter where and what time it is. Avoid as best as you can going against the flow of the general traffic.

One of the more amazing behaviours of certain pilgrims is when they are late, they persist in moving towards the front (even though there is no place), and when the *Salah* is finished they are the first to rush back out again. If you are late, your rightful place is at the back!

Even though *Hajj* itself is a very spiritual uplifting experience, the terrible behaviour of some of the pilgrims certainly leaves one wondering. Don't be tempted to behave like them!

About *Salah*

Timings

The gold clocks inside the *Haram* and the outside clock towers have digital displays of all the *Salah* times.

The time between *Adhaan* and *Iqaama* varies for the different *Salawaat*. The longest is 15 minutes and the shortest is 5 minutes. During *Hajj* they change them, so keep track of the timings so you can always be in time for *Takbiratul-Ihram* (first *Takbir*).

About 15 to 20 minutes before *Adhaan* time, you will notice (hear) a "blowing sound" through the microphones in the *Haram*. They are testing the microphones, and the women can use this as a guide to start moving towards the back, so they can perform their *Salah* in the designated areas for ladies, and not among the men.

There are many designated *Salah* areas for women inside the *Haram*. (Sometimes during *Jumu'ah* even these areas are taken over by the men.)

There are two *Adhaans* in the morning. One is called one hour before the *Adhaan* of *Salatul-Fajr*, and the second is the *Adhaan* for *Salatul-Fajr*.

It is narrated by Abdullah bin Umar ﷺ that the Prophet (ﷺ) said:

«إِنَّ بِلَالًا يُنَادِي بِلَيْلٍ، فَكُلُوا وَاشْرَبُوا حَتَّى يُنَادِيَ ابْنُ أُمِّ مَكْتُومٍ» .

"Bilal pronounces the Adhaan at night so that you may eat and drink till Ibn Umm Maktum pronounces the Adhaan (for the Fajr prayer)."

(Bukhari:620)

For women it is very important to keep track of the *Salah* times to avoid being "caught" in the *Tawaaf* area at *Fard Salah* time. It is also the men's responsibility to assist their partners in this. Although it is quite common during the very busy periods of *Hajj*, the women should avoid performing *Salah* among or in front of men.

Always try to be early for the *Salah* as the *Haram* gets very crowded.

About two weeks before *Hajj*, you need to leave for the *Haram* at least half to one hour before the *Salah*, in order to obtain a place inside the *Masjid*.

For *Jumu'ah* you need to be there at least two hours before the *Adhaan* to get a 'good' place.

Be kind and always try to accommodate others for space.

Stay out of the sun to avoid heat stroke. Use your umbrella. (Do not use the heat as an excuse for not going to the *Haram* for *Salatul-Zuhr* or *'Asr*. Many pilgrims (healthy young males) perform *Salah* at small mosques near their hotels, or worse, they pray in their rooms. Don't short-change yourself by intentionally missing out on the 100,000 times reward in the *Haram*).

Adhaan:

What to say on hearing the *Adhaan*:

It is narrated by Abu Sa'id Al-Khudri (﷐) that Allah's Messenger (ﷺ) said:

«إِذَا سَمِعْتُمُ النِّدَاءَ فَقُولُوا . مِثْلَ مَا يَقُولُ الْمُؤَذِّنُ»

"Whenever you hear the Adhaan say just as the Muadhdhin is saying."

(Bukhari:611)

«أَنَّهُ سَمِعَ مُعَاوِيَةَ يَوْمًا فَقَالَ مِثْلَهُ إِلَى قَوْلِهِ: «وَأَشْهَدُ أَنَّ مُحَمَّدًا رَسُولُ اللهِ» قَالَ يَحْيَى: وَحَدَّثَنِي بَعْضُ إِخْوَانِنَا أَنَّهُ قَالَ: لَمَّا قَالَ: حَيَّ عَلَى الصَّلَاةِ، قَالَ: لَا حَوْلَ وَلَا قُوَّةَ إِلَّا بِاللهِ، وَقَالَ: هَكَذَا سَمِعْنَا نَبِيَّكُمْ ﷺ يَقُولُ»

"Narrated Mu'awiyah (﷐) similar to the above Hadith until 'Wa ash-hadu anna Muhammadan Rasul-ullah' (and I testify that Muhammad is the Messenger of Allah). When the Muadhdhin said, 'Haya 'alas-Salah,' Mu'awiyah said, 'La hawla wa la quwata illa billah (There is neither might nor any power except with Allah),' and added, 'We heard your Prophet (ﷺ) saying the same.'"

(Bukhari:612 and 613)

There are five recommended actions in relation to the *Adhaan*:

1. Repeat after the *Muadhdhin* as described above (1st *Hadith*).

2. Repeat ("and I testify") after the *Muadhdhin* as described above (2nd *Hadith*).

3. On completion of the *Adhaan*, read the *Dua'*-"*Allahumma Rabba hadhihid-da watit-tammati...*"

4. Followed by reading *"Allahumma sal-li ala Muhammadin wa ala ali Muhammadin..."*

5. Followed by making *Dua'* for yourself and for your fellow Muslims.

Aurah:

The *Aurah* means the essential parts of one's body that must be covered in public at all times and not only for *Salah*.

For men it is from the navel to the knees (inclusive).

For the women it is easy as their *Ihraam* clothes ensure that their *Aurah* is covered. However, many women leave their feet uncovered. The feet should be covered! See chapter 3 for more details.

Apart from being dressed correctly, it is essential that your clothes are clean.

Would you attend a meeting with an important person with only a pair of trousers and no shirt, or with your shirt open exposing your stomach or in shorts, or with dirty clothes? I am sure most people wouldn't.

Remember you are now in the presence of Allah as well as being a guest of Allah. Also you would like to obtain as much of the 100,000 reward as possible.

Sutrah:

Many people do not know about the importance of *Sutrah* while performing *Salah*. Review the following *Ahadith* and you will realise its importance.

What is *Sutrah*? An object like a pillar, wall, stick or spear, etc., the height of which should not be less than a foot and must be in front of a person offering salah to act as a symbolical barrier between him and others.

The *Sutrah* rule does not apply to *Fard Salah* for the *Jamah* (congregation), as the *Imam's Sutrah* is valid for the entire congregation, except for the portion of the *Salah* done on your own if you came late.

«عَنْ سَهْلٍ قَالَ: كَانَ بَيْنَ مُصَلَّى رَسُولِ اللهِ ﷺ وَبَيْنَ الجِدَارِ مَمَرُّ الشَّاةِ. »

"Narrated Sahl (bin Sa'd) (ﷺ): 'The distance between the Musalla (praying place) of Allah's Messenger (ﷺ) and the wall (Sutrah) was just sufficient for a sheep to pass through.'"

(Bukhari:496, Muslim:508)

Narrated Abu Juhaifah (ﷺ):

«أَنَّ النَّبِيَّ ﷺ صَلَّى بِهِمْ بِالبَطْحَاءِ - وَبَيْنَ يَدَيْهِ عَنَزَةٌ - الظُّهْرَ رَكْعَتَيْنِ، وَالعَصْرَ رَكْعَتَيْنِ، يَمُرُّ بَيْنَ يَدَيْهِ المَرْأَةُ والحِمَارُ. »

"The Prophet (ﷺ) led us and prayed a two-Rak'at Zuhr prayer and then a two-Rak'at 'Asr prayer at Al-Batha with an Anazah (type of stick) (planted) in front of him (as a Sutrah) while women and donkeys were passing in front of him (beyond the Anazah)."

(Bukhari:495, Muslim:503)

Narrated Abu Juhaim (ﷺ) that the Prophet (ﷺ) said:

«لَوْ يَعْلَمُ المَارُّ بَيْنَ يَدَيِ المُصَلِّي مَاذَا عَلَيْهِ لَكَانَ أَنْ يَقِفَ أَرْبَعِينَ خَيْرًا لَهُ مِنْ أَنْ يَمُرَّ بَيْنَ يَدَيْهِ». قَالَ أَبُو النَّضْرِ: لَا أَدْرِي قَالَ: أَرْبَعِينَ يَوْمًا أَوْ شَهْرًا أَوْ سَنَةً. »

"If the person who passes in front of another person in Salah knew the magnitude of his sin, he would prefer to wait for 40 (days, months or years) rather than to pass in front of him." Abu An-Nadr said, "I do not remember exactly whether he said 40 days, months or years."

(Bukhari:510)

«إِذَا صَلَّى أَحَدُكُمْ إِلَى شَيْءٍ يَسْتُرُه مِنَ النَّاسِ فَأَرَادَ أَحَدٌ أَنْ

يَجْتَازَ بَيْنَ يَدَيْهِ، فَلْيَدْفَعْهُ فَإِنْ أَبَىٰ فَلْيُقَاتِلْهُ فَإِنَّمَا هُوَ شَيْطَانٌ» .

"When one of you prays behind anything which screens from the people, then if someone wants to pass between him and the Sutrah, he should repel him by pushing at his chest. And if he refuses to defer then fight him, for he is a devil."

(Bukhari:509)

Many people believe that the two *Harams* are exempted from the above *Ahadith* about not walking in front of a person performing *Salah*. Unfortunately there is also no unanimous opinion by the scholars on this issue that I could find. Some scholars say it is acceptable due to the crowds while others say it's not.

You may use the pillars, Qur'an stands, *Zamzam* drums, or even the person in front of you as a *Sutrah*.

Women should take even more care about walking in front of men performing *Sunnah* or *Nafl Salah*, as per the *Hadith*, it "breaks" the person's *Salah*.

During the very busy periods of *Hajj* it becomes almost impossible to avoid performing *Salah* with women next to or in front of you, let alone being able to avoid "breaking" a person's *Sutrah*. The most sensible advice I heard on the issue is to try and avoid both actions and to make it the exception rather than the rule: meaning that one should try and avoid walking in front of a person performing *Salah* unless it is absolutely necessary. About making *Salah* next to or behind women, one should endeavour to move closer to the front or to an area where there are only men and not merely stop where everybody else does. On many occasions I have experienced that there are plenty of spaces inside the *Haram* or in the front male areas, whereas people perform *Salah* (mixed) in the street.

Do your best and ensure that your *Niyah* is to do the right thing. Being early in the mosque somewhat alleviates this problem.

Avoid performing your *Salah* in doorways, walkways and the *Tawaaf* areas. People have the right to walk in these areas; therefore you should expect people not only to walk in front of you, but also over you.

If you do end up performing your *Fard Salah* in these areas, try to move out of the way immediately after the *Salah* is completed. Do not perform your *Sunnah Salah* here as your *Sutrah* will definitely be "broken". Move to a less obstructive place.

Rewards

Perform your *Wudu*, apply perfume (men only, and when not in *Ihraam*), put on clean clothes and make a habit of using a *Miswak* (tooth-stick), prior to going to the *Haram*:

Abu Hurrairah (ﷺ) relates that Allah's Messenger (ﷺ) remarked:

«لَوْلا أَنْ أَشُقَّ عَلى أُمَّتي – أَوْ لَوْلا أَنْ أَشُقَّ عَلى النَّاسِ –
لأَمَرْتُهُمْ بِالسِّوَاكِ مَعَ كُلِّ صَلاةٍ»

"Had I not feared that it would cause inconvenience to my Ummah (people) then I would have prescribed the brushing of teeth with a Miswak before every prayer."

(Bukhari & Muslim: 887:252)

Always try to be early to start the *Salah* with the *Imam*, and to be in the front row or close to it. Also there is much reward in waiting for the next *Salah*:

Abu Hurrairah (ﷺ) states that Allah's Messenger (ﷺ) said:

«خَيْرُ صُفُوفِ الرِّجَالِ أَوَّلُهَا، وَشَرُّهَا آخِرُهَا، وَخَيْرُ صُفُوفِ
النِّسَاءِ آخِرُهَا، وَشَرُّهَا أَوَّلُهَا»

"The best rows of the males in prayer in (congregational prayer) are the first ones and the worst are the last ones, and the best rows among females in prayer are the last ones and the worst are the first ones."

(Muslim:440)

«لَا يَزَالُ أَحَدُكُمْ فِي صَلَاةٍ مَا دَامَتِ الصَّلَاةُ تَحْبِسُهُ، لَا يَمْنَعُهُ أَنْ يَنْقَلِبَ إِلَىٰ أَهْلِهِ إِلَّا الصَّلَاةُ»

"As long as you stay in a mosque waiting for prayer (congregation), and are held up there only for the sake of prayer, and only this thing prevents you from returning home, you will be treated as continuously in prayer."

(Muslim:649)

«لَوْ يَعْلَمُ النَّاسُ مَا فِي النِّدَاءِ وَالصَّفِّ الْأَوَّلِ ثُمَّ لَمْ يَجِدُوا إِلَّا أَنْ يَسْتَهِمُوا عَلَيْهِ لَاسْتَهَمُوا، وَلَوْ يَعْلَمُونَ مَا فِي التَّهْجِيرِ لَاسْتَبَقُوا إِلَيْهِ، وَلَوْ يَعْلَمُونَ مَا فِي الْعَتَمَةِ وَالصُّبْحِ لَأَتَوْهُمَا وَلَوْ حَبْوًا»

"If the people knew the reward for pronouncing the Adhaan and for standing in the first row (in congregational prayers) and found no other way to get that except by drawing lots they would draw lots; and if they knew the reward of the Zuhr prayer (in the early moments of its stated time) they would race for it (go early); and if they knew the reward of 'Eshaa and Fajr (morning) prayers in congregation, they would come to offer them even if they had to crawl."

(Bukhari:615)

Remember that the reward is 100,000 times more than in any other mosque except the *Haram* in *Madinah* (1,000) and *Masjid-Al-Aqsa* (500) in Jerusalem.

Ensure that you are facing *Qiblah*, and are standing in straight lines.

Do not perform any *Sunnah* or *Nafl Salah* once the *Iqaamah* is called. Join the congregation as soon as the *Iqaamah* is called and if you are late, join the *Salah* in the position you find it, even though you may have to redo that *Ra'kah*.

Abu Hurrairah (ﷺ) relates that Allah's Messenger (ﷺ) said:

«إِذَا أُقِيمَتِ الصَّلَاةُ فَلَا صَلَاةَ إِلَّا الْمَكْتُوبَةُ»

"When iqaama (call for beginning the prayer) is called out, no prayer is permissible except the obligatory (Fardh) one."

(Muslim:710)

Perform your *Salah* with calmness, humility and concentration. Avoid looking around and raising your head from bowing and prostration ahead of the *Imam*.

Complete all your actions in a slow and dignified manner. There are numerous *Ahadith* about these points. The Prophet (ﷺ) said that the worst thief is the one who steals from his *Salah*. Meaning the one who performs the *Salah* actions in a fast and hurried manner. (One should pause for a short while in each position.)

Fortunately in Makkah (and Madinah) you will notice the practical application of these actions during *Salah*. Some differences (compared with my experiences in many other parts of the world) you will notice are:

- It is the only place in the world where there are circular lines for *Salah*.
- There is no *Dhikr* in congregation after *Salah*.
- There is no *Dua'* in congregation (except when there is *Qunoot*).
- There is no *Qunoot* (*Dua'* in *Salah*) in *Salatul-Fajr*.
- The *Salah* is performed in a very slow and calm manner.
- Though wrong, men and women perform *Salah* intermingled during the busy periods. Often females stand in front of males.
- Though wrong, you will see pilgrims sleeping in the mosque, and get up at *Iqaamah* time, and perform *Salah* without first performing *Wudu*.

- Most of the time there is a *Janazah Salah* after the *Fard Salah*.

It is not my intention to delve into the various views about any of these differences. I am merely pointing them out for the reader's awareness.

After the *Fard Salah*, it is best not to rush to perform *Sunnah* or *Nafl Salah*. Instead sit and make *Dhikr* as per the *Sunnah*. Also this way you will not miss the *Janazah Salah*, if it is to be performed.

When you perform your *Salah* and you wish to sit to your side in the last (sitting) *Tashahud* (as per the *Sunnah*), keep in mind that it may not always be feasible due to the sheer number of people. Avoid forcing the issue as you may end up sitting on top of the person next to you, and you may even hurt his or her leg.

When the *Salah* is completed, the exit doors are congested for a long time with people trying to leave. Make a habit of sitting for at least half an hour, either reciting the *Qur'an*, or making *Dhikr* or performing *Nafl Salah*. This will allow you to avoid the crowds at the doors. Sometimes it will take you at least that long to get out, so you may as well earn some more reward, and leave when it is easier.

Do not always follow the crowd through the doors or stairs. Look to your left or right or further ahead; most of the time you may find another door or steps that are less crowded. A large proportion of people tend to follow the crowd.

Jumu'ah Salah

It is needless to mention the importance of *Jumu'ah Salah*, except to remind you of a few points:

√ It is *Sunnah* to have a *Ghusl* (shower).

√ To apply perfume (men) and to wear clean clothes.

√ To go to the *Haram* very early.

√ Not to speak during the *Khutbah*.

✓ Not to sit with your knees up against your chest.

«عن سَهْلِ بنِ مُعَاذِ بنِ أَنَس، عن أَبِيهِ: أَنَّ رسولَ الله ﷺ
نَهَى عن الْحِبْوَةِ يَوْمَ الْجُمُعَةِ وَالإِمَامُ يَخْطُبُ»

*Muadh bin Anas Al-Juhani (☻) says that Allah's Messenger
(ﷺ) has forbidden a person to draw up his knees so they are
touching his abdomen while the Imam is delivering the Friday
Sermon.*

(Abu Dawud & Tirmidhi: 1110:514)

Janazah Salah (prayer for the deceased)

Women should not miss this opportunity to perform the
Janazah Salah, as they are equally rewarded. Also there are not
many other places or instances where they may have this
opportunity.

How to perform *Janazah Salah*:

- ☑ Follow the *Imam*
- ☑ There are 4 *Takbir's*
- ☑ After the 1st *Takbir*, read *Suratul-Fatihah*
- ☑ After the 2nd *Takbir*, read the *Salawaat* - ''*Allaahumma
  sallee alaa Muhammad...*''
- ☑ After the 3rd *Takbir*, make *Dua'* for the deceased
- ☑ After the 4th *Takbir*, make *Dua'* for the Muslims in general
- ☑ Make *Tasleem*, to the right only

Let us see the reward for performing this *Salah* and also for
following the bier. (Uhud is a mountain in Madinah, where
the battle of Uhud was fought.) So sisters, don't miss out on
the *Salah*!

Abu Hurrairah (☻) reports that Allah's Messenger (ﷺ) *said:*

«مَنْ صَلَّى عَلَى جَنَازَةٍ وَلَمْ يَتْبَعْهَا فَلَهُ قِيرَاطٌ، فَإِنْ تَبِعَهَا فَلَهُ
قِيرَاطَانِ» قِيلَ: وَمَا الْقِيرَاطَانِ؟ قَالَ «أَصْغَرُهُمَا مِثْلُ أُحُدٍ»

> *"He who offered prayer over the dead, but did not follow the*
> *bier, for him is the reward of one qirat, and he who followed it,*
> *for him is the reward of two qirats. It was asked what the*
> *qirats were. He said the smaller among the two is equivalent*
> *to Uhud."*

(Muslim:945)

There are many pilgrims that either sit or perform *Sunnah* or *Nafl Salah* during the *Janazah Salah*. You can always perform your *Sunnah Salah* later.

Sunnah & Nafl (voluntary) Salah

Though *Nafl Tawaaf* is superior to *Nafl Salah* in Makkah, it may not always be possible to perform *Tawaaf* due to the excessive crowds.

We are now at another junction (topic) where people's views and understanding differ a great deal. The topic of *Salah* while travelling (*Musafir*).

The issues are:

1. How long can I stay in one place to be still regarded as a traveller?

2. Why should I shorten my *Salah* when I have plenty of time to do it in "full"?

Regarding the first point, the discussion is wide and varied and I do not intend to address it in this book.

About the second point:

Allah's Messenger (ﷺ) said:

«صَدَقَةٌ تَصَدَّقَ اللهُ بِهَا عَلَيْكُمْ، فَاقْبَلُوا صَدَقَتَهُ»

"It is a gift from Allah which He has bestowed upon you; so you should accept it."

(Muslim:686)

Regardless of the view you hold on this issue, I would like to take this opportunity to remind you of the numerous rewards associated with *Sunnah* and *Nafl Salah*. Implement this in your daily life, if you haven't already done so. That is the 12 *Raatibah Rak'at* (*Sunnah Muakadah Salawaat* associated with the *Fard Salah*).

Umm Habeebah (🌸) related that she heard the Prophet (ﷺ) say:

«مَا مِنْ عَبْدٍ مُسْلِمٍ يُصَلِّي للهِ كُلَّ يَوْمٍ ثِنْتَيْ عَشْرَةَ رَكْعَةً تَطَوُّعًا، غَيْرَ فَرِيضَةٍ، إِلَّا بَنَى اللهُ لَهُ بَيْتًا فِي الْجَنَّةِ، أَوْ إِلَّا بُنِيَ لَهُ بَيْتٌ فِي الْجَنَّةِ»

"Allah prepares a house in Paradise for every believer who offers twelve Rak'at of Nafl (voluntary) prayer beyond that which is obligatory upon him."

(Muslim:728)

Abu Hurrairah (🌸) reported that the Prophet (ﷺ) said:

«إِنَّ اللهَ تَعَالَى قَالَ: مَنْ عَادَى لِي وَلِيًّا فَقَدْ آذَنْتُهُ بِالْحَرْبِ، وَمَا تَقَرَّبَ إِلَيَّ عَبْدِي بِشَيْءٍ أَحَبَّ إِلَيَّ مِمَّا افْتَرَضْتُهُ عَلَيْهِ. وَمَا زَالَ عَبْدِي يَتَقَرَّبُ إِلَيَّ بِالنَّوَافِلِ حَتَّى أَحْبَبْتُهُ فَكُنْتُ سَمْعَهُ الذِي يَسْمَعُ بِهِ، وَبَصَرَهُ الذِي يُبْصِرُ بِهِ، وَيَدَهُ الَّتِي يَبْطِشُ بِهَا، وَرِجْلَهُ الَّتِي يَمْشِي بِهَا، وَإِنْ سَأَلَنِي لَأُعْطِيَنَّهُ، وَلَئِنِ اسْتَعَاذَنِي لَأُعِيذَنَّهُ»

"Allah the Almighty says: 'No servant of mine can seek nearness to Me with anything better than what I have made obligatory upon him; and My servant continues to seek nearness to Me with Nafl prayers until I love him. When I love him, I become his ears with which he hears, his eyes with which he sees, his hands with which he holds, and his legs with which he walks. If he begs Me for anything, I give it to him, and if he seeks My refuge, I give it to him'."

(Bukhari:6502)

So wouldn't you like Allah to love you?

Sad as it is, Muslims cannot even agree on the 12 *Rak'at*. So my suggestion is the following: Out of the 12, 10 are generally agreed upon, and they are:

√ 2 before *Fajr*

√ at least 2 before *Zuhr*

√ at least 2 after *Zuhr*

√ 2 after *Maghrib*

√ 2 after *'Eshaa*

That is 10. So you can make the other 2, either before or after *Zuhr*, or before *'Asr*.

The Prophet (ﷺ) NEVER omitted the two *Sunnah Rak'at* before *Salatul-Fajr* and always performed *Salatul-Witr*, even while travelling.

Some other *Sunnah/Nafl Salawaat* that have great rewards:

√ *Salatul-Tahajjud* – at night, after *'Eshaa* until *Fajr*.

√ *Salatul-Duha* - after sunrise until *Salatul-Zuhr*.

√ *Salatul-Wudu* - after performing *Wudu*.

√ *Salatul-Tahiyatul-Masjid* – Necessary upon entering a mosque prior to sitting down (as mentioned before, if you plan to perform *Tawaaf* then you should proceed directly to do so as this is the *Sunnah*. However if you are not going to perform *Tawaaf*, then *Tahiyatul Masjid Salah* becomes necessary.)

Abu Qatadah (ﷺ) related that Allah's Messenger (ﷺ) said:

«إِذَا دَخَلَ أَحَدُكُمُ الْمَسْجِدَ فَلَا يَجْلِسْ حَتَّى يُصَلِّيَ رَكْعَتَيْنِ»

"When one of you enters the mosque you should pray two Rak'at Salah before sitting down."

(Bukhari & Muslim: 1163:714)

Forbidden times for *Salah*

Uqbah bin Amir (ﷺ) said:

«ثَلَاثُ سَاعَاتٍ كَانَ رَسُولُ اللهِ ﷺ يَنْهَانَا أَنْ نُصَلِّيَ فِيهِنَّ، أَوْ
أَنْ نَقْبُرَ فِيهِنَّ مَوْتَانَا: حِينَ تَطْلُعُ الشَّمْسُ بَازِغَةً حَتَّىٰ تَرْتَفِعَ،
وَحِينَ يَقُومُ قَائِمُ الظَّهِيرَةِ حَتَّىٰ تَمِيلَ الشَّمْسُ، وَحِينَ تَضَيَّفُ
الشَّمْسُ لِلْغُرُوبِ حَتَّىٰ تَغْرُبَ»

*"There are three times at which Allah's Messenger (ﷺ) used
to forbid us to pray or bury our dead.*

1. *When the sun began to rise until it was fully up.*

2. *When the sun was at its height at midday till it passed the
meridian.*

3. *When the sun drew near to setting till it had set."*

(Muslim:831)

- Note that it also mentions burying of the dead.

- Abu Sa'eed Al-Khudree (ﷺ) reported Allah's Messenger
(ﷺ) as saying:

«لَا صَلَاةَ بَعْدَ الصُّبْحِ حَتَّى تَرْتَفِعَ الشَّمْسُ، وَلَا صَلَاةَ بَعْدَ
العَصْرِ حَتَّى تَغِيبَ الشَّمْسُ»

*"No prayer is to be offered after Salatul-Fajr until the sun
rises, or after Salatul-'Asr until the sun sets."*

(Bukhari & Muslim: 586:827)

Any unintentionally missed *Salah*, due to sleep or
forgetfulness, can and should be performed immediately,
even if it 'falls' in the forbidden times. Also *Salah* with a
purpose, such as the two *Rak'at* after *Tawaaf* and also *Salatul-
Tahiyatul-Masjid* are also exempted.

Allah's Messenger (ﷺ) said:

«مَنْ نَسِيَ صَلَاةً فَلْيُصَلِّهَا إِذَا ذَكَرَهَا»

"Who has forgotten the prayer he should pray it whenever he remembers it."

(Bukhari & Muslim: 597:684)

Being late

If you are late for the *Salah* do not run towards the mosque or the congregation in order to join it; instead walk calmly and at your normal pace.

Join the congregation immediately in whatever position they are in. Be it *Sujood* or *Tashahud* (even though you need to redo that *Rakah*).

You will need to complete each *Rakah* that you have missed. A *Rakah* is considered missed if you did not perform the Ruku (and recite at least once *"Subahana rabbi'aladheem"*) for that *Rakah*.

Abu Hurrairah (؆) relates that Allah's Messenger (؄) said:

«إِذَا أُقِيمَتِ الصَّلَاةُ فَلَا تَأْتُوهَا تَسْعَوْنَ، وَأْتُوهَا تَمْشُونَ، وَعَلَيْكُمُ السَّكِينَةُ ، فَمَا أَدْرَكْتُمْ فَصَلُّوا، وَمَا فَاتَكُمْ فَأَتِمُّوا»

"If the prayer is started, do not run for it. Walk calmly, join the prayer at the point you enter the mosque and make up what you missed afterwards."

«فَإِنَّ أَحَدَكُمْ إِذَا كَانَ يَعْمِدُ إِلَىٰ الصَّلَاةِ فَهُوَ فِي صَلَاةٍ»

Other narration in Muslim adds: "...for once one of you make the intention to pray, he is considered in prayer."

(Muslim:602)

Sunnah before *Maghrib*

Some people dispute the validity of performing *Sunnah Salah* before *Salatul-Maghrib*. There are numerous *Ahadith* about its validity. I will mention only one.

Instead of disputing or discussing with the person next to you about those that choose to perform it, recite Qur'an, make *Zikr* or *Dua'*, or perform it.

Abdullah bin Mughaffal (ﷺ) relates that Allah's Messenger (ﷺ) said:

«صَلُّوا قَبْلَ صَلاةِ المَغْرِبِ». قالَ في الثَّالِثَةِ: «لِمَنْ شاءَ، كَرَاهِيَةَ أنْ يَتَّخِذَها النَّاسُ سُنَّةً»

"Offer two (Sunnah) Rak'at before Salatul-Maghrib (sunset prayer) and he repeated this direction twice. On the third time he added:

One who likes may do so so that people may not take this direction as Muakkadah (essential)."

(Bukhari:1183)

Other recommended actions

Reciting Qur'an

'Aishah (ﷺ) says that Allah's Messenger (ﷺ) said:

«الْمَاهِرُ بِالْقُرْآنِ مَعَ السَّفَرَةِ الْكِرَامِ الْبَرَرَةِ، وَالَّذِي يَقْرَأُ الْقُرْآنَ وَيَتَتَعْتَعُ فِيهِ، وَهُوَ عَلَيْهِ شَاقٌّ، لَهُ أَجْرَانِ»

"A person who recites the Qur'an, and reads it fluently, will be in the company of the obedient and noble angels, and who reads the Qur'an haltingly and with difficulty will have a double recompense."

(Bukhari & Muslim: 4937:798)

There is no evidence from the Qur'an or the *Sunnah* about kissing or touching the Qur'an with your forehead, before or after reading it.

For those ardent readers, keep the following *Hadith* in mind:

Abdullah bin Amr bin Al-'Aas (ﷺ) narrated that Allah's Messenger (ﷺ) told him that:

«لَا يَفْقَهُ منْ قَرَأَ الْقُرآنَ فِي أَقَلَّ مِنْ ثَلَاثٍ»

"One will not be able to comprehend fully the meaning if one recites the whole Qur'an in less than three days."

(Abu Dawud, Ahmed: 1394:6535)

Utilise your time in Makkah to recite as much Qur'an as possible.

When you are in the *Haram*, do not read aloud, as you may disturb the person next to you, who may be engaged in *Salah* or other forms of *Ibadah*.

Regarding the print type and positioning of the Qur'ans inside the *Haram* see earlier in this chapter under "Inside the *Haram*".

Dua' (supplication)

And your Lord said:

$$﴿ ادْعُونِي أَسْتَجِبْ لَكُمْ ﴾$$

"Invoke Me, I will respond to your (invocation)..."

Surah Ghafir (40:60)

The manner of supplication

A common mistake made by many is that when they supplicate they say *"In Sha Allah"* after it. One should say *"Aameen"* instead.

Anas bin Malik (ﷺ) relates that Allah's Messenger (ﷺ) said:

«إذا دَعا أَحَدُكمْ فَلِيعْزِم المَسألَةَ وَلا يَقُولَنَّ: اللَّهُمَّ إِنْ شِئْتَ فأعْطِني، فإنَّهُ لا مُسْتَكْرَهَ لهُ»

"When one of you is to supplicate he should do so with full confidence and should not say. "O' Allah, grant me if Thou will" for there is no power which can force Allah."

(Bukhari:6338 & Muslim:2678)

$$﴿ ادْعُوا رَبَّكُمْ تَضَرُّعًا وَخُفْيَةً إِنَّهُ لَا يُحِبُّ الْمُعْتَدِينَ ﴾$$

"Invoke your Lord with humility and in secret..."

Surah Al-A'raf (7:55)

➤ Sincerity is the most important ingredient, so do it with humility and sincerity.

➤ Face *Qiblah* if possible, though it is not obligatory.

➤ Begin by praising Allah.

➤ Then ask for blessings on the Prophet (ﷺ).

➤ Then supplicate.

➤ Implore Allah by His names and attributes which are mentioned in the Qur'an and *Sunnah* (e.g.: "O Most Merciful, have mercy on me"; "O Most Forgiving, forgive me for my sins"; O Allah, I ask You O Allah, as You are the One, the Only, *As-Samad* (the Self-Sufficient Master, Possessor of perfect attributes whom all of creation turn to in all their needs)".

➤ Plead to Allah and be persistent in the request.

➤ Ask with confidence and do not say: "If Allah wills".

➤ Ask for the best (if you ask for *Jannah*, ask for *Janatul-Firdhous*).

➤ Finish by saying "*Aameen*".

Choose the best times (and places) when response is most likely. Below are some of the best times to make supplication:

√ The last third of the night.

√ The time between the *Adhaan* and the *Iqaamah*.

√ At the time of breaking fast.

√ While travelling (*Musafir*).

√ During *Salah*:

  ○ In the last *Tashahud*, before *Tasleem*.

  ○ While in *Sujood*.

√ On a Friday (special time, hour before *Maghrib*).

√ During *Tawaaf*.

√ During *Sa'ee*.

√ Day of *Arafat*.

√ After *Salatul-Fajr* in *Muzdalifah.*

√ After throwing (*Ramy*) at the small and middle *Jamr'at* in Mina.

The above list is definitely not conclusive, but you can see that there are many places where you have a 'better chance' of your *Dua'* being accepted. Utilise it!

Also very few Muslims know about *Tawassul*. What is it you may ask? Simply stated, it is a way of seeking nearness to Allah and also how you can 'improve' your chances of your *Dua'* being accepted. Following is a very brief explanation, taken from the book: *Tawassul*, its types and rulings by the late Shaikh Muhammad Naasiruddeen Al-Albaanee (اللّٰه).

There are three (agreed) means of *Tawassul*, and they are:

- *Tawassul* by means of the Names of Allah, the Blessed and the Most High, and His Attributes. Such as the Muslim saying in his supplication: "O Allah I ask You by Your being the Most Merciful, the Bestower of Mercy, the Most Gracious Knower of all that is hidden, the Fully-acquainted: that You grant me safety and well-being."

- *Tawassul* to Allah, the Most High, by means of righteous deed which the person supplicating has done. Such as the Muslim saying: "O Allah by my *Eemaan* in You, and my love for You, and my following of Your Messenger, forgive me..."

- *Tawassul* to Allah, the Most High, by the supplication of a righteous man.

In chapter 11 of this book there are some supplications from the Qur'an and the *Sunnah*.

Remembrance and mentioning (*Dhikr*) of Allah

Remember (mention) Allah at all times. *Dhikr* is normally

translated as remembering Allah, but in real terms it means remembering as well as mentioning (praising) Allah.

'Abu Hurrairah (☻) relates that Allah's Messenger (ﷺ) said:

«قال اللهُ تَعالى: أنا مَعَ عَبْدِي إذا ذَكَرَني وتَحَرَّكَتْ بي شَفتاه»

"Allah says, 'I am with My servant when he remembers Me and his lips move in My remembrance.'"

(Bukhari: The book of Tawhid Chapter No:43)

Make *Dhikr* instead of idle talk.

Do not neglect the *Dhikr* after the *Fard Salah*.

Allah, the Exalted said:

﴿فَٱذْكُرُونِىٓ أَذْكُرْكُمْ وَٱشْكُرُواْ لِى وَلَا تَكْفُرُونِ﴾

"Therefore remember Me (by praying, glorifying), I will remember you, and be grateful to Me (for My countless Favors on you) and never be ungrateful to Me."

Surah Al-Baqarah (2:152)

﴿وَٱذْكُرُواْ ٱللَّهَ كَثِيرًا لَّعَلَّكُمْ تُفْلِحُونَ﴾

"...And remember Allah much, that you may be successful."

Surah Al-Jumu'ah (62:10)

Fasting

Fast as many days as possible in the first 7 days of Dhul-Hijjah. Remember the first 10 days of Dhul-Hijjah are some of the best days in the Sight of Allah:

The Prophet (ﷺ) said:

«مَامِنْ أَيَّامٍ أَعظَمَ عِنْدَ اللهِ ولاَ أحبَّ إليه منَ العمل فِيهِنَّ، مِنَ هٰذه الأيَّامِ العَشْرِ، فأكثِرُوا فِيهِنَّ مِن التَّهْلِيلِ وَالتَّكْبِيرِ وَالتَّحْمِيدِ»

"There are no days greater or more loved by Allah in which to

perform good deeds other than these 10 days, therefore praise and glorify Allah abundantly in these days."

(Ahmad:5446)

If you are performing the *Tamattu* method of *Hajj* and you cannot afford the sacrifice, then you MUST fast for 3 days during *Hajj* (before the 8th if possible) and 7 days when returning home (10 in total), as per the instruction from Allah in *Surah Al-Baqarah, Ayah* 196.

Fast as many days as you can, it has many rewards:

Abu Sa'id Al-Khudri (⬥) reported Allah's Messenger (ﷺ) as saying:

«مَنْ صَامَ يَوْمًا فِي سَبِيلِ اللهِ، بَاعَدَ اللهُ وَجْهَهُ عَنِ النَّارِ سَبْعِينَ خَرِيفًا»

"He who observes fast for a day in the way of Allah He would remove his face from the Hell to the extent of seventy years distance."

(Muslim:1153)

«الصَّوْمُ لِي وَأَنَا أَجْزِي بِهِ، يَدَعُ شَهْوَتَهُ وَأَكْلَهُ وَشُرْبَهُ مِنْ أَجْلِي»

"Fasting is preformed for My sake and I Myself shall decide its reward (for each person) for he (the servant) has abstained from his desire, eating and drinking for My sake."

(Bukhari:7492 and Muslim:1151)

Sadaqah (charity)

Perform as many charitable acts as possible and also distribute charity (money, food etc.) to the poor while you are in Makkah or Madinah.

Remember that helping others and even greeting your fellow Muslim with a smile is an act of charity.

You will notice many poor people to which you can give

Sadaqah to. A suggestion is to give some of your *Sadaqah* to the cleaners in the *Haram* and also the street cleaners.

Visiting (*Ziyarah*)

Visit any sick pilgrims, be it in their hotel or in the hospital. Keep in mind the etiquette of visiting the sick, by not staying too long or talking too loud or too much. Make *Dua'* for them and encourage them to be patient.

Visit the cemeteries (graveyards). This is to remind us of death.

There are no places to visit in Makkah as part of *Hajj*. (So, if you do not wish to go anywhere, except spending your time in the *Haram*, then do so).

However, there are many pilgrims who are interested in some of the historical places. Many people save their money over a lifetime to come to Makkah and have learnt about some of these places over the years at school and from *Ahadith* and so on, therefore they are really keen to visit them. Don't necessarily believe everything the guide tells you, as there are many of them that relate fake stories. Just recently I heard that some groups are brought to Jeddah to show them the bicycle of Prophet Adam. How ludicrous, but the 'poor' pilgrims are just so gullible.

One place of interest to visit is the factory where they make the cloth (*Kiswat*) that covers the Ka'bah. You need to make an appointment to visit the factory. Most agents know the procedures to follow to obtain permission for a visit to this factory.

If you plan to go somewhere and the trip means missing a *Fard Salah* in the *Haram*, avoid it. Remember the reward is 100,000 times for each *Salah*. Do not "short-change" yourself.

Preferably avoid the trips to climb Jabal-Thur or Jabal-Nur (Mountains). This is dangerous and tiring. There is a probability of you hurting your ankles doing this, so avoid it as you will need your health and strength for *Hajj*.

Furthermore there is no reward for climbing these mountains. If you insist, and are looking forward to see an historical sight, be warned; I think the shops and photographers up on the mountain reduces the spiritual significance of the site.

Most groups take a trip to Arafat and Mina. This may be worthwhile as it gives you a chance to see these places when they are less crowded.

DO NOT perform *Salah* on Jabal-Rahmah (Mountain of Mercy) in Arafat as many people do or cast pebbles at the *Jamr'at* in Mina. Also refrain from writing your name on the stone structure on Jabal-Rahmah.

Once again, none of these visits is necessary and if you decide to go (from an historical point), ensure that you are back in time for *Salah* in the *Haram*.

About *Tawaaf*

General guidelines

See later in this section – "How to perform *Tawaaf*".

Tawaaf is the best *Ibadah* to perform other than the *Fard Salah* in the *Haram*.

Tawaaf is superior to *Nafl Salah* in the *Haram*.

There is no fixed time for *Tawaaf*.

If you plan to perform *Tawaaf*, then you should proceed directly to perform it when entering the *Haram*. *Tahiyatul-Masjid Salah* is only performed if you plan to sit down prior to the *Tawaaf*.

You do not need to be in *Ihraam* to perform *Nafl Tawaaf*.

There is no *Sa'ee* after *Nafl Tawaaf*. (There is no *Nafl Sa'ee*.)

The number of circuits to perform is always seven, regardless of the type of *Tawaaf* (i.e. *Umrah*, *Hajj* or *Nafl*).

There is no *Niyah* to be uttered audibly. The *Niyah* is in the heart as with all other acts of *Ibadah*.

Tawaaf begins at *Hajrul-Aswad* (Black Stone) and proceeds in an anti-clockwise direction.

The *Tawaaf* also finishes at the *Hajrul-Aswad*.

One should encircle (walk around the outside) the area called *Hijr* (the open area, under the roof's water spout, surrounded by a low wall).

There is no evidence from the Qur'an or the *Sunnah* that one can perform *Nafl Tawaaf* on behalf of deceased (or living) relatives or friends.

Dua' in your own language, *Dhikr*, and reciting Qur'an are all acceptable forms of *Ibadah* while performing *Tawaaf*.

Tawaaf MUST be interrupted for *Fard Salah* and recommended for *Janazah Salah*. Resume from where you have stopped. If you stopped half way through one circuit, ensure that you continue at the right place. This is important if you stopped for *Salah* and moved positions several times before the actual *Salah*. So it is important to remember exactly where you have stopped, otherwise start again with that round.

If you are in doubt about the number of rounds you have made, rely on the lesser number you remember.

It is permissible to talk while performing *Tawaaf*. Most scholars agree that one should only discuss necessary things and not merely engage in idle chat.

Avoid performing *Tawaaf* in groups or following and reciting behind a "leader". The Prophet (ﷺ) was the best of teachers and he did not lead anybody, or any group, in *Tawaaf*, nor did he instruct his Companions (ﷺ) do so.

You must have *Wudu'* (as with *Salah*) to perform *Tawaaf*.

Avoid raising your voice while performing *Tawaaf*:

Narrated Abu Musa Al-Ash'ari (ﷺ):

The Prophet (ﷺ) started ascending a high place or hill. A man (among his companions) ascended it and shouted in a loud voice: 'La ilaha illal-lahu wallahu Akbar'. (At that time)

Allah's Messenger (ﷺ) was riding his mule. Allah's Messenger (ﷺ) said:

«فَإِنَّكُمْ لَا تَدْعُونَ أَصَمَّ وَلَا غَائِبًا»

"You are not calling upon a deaf or an absent One."

(Bukhari:6409)

Avoid walking against the flow of people. Rather walk right around to the starting place.

There is no need to actually stop at the starting area. This is not a place to stop or make *Salah*. Many people stop here and make all sorts of gestures towards the Black Stone, causing a great deal of congestion and confusion.

It is important to note that if one is unable to reach the Black Stone, one's *Umrah* or *Tawaaf* is NOT decreased in merit in any way, but if one pushes and shoves his Muslim brethren in order to do so, he risks incurring Allah the Almighty's displeasure.

Why are we kissing the Black Stone?

Ibn Umar (ﷺ) reported that Umar (ﷺ) kissed the stone and said:

«إِنِّي لَأُقَبِّلُكَ وَإِنِّي لَأَعْلَمُ أَنَّكَ حَجَرٌ، وَلَكِنِّي رَأَيْتُ رَسُولَ اللهِ ﷺ يُقَبِّلُكَ»

"I am kissing you, whereas I know you are a stone, but I saw Allah's Messenger (ﷺ) kissing you (that is why I kiss you)."'

(Muslim:1270)

See the diagram later in this chapter on some hints for *Tawaaf*.

Types of *Tawaaf*

➤ *Umrah Tawaaf* ❶

➤ Welcome *Tawaaf* (*Tawaaful-Qudoom*) ❷

➤ *Tawaaf* for *Hajj* (*Tawaaful-Ifadah* also known as *Tawaaf-uz-*

Ziyarah or *Tawaaful-Hajj*)❸

➤ Farewell *Tawaaf* (*Tawaaful-Wadaa'*)❹

➤ *Nafl Tawaaf* ❺

❶ & ❷ You should be in *Ihraam*.

❷ This *Tawaaf* is performed by those pilgrims performing the *Qiran* or *Ifrad* method of *Hajj*.

❶ & ❷ *Ramal* (to walk briskly in the first three rounds) and *Idtiba* (to have your right shoulder open) are required for these *Tawaafs*.

Narrated Ibn Abbas (☞):

«قَدِمَ رَسُولُ اللهِ ﷺ وأصحابُهُ فَقالَ المُشرِكونَ: إنَّهُ يَقْدَمُ
عَلَيْكُمْ وَفْدٌ وَهَنَهُمْ حُمَّى يَثْرِبَ، فأمَرَهُمُ النَّبِيُّ ﷺ أنْ يَرْمُلُوا
الأَشْوَاطَ الثَّلاثَةَ وأنْ يَمْشُوا ما بَينَ الرُّكْنَينِ، ولَمْ يَمْنَعْهُ أنْ
يأْمُرَهُمْ أنْ يَرْمُلُوا الأَشْوَاطَ كُلَّها إلَّا الإبْقاءُ عَلَيْهِمْ»

"When Allah's Messenger (ﷺ) and his companions came to Makkah, the pagans circulated the news that a group of people were coming to them and they had been weakened by the fever of Yathrib (Al-Madinah). So the Prophet (ﷺ) ordered his companions to do Ramal in the first three rounds of Tawaaf of the Ka'bah and to walk between the two corners (the Yemenite Corner and the Black Stone). The Prophet (ﷺ) did not order them to do Ramal in all the rounds of Tawaaf out of pity for them."

(Bukhari:1602)

❸ This is one of the pillars of *Hajj* and MUST be performed by ALL pilgrims.

❹ This is the last act to be performed before leaving Makkah.

❺ This *Tawaaf* can be performed at any time and as many times as possible.

❸, ❹ & ❺ No *Ihraam*, no *Ramal* and no *Idtiba* for these *Tawaafs*.

How to Perform *Tawaaf*

The *Niyah* is in the heart (*Umrah, Ifadah, Wadaa' etc.*)

Start at the *Hajrul-Aswad* (Black Stone):

> ➤ Kiss it if possible;

> ➤ If not, touch it with your right hand (*Istilam*) and kiss your hand;

> ➤ If this is not possible, then face the Black Stone and with your right hand gesture towards it ONCE only, and DO NOT kiss your hand.

Say once only:

بِسْمِ اللهِ وَ اللهُ أَكْبَرُ

"Bismillahi-wallahu-akbar"

(In the Name of Allah, Allah is the Greatest.)

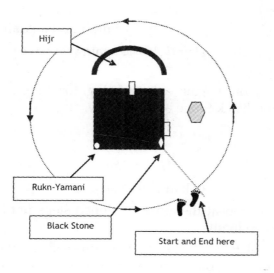

Proceed in an anti-clockwise (towards the *Maqaam Ibraheem*) direction.

Supplicate, make *Dhikr*, recite Qur'an.

Walk around the *Hijr* area and not through it.

Once you reach the **Rukn–Yamani** (the southern corner) touch it with your right hand (*Istilam*) and say الله أَكْبَرُ (*Allahu Akbar*). Do NOT kiss it. If you are unable to touch it, do not gesture towards it, but proceed towards the *Hajr-al-Aswad*, without saying الله أَكْبَرُ .

It is *Sunnah* to recite the following between the *Rukn–Yamani* and the Black Stone Corner (note that the Dua' stops at...*adhaabannaar*):

﴿رَبَّنَآ ءَاتِنَا فِى ٱلدُّنْيَا حَسَنَةً وَفِى ٱلْأَخِرَةِ حَسَنَةً وَقِنَا عَذَابَ ٱلنَّارِ﴾

"Rabbanaa aatina fidunya hasanatan wa fil aakhirati hasanatan wa qinaa adhaabanaar"

(Oh Allah, give us the good of this world and the good of the Hereafter and protect us from the punishment of Hellfire.)

Surah Al-Baqarah (2:201)

Once you reach the *Hajrul-Aswad* again you have completed 1 circuit.

Continue by once again either kissing, touching or gesturing towards the Black Stone and say only:

الله أَكْبَرُ

"Allahu Akbar"

(Allah is the Greatest)

Proceed and repeat the aforementioned steps until you have completed 7 circuits.

Upon completion of the *Tawaaf*, proceed to the *Maqaam Ibraheem* or any place in the mosque if this area is too crowded.

It is commendable to say:

«وَاتَّخِذُوا مِنْ مَقَامِ إِبْرَاهِيمَ مُصَلًّى»

"Wattakhithu min Maqaami Ibraheema musalla"
(And take the station of Ibraheem as a place of prayer.)

Cover your right shoulder and perform 2 *Rak'at* of prayer. I cannot stress enough that it is acceptable to perform the 2 *Rak'at* anywhere in the mosque. As with the kissing of the Black Stone, remember it is best to avoid harming and causing difficulties to fellow Muslims.

If you are fortunate enough to perform it near the *Maqaam*, then stand with the *Maqaam* between you and the Ka'bah (if possible).

It is *Sunnah* to recite *Suratul-Kafirun* (109) after *Suratul-Fatiha* in the first *Rakah* and *Suratul-Ikhlas* (112), after *Suratul-Fatiha* in the second *Rakah*.

> For *Nafl Tawaaf* or *Tawaaful-Wadaa'*: At this point you are completed.

Some hints for *Tawaaf*

During the very busy periods of *Hajj* the *Tawaaf* area around the Ka'bah is extremely crowded with people performing *Tawaaf*. It is like being in a can of sardines and one can get severely squashed and bruised.

If you cannot stand being pushed and squashed I suggest you perform your *Tawaaf* on the roof level. It is much easier than the middle floor level as the middle floor has lots of people and pillars to negotiate. The roof can also get very crowded but from experience it is much more comfortable. It may take a while longer due to the bigger area you need to cover. Walking normally, with a fair crowd, one circuit can take about 15 to 20 minutes to complete.

Apart from the pushing, it is not recommended for women to be in such crowds, if it can be avoided. It is a sin for them to be touched by strange men. And believe me some men are in the *Tawaaf* area for that!

The bottom level around the Ka'bah is the quickest, but it is also for the bravest, during these busy times.

If you start your *Tawaaf* on the ground level, and find it too difficult to continue, it is acceptable to go to the other floors to complete the seven circuits. It is best to try and complete a circuit prior to going upstairs. If you go halfway through a circuit, then you should redo that circuit. (The distance covered to get upstairs does not count as part of the *Tawaaf*.)

It is also acceptable to go outside the mosque to use the escalators (which is sometimes easier) to get upstairs.

Start your *Tawaaf* as far out as possible (as indicated - start *Tawaaf* / 1st Circuit)

Proceed to walk slowly inwards, closer to the Ka'bah.

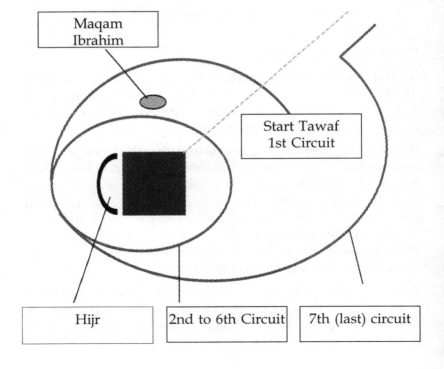

Try to maintain this position and complete the 1st circuit followed by circuits 2 to 6.

On the 7th circuit start moving slowly towards the outer side again.

At the end of the 7th round, walk quickly diagonally along the starting area, in front of the people.

Because everybody stops in this area, if you walk quickly, you will find a clear path most of the way.

If you encounter any "human-chains", just wait until they pass and then move on.

If you have women with you, I suggest you remain on the outside for all seven circuits.

About getting to kiss the Black Stone. Sometimes the pilgrims actually form a queue. You may wait very long in this queue as there are thousands of others that push in at the front. There is no easy way other than waiting your turn. Do not even consider taking the females to try and kiss the stone. This is looking for trouble. Rather go at a less busy time if possible.

Touching of the *Rukn–Yamani* Corner is also virtually impossible.

Do NOT walk against the flow of people!

After finishing the two *Rak'at Salah* it is *Sunnah* to proceed to the well of *Zamzam* and drink your fill. The well entrance is gone now, so you need to drink from the taps against the wall.

Then return to the Black Stone and kiss it if possible, saying "*Allahu Akbar''*. If it is not possible proceed to the *Sa'ee* area without gesturing or saying "*Allahu Akbar''*.

About *Sa'ee*

Guidelines

See later in this section – "How to perform *Sa'ee''*.

There is no *Sa'ee* after a *Nafl Tawaaf* or after *Tawaaful-Wadaa'*.

The *Sa'ee* comprises of seven laps.

The distance between Safaa and Marwah is about 450 meters (492 yards).

Starting at Safaa one proceeds to Marwah. This is one lap.

From Marwah you return to Safaa (this is lap two) and so on,

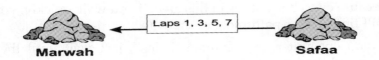

finishing lap seven at Marwah.

When you are in doubt about the number of rounds you have

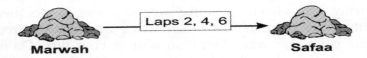

made, rely on the lesser number you remember.

Dua' in your own language, *Dhikr*, *Tasbih*, are all acceptable forms of *Ibadah* while performing *Sa'ee*.

Between the green lights (indicated on the side of the walls nearer to Safaa), the male pilgrims walk briskly (or run). Sometimes due to crowds it is impossible to do so. Also if you are taking care of elderly or female pilgrims, you can refrain from running between the green lit areas. Some male pilgrims run all the way from Safaa to Marwah. Maybe they are in a hurry, but this is contrary to the *Sunnah*. Do nut run near the *Zamzam* containers as the floor is often wet and slippery.

Sa'ee MUST be interrupted for *Fard Salah* and recommended for *Janazah Salah*. Resume from where you have stopped. If you stopped half way through one lap, ensure that you continue at the right place. This is important if you stopped for *Salah* and moved positions several times before the actual

Salah. So it is important to remember exactly where you have stopped, otherwise start that lap again. If you are not sure about the number, remember that the *Sa'ee* finishes at *Marwah*, hence you should take care of the numbers. If you are confused then count as follows. If you were going towards *Marwah*, then the count can either be 1, 3, 5 or 7, and if you were going towards Safaa, then it is 2, 4 or 6.

It is permissible to talk while performing *Sa'ee*. Most scholars agree that one should only discuss necessary things and not merely engage in idle chat.

Avoid performing *Sa'ee* in groups or following and reciting behind a leader. The Prophet (ﷺ) was the best of teachers and he did not lead anybody, or any group, in *Sa'ee*, nor did he instruct his companions (ﷺ) to do so.

Avoid raising your voice while performing *Sa'ee*.

It is preferable but not a requirement to have *Wudu* while performing *Sa'ee*.

Where is the Sa'ee area?

With your back facing the *Maqaam Ibraheem*, Safaa is located towards your right. There is a big white sign indicating the direction. Also if you proceed straight towards the back of the *Haram* from the green light or starting area, you will be going in the right direction.

Sa'ee can also be performed on the middle and roof areas.

Once again I suggest the roof area to be the best. However, the middle floor may be better if you are performing *Sa'ee* during the day and it is hot.

Sometimes the stairs to the upper floors of the *Sa'ee* area are just as crowded as the *Sa'ee* itself. If this is the case, I suggest you exit from door no. 11 (Baabus-Safaa) and turn right to enter from door no. 8 (Ajyad Escalator), to go to the roof or middle floor.

Many pilgrims make the mistake of counting from Safaa to

Safaa as one lap. This means you will end up performing 14 laps. Try to picture the previous diagrams when you are in doubt.

Types of *Sa'ee*

➤ After *Tawaaf* for *Umrah* ❶

➤ After *Tawaaful-Qudoom* ❷ (*Sa'ee* for *Hajj*, recommended at this point for the *Qaarin* and optional for the *Mufrid*)

➤ After *Tawaaful-Ifadah* ❸ (For those performing the *Tamattu* method. Also for the *Qaarin* and *Mufrid* if they did not do it after *Tawaaful-Qudoom*.)

There is no *Nafl Sa'ee*.

❶ & ❷ You should be in *Ihraam*.

❸ Normally not in *Ihraam*, unless you perform it prior to the cutting of your hair.

How to Perform *Sa'ee*

Proceed to Safaa. When you get close to Safaa it is *Sunnah* to say:

$$﴿إِنَّ ٱلصَّفَا وَٱلۡمَرۡوَةَ مِن شَعَآئِرِ ٱللَّهِ﴾$$

"Innassafa walmarwata min sha'aa' irillah."

(Indeed Safaa and Marwah are among the signs of Allah.)

Surah Al-Baqarah (2:158)

Followed by saying:

$$«أَبۡدَأُ بِمَا بَدَأَ اللهُ بِهِ»$$

"Abda'u bima bada'a Allahu bihi."

(I begin with that which Allah has begun.)

Please note that both the above are only to be said **ONCE**, that is at the beginning of the *Sa'ee* and not at the beginning of every lap.

In case you wondered why the *Sa'ee* starts at Safaa; this is the answer...because Allah starts with it!

When ascending Safaa, go up until the Ka'bah is visible (if possible) and facing it, it is *Sunnah* to repeat the following 3 times while raising your hands as in making *Dua'* (supplication), and not with your palms facing the Ka'bah. Also do not gesture towards the Ka'bah with your hands as in *Tawaaf*. In between these 3 times you may make your own supplications (i.e. say the following; supplicate; say the following; supplicate; say the following):

« الْحَمْدُ لِلهِ وَلَا إِلهَ إِلَّا اللهُ وَاللهُ أَكْبَرُ، لَا إِلهَ إِلَّا اللهُ وَحْدَهُ لَا شَرِيكَ لَهُ، لَهُ الْمُلْكُ وَلَهُ الْحَمْدُ يُحْيِي وَيُمِيتُ وَهُوَ عَلَى كُلِّ شَيْءٍ قَدِيرٌ، لَا إِلهَ إِلَّا اللهُ وَحْدَهُ، صَدَقَ وَعْدَهُ، وَنَصَرَ عَبْدَهُ، وَهَزَمَ الْأَحْزَابَ وَحْدَهُ» .

"Alhamdu lillah, wala ilaha illallah, wallahu Akbar. Laa ilaha illallahu wahdahu la shareeka lahu, lahulmulku wa lahulhamdu, yuhyee wa yumeetu wa Huwa ala kulli shay'in Qadeer. La ilaha illallahu wahdahu, sadaqa wa'dahu, wa nasara abdahu, wa hazamal-ahzaaba wahdahu."

(All praise is due to Allah, there is no God but Allah, and Allah is Greater. There is none worthy of worship but Allah alone, no partners are unto Him, His is the dominion (kingdom) and His is the praise. He gives life and He gives death and He is capable of everything. There is none worthy of worship but Allah alone, who fulfilled His promise, and gave victory to His servant and defeated the confederates alone.)

Walk towards Marwah. When you arrive at the green fluorescent light, the men should run briskly (if convenient), until the next green light. Women should **NOT** run.

Marwah   Laps 1, 3, 5, 7   Safaa

There is no prescribed supplication during the *Sa'ee* or between the two green lights, though you can supplicate and mention Allah as you like. It is also good to recite the Qur'an during the *Sa'ee*. There is nothing from the Prophet (ﷺ) establishing any particular prayer during the *Sa'ee*, but it has been established that Ibn Masood and Ibn Umar (ﷺ) used to say:

«رَبِّ اغْفِرْ وَارْحَمْ إِنَّك أَنْتَ الأَعَزَّ الأَكْرَمُ»

"Rabbighfir warham innaka Antal Azul-Akram."

(Oh Allah forgive me and have mercy upon me, for You are the most Mighty and Honourable.)

C But this is without any reference to any particular place where it should be said.

Upon reaching Marwah, the 1st lap is complete. Ascend Marwah, face the Ka'bah, and it is commendable to do what was done at Safaa.

Proceed back to Safaa (once again men run at the green lights

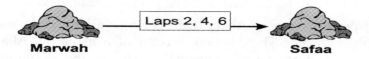

Marwah   Laps 2, 4, 6   **Safaa**

if convenient). The 2nd lap is now complete. Repeat this procedure at Safaa and Marwah until you finish at Marwah, which should be your 7th lap.

There is no *Dua'* at the end of the 7th lap at Marwah.

Sa'ee is now complete.

At Marwah, and if you are performing *Sa'ee* on the second floor or on the roof, you will not be able to see the Ka'bah, so you need to ensure that you face the correct direction while supplicating.

You will find people with scissors at Marwah, offering (for a small fee) to cut your hair. Many women opt for this, and by doing so, often expose their hair. It is better that they wait until they return to their rooms, and do it in privacy.

Men should also refrain from using this "service" as it causes them to cut only a few strands of hair.

Leaving the *Haram*

There is no special supplication upon leaving *Al-Masjid Al-Haram*. However, the one offered upon leaving any mosque should be recited:

«بِسْمِ اللهِ وَالصَّلَاةُ وَالسَّلَامُ عَلَى رَسُولِ اللهِ، اللَّهُمَّ إِنِّي أَسْأَلُكَ مِنْ فَضْلِكَ»

"Bismillahi wassalaatu wa salaamu alaa rasullillahi; Allahumma innee asaluka min fadhlika."

(In the Name of Allah. Blessings and peace be upon the Messenger of Allah. Oh Allah, I ask of You Your favour.)

(Muslim:713, Abu Dawud: 465, Nasa'i: 730 & Ibn Majah: 772)

Do not walk backwards out of the *Haram*. There is no evidence for this practice in the *Sunnah*. As a matter of fact, it is dangerous, as you may trip and fall over somebody.

Chapter 9

Umrah

Before I cover the actual performance of *Umrah*, I would like to recap on the overall *Hajj* procedure.

Recap:

Hajj is the fifth pillar of Islam. It is obligatory for those Muslims who can afford to make the journey to Makkah once in a lifetime. It is performed from the 8th to the 13th of Dhul-Hijjah, which is the 12th month of the *Hijrah* (lunar) calendar. The history of *Hajj* goes back to Prophet Ibraheem (عليه السلام).

Eligibility for performing *Hajj*:

1. To be a Muslim
2. To have reached puberty
3. To be of sound mind
4. To be free (not a slave)
5. To have the financial means
6. To possess the physical means
7. To have a *Mahram* (for women)

There are three methods of *Hajj* that one can perform. The one that most people perform is called *Hajj Tamattu*. This is the *Hajj* the Prophet (ﷺ) instructed his companions to perform. This is *Hajj* joined with *Umrah*, with two separate *Niy'at*. This method of *Hajj* is covered in great detail as this is the most common type performed by those coming from abroad. The other two types are *Hajj Qiran* (*Umrah* and *Hajj*, with one *Niyah*) and *Hajj Ifrad* (*Hajj* only).

Some people may dispute whether the *Tamattu* method is the best as the Prophet (ﷺ) himself performed *Hajj Qiran*. The following incident as related in *Sahih Muslim* should clarify this point:

«أَحِلُّوا مِنْ إِحْرَامِكُمْ بِطَوَافِ البَيْتِ، وَبَيْنَ الصَّفا والمَرْوَةِ،
وَقَصِّرُوا ثُمَّ أَقِيمُوا حَلالًا حَتَّى إِذَا كَانَ يَوْمُ التَّرْوِيَةِ فَأَهِلُّوا
بِالحَجِّ وَاجْعَلُوا الَّتِي قَدِمْتُمْ بِها مُتْعَةً». فَقالُوا: كَيْفَ نَجْعَلُها
مُتْعَةً وَقَدْ سَمَّيْنا الحَجَّ؟ فَقالَ: «افْعَلُوا ما أَمَرْتُكُمْ فَلَوْلا أَنِّي
سُقْتُ الهَدْيَ لَفَعَلْتُ مِثْلَ الَّذِي أَمَرْتُكُمْ»

*"When the Prophet (ﷺ) performed Tawaaf and Sa'ee during
the year of the Farewell Hajj with his Companions, he ordered
all those who hadn't brought sacrificial animals to change
their Niyah for Hajj to Niyah for Umrah, cut their hair and
disengage from Ihraam until Hajj. He said:*

*'If I had not brought the sacrificial animal, I would have done
what I've ordered you to do'."*

(Bukhari:1568)

It is agreed by most scholars that once you perform *Umrah* in
the *Hajj* months (Shawaal, Dhul-Qadah, up to 9th of Dhul-
Hijjah) then you are automatically a *Mutamatti*. Meaning that
you have no choice but to perform the *Tamattu* method of *Hajj*.

The basic actions/differences of the three types of *Hajj*:

Action	Tamattu	Qiran	Ifrad
Adopt *Ihraam* at *Meqaat*	Yes	Yes	Yes
Niyah for *Umrah* Only	Yes	No	No
Niyah for *Umrah* & *Hajj*	No	Yes	No
Niyah for *Hajj* Only	No	No	Yes
Tawaaf for *Umrah*	Yes	No	No
Sa'ee for *Umrah*	Yes	No	No
Tawaaful-Qudoom (Welcome *Tawaaf*)	No	Yes	Yes
Perform *Sa'ee* for *Hajj*	No	Yes (recommended)	Yes (optional)
Haircut after *Sa'ee*	Yes	No	No
Relief from *Ihraam* restrictions	Yes	No	No

8th of Dhul-Hijjah:			
Adopt *Ihraam* from where you are	Yes	Not Applic.	Not Applic.
Niyah for *Hajj*	Yes	Not Applic.	Not Applic.
Proceed to Mina	Yes	Yes	Yes
9th of Dhul-Hijja:			
Proceed to Arafat	Yes	Yes	Yes
After *Maghrib* on the 9th of Dhul-Hijjah:			
Proceed to Muzdalifah (spend the night)	Yes	Yes	Yes
Before Sunrise on the 10th of Dhul-Hijjah:			
Proceed to Mina	Yes	Yes	Yes
Ramy the Big *Jamrah* (*Aqaba*)	Yes	Yes	Yes
Perform Sacrifice (*Hady*)	Yes	Yes	Optional
Shave or cut your hair	Yes	Yes	Yes
First part of *Ihraam* restrictions lifted	Yes	Yes	Yes
Proceed to Makkah - *Tawaaful-Ifadah*	Yes	Yes	Yes
Sa'ee for *Hajj* (* Yes for *Qiran* and *Ifrad* if it was not done with *Tawaaful-Qudoom*)	Yes	Yes*	Yes*
All *Ihraam* restrictions lifted	Yes	Yes	Yes
Return to Mina on the 10th	Yes	Yes	Yes
11th, 12th in Mina	Yes	Yes	Yes
Ramy all three *Jamr'at* after *Zawaal*	Yes	Yes	Yes
Spend the nights in Mina	Yes	Yes	Yes
Proceed to Makkah before sunset (12th)	Yes	Yes	Yes
Remain until 13th (optional)	Yes	Yes	Yes
Ramy all three *Jamr'at* after *Zawaal*	Yes	Yes	Yes
Proceed to Makkah	Yes	Yes	Yes
Perform *Tawaaful-Wadaa'*	Yes	Yes	Yes
Can change *Niyah*?	Conditional	Yes	Yes

Changing of your *Niyah* (Intention):

There are some instances when a pilgrim may wish to change his *Niyah*; meaning he opts for another method of *Hajj* from the one he originally started with. Remember, if circumstances permit, then one should change one's *Niyah* to *Tamattu*, if that's not the method one started with. If the pilgrim hasn't performed any *Hajj* rites yet, or is not in *Ihraam* state (has not uttered the *Niyah*) yet, then it is not an issue, otherwise there are some rules to abide by. In basic terms one cannot change ones *Niyah* to something "lesser", without a compelling reason. So the order is: *Tamattu* (*Hajj* and *Umrah*) followed by *Qiran* (*Hajj* and *Umrah*); then *Ifrad* (*Hajj* only). The rules are as follows:

The residents of Makkah can ONLY perform *Ifrad*.

The *Mutamatti* (*Tamattu* method pilgrim) or the *Qaarin* (*Qiran* method pilgrim) CANNOT change his or her *Niyah* to *Ifrad*.

The *Mutamatti* (*Tamattu* method pilgrim) CAN change his or her *Niyah* to *Qiran* only if:

1. The pilgrim's menstruation starts prior to having done *Umrah* and she is due to proceed to Mina or Arafat.

2. The pilgrim is unable to get to Makkah or does not have enough time to complete an *Umrah* prior to proceeding to Mina or Arafat.

The *Qaarin* should change his *Niyah* to *Tamattu*. Also as stated before, some scholars rule that it is a must: if he did not have his sacrificial animals with him.

Example 1:

A pilgrim decides to perform the *Qiran* method. At the *Meqaat* he makes *Niyah* for *Umrah* and *Hajj*. He enters Makkah and performs *Tawaaful-Qudoom* and *Sa'ee* for *Hajj*. He remains in *Ihraam*. He then opts to perform *Tamattu* instead (as he does not have his animals with him). All he has to do is cut his hair and relieve himself from the *Ihraam*. (The *Tawaaf* and *Sa'ee* already completed will be regarded as that of *Umrah*. *Sa'ee* for *Hajj* must be performed again with *Tawaaful-Ifadah*.)

If he did not perform *Sa'ee* for *Hajj* and did only the welcome

Tawaaf, then he should do the following: proceed to perform *Sa'ee* for *Umrah* and then cut his hair.

On the 8th of Dhul-Hijjah he makes *Niyah* for *Hajj* and continues to follow the *Tamattu* rules.

The *Mufrid* (*Ifrad* method pilgrim) can and should change his *Niyah* to *Tamattu* or *Qiran* if possible. This is only for those who are not residents of Makkah:

○ If he changes his *Niyah* to *Tamattu*, he then has to follow the *Tamattu* rules.

○ If he changes his *Niyah* to *Qiran*, he then has to follow the *Qiran* rules.

Example 2

A pilgrim decides to perform the *Ifrad* method. At the *Meqaat* he makes *Niyah* for *Hajj* only. He enters Makkah and performs *Tawaaful-Qudoom* and *Sa'ee* for *Hajj*. He remains in *Ihraam*. If he is able he should change to perform *Tamattu* instead. All he has to do is cut his hair and relieve himself from the *Ihraam*. (The *Tawaaf* and *Sa'ee* already completed will be regarded as that of *Umrah*. *Sa'ee* for *Hajj* must be performed again with *Tawaaful-Ifadah*.) If he did not perform Sa'ee for *Hajj* and did only the welcome *Tawaaf*, then he should do the following: Perform *Sa'ee* for *Umrah* and cut his hair. On the 8th of Dhul-Hijjah he makes *Niyah* for *Hajj* and continues to follow the *Tamattu* rules.

Example 3

A pilgrim decides to perform the *Ifrad* method. At the *Meqaat* he makes *Niyah* for *Hajj* only. He enters Makkah and performs *Tawaaful-Qudoom* and *Sa'ee* for *Hajj*. He remains in *Ihraam*. He then decides that he wishes to perform *Qiran* instead. All he has to do is on the 8th of Dhul-Hijjah make *Niyah* for *Hajj* and continue to follow the *Qiran* rules, and then the same steps as the previous examples apply. However, in this instance he should change his *Niyah* to *Tamattu* instead.

Summary of the numbers

Tamattu has 3 sets of *Tawaaf* (*Umrah, Ifadah, Wadaa'*) and 2 sets of *Sa'ee* (*Umrah, Hajj*) and 1 sacrifice (*Hady*) is compulsory.

Qiran has possibly 3 sets of *Tawaaf* (*Qudoom*, which is optional; *Ifadah; Wadaa'*) and 1 set of *Sa'ee* (*Hajj*) and 1 sacrifice (*Hady*) is compulsory.

Ifrad has possibly 3 sets of *Tawaaf* (*Qudoom*, which is optional; *Ifadah; Wadaa'*) and 1 set of *Sa'ee* (*Hajj*) and there is no requirement to sacrifice (*Hady*).

If you are departing for home almost immediately after returning from Mina and you have delayed performing *Tawaaful-Ifadah* then you can "join" *Tawaaful-Wadaa'* with it; meaning that you do only one set of *Tawaaf*, with the *Niyah* for *Ifadah*. This has to be your last rite, prior to leaving for home.

If you arrive "very late" in Makkah (8th or 9th of Dhul-Hijjah) or you live in Jeddah for example, and you still wish to perform *Hajj Tamattu*, then you proceed to perform *Umrah* (*Tawaaf* & *Sa'ee*); cut your hair (this relieves you from *Ihraam*); make *Niyah* for *Hajj*; proceed to Mina... The two points I am making here are: one; that you do not need to take off your *Ihraam* clothes after *Umrah* as many people believe. The cutting of your hair is what "removes" you from the state of *Ihraam* and not the removal of the clothes; and two, you can still perform *Hajj Tamattu* even if you start your *Hajj* rituals very late.

The *Tamattu* method encompasses all the actions; meaning that *Qiran* and *Ifrad* are sort of subsets of *Tamattu*. Therefore, if you are unsure of which method to follow, *Tamattu* is the safest and also the recommended method (as stated earlier).

Performance of *Umrah*

If you wish to keep some form of guide (book) with you in

order to follow the correct steps for *Umrah*, keep in mind that I have published an *Umrah* pocket guide for this purpose.

What follows is the procedure for the *Mutamatti* pilgrim (*Hajj Tamattu*).

When you enter the *Haram* proceed directly towards the Ka'bah to perform your *Tawaaf*, unless it is time for *Fardh Salah*. Do perform two *Rak'at Tahiyatul-Masjid Salah*, if you plan to sit down prior to performing your *Tawaaf*.

The actions for *Tawaaf* and *Sa'ee* are covered in detail in the previous chapter. I have repeated only some of the points:

1. Perform *Tawaaf*

Uncover your right shoulder (men).

Start at the *Hajr-Aswad* (Black Stone) and continue as explained in the previous chapter.

2. Perform Two *Rak'at Salah*

Cover your right shoulder at this point (men). Perform two *Rak'at Salah* here (the *Maqaam Ibraheem* between you and the Ka'bah) if possible, otherwise anywhere else in the *Haram* is acceptable.

It is *Sunnah* to recite *Suratul-Kafirun* (109) after *Suratul-Fatiha* in the first *Rakah* and *Suratul-Ikhlas* (112) after *Suratul-Fatiha* in the second *Rakah*.

After finishing the two *Rak'at* at the *Maqaam Ibraheem* it is *Sunnah* to proceed to the Zamzam and drink your fill.

Then return to the Black Stone and kiss it if possible and say "*Allahu Akbar*".

If it is not possible, proceed to the *Sa'ee* area without gesturing or saying "*Allahu Akbar*".

3. Perform *Sa'ee*

Proceed to Safaa. When you get close to Safaa it is *Sunnah* to say:

﴾ إِنَّ ٱلصَّفَا وَٱلْمَرْوَةَ مِن شَعَآئِرِ ٱللَّهِ ﴿

"*Innassafa walmarwata min sha'aa irillah*"

(Indeed Safaa and Marwah are among the signs of Allah.)

Surah Al-Baqarah (2:158)

Followed by saying:

﴾ أَبْدَأُ بِمَا بَدَأَ اللهُ بِهِ ﴿

"*Abda'u bima bada'a Allahu bihi*"

(I begin with that which Allah has begun.)

Both of the above are only to be said at the beginning of the *Sa'ee* and not at the start of every lap. The reference for the above is narrated by Muslim.

Continue the *Sa'ee* as explained in the previous chapter.

4. Proceed to have your hair cut

For men, it is recommended not to have your head shaved at this stage, as you will be doing so on the 10th of Dhul-Hijjah. However, if the time between your *Umrah* and *Hajj* is sufficient for enough hair to grow back, then it is recommended to shave it.

It is not enough to cut a small piece of hair from one side only. You should cut from all over your head. In other words, have a haircut (men).

The women should cut no more than one inch of hair (one place only).

You will find people with scissors at Marwah, offering (for a small fee) to cut your hair. Many women opt for this, and by doing so, often expose their hair. It is better that they wait until they return to their rooms, and do it in privacy.

The *Umrah* is now complete and you are out of the state and restrictions of *Ihraam*.

You may now adopt your normal clothes again.

If you feel somewhat concerned or disappointed that you have not performed your *Umrah* "correctly", don't. Most pilgrims feel this way after their first *Umrah*.

About the other two methods

The *Qaarin* and the *Mufrid* does not perform *Umrah* upon arrival in Makkah.

Instead they perform *Tawaaful-Qudoom* (welcome *Tawaaf*) and it is recommended for the *Qaarin* to also perform *Sa'ee* for *Hajj* (this is the *Umrah* + part of *Hajj*). The *Sa'ee* is optional here for the *Mufrid*, as it is recommended to perform it with *Tawaaful-Ifadah* instead.

They may also opt to go directly to Mina on the 8th or Arafat on the 9th from the *Meqaat*.

Both the *Qaarin* and *Mufrid* remain in *Ihraam*.

Between *Umrah* and *Hajj*:

What are the best actions?:

The *Tamattu* pilgrims can now wear their normal clothes again.

Spend your time attending *Salah* at the *Haram* (remember each *Fard Salah* in the *Haram* is 100,000 times reward, compared to any other mosque, except the Prophets Mosque in Madinah (1,000) and *Al-Quds* (500) in Jerusalem).

Also keep yourself busy with recitation of the Qur'an, *Nafl Salah* and *Nafl Tawaaf*. As mentioned earlier, *Nafl Tawaaf* is one of the best forms of *Ibadah* while in Makkah.

Many people spend lots of time shopping. Try not to waste your time shopping and in idle discussions. Time is precious now.

Summary (*Umrah*) Flow Diagram:

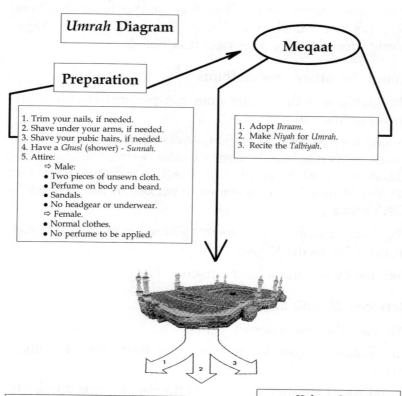

| **Umrah Diagram** | | **Meqaat** |

Preparation

1. Trim your nails, if needed.
2. Shave under your arms, if needed.
3. Shave your pubic hairs, if needed.
4. Have a *Ghusl* (shower) - *Sunnah*.
5. Attire:
   ⇨ Male:
   • Two pieces of unsewn cloth.
   • Perfume on body and beard.
   • Sandals.
   • No headgear or underwear.
   ⇨ Female.
   • Normal clothes.
   • No perfume to be applied.

1. Adopt *Ihraam*.
2. Make *Niyah* for *Umrah*.
3. Recite the *Talbiyah*.

Tawaaf:

1. Right shoulder exposed for men.
2. Start by kissing the Black Stone, if possible. Saying "Allahu-Akbar". This is done on each round, if possible.
3. Men walk briskly *(Raml)* in the first 3 rounds only.
4. Make supplication, read Qur'an, etc.
5. Touch (not kiss) the Rukn-al-Yamani corner, if possible.
6. Read *"Rabanaa Aatinaa, fi-dunya... naar"* between the Al-Yamani corner and the Black Stone.
7. Complete 7 circuits.
8. Cover the right shoulder.
9. Perform 2 *Rak'at* at the Maqaam Ibrahim.
10. Drink Zamzam to your fill.
11. Kiss the Black Stone, if possible and proceed to Safaa.

Halq or *Qasr:*

1. Shave your head or cut hair from all sides but shaving is preferable. (men).
2. Women should cut approximately 1 inch from one place only.
3. All *Ihraam* restriction now lifted.
4. Adopt normal clothes.

Sa'ee:

1. Start at Safaa and proceed towards Marwah.
2. Men walk briskly between the green lite area.
3. Make supplication, read Qur'an, etc.
4. Complete 7 laps (from Safaa to Marwah = 1 lap).
5. Finish at Marwah.

Performing multiple *Umrahs*

If we look at the practice of the Prophet (ﷺ) and of his Companions (﴿), we do not find them doing this at all. They did not try to accumulate many *Umrahs* on the same trip. Had there been any virtue in doing so, they would not have omitted that. Therefore, doing many *Umrahs* on the same trip is not recommended. One may do so only when one wants to do the *Umrah* on behalf of someone else, or in fulfilment of a pledge.

A pilgrim who has already done the *Umrah* in the *Hajj* months (Shawaal, Dhul-Qadah and Dhul-Hijjah), and is waiting in Makkah for the *Hajj* days in order to perform *Hajj* has opted for the *Tamattu* method. This involves doing the *Umrah* upon arrival (as described previously) and releasing oneself from the state of consecration, or *Ihraam*, and waiting until the time of pilgrimage. If he is to do another *Umrah*, he is required to leave Makkah and the *Haram* area, enter into *Ihraam* again, and come back to do the same duties again. This is not logical, considering that he is already in the area, which is most blessed on earth, with access to the Ka'bah.

If you consider the duties that the *Umrah* involves, you will find that they are four: entering into the state of *Ihraam*; *Tawaaf*; *Sa'ee*; and then releasing oneself from *Ihraam* by shaving one's head or cutting one's hair. So apart from the *Ihraam* (being in the state of consecration and releasing oneself from it), there are only the *Tawaaf* and *Sa'ee* left. As mentioned previously, the Prophet (ﷺ) described *Tawaaf* as a form of prayer and that it is highly recommended to perform as many voluntary *Tawaafs* as possible while in Makkah.

Sa'ee on the other hand, is a duty of *Umrah* and *Hajj* only. It cannot be done except as part of either duty. It may not be offered voluntarily for any reason. Therefore a person who goes out of Makkah in order to do a second *Umrah* is not able to do anything which he may not do while in Makkah, except for *Sa'ee*, which is not something we are encouraged to do on its own. One can easily do as many *Tawaafs* as one wishes while one is inside Makkah, without going through the rituals that a second *Umrah* involves.

Many pilgrims perform *Umrah* almost daily but sleep through the *Fard Salah* times, due to tiredness. This is a good example of misplaced priorities and a total lack of understanding of our basic Islamic duties.

Save yourself some energy and do the following instead:

Anas (اللها) narrated that the Prophet (ﷺ) said:

«مَنْ صَلَّى الْفَجْرَ في جَمَاعَةٍ ثُمَّ قَعَدَ يَذْكُرُ الله حَتَّى تَطْلُعَ الشَّمْسُ ثُمَّ صَلَّى رَكْعَتَيْنِ كانَتْ لَهُ كَأَجْرِ حَجَّةٍ وعُمْرَةٍ»

"Whoever performs Salatul-Fajr in congregation and remains in the place (Masjid) busy with Dhikr of Allah, and then performs two Rak'at after sunrise, he will get the reward equal to that of performing Hajj and Umrah."

(Tirmidhi:586)

How Great and Merciful is Allah! Do not make things difficult for yourself by exerting your energy in actions that have no basis in the *Sunnah*. This *Salah* is called *Salatul-Ishraq*. It is also referred to as *Salatul-Duha*. If you are not sure of the exact starting time of this, then you can look at the time on the digital clocks as it shows the sunrise time, or generally it is when the lights in the *Haram* are turned off in the morning.

Even though you will find many taxis outside the *Haram* shouting "Small *Umrah*" (from Tana'ym) and "Big *Umrah*" (from Jiranah), do not be tempted. Also many packages include a "big" and a "Small *Umrah*" as an incentive (to take the package).

Question: How many *Umrahs* did the Prophet (ﷺ) perform in his lifetime? (You will find the answer in chapter 14, "Revision".)

I have also witnessed some pilgrims shave their hair in strips at a time, for each time they perform an *Umrah*. See the *Hadith* in chapter 10 about not shaving only part of one's hair. (What about those fancy, partly shaven heads some of our Muslim youth have these days? I guess that's another subject.)

Please remember the *Ahadith* about following only what the Prophet (ﷺ) did or instructed us to do. Also about doing "good deeds" that have no basis in the *Sunnah*.

Aishah (ﵛ) narrated that the Prophet (ﷺ) said:

«مَنْ أَحْدثَ في أَمْرِنا هذَا ما لَيْسَ فِيهِ فَهُوَ رَدٌّ»

"If somebody innovates something which is not in harmony with the principles of our religion, that thing is rejected."

(Bukhari:2697)

Umrah after *Hajj*

There is no basis in the *Sunnah* for this practice either, i.e. people performing *Umrah* frequently after having completed *Hajj* by going to Tana'ym or Jiranah. Many people that do this will relate the story of 'Aishah (ﵛ). So anyone having the same excuse as her is entitled to do so. However, the pilgrims' preoccupation with this new *Umrah* puts everyone to inconvenience and results in further overcrowding.

If a *Mutamatti* was unable to perform her *Umrah* before *Hajj*, due to her menstruation, then she should have changed her *Niyah* to *Qiran*. An *Umrah* after *Hajj* does not "make" it *Tamattu*. See chapter 3 for more details and case examples regarding menstruation.

Do your *Hajj* rites right the first time...

YOU MAY NOT HAVE ANOTHER CHANCE!

Chapter 10

Hajj

Finally we are at the doorstep of the actual *Hajj*. As this is the most important aspect of your journey, I will be covering the *Hajj* from various angles: starting with the compulsory and obligatory actions of *Hajj*; followed by what to expect during the *Hajj* days; continuing with the issues, options and actions regarding each rite of *Hajj*, then by place and what the Prophet (ﷺ) did and instructed us to do in these places; finishing with the performance of *Hajj* on a day-by-day basis. In addition to this there are diagrams of the procedures and actions for all three methods of *Hajj*, a one-page summary of the *Hajj* days and many common questions (with answers) in chapter 14 ("Revision"). In the checklist section (chapter 15) all the actions of *Umrah* and *Hajj* are repeated item by item, which you can tick off, as you complete them. So there is something for all "tastes".

Although some points are repeated, each section builds on the previous one, allowing you to slowly formulate the actions required for the performance of *Hajj*. If you wish to keep some form of guide (book) with you in order to follow the correct steps for *Hajj*, keep in mind that I have published *Hajj* pocket guide for this purpose.

The Pillars (*Arkan*) of *Hajj*

The pillars of *Hajj* are the rites that are compulsory for the validity and completion of the *Hajj*.

1. *Ihraam* (with *Niyah*).

2. *Wuqoof-bil-Arafat* (Standing at Arafat).

3. *Tawaaful-Ifadah* (*Tawaaf* for *Hajj*).

4. *Sa'ee* for *Hajj*.

The *Wajib* (obligatory) rites of *Hajj*

The obligatory rites of *Hajj* are the rites that if omitted require the pilgrim to offer a *Fidyah* (expiation). This is a sacrifice commonly known as dumm. Many scholars rule that if these rites are omitted intentionally (premeditated) without any valid reason, then the *Hajj* is incomplete.

1. Ihraam at the *Meqaat*.
2. Being at Arafat until sunset.
3. To spend the night (or part of) in Muzdalifah.
4. To ramy (cast pebbles) at the *Jamr'at*.
5. To shave the head or cut the hair.
6. To spend the nights of *Tashreek* in Mina.
7. To perform *Tawaaful-Wadaa'*. (Menstruating women may omit this without expiation.)

1st of Dhul-Hijjah

Issue of the moon

In Saudi Arabia there is an official calendar that is used for business and other date-required events, except for the start of Ramadan, Shawaal and Dhul-Hijjah.

For the start and end of Ramadan and for the start of Dhul-Hijjah the practice is for any citizen to try and see the *Hilal* (crescent) and report it to the authorities. They will "verify" it and make the announcements on the radio and the television. If nobody sights the moon on the 29th then the month is automatically 30 days (as per the *Sunnah*).

Contrary to what many people believe, the authorities do not change the day in order to avoid or allow *Hajj* to be or not to be on a Friday, or to have *Eidul-Fitr* on a more "convenient" day.

Sometimes the official calendar coincides with the actual date, but there are many instances where it is a day or so different due to the moon sightings.

There are times when the calendar date shows that Arafat day will be on a Friday and, due to the sighting of the moon, it is on the Thursday. I have witnessed many pilgrims get extremely upset and start making accusations about the authorities being afraid of big crowds, etc.

I have also witnessed when the calendar shows that Arafat day will be on Thursday (or Saturday) and, due to the moon sighting, it falls on a Friday. In this instance the pilgrims do not say anything and believe for this year that the authorities are actually going according to the moon sighting.

In summary: My fellow Muslims, for what it's worth and without bias: The Saudi Arabian authorities do try to follow the sighting of the moon for these important dates and events.

Washing of the Holy Ka'bah

On the 1st of Dhul-Hijjah a ceremony is held in which the Holy Ka'bah is washed on behalf of the King (Custodian of the Two Holy Mosques), by the governor of Makkah Region. During this ceremony dignitaries and Ambassadors of the Muslim world are invited to have the honour of entering into the Holy Ka'bah. Apart from them some ordinary pilgrims who are present at that time are allowed inside the Holy sanctuary which is really a great honour for them.

It is normally done immediately after *Salatul-Fajr*.

The cover of the Holy Ka'bah, which is made of pure silk and embroidered with Qur'anic ayât with pure gold is changed on the day of Arafat, 9th of Dhul-Hijjah. (You will not be able to see this, as you will be on Arafat.) This cover is called *Kiswah*.

On the 10th of Dhul-Hijjah when you are back in the Haram for *Tawaaful-Ifadah*, you will notice the striking black (with gold inscriptions) new cloth on the Ka'bah. (It is sight to remember!)

Arafat Day announcement and *Hajji-Akbar*

Most years the announcement of which day Arafat will be is made about 3-4 days into the month (Dhul-Hijjah). I think it happens when no one sights the moon, and they wait to see the size of the moon. I am speculating as I could not find anyone who could explain why the delay.

Is there such a thing as *"Hajji-Akbar"*?

Many people believe that if Arafat is on a Friday, there is more reward and they call it *"Hajji-Akbar* (Big *Hajj)"*.

No, there is no such thing as *"Hajji-Akbar"*.

Yes, it is true that Arafat day was on a Friday during the Farewell Pilgrimage of the Prophet (ﷺ). However, there is no evidence from Qur'an or the *Sunnah* that there is anything special about Arafat being on a Friday, apart from the best day of the week, and the best day of the year, being on the same day.

Disappointed? Don't be! Look at it this way. If Arafat is on Thursday or Saturday, then you have the best day of the week (Friday) and the best day of the year (Arafat) to seek Allah's Mercy and Blessings.

There is more good news: "Every year is *Hajji-Akbar"*. The 10th day of Dhul-Hijja is mentioned in the Qur'an by Allah as: *"Yaumul-Hajjil-Akbar"*.

According to the scholars this day is called the greatest day, owing to the number of rites to be performed on this day (i.e. stoning, sacrifice, *Halq* or *Qasr*, *Tawaaful-Ifadah* and *Sa'ee* for *Hajj*).

$$\text{﴿وَأَذَٰنٌ مِّنَ ٱللَّهِ وَرَسُولِهِۦ إِلَى ٱلنَّاسِ يَوْمَ ٱلْحَجِّ ٱلْأَكْبَرِ أَنَّ ٱللَّهَ بَرِىٓءٌ مِّنَ ٱلْمُشْرِكِينَ وَرَسُولُهُۥ﴾}$$

"And a declaration from Allah and His Messenger to mankind on the greatest day (the 10th of Dhul-Hijjah) that Allah is free from (all) obligations to the Mushrikin and so is His Messenger..."

Surah At-Taubah (9:3)

What to Expect

Expect the Unexpected! Experience has taught me that the best of plans and preparation can go wrong at the last moment due to circumstances that will be totally beyond your control. Leave it all up to Allah...

Crowds

The official statistics show that in 1983 a record number of pilgrims performed *Hajj*, which was in excess of 3 million. There are on average 2 million people performing *Hajj* each year.

If *Hajj* (Arafat day) is on a Friday, this number increases dramatically and can reach 2.5 to 2.8 million people. (These numbers include the local residents who are performing *Hajj*.)

It is unlikely that the number of pilgrims will go much higher than this as the Saudi authorities have implemented a quota system to regulate the number of pilgrims from the various countries. Since 1999 a new rule was implemented to restrict all local residents as well to once every 5 years.

Believe me, it is only 2 million people or less, even though it may look and feel like 10 million.

You have to be patient and be mentally prepared. Remember that all these people are here for the same reason you are. You cannot avoid it!

To give you an idea of the number of people in Makkah by the last week of *Hajj*: during the *Hajj* of 1420, on the night of the 7th Dhul-Hijjah, we prayed *Salatul-'Eshaa* in the street about 2km away from the *Haram* and the lines of people stretched all the way.

Food

Most packages provide food for the *Hajj* days. If it was not included in your original package then you may have to pay extra for it. It cost about SR150 per person for the five days.

Over the last few years some entrepreneurs came up with the idea of 'special services' in Mina which cost over SR500 extra per pilgrim. You not only get buffet dinners, but also a bed (or thicker mattress). Skip it, it is not worth it!

Even though there are many arguments about the quality and timing of the food, I strongly recommend you take at least one for every two people. You may wish to check with the agent providing the food whether it will be pre-packed meals or meals cooked in big pots and served by plate directly from the pot. If it is pre-packed meals, then be sure that you will be eating cold food for the next 5 days.

Be prepared to have lunch at 3pm, dinner at 11pm etc. So as I said before, lunch is when the food arrives.

There are no "real" food shops in Arafat and Muzdalifah. If you did not opt to take the food, make sure you have enough eatables for Arafat and Muzdalifah. You will be very hungry in Muzdalifah, so take something for late dinner as well as breakfast.

Although there are many shops in Mina to buy food from, keep some dry biscuits, dates, water and fruit with you. On one occasion there was a cholera outbreak in Mina, so the pilgrims were advised not to buy any food from the streets.

The price of everything doubles in Mina. Officially it is not supposed to, but be prepared to pay double for drinks and tea, and also double the normal price for most fruit.

Always keep a flask of water with you and drink plenty of liquids to avoid dehydration. Also only eat fruit that requires it to be peeled, such as oranges and bananas.

Some of the bus journeys can be very long, so the water and biscuits come in handy. A small packet of sweets is also useful to give you some glucose.

Avoid getting into any arguments in Mina and Arafat about the food.

The Days of *Hajj*

Day No:	Date (Dhul-Hijjah):	Day known as:	Meaning:
1	8th	*Yaumut-Tarweya*	Day of Quenching*
2	9th	*Wuqoof-bil-Arafat*	Standing at Arafat
3	10th	*Yaumun-Nahr; Yaumul-Eid; Yaumul-Hajjil-Akbar*	Day of Sacrifice; Day of Eid *(Eidul-Adha)*; Greatest day of *Hajj*
4, 5 & 6	11th, 12th & 13th	*Ayaamut-Tashreek*	Days of drying of the meat**

* Day of Quenching: This was the day all the animals (used during *Hajj*) would be given the chance to quench their thirst.

** As there was plenty of meat and no refrigerators at that time, the method of drying the meat in the sun was used, to preserve it from going bad.

Packages vary as to the days they spend in the various places.

- 6 days - 8th (Mina) until the 13th (Mina)
- 5 days - 8th (Mina) until the 12th (Mina)
- 5 days - 9th (Arafat) until the 13th (Mina)
- 4 days - 9th (Arafat) until the 12th (Mina)

The 5-day package (8th to 12th) is the most common.

All of these packages are acceptable and fulfil the requirements of *Hajj*.

The 6 days are as the Prophet (ﷺ) performed *Hajj*.

Transportation

Most of the pilgrims are transported by bus from one place to another during the *Hajj* days. These are the government appointed buses. Some groups have private buses.

As mentioned before, a system of bus rotation is being used. Meaning for every 100 people, instead of using two buses, the same bus makes two trips. This works fine if the bus does not get stuck in traffic. Either way, it means your wait for the bus is longer. This method may change as they are experimenting to try and find the best method of traffic control. During the Hajj of 2004 and 2006 (1426) I experienced the bus rotation system and it seemed to work well if your camp was located close to the edge (near Muzdalifah) of Mina. However for those camps in the middle and closer to the *Jamrah*, the wait was still agonisingly long.

The various trips by bus can be very short (30 minutes) or very long (up to 12 hours) for the same distance, depending on the traffic, your location and the time you leave. Be patient as there are many delays with the buses.

They also try to restrict the size of cars (only 8-seaters and above are allowed) to enter the *Hajj* areas during these days. Even though there is a restriction you still find many smaller cars and taxis transporting pilgrims.

The transport cost is included in your package, unless you choose to take a taxi.

The transport to and from Makkah on the 10th (to perform *Tawaaful-Ifadah*) is normally at your own cost.

So yes, transportation during the *Hajj* days is the biggest nightmare.

Walking

There are special roads for the walking pilgrims. The part from Mina to Makkah is shaded almost all the way, the end part being through a 1.5km tunnel.

By foot is always one of the best modes of transport. There are many pilgrims who walk to Arafat and back. The following table is an illustration of the time it may take to walk, from my experience. This is walking at a normal calm pace.

Location:	Distance:	Approximate time:
Arafat to Muzdalifah:	about 9km (6 miles)	2.5 hours
Muzdalifah to Mina (*Jamr'at*):	about 6km (4 miles)	2 Hours (due to crowds)
Mina (*Jamr'at*) to Makkah (*Haram*):	about 8km (5 miles)	2 hours
Makkah to Arafat	about 22km (14 miles)	5 hours

If you have women, children, elderly pilgrims or luggage with you, then the walking journey may take much longer.

Many pilgrims walk. Some by choice and many not by choice. So be prepared to walk. Therefore you need to conserve your energy and health in the days leading up to *Hajj*.

To give you an idea, during the *Hajj* of 1420, we had no plans of walking, yet we ended up walking from Muzdalifah to Mina, Mina to Makkah twice and Makkah to Mina once. This was due to the traffic congestion and the bus rotation has one drawback- the bus cannot stay with you in Muzdalifah as it has to go back to Arafat to get the rest of the group.

Many pilgrims choose to walk all the way in the hot sun, even though they are able to go by bus, as they believe that there is more reward in doing so. This is not so, as Allah does not wish to make things difficult for you.

There are times when your bus may break down and you are forced to walk. If this happens, leave your luggage on the bus if possible, and take only water and some dry food items with you. Do not forget your umbrella.

For this reason it is very important to have a comfortable pair of slippers. Do not buy a new pair of slippers for *Hajj* just prior to the *Hajj* days. Instead, use slippers that your feet are already used to.

Most years we walk from Mina to Makkah on the last day, as it takes only about 2 hours. The bus journey on this day can be extremely long. In 2004 it took 8 to 10 hours to get to Makkah by bus. You better believe it! This is why I was so impressed with Aziziah option during 2006, as it took us no time at all to get back to the base.

Accommodation

In Arafat and Mina the pilgrims are divided into groups (by country) and their locations are pre-allocated.

The streets and camps are numbered. So remember your location by noting down the number of your camp.

In Mina most of the accommodation use to be in small tents. Since the major fire in Mina during the *Hajj* of 1417, the tents have been replaced with fire-proof tents. By 1420 (2000), all the tents in Mina have been replaced. The new tents have air-conditioning, lights, electric plugs, etc., and are very comfortable.

In Arafat the accommodation is normally a big, wide open tent. Some tents have fans or desert coolers (device that uses water and air to blow cool air), and other tents have nothing.

The men and women are normally in separate tents in Arafat and Mina.

Once again it depends on your *Hajj* package, which determines what type of accommodation and food you will receive.

Arafat day and the days in Mina are normally very hot, so you will need some sort of cooling device. As I mentioned in the beginning of this book, check all these things with your agent. Knowing what you're getting will help reduce any anxieties and prevent arguments during *Hajj*.

In Muzdalifah, well...wait and see. Normally there is no accommodation provided for the night in Muzdalifah.

Sleeping

What about sleeping arrangements? Well what can I say other

than: "You will never again complain about your mattress at home."

You will notice many pilgrims sleeping and staying in the streets, and under the bridges and in the tunnels. The more amazing ones are the ones that stay on top of the mountains in Mina.

Some of the tents in Mina provide some carpet, but this is where your inflatable air mattress takes on a new meaning.

If you do not have a mattress, then the straw *Hajji* mat is a must.

The night sleep in Muzdalifah is one of the highlights of the trip. Your bed is the pavement, the street or just anywhere where you can find a place. Believe me, you will sleep, even with all the lights, noise, traffic and smells. Many pilgrims felt that they will not be able to sleep, but within minutes they would be fast asleep like babies... A night to remember!

Some tips

If you were unhappy with your accommodation in Makkah, your tent in Mina will certainly make you appreciate it. If you were unhappy with your accommodation in Mina, the night stay in Muzdalifah will certainly make you appreciate it. If you were unhappy with the air-conditioner in Mina or Makkah, the day in your big tent in Arafat will most certainly make you think again. There is a lesson in all of this!

Assuming that you have a choice, do not choose a tent near the toilets or any cooking area.

Also, areas near the entrances are always busy. Try to choose a tent near the middle or back of the camp

If you are accommodated in a big tent in Mina, choose a sleeping area closer to the rear of the tent. Also try to find a spot in the back or side that is 'away' from *Qiblah*, so that your spot is not in the front row, but the back row for *Salah*. The front and middle areas are normally used for eating, *Salah* and lectures, which mean you will constantly have to move your bags.

There tend to be "fights" for positions and space in the tents in Mina. So, as soon as you enter the tent for the first time, throw open your mat on the selected area and sit or lay down on it. Ignore the arguments around you and just "stick" to your spot. However, don't take a big space.

If you have your spouse with you on *Hajj*, you may wish to choose the corner of the tent where you can be on the one side and your partner on the other side of the tent's partition. This facilitates for easy communication and easier sharing of food.

In Arafat, it is normally a large canopy-type tent. Also try to choose a quiet position that will allow you some privacy. I found the position between the air-conditioned units a perfect place to put a mat down and sit. This also provides a backrest. If there are no units, the back of the tent is normally more private. Once again see which way is *Qiblah* and choose the back sides.

Be early and avoid the crowds for *Wudu* and for taking a shower, especially in the morning for *Fajr*. The queues can get very long at the bathrooms and tempers start fraying. Try to avoid the bathrooms about 20 minutes before *Salah* or immediately after a meal.

Set your alarm (especially for *Fajr*) at least one hour earlier to avoid the rush at the bathrooms in the morning. Also use the showers and bathrooms at times, when everybody is sleeping, eating or listening to a lecture.

Pack your small bag in a way that you can possibly use it as a pillow. During the winter months, Muzdalifah can be very cold. Though it is only one night, a small blanket or sleeping bag is very useful.

The days of *Hajj* are certainly an education for many, in many ways!

The Boundaries

The rites of *Hajj* clearly stipulate the place and time where one should be during the days of *Hajj*. It is therefore of the utmost importance that you are within the specified boundaries.

The boundary of each area is clearly marked by huge signposts. The signs indicate the start and end of each area (i.e. Arafat begins here; Mina ends here).

The signposts are as big as advertising boards, and are in different colours for each location (Mina = green; Muzdalifah = purple; Arafat = yellow).

For the general layout of the boundaries, see the *Hajj* itinerary diagram later in this chapter.

Ensure that you are in the boundaries; Arafat on the 9th, Muzdalifah after that, Mina on the 10th, 11th, 12th and possibly the 13th.

There are many pilgrims and groups who are wrongly located outside these boundaries, so be aware.

I have seen pilgrims sit underneath the signpost and still set up camp on the wrong side.

Facilities – Mina / Muzdalifah / Arafat

Mosques

In Mina there are a few mosques. One important mosque is "Masjidul-Khaif". It is located near the *Jamr'at* area, and it is reported that at least 70 Prophets performed *Salah* here.

"Masjid Namira" is the only mosque in Arafat. Part of this mosque is outside the boundaries of Arafat.

The location of the only mosque in Muzdalifah, known as ''*Mash'ar-il-Haram*'', used to be a small mountain.

Hospitals

There are medical facilities (including mobile clinics) available in Mina and Arafat.

In Mina there is a hospital located opposite "Masjidul-Khaif" and another one near the old slaughter house.

There is a big hospital in Arafat, located very close to the mountain *(Jabal-Rahmah)*.

Wudu and Toilets

There are plenty of *Wudu* and public toilet facilities in Mina, Arafat and Muzdalifah.

The *Wudu* places are normally located right next to the toilets.

All the camps in Mina have toilet facilities. Individual camps in Arafat also provide toilets apart from the public ones.

Innumerable toilets have been built all over the holy places and there used to be hundreds of maintenance staff who take care of the cleaning responsibility during the Hajj days and they are cleaned and maintained 24 hours.

All toilets have been equipped with shower facilities with running water available for 24 hors to take a bath any time. You will not face scarcity of water.

The toilets in all the places are extremely crowded, so try to be patient.

In most cases there is at least one upright toilet in each row of toilets.

Even though there are plenty of toilet facilities in Muzdalifah, they are definitely not enough. The queues are very long and it sometimes takes much time to get your turn.

I suggest you minimise your food intake in Arafat, to avoid the need for the toilet in Muzdalifah. If you only wish to urinate, then sometimes you are forced to do so in the bushes or somewhere on the mountain.

This is one more reason why you should use the toilets in Arafat before you leave.

Telephones

There are public telephones available in Arafat and Mina. I have not seen any in Muzdalifah.

The phone cards are easily available in different denominations, starting from SR10, SR20, SR30, SR50, SR100 and above. The phone service is excellent. All of the public phones are card phones.

"Reverse Charge" calls facilities are not available.

The queues can be long, so as with the toilets, use the phones at less busy times (before *Salah*, during meal times, etc.).

Be prepared to share your telephone conversation with the rest of the queue, as the person behind you, more than likely will be standing almost on top of you, waiting for you to finish. A way around this is to either bend down and talk or stand behind the phone booth. This means you may have to climb through the barrier. This also helps to minimise the noise.

Get yourself a mobile (cell) phone card instead. Minimum charge is SR100.

Other

There is a mortuary next to the mosque in Mina. (If you "lose" somebody for a long period of time, one of the places to look is here.)

The sacrificial slaughter houses are located at the end of the walking tunnel, near Muzdalifah.

The SAPTCO bus service (to go to Makkah and back) is located in Mina about 200 metres (218 yards) from the *Jamr'at* bridge, at the big *Jamrah* side.

There are also LOST pilgrim offices in all the locations.

The *Jamr'at* in Mina

The three stone structures in Mina, known as the *Jamr'at*, are the symbols of the three places where *Shaytaan* tried to make

Prophet Ibraheem (عليه السلام) change his mind about sacrificing his son, Ismail (عليه السلام).

The stone structures are not the actual *Shaytaan*. You are not casting stones at *Shaytaan* per se. It is only a symbolic act and you should not get over excited as many pilgrims do. Some pilgrims throw shoes and umbrellas at the *Jamr'at*. This is wrong and should be avoided.

The *Jamr'at* are located at the end (nearest to Makkah) of Mina. There are three of them: the big *Jamrah* (*Aqaba*); the middle or medium *Jamrah* (*Wusta*); and the small *Jamrah* (*Sughrah*).

There is a bridge built over the top of the *Jamr'at*, so one can either throw from the top or from the bottom (underneath the bridge). By the time you go, there may be more than one top level. There has been many suggestions and proposals over the years, and it seems that they have decided to act on one suggestion, and that is to make more than two levels. The idea is to have up to seven levels, which means less poeple in each area at any given time. They are also planning new roads and tunnels leading to the *Jam'rat*. In 2005 the actual *Jam'rat* structures were rebuilt. Instead of a tall skinny structure, each one was built into a huge wall structure. This worked great as pelting was so much easier (as the target was much bigger). Hence I had to remove the pictures and diagrams from this edition, because no one seems to know exactly what the end result will be.

The bridge is very wide and is policed at the entrance to avoid over crowding on the top. There are also police on the bridge to stop pilgrims from walking in the opposite direction.

One should take special care at the *Jamr'at* as there are many incidents where pilgrims have been hurt due to the crowd and the general misbehaviour of some pilgrims. Even with the new wall structure, I found that my pelting suggestions (see later in this chapter) still apply.

Pilgrims have died at the *Jamr'at*. Unfortunately this seems to have become a yearly tragedy. Even in 2006 (1426) with the new wall structure, there was yet again a stampede where many pilgrims died. There are many reasons for this and one of them is the behaviour of the pilgrims. On the last day some pilgrims came to *Jam'rat* place with their huge baggage in their hands with the idea in mind that as soon as they finish pelting they would proceed to their respective places. This caused a nuisance among the heavy crowd and this was, people say, one of the reasons of 2006's stampede in Mina.

Do not sit under the bridges or in the walkways in Mina. These are crowded enough as it is, and people sitting in these places cause a great deal of problems for the efficient flow of people.

Many pilgrims get lost at the *Jamr'at* area. Try and assist pilgrims who are lost. Remember you do not have to know where they need to go, just comfort them and take them to the police who can assist them further. Keep your identification card with you at all times, and fasten it tightly to your clothes as it may get lost in the pushing and shoving at the *Jamr'at*.

I often joke at my lectures that it seems many pilgrims did not fulfil the one obligation to be eligible for *Hajj*, and that is to be of sound mind. You will agree with me when you return from the *Jamr'at*.

Hajj – by Major Rites

Following are the major rites the pilgrim will perform. The day of Arafat is covered later in the chapter.

Ramy (casting of pebbles)

You need to collect seven pebbles for each *Jamrah* for each day (i.e. on the 10th you need 7 only; on the 11th, 12th and 13th you need 21 for each day).

Many pilgrims insist on collecting the pebbles in Muzdalifah and put themselves through a great deal of hardship during the night to do this. The pebbles can be collected in Muzdalifah or Mina. It is reported that the Prophet (ﷺ)

collected the pebbles on his way to the *Jamr'at*. There are narrations that specifically say, in Mina (and not in Muzdalifah). So collect it where it is convenient for you.

There is no need to wash the pebbles.

The size of the pebbles

Jabir bin Abdullah (ﷺ) reported:

«رَأَيْتُ النَّبِيَّ ﷺ رَمَى الْجَمْرَةَ بِمِثْلِ حَصَى الْخَذْفِ»

"I saw the Prophet (ﷺ) throwing stones (at Jamrah Al-Aqaba), like pelting of small pebbles."

(Muslim:1299)

The timing

Jabir bin Abdullah (ﷺ) reported:

«رَمَىٰ رَسُولُ اللهِ ﷺ الْجَمْرَةَ يَوْمَ النَّحْرِ ضُحًى، وَأَمَّا بَعْدُ، فَإِذَا زَالَتِ الشَّمْسُ»

"That the Prophet (ﷺ) flung pebbles at the Jamr'at on the day of Nahr after sunrise, and after that (i.e. on the 11th, 12th and 13th of Dhul-Hijjah) when the sun had declined."

(Muslim:1299)

Date	Time:	Small	Middle	Big	Pebbles:	Approx. Size:
10th	from after sunrise	No	No	Yes	7	
11th	from after *Zawaal**	Yes	Yes	Yes	21 (3 x 7)	
12th	from after *Zawaal**	Yes	Yes	Yes	21 (3 x 7)	
13th	from after *Zawaal**	Yes	Yes	Yes	21 (3 x 7)	

**Zawaal* = Midday, when the sun is at its zenith.

The preceding table shows the starting time as per the *Sunnah*. According to the scholars the preferred end time is generally before *Maghrib*. However, due to the massive crowds, it is acceptable for the women, weak and elderly to cast even until late at night, as the Prophet (ﷺ) did not specify an end time.

Even on the 10th, it is acceptable to stone in the afternoon or evening. Most of the stampedes happen on this day due to the incorrect understanding that the stoning must be done before midday.

Many pilgrims stone in the morning due to the crowds. This is incorrect as the start time is only after *Zawaal* and one cannot perform any act of *Ibadah* ahead of its prescribed time.

Many pilgrims also insist that on the 13th it is acceptable to stone in the morning. As per the *Hadith*, it is clear that it is after *Zawaal* (the decline of the sun) on all three days. (If you are staying for three days (until the 13th), what is the sudden rush to throw in the morning?)

On the 10th the pilgrims only stone the big *Jamrah*. There is a difference of opinion among the scholars about the stoning for the women and elderly that left Muzdalifah after moonset. Some say they can throw as soon as they reach Mina, whereas some say they have to wait until after sunrise. Nonetheless, it may be better to wait as you will still miss the crowd as they will only leave Muzdalifah at the time you will be throwing.

The actual stoning of the *Jamr'at*

The stoning order on the 11th, 12th and the 13th is to start from the small *Jamrah* and to finish at the big one. There is no special *Niyah*.

The pilgrim casts seven pebbles, one at a time, saying:

اللهُ اكْبَرُ

"Allahu Akbar."

(Allah is the Greatest.)

Move towards the next *Jamrah* and repeat the process.

The pilgrim should ensure that the pebble either hits the target or falls in the encircled area; otherwise it has to be redone. (This is when those extra pebbles become a necessity.)

You should not reuse any pebble that has already been cast into the circled area.

Supplication

It is *Sunnah* to face *Qiblah* after throwing at the small and middle *Jamr'at* and to make supplication. Move away from the *Jamrah* itself and stand away from the crowd.

It is reported that the Prophet (ﷺ) stood and supplicated here for a very long time.

There is no supplication after throwing at the big *Jamrah*.

Deputising

You may deputise someone to cast the pebbles for you.

This is only valid if you are old, sick, pregnant or very weak.

You cannot ask or pay someone else because you are afraid of the crowds. Able women should perform the *Ramy* themselves. They should choose a less crowded time and avoid going to the *Jamr'at* by themselves (without a *Mahram*).

If you are stoning on behalf of someone else, the method is as follows:

- First cast (stone) your seven pebbles at the *Jamrah*, one at a time;

- Follow this by casting seven pebbles on behalf of the other person, one at a time.

- Move towards the next *Jamrah* and repeat the process.

- There is no special *Niyah*, and you should say *"Allahu Akbar"* as you throw each stone (pebble).

Tips

I am leaving these tips here as they may still apply, even with the new layout at the *Jamr'at*.

In my experience and especially now that the bridge is widened and policed, throwing from the top is definitely easier.

The best times to stone: Definitely the busiest time is immediately after midday. Just before and immediately after *Salatul-'Asr* seems to be when the crowds are less. Also at night it is less crowded. This applies for the 11th and 12th. On the 13th anytime after about 1.30pm is okay. On all 3 days, avoid the time immediately after *Zawaal*, if you have women or children with you. On the 10th (first day of stoning), it is better to wait until after *Zuhr*.

If one of the days of *Tashreek* is on a Friday, then the best time to throw is after *Zuhr*, as many pilgrims tend to go to Makkah for *Jumuah*. The busiest time on this day is before and after *'Asr*, as the pilgrims return from Makkah.

It is only on the 10th that you are in *Ihraam* when throwing at the big *Jamrah*. After that you are out of *Ihraam*; therefore it is better to wear shoes (runners, joggers, tennis shoes), as this will give you better balance and grip in the crowds.

After you have cast your pebbles, and you turn around to come out, lower your head to avoid being hit by a pebble in your face.

It is *Sunnah* to make supplication after the stoning of the small and middle *Jamr'at*. Do not stand in the middle of the crowd. Move to a less crowded space, face *Qiblah* and make supplication.

Number of pebbles: If you are staying until the 13th you need a total of 7+21+21+21=70 pebbles, and if you are staying only until the 12th, you need a total of 7+21+21=49.

You may collect them all at once or on a daily basis. Remember you cannot reuse any pebble that has already been cast. I suggest you collect a few extra pebbles in case you drop some or "miss the target".

If you do not have a stone bag to keep the pebbles in, you can use a small empty drinking water bottle as a means of storage.

Take your 21 pebbles and keep them in your pocket or in a small packet. When you get near the *Jamrah*, take seven only and keep these in your left hand. Take one at a time with your right hand and throw it at the *Jamrah*. This way you need not keep count as you are throwing. When your left hand is empty, you should have thrown seven. If you missed or dropped some, remove the exact number from your pocket. Alternatively you can keep all your pebbles in your hand and count as you throw. However, if somebody knocks your hand you may lose all your pebbles. It is almost impossible to bend and pick up pebbles while you are near the *Jamrah*.

If you are caught in a crowd and your shoe or slipper comes off, avoid bending down to pick it up as you may fall over and get crushed.

Try to go as close as possible to rim of the *Jamrah*, as it easier to pelt from there. Always keep the women behind you as you "go in", and move them in front of you when they are ready to pelt.

On the top when it is very busy, walk past the crowd and enter from the furthest side of the wall. This works for all three *Jamr'at*.

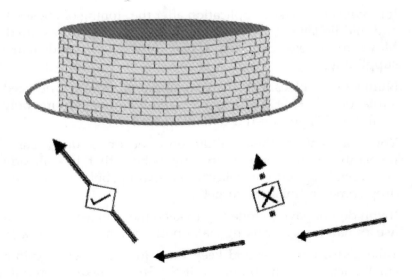

On the bottom, look which end of the wall has the least amount of people (as people walk in both directions). Whatever shape it is, there are always less people on the opposite side from where the crowd enters.

Do not go in a big group. Smaller groups of 4 people are much easier. If you are 4 (2 males and 2 females), do the following: make a chain; with one male in front; followed by a female holding him from the back; the other female then holding onto her from the back followed by her *Mahram* protecting her from the back. Once you reach the rim, move the females to the front while you stand behind them. Only exit once all of you have pelted. Once completed, form the same chain and exit lowering your head.

Do not try to break or pass through any "human-chains", instead you give way.

The Sacrifice

See chapter 6 for more details about the sacrifices (and remember HUF).

The sacrifice (*Hady*) is compulsory for the pilgrims performing *Hajj Tamattu* and *Hajj Qiran*.

The pilgrims may eat from the *Hady* meat.

A sacrifice (*Fidyah*) is also obligatory on a pilgrim:

➢ Who failed to perform a *Wajib* (obligatory) act of *Hajj*, such as not stoning the *Jamr'at*, or not adopting *Ihraam* at the *Meqaat* etc. (see the *Wajib* acts of *Hajj* in chapter 9).

➢ Who did something prohibited, while in the state of *Ihraam*, such as using perfume or cutting the hair, etc.

➢ Who transgressed the sanctity of the *Haram* area, such as hunting an animal or cutting a tree within its boundaries.

➢ For those with an excuse, such as having to shave his head due to some illness in his scalp.

All the meat of the *Fidyah* is to be distributed among the poor in the Makkah area.

About the animals

The sacrificial animals can be: camels; cattle, sheep or goats.

The pilgrim can either sacrifice a sheep or a goat or share with six other pilgrims (total of 7) in a cow or a camel.

The age and health of the animal are important:

- ○ a camel should be at least five years old;
- ○ a cow should be at least two years old;
- ○ a goat should be at least one-year-old;
- ○ a sheep should be at least six months old (some say one year);
- ○ the animal must be free of defects as it is not acceptable if it is one eyed, or lame, or thin.

The proper time for slaughtering the *Hady* is on the 10th of Dhul-Hijjah and the three days after that which are called *Ayaamut-Tashreek* (which means to cut meat into strips for drying).

The proper time for slaughtering the *Udhiyah* is on the 10th of Dhul-Hijjah.

The *Fidyah* can be done as required (after the 10th) or even before if the transgression was in relation to the *Umrah*.

Place of slaughtering

The proper place for slaughtering the *Hady* is in either, Mina, Muzdalifah or Makkah.

The Prophet (ﷺ) *said*:

«نَحَرْتُ هَا هُنَا، ومِنَّى كُلُّهَا مَنْحَرٌ»

"I slaughtered here, but the whole of Mina is a place of sacrifice."

(Muslim:1218)

Performing the *Hady* and *Fidyah* in your home country is not valid.

The sacrifice MUST be performed in the Mina/Makkah/Muzdalifah area and the claim that there are many poor people in your home country, hence the decision to slaughter there, is not valid according the *Sunnah*. *Udhiyah* can be done in your home country.

«وَفِطْرُكُمْ يَوْمَ تُفْطِرُونَ وَأَضْحَاكُمْ يَوْمَ تُضَحُّونَ وَكُلُّ عَرَفَةَ مَوْقِفٌ وَكُلُّ مِنَّى مَنْحَرٌ، وَكُلُّ فِجَاجِ مَكَّةَ مَنْحَرٌ وَكُلُّ جَمْعٍ مَوْقِفٌ»

The festival of sacrifice (Eidul-Adha) is on the day when you sacrifice. All of Arafat is the place of staying, and all of Mina is the place of sacrifice, and all the places within the limits of the sacred Makkah are the place of sacrifice, and all of Muzdalifah is the place of staying.

(Abu Dawud:2324)

While slaughtering the animal you should say:

﴿بِسْمِ اللهِ وَاللهُ أَكْبَرُ﴾

"Bismillahi-wallahu-akbar"
(In the Name of Allah, Allah is the Greatest.)

At the time of the *Eid* sacrifice the Prophet (ﷺ) supplicated:

(اللَّهُمَّ تَقَبَّلْ مِنْ مُحَمَّدٍ وَآلِ محمَّدٍ وَمِنْ أُمَّةِ محمَّدٍ)

"Allahuma takabal min Muhammadin wa aali Muhammadin wamin ummati Muhammadin."

(O Allah, accept this sacrifice on behalf of Muhammad, the family of Muhammad and the followers of Muhammad.)

(Muslim:1967)

As illustrated by the above method, one should ask Allah to accept the sacrifice, and one should also name the person on whose behalf the sacrifice is made.

There are very good programmes in place for the slaughtering of the animals and the distribution of the meat.

Tons and tons of meat are frozen immediately and flown to the poorer Muslim countries for distribution.

A huge new slaughter house was opened in Mina during the *Hajj* of 1420 with the capacity to slaughter more than 600,000 animals in 4 days.

Many pilgrims insist on doing their own sacrifice. The authorities will not allow everybody to enter. However, they do allow a delegate for about every 20 people or so, to do the slaughtering.

A word of caution: this area is not for the timid or sometimes not even the brave can handle the sight. Remember that they are slaughtering close to 1 million animals.

Also if you do it yourself via a private farmer, you are expected to take the animal with you. Picture yourself: nice clean outfit with a blood-stained sheep hanging over your shoulder walking around Mina trying to find your camp or somebody to give the dead animal to. I have seen this happening.

If you choose to leave the animal at the farm, be aware that the meat may not reach its intended recipients. After the *Hajj* of 1420, the authorities found hundreds of slaughtered animals dumped, as the farmers could not cope with the sheer numbers.

So, if you are not too fussed and believe in the procedures set up by the authorities in Saudi Arabia then leave it to them. You can enjoy the meal instead.

Questions

How many camels did the Prophet (ﷺ) offer for sacrifice during his farewell pilgrimage?

How many did he slaughter by his own hand and what is the significance of this number?

Who did the rest of the slaughtering for him?

Answers: You can find the answers in chapter 14 ("Revision").

Substitute for sacrifice

Fasting is only permitted if the pilgrim cannot afford the sacrifice (*Hady*).

﴿فَمَن لَّمْ يَجِدْ فَصِيَامُ ثَلَاثَةِ أَيَّامٍ فِي الْحَجِّ وَسَبْعَةٍ إِذَا رَجَعْتُمْ تِلْكَ عَشَرَةٌ كَامِلَةٌ﴾

"...But if someone cannot afford a sacrifice, he can fast three days during Hajj and seven days after returning home. That is ten days in all."

Surah Al-Baqarah (2:196)

It is recommended to fast the 3 days before the 8th of Dhul-Hijjah if possible, as the Prophet (ﷺ) indicated that the days of *Tashreek* are for eating (celebrating). However if these (*Tashreek*) are the only days you are able to fast then you should do so.

Do not forget to fast the rest of the days (7) upon your return home.

Many pilgrims opt to fast as they claim that they cannot afford it, but the amount of shopping they do before and after *Hajj* totally contradicts their claim. You are only fooling yourself!

Cutting of your Hair

After slaughtering the sacrificial animals the Prophet (ﷺ) had his head shaved. Then he supplicated to Allah three times to forgive those who had their heads shaved (*Halq*) and once for those who had their hair cut short (*Qasr*).

Ibn Umar (﷽) reported that the Prophet (﷽) said:

«رَحِمَ اللهُ الْمُحَلِّقِينَ» قَالُوا: وَالْمُقَصِّرِينَ؟ يَا رَسُولَ اللهِ! قَالَ:
«رَحِمَ اللهُ الْمُحَلِّقِينَ» قَالُوا: وَالْمُقَصِّرِينَ؟ يَا رَسُولَ اللهِ! قَالَ:
«رَحِمَ اللهُ الْمُحَلِّقِينَ» قَالُوا: وَالْمُقَصِّرِينَ؟ يَا رَسُولَ اللهِ! قَالَ:
«وَالْمُقَصِّرِينَ»

"May Allah have mercy upon those who had their heads shaved.' They said: 'Messenger of Allah, what about those who had their hair clipped?' He said: 'May Allah have mercy upon those who had their heads shaved.' They said: 'Messenger of Allah, what about those who had their hair clipped?' He said: 'May Allah have mercy upon those who had their heads shaved.' They said: 'Messenger of Allah, what about those who had their hair clipped?' He said: '(Oh Allah, have mercy upon) those who had their hair clipped'."

(Muslim:1301)

Shaving is referred to as *Halq* and cutting as *Qasr* (or *Taqseer*).

Women cut only about one inch of hair from one place only.

For those pilgrims who are in Makkah long before the *Hajj* days and plan to shave their head, keep the following in mind. This also applies at anytime you shave your head (after *Umrah* or *Hajj*).

Do not shave only parts of it

«عَنِ ابنِ عُمَرَ: أَنَّ رَسُولَ اللهِ ﷺ نَهَى عَنِ القَزَعِ»

"Ibn Umar (﷽) said that the Prophet (﷽) has forbidden shaving only a part of the head and leaving unshaved another part."

(Bukhari & Muslim: 5921:2120)

Start from the right side

«عَنْ أَنَسِ بْنِ مَالِكِ أَنَّ رَسُولَ اللهِ ﷺ أَتَى مِنًى، فَأَتَى الْجَمْرَةَ
فَرَمَاهَا، ثُمَّ أَتَى مَنْزِلَهُ بِمِنًى وَنَحَرَ، ثُمَّ قَالَ لِلْحَلَّاقِ : «خُذْ»
وَأَشَارَ إِلَى جَانِبِهِ الْأَيْمَنِ، ثُمَّ الْأَيْسَرِ، ثُمَّ جَعَلَ يُعْطِيهِ النَّاسَ»

"Anas bin Malik (ﷺ) reported that the Prophet (ﷺ) came to Mina; he went to the Jamrah and threw the pebbles at it, after which he went to his lodging in Mina, and sacrificed the animal. He then called for a barber and, turning his right side to him, let him shave it; after which he turned his left side. He then gave (his hair) to the people."

(Muslim:1305:323)

There are a group of barbers when you exit from the bridge at *Jamrah Aqaba*. These are similar to the ones outside Marwah in Makkah. The prices are also the same, 5 to 10 riyals to shave your head and about 10 to 15 riyals for a haircut. In 2006 (1426), all foreign barbers were replaced with locals, so we paid 35 riyals and more for a head shave.

There is also a big group of barbers right opposite the slaughtering houses.

Alternatively you may choose one of the makeshift barbers you find on and under the bridge. You will save some money, but you may have a few scars on your head as these guys use blades to scrape (not shave) your head. Some of them do a reasonable job, but I suggest you give it a miss. This is also not very hygienic and open to transmission of infections.

You may also choose to wait until you get to Makkah.

If you have thick hair, another option is to use a beard shaver and set it to number zero, and get a fellow pilgrim to cut your hair (starting on the right side), and then use the blades to do the rest. To fulfill the duty of *Halq*, one must shave. Brush cut only does not suffice!

Tawaaful-Ifadah and *Sa'ee* for *Hajj*

Also known as *Tawaafuz-Ziyarah* or *Tawaaful-Hajj*:

This *Tawaaf* is a pillar of *Hajj* (just as *Arafat* is) and CANNOT be omitted by any pilgrim. Women in their menses can delay this *Tawaaf* but must not omit it as they will remain "illegal" to their husbands until such time as it is performed. Some pilgrims confuse this *Tawaaf* with *Tawaaful-Wadaa'*. This is a grave error and must be avoided. Delay your departure for home until the women are out of their menses, even if it means that you will miss your flight. (Hence good planning is essential.)

$$﴿ثُمَّ لَيَقْضُوا تَفَثَهُمْ وَلْيُوفُوا نُذُورَهُمْ وَلْيَطَّوَّفُوا بِالْبَيْتِ الْعَتِيقِ﴾$$

"Then let them complete the prescribed duties (Manasik of Hajj) for them, and perform their vows, and circumambulate the Ancient House."

Surah Al-Hajj (22:29)

Following the *Sunnah*, *Tawaaful-Ifadah* should be performed on the 10th of Dhul-Hijjah. If it cannot be done on this day, it should be performed on any day during *Ayaamut-Tashreek* or even later if you have a valid reason.

$$«عَنِ ابْنِ عُمَرَ؛ أَنَّ رَسُولَ اللهِ ﷺ أَفَاضَ يَوْمَ النَّحْرِ، ثُمَّ رَجَعَ فَصَلَّى الظُّهْرَ بِمِنًى»$$

"Ibn 'Umar (﴿) reported that the Prophet (ﷺ) observed the circumambulation of Ifadah on the Day of Nahr (10th of Dhul-Hijjah), and then came back and observed the noon prayer at Mina."

(Muslim:1308)

Tamattu pilgrims MUST perform *Sa'ee* as well. Some *Tamattu* pilgrims perform *Nafl Tawaaf* on the 8th of Dhul-Hijjah, followed by *Sa'ee* for *Hajj*. This is contrary to the *Sunnah*.

Also *Qiran* and *Ifrad* pilgrims who did not perform the *Sa'ee* with the welcome *Tawaaf*, MUST perform the *Sa'ee* for *Hajj*.

Some pilgrims mistakenly think that this *Sa'ee* is not required and quote the narration of Jabir (﷽) who said that the Prophet (﷽) and his companions only performed one *Sa'ee* between Safaa and Marwah (*Muslim*).

The Prophet (﷽) did not perform *Sa'ee* as he was performing the *Qiran* method and did the *Sa'ee* with the welcome *Tawaaf*.

For this *Tawaaf*, you will find Makkah extremely crowded. Review the notes in the previous chapter about the best place and the hints for *Tawaaf*. You will need it.

If you plan to perform this *Tawaaf* on *Yaumul-Eid* (10th), I suggest you try to get to Makkah before 10.00am, after which it gets very crowded. Also, immediately after *Salatul-'Eshaa* (don't delay or perform *Sunnah Salah*), it is less crowded. If you plan to delay this *Tawaaf* until the 13th, then try to perform it before *Salatul-Maghrib*, as it becomes almost impossible to enter the mosque after this time. On the 12th, there is no good time as the mosque is full from the afternoon until the next morning. Remember there are many pilgrims (mainly locals) that are performing *Tawaaful-Wadaa'* at these times on the 12th and 13th.

When you enter the *Haram*, you will notice the striking black and gold new cloth (*Kiswat*) over the Ka'bah. It is a beautiful sight!

Putting it all together

I suggest you review all the tips and points about *Hajj*, such as: what to buy (i.e. liquid soap instead of a soap bar; *Miswak* instead of toothpaste; where to sit and locate yourself in Mina and Arafat; not to buy new slippers or shoes for *Hajj*; when to use the bathrooms, and what medication to take, etc.).

What to take to Mina and Arafat

In chapter 15 ("Checklists") is a list of recommended items to take with you to Mina and Arafat. It may appear to a big list, but most of these items are small yet essential.

If you are going to Mina on the 8th, I suggest you take two bags, one with all your Mina requirements and a smaller one for your Arafat needs. This way you can leave the one bag in Mina when you go to Arafat on the 9th.

However, if you are going directly to Arafat from Makkah on the 9th, then you need only one bag with your Arafat, Mina and Muzdalifah needs.

This is one more reason why moving to Aziziah before Hajj is such a great logistical move as you need not carry much to Mina.

Depending on what your package offers, you may need to take your favourite pillow and a small fold-up mattress as well. A sleeping bag or an inflatable air mattress is a very useful item for this part of *Hajj*.

Take all the necessary toiletries, and I suggest the women take sanitary pads also, even though they may not expect their menstruation to start.

Take all the required medicine.

Some pilgrims leave their clothes in Makkah and collect them on the 10th after they have completed *Tawaaful-Ifadah*. If you plan to go to Makkah on the 10th then these is fine but if you do not, remember that you will be in Ihraam, and after two days it will be quite dirty, so take some clothes with you.

One more important item I would like to repeat. Take enough food (biscuits, fruit, dates, etc.) for the night stay in Muzdalifah. As it is very likely that you will walk to Mina from Muzdalifah, also take something to eat for breakfast as well as a water flask and an umbrella.

Over the last few years I 'discovered' a very handy item to take with if you don't mind carrying it. It is a fold-up (flip open) two person tent. We have been using it very effectively for privacy (change, sleep, eating) in Arafat and you cannot believe its 'value' in Muzdalifah. Last *Hajj* some pilgrims complained that I did not have this in my book, well here it is now. These tents are nor readily available, but I normally find them with some street vendors during *Hajj*. So you may have to do some searching, but believe me, leave the pillow and the clothes, but take this item, you will not regret it.

Hajj **Place by Place**

The following diagram outlines the flow of the *Hajj* programme:

The *Hajj* events are now explained as the Prophet (ﷺ) performed them during his farewell pilgrimage. In this section I address the required actions for each place, followed in the next section by the actual *Hajj* performance day by day:

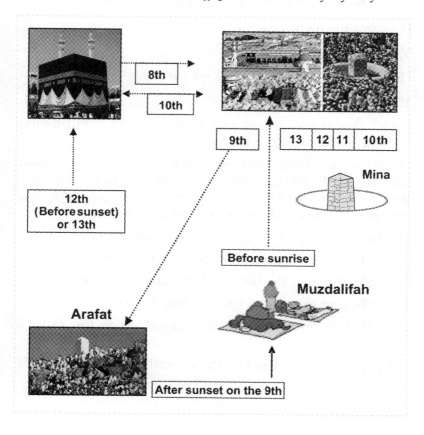

Mina

The Prophet (ﷺ) did the following in Mina:

8th Dhul-Hijjah

He performed *Salatul Zuhr* (2 *Rak'at*); *'Asr* (2 *Rak'at*); *Maghrib* (normal); and *'Eshaa* (2 *Rak'at*), not joined.

He spent the night here.

9th Dhul-Hijjah

He performed *Salatul Fajr* and left for Arafat after sunrise.

10th Dhul-Hijjah

He left Arafat after sunset and spent the night in Muzdalifah and left for Mina before sunrise.

He performed *Ramy* (casting of pebbles) of the big *Jamrah*; followed by the sacrifice; followed by shaving of his head; and then proceeded to Makkah to perform *Tawaaful-Ifadah*; and returned to Mina and performed the noon prayer.

On the 10th, the preferred order of the actions are:

1. Throwing the seven stones at *Jamrah Aqaba*.

2. Slaughtering the sacrificial animal, if applicable.

3. Shaving the head (or shortening the hair).

4. Performing *Tawaaful-Ifadah* (and *Sa'ee* for *Hajj*, if applicable).

If a pilgrim does not follow the prescribed order there is no harm:

«عَنْ عَبْدِ اللهِ ابْنِ عَمْرِو بْنِ الْعَاصِ قَالَ: وَقَفَ رَسُولُ
اللهِ ﷺ، فِي حَجَّةِ الْوَدَاعِ، بِمِنًى، لِلنَّاسِ يَسْأَلُونَهُ، فَجَاءَ
رَجُلٌ فَقَالَ: يَا رَسُولَ اللهِ! لَمْ أَشْعُرْ، فَحَلَقْتُ قَبْلَ أَنْ أَنْحَرَ،
فَقَالَ: «اذْبَحْ وَلَا حَرَجَ» ثُمَّ جَاءَهُ رَجُلٌ آخَرُ فَقَالَ: يَا رَسُولَ
اللهِ! لَمْ أَشْعُرْ فَنَحَرْتُ قَبْلَ أَنْ أَرْمِيَ، فَقَالَ: «ارْمِ وَلَا حَرَجَ»

"Narrated 'Abdullah bin Amr bin Al 'Aas (ﷺ): 'The Prophet (ﷺ) stopped (for a while near the Jimar) at Mina during his last Hajj for the people and they were asking him questions.

A man said, 'I forgot and had my head shaved before slaughtering the Hady'.

'The Prophet (ﷺ) said: 'There is no harm, go and do the slaughtering now.''Then another person came and said, 'I forgot and slaughtered before the Ramy.' The Prophet (ﷺ) said, 'Do the Ramy now and there is no harm.' The narrator added: 'So on that day, when the Prophet (ﷺ) was asked about anything (as regards the ceremonies) of Hajj performed before or after its due time, his reply was: 'Do it (now) and there is no harm'.''

(Bukhari:1306)

11th - 13th Dhul-Hijjah

11th - After *Zawaal* he performed *Ramy* of all three *Jamr'at* starting at the small one and finishing at the big one and making supplication after *Ramy* of the small and middle ones only.

12th - He did exactly the same as on the previous day.

13th - He did exactly the same as on the previous day and then proceeded to Makkah.

Some other important points regarding Mina

﴿ وَٱذْكُرُواْ ٱللَّهَ فِيٓ أَيَّامٍ مَّعْدُودَٰتٍ فَمَن تَعَجَّلَ فِي يَوْمَيْنِ فَلَآ إِثْمَ

عَلَيْهِ وَمَن تَأَخَّرَ فَلاَ إِثْمَ عَلَيْهِ لِمَنِ ٱتَّقَىٰ وَٱتَّقُوا ٱللَّهَ وَٱعْلَمُوٓا
أَنَّكُمْ إِلَيْهِ تُحْشَرُونَ ۞

*"And remember Allah during the appointed days. But
whosoever hastens to leave in two days, there is no sin on
him and whosoever stays on, there is no sin on him, if his aim
is to do good and obey Allah (fear Him), and know that you
will be surely gathered unto Him."*

Surah Al-Baqarah (2:203)

If you plan to leave Mina on the 12th, you should do so before
sunset. If you are still in Mina after sunset you should stay
until the 13th. However if you are in the process of leaving and
are stuck in the traffic you may still leave even if it is after
sunset. The rule is basically that you cannot decide to leave
after sunset.

The prayers in Mina are shortened but not joined. (*Zuhr*, *'Asr* &
'Eshaa = 2 *Rak'at* each) for all the days you are there, 8th, 10th -13th.

The *Sunnah* for *Salatul-Fajr* should be performed.

Salatul-Witr should be performed.

You do not have to face *Qiblah* while throwing the *Jamr'at*. However, you need to turn to face *Qiblah* to make *Dua* at the small and middle *Jamr'at*. Move out of the *Jamr'at* vicinity as soon as you are finished with your ramy.

The 10th day is *Al-Yaumun-Nahr* and is not counted as part of the days of *Tashreek*. This day is *Eid* day for all the non-pilgrims. The pilgrim does not have any *Eid* obligations, even though many pilgrims rush to Makkah to "catch" the *Eid Salah*. This is not required.

Arafat

The Prophet (ﷺ) left for Arafat on the morning of the 9th (a Friday) where he stopped at the valley of Uranah. A tent had been set up for him at Namirah, where he rested until the sun had passed the meridian.

When the sun had declined he mounted his she-camel, Al-Qaswa and went down into the valley, where he delivered the *Khutbah* (speech) as illustrated in chapter 1 of this book.

After the *Khutbah*, Bilal pronounced *Adhaan* and the *Iqaama*. The Prophet (ﷺ) led the *Zuhr* prayer, performing only two *Rak'at* without reciting aloud, although it was Friday. It is therefore concluded from this action that the prayer offered was not the two *Rak'at Salah* of the Friday prayer but the *Zuhr* prayer for a traveller. Immediately afterwards Bilal again recited the *Iqaamah*, and the Prophet (ﷺ) led the *'Asr* prayer, performing again only two *Rak'at*. No voluntary prayers were offered between these two prayers. And even those among the residents of Makkah joined the other pilgrims in shortening and combining the two prayers.

After the prayers the Prophet (ﷺ) went to the plain of Arafat. Standing near the rocks at the foot of the hill, he (ﷺ) said:

$$\text{«وَوَقَفْتُ هَهُنَا ، وَعَرَفَةُ كُلُّهَا مَوْقِفٌ»}$$

"I stand here, but the whole of Arafat is a standing place."

(Muslim:1218)

Therefore there is no requirement to be near or climb on top of Jabal-Rahmah (Mount of Mercy).

The Prophet (ﷺ) then faced *Qiblah*, and raising his hands up to the level of his chest, he supplicated earnestly until sunset. He informed the people that the best supplication is that of the day of Arafat and the best which he and the other Prophets before him have said is:

«لَا إِلَهَ إِلَّا اللهُ وَحْدَهُ لَا شَرِيكَ لَهُ، لَهُ الملكُ وَلَهُ الحَمْدُ، وَهُوَ عَلى كُلِّ شَيءٍ قَدِيرٌ»

"Laa illaha illallahu wahdahu laa shareekalah lahulmulk wa lahulhamdu wahuwa alaa kullishayin qadeer."

(None has the right to be worshipped except Allah, alone, without partner. To Him belongs all praise and sovereignty and He is over all things Omnipotent.)

(Bukhari & Tirmidhi: 2995:3428)

Some other points of importance regarding Arafat

All pilgrims MUST be on Arafat on the 9th of Dhul-Hijjah. Without this rite, *Hajj* is not valid.

This rite cannot be done on any other day nor is there expiation if it is missed.

The Prophet (ﷺ) was asked about *Hajj* and he said:

«الحَجُّ عَرَفَةُ»

"The Hajj is Arafat..."

(Tirmidhi, & Abu Dawud: 889:1949)

This day is one of the most blessed days. It is narrated:

«مَا مِنْ يَوْمٍ أَكْثَرَ مِنْ أَنْ يُعْتِقَ اللهُ عَزَّ وَجَلَّ فِيهِ عَبْدًا مِنَ النَّارِ،

مِنْ يَوْم عَرَفَةَ، وَإِنَّهُ لَيَدْنُو ثُمَّ يُبَاهِي بِهِمُ الْمَلَائِكَةَ، فَيَقُولُ: مَا أَرَادَ هُؤُلَاءِ؟»

"On no other day does Allah set free as many of His servants from the Fire as on the day of Arafat. On that day He is face to face with His Servants and is proud before the angels of the pilgrims and says, 'What is it they want?'"

(Muslim:1348)

Pilgrims MUST NOT fast on Arafat day. Only non-pilgrims are encouraged to fast on this day.

If you are inside Masjid Namirah (mosque in Arafat), be aware that there is a large portion of the mosque (front portion) that is outside the boundary of Arafat. It is acceptable to be in this area during the *Khutbah*. However, you must move into the precincts of Arafat afterwards. There are clear signs inside the mosque. Once again, do not follow the crowd. You MUST ensure that YOU are in Arafat.

Pilgrims, this is the day you have come for. I will not say do not "short-change" yourself, no, do not "throw" all that time, effort and money away, by wasting this day in idle talk or by sleeping.

Allah has "widened" the day for you by removing all *Fard* obligations for you from *Zuhr* until *'Eshaa*. It is therefore important that you follow the *Sunnah* and join the *Zuhr* and *'Asr* prayers, regardless of where you are located in *Arafat*.

Some people believe that if they are not in Masjid Namira, they cannot join their prayers in the tents. This is not correct!

This is where the radio is useful, as you can listen to the *Khutbah* on the radio, if you are too far from the mosque. Hopefully there is someone in the group that understands Arabic that can translate it for the camp.

Saudi channel 2 broadcasts the *Khutbah* with the English translation. That means you need a TV.

Lunch is normally served after the *Salah*. Do not waste too much time eating. You only have a few hours at your disposal.

The time of *Wuqoof* (meaning the time to supplicate), only starts AFTER the performance of *Salatul-Zuhr* and *'Asr* (joined). This is a very important point as I have seen many pilgrims who arrive very early (after *Fajr*) at Arafat, spend a lot of time in the morning supplicating and *Dhikr*, *Tasbih*, etc. By the afternoon they are tired and spend most of their time sleeping. The afternoon, until sunset, is the time of Arafat, and not in the morning. It is better to rest or sleep in the morning if you so wish.

My fellow Muslims, do not sleep, supplicate...

- Seek Allah's Forgiveness, Mercy and Blessings;
- Ask what your heart desires;
- For your parents and children;
- For relatives and friends;
- For the general Muslim communities;
- For the *Mujahideen*;
- For the Muslims in troubled countries;
- For me and my family;
- Make *Istighfaar*;
- etc.

See chapter 8 for the correct manner of supplication. In the late afternoon, it is very nice to stand outside the tent and supplicate.

Arafat is not a picnic, this is the day you've been planning and waiting for!

If you think about it, all the money spent, time and effort was for this time. So let us say you paid $5000.00 for your trip, and there are five hours from *Zuhr* until sunset. That means each hour is 'worth' $1000.00. So if you spend one hour eating and one hour sleeping or chatting, then that would be your most expensive lunch or nap you would ever have. Get my point?

Nafarah

This is the term used for the movement of pilgrims from Arafat after sunset.

It is *Wajib* to stay in Arafat until after sunset.

Maghrib Salah is NOT performed in Arafat, unless you are still there at midnight.

Do not push or rush as the Prophet (ﷺ) ordered the people to be calm and patient:

«أَيُّها النَّاسُ، عَلَيْكُمْ بِالسَّكِينَةِ فإِنَّ البِرَّ لَيْسَ بِالإِيضَاعِ»

"O people, be calm. Hastening is not a sign of righteousness."

(Bukhari:1671)

Before departing from Arafat, use the toilets, no matter how "bad" they are. Also perform *Wudu* as you will be performing *Salah* once you reach Muzdalifah. Although there are many toilets and *Wudu* facilities in Muzdalifah, they are extremely crowded most times.

The journey to Muzdalifah could be short or very, very, very long. Be patient.

Keep some drinking water and biscuits with you on the bus.

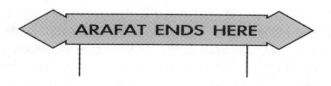

ARAFAT ENDS HERE

Muzdalifah

When the Prophet (ﷺ) reached Muzdalifah, he made ablution. Then the *Adhaan* and *Iqaamah* were pronounced, and he offered the *Maghrib Salah* followed by the *'Eshaa Salah* after the *Iqaamah* was pronounced again. The *'Eshaa Salah* was shortened to two *Rak'at* and no voluntary prayers were offered between *Maghrib* and *'Eshaa*.

After the prayers the Prophet (ﷺ) lay down until dawn. Many books teach the pilgrim to stay up on this night and spend it in supplication. The authentic proof is that it is to be spent in rest or sleep, as the Prophet (ﷺ) did.

After the moon had set, he sent the weak among his family (women and children) to Mina. There are numerous *Ahadith* narrated by Muslim and Bukhari regarding the issue about the weak and aged leaving Muzdalifah early. At the same time the *Ahadith* clearly indicate that the young and able should spend the night in Muzdalifah. (The time indicated here is generally agreed to be, between midnight and *Fajr*).

The Prophet (ﷺ) got up at dawn and led the congregational *Fajr Salah*. He then mounted Al-Qaswa and went to *Al-Mash'ar-il-Haram*, where he faced *Qiblah* and made supplication.

﴿فَإِذَآ أَفَضْتُم مِّنْ عَرَفَٰتٍ فَٱذْكُرُوا۟ ٱللَّهَ عِندَ ٱلْمَشْعَرِ ٱلْحَرَامِ ۖ وَٱذْكُرُوهُ كَمَا هَدَىٰكُمْ وَإِن كُنتُم مِّن قَبْلِهِۦ لَمِنَ ٱلضَّآلِّينَ ○ ثُمَّ أَفِيضُوا۟ مِنْ حَيْثُ أَفَاضَ ٱلنَّاسُ وَٱسْتَغْفِرُوا۟ ٱللَّهَ ۚ إِنَّ ٱللَّهَ غَفُورٌ رَّحِيمٌ﴾

"...Then when you leave Arafat, remember Allah at the Mash'ar-il-Haram. And remember Him as He has guided you, and verily, you were, before, of those who were astray. Then depart from the place whence all the people depart and ask Allah for His Forgiveness. Truly, Allah is Oft-Forgiving, Most-Merciful."

Surah Al-Baqarah (2:198-199)

Once again, as with Arafat, it is not a requirement for all pilgrims to be at this very place as the Prophet (ﷺ) said:

«وَوَقَفْتُ هَٰهُنَا ، وَجَمْعٌ كُلُّهَا مَوْقِفٌ»

"I am standing here, but the whole of Muzdalifah is a place of standing."

(Muslim:1218)

With all this evidence, I am sure that there should be no more doubt or confusion as to where you are supposed to be after Arafat and for how long...

Some other important points regarding Muzdalifah

You need not collect your stones here, as it is acceptable to collect them in Mina, and there is no obligation to collect them in Muzdalifah. However due to the new paving in the camps in Mina it is more difficult to obtain stones there. So if you have time and a torchlight, collect your stones.

If you have not reached Muzdalifah by midnight, then you should perform the prayers at the place you are, if possible, as you will pass the end time for *'Eshaa Salah*. Many times you may still be in Arafat or in the bus stuck in the traffic. On one occasion we were unable to perform our *Salah* until 2:30am due to the traffic. So stop and perform your *Salah* at the first opportunity. *'Eshaa* does not end at *Fajr*!

Sleep. The next day has a very hectic agenda, so rest. When the light of dawn was very clear, the Prophet (ﷺ) departed quickly before the sun rose. When they arrived at the valley of Muhassir he increased his camel's pace, hastening through the valley.

This is the only place throughout the *Hajj* that you will be able to see so many of the pilgrims (in *Ihraam*) in one place, as it is an open area and everybody is sleeping in the open. A sight to remember!

Keep some water to perform *Wudu* in the morning for *Fajr Salah*, unless you are close to water or the toilets.

This is where your *Hajji* mat or air-mattress, and those eye covers (you received on the aeroplane) are needed. And that two person tent!

Now you will appreciate the food that you have been carrying all this time. Many pilgrims do not bring any food with them, so be prepared to share with the rest of the group.

If you plan to walk to Mina, I suggest you "camp" closer to the Mina border, so you have a shorter distance to walk. The walk should take you about 1 to 2 hours to the *Jamr'at*.

Also do not delay too long in the morning, leave as soon as you have completed your *Dua'*. This way you may avoid the big crowd and traffic. This may mean you have to skip breakfast. Alternatively you can have something to eat before *Fajr*.

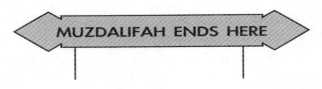

MUZDALIFAH ENDS HERE

You should constantly be reciting the *Talbiyah* from the 8th until after the stoning on the 10th

Hajj - Day by Day

The actual *Hajj* days are from the 8th to the 13th of Dhul-Hijjah.

Day 1 - 8th Dhul-Hijjah (*Yaumut-Tarweya*)

On the 8th day of Dhul-Hijjah the pilgrim (*Tamattu*) re enters into the state of *Ihraam* from his place (normally in Makkah) with the *Niyah* for *Hajj* (*Labbayk Allahumma Hajjan*). The *Talbiyah* is now recited by all pilgrims as they head for Mina (Muna) north-east of Makkah, after sunrise. Here they stay from the morning on the 8th until after *Fajr* on the 9th. All prayers are performed on time, but *Zuhr*, *'Asr* and *'Eshaa* are shortened to two *Rak'at* each.

Day 2 - 9th Dhul-Hijjah (Standing at Arafat)

After performing *Salatul-Fajr* in Mina and waiting until after sunrise, the pilgrim leaves Mina for Arafat. Due to the traffic it is difficult to predict the time of arrival at your arranged place on the plain of Arafat. Most pilgrims arrive prior to or just after *Zuhr*, depending on the time they left Mina. Not all pilgrims are able to go to the mosque or stay near Jabal Ar-Rahmah (Mountain of Mercy). The plain of Arafat is not very big but all the pilgrims are accommodated with no major problem. This is the day you have come for. There is no *Hajj* without Arafat. If this *Wuqoof* is missed, the whole *Hajj* is invalidated according to the saying of the Prophet (ﷺ), "*Hajj* is 'Arafat". There is a *Khutbah* before the *Salah* in Masjid Namirah (the big *Masjid* in Arafat, built on the place where the Prophet (ﷺ) stood and delivered his *Khutbah* during his Farewell *Hajj*). For those who are in the *Masjid* or are within hearing distance, listen attentively to the *Khutbah*. After the khutbah the pilgrim prays *Zuhr* and *"Asr Salah*, joined and shortened to two *Rak'at* each, with one *Adhaan* and two *Iqaama's*. In most tents, lunch will be served to the pilgrims by their *Hajj* organiser. The time between *Zuhr* and *Maghrib* should now be spent in sincere supplication, *Dhikr*, etc., and not sleeping or idle talk. The *Fard* obligation of 'Asr Salah has been removed by joining it with *Zuhr* as well as *Maghrib Salah*, which is joined with *'Eshaa*, in Muzdalifah. Allah has now provided the pilgrim with enough time to seek His Forgiveness and His Mercy. Many pilgrims tend to forget that this is the most important time of their entire *Hajj*.

Fellow Muslims, do not waste this precious time!

Immediately after sunset the pilgrims start leaving Arafat for Muzdalifah. This process is known as *Nafarah*. *Maghrib Salah* is not performed in Arafat. It is not permissible to leave Arafat before sunset.

Day 2 - Night (Staying in Muzdalifah)

The distance to Muzdalifah is only about 9km (6 miles). However this journey can take you from 1 hour to 16 hours depending on the traffic and where you were located in

Arafat. Patience is the best medicine at this time. Many pilgrims choose to walk from Arafat to Muzdalifah. At Muzdalifah the pilgrims pray *Maghrib* (3) and *'Eshaa* (2) together, one *Adhaan* and 2 *Iqaama's*. After which they find a nice comfortable place on the ground to sleep. The sight in Muzdalifah is like no other sight in the world. It is a flat plain and as you look far and wide, all you see are pilgrims in their white *Ihraams* ("a sight worth remembering"). The facilities in Muzdalifah are definitely not 5 star or not even 1 star, but you will not find anyone complaining, as the pilgrims know that they have been blessed to have been present on Arafat on the 9th of Dhul-Hijjah. Men who are physically weak, women and children are allowed to leave Muzdalifah after moonset (some time after midnight) and before *Fajr*. Unfortunately, many able pilgrims leave before the morning or do not even stop in Muzdalifah at all. Sometimes this is outside your control, and you are at the mercy of your *Hajj* organiser. Obtain beforehand the details about the programme from your *Hajj* organiser, so you can make alternate plans if required. Needless to say the Prophet (ﷺ) spent the night in Muzdalifah. You may collect your stones for the *Ramy* (casting of seven pebbles at each *Jamrah* in Mina) here. It is not a must that you to do it here as they can be collected in Mina. There is also no requirement to wash them.

Day 3 - 10th Dhul-Hijjah (Day of Sacrifice)

The day of *Nahr*. This is *Eid* day (There is no *Eid* for the pilgrims). After performing *Fajr Salah* and supplicating in Muzdalifah the pilgrim sets out for Mina shortly before sunrise. Once again many pilgrims choose to walk to Mina. The *Talbiyah* is still recited at this time by the pilgrims. All the pilgrims head for the largest *Jamrah*, known as *Al-Aqabah* where they perform *Ramy* (casting of seven pebbles, one at a time, at the *Jamrah* in Mina). The pilgrim says: "*Allahu Akbar*" ("Allah is the Greatest") as he throws each pebble. After the

Ramy the pilgrim stops the *Talbiyah* and starts reciting the takbir. After the *Ramy* the pilgrim performs the slaughtering of a sheep or goat (*Hady*). After this the male pilgrims shave or cut their hair. The women cut only approximately one inch of hair. These three rites should be done in the above order if convenient, but there is no harm if the one precedes the other. The pilgrim is now free from all *Ihraam* restrictions except marital relations (which are "lifted" after *Tawaaful-Ifadah*). The pilgrim can now wear normal clothes. The pilgrim should recite the *Takbir* as often as possible. The *Takbir* should be recited until after *Asr* on the 13th of Dhul-Hijjah, specially after the *Fard* prayers.

The *Takbir:*

(اللهُ أكبرُ، اللهُ أكبرُ، لاإله إلاالله، اللهُ أكبرُ، اللهُ أكبرُ ولله الحمدُ)

"Allahu Akbar, Allahu Akbar, La ilaha illalah, Allahu Akbar, Allahu Akbar, wa lillah-il-hamd."

(Allah is the Greatest, Allah is the Greatest, None has the right to be worshipped but Allah, Allah is the Greatest, Allah is the Greatest, All praise is due to Allah.)

The pilgrim now heads for Makkah to perform the second most important pillar of *Hajj*: *Tawaaful-Ifadah* (*Tawaaful-Hajj*; *Tawaaf-uz-Ziyarah*). Many pilgrims confuse this *Tawaaf* with *Tawaaful-Wadaa'* (farewell). Women who have their menses or postnatal bleeding can omit *Tawaaful-Wadaa'*, if circumstances require it, but nobody can omit *Tawaaful-Ifadah*. Complete seven circumambulations, *Salah* at *Maqaam Ibraheem*, and then for the *Mutamatti*, seven circuits between Safaa and Marwah (*Sa'ee*). The *Qaarin* and *Mufrid* who did not perform *Sa'ee* for *Hajj* with the welcome *Tawaaf* MUST also perform *Sa'ee* now. On completion of this, the pilgrim is now free from all *Ihraam* restrictions. He now returns to Mina to spend the next two or three days and nights.

Day 4 - 11th Dhul-Hijjah (Day one of *Tashreek*)

It is important for the pilgrim to spend the nights and most of his time, if not all, in Mina during these three days. In Mina the pilgrim collects his pebbles (7 x 3 = 21, remember the size) to *Ramy* all three *Jamr'at*. After *Zawaal* the pilgrim proceeds to *Ramy* (stone), starting with the small *Jamrah*, followed by *Dua'* facing *Qiblah*, then the middle one, *Jamratul-Wustaa*, followed by *Dua'* facing *Qiblah*, and finishing with the big one, *Al-Aqaba* (no *Dua'* after this one). There are clear signs to indicate them. *Ramy* is not to be done prior to *Zawaal* time, for all three days, but can be done at night, due to over crowding. The rest of the day and night is spent in Mina, in praise of Allah. If the pilgrim did not perform *Tawaaful-Ifadah* the previous day, he may do so on this day.

Day 5 - 12th Dhul-Hijjah (Day two of *Tashreek*)

On this day the pilgrim does the same as the day before. On completion of the *Ramy*, the pilgrim is allowed to leave Mina for Makkah. The pilgrim who wishes to leave, should do so prior to *Maghrib*, otherwise the pilgrim should stay until the next day. If the pilgrim decided to leave, but was still in Mina after sunset, due to reasons beyond his control (i.e. traffic, organiser delays, etc.), he may still leave after sunset. If the pilgrim did not perform *Tawaaful-Ifadah* the previous day, he may do so on this day.

Day 6 - 13th Dhul-Hijjah (Day three of *Tashreek*)

On this day the pilgrim does the same as the day before. (*Ramy* is also after *Zawaal* on this day, contrary to many *Hajj* books, which indicate that it can be done in the morning.) On completion of the *Ramy*, the pilgrim now leaves Mina for Makkah.

Tawaaful-Wadaa'

If the pilgrim is to leave Makkah, the last rite to be performed is *Tawaaful-Wadaa'* (the farewell *Tawaaf*). Menstruating or postnatal bleeding women are not obligated to perform this *Tawaaf*. If the pilgrim has not performed *Tawaaful-Ifadah* yet, and it is the last rite to do before leaving for home, then *Tawaaful-Ifadah* and *Tawaaful-Wadaa'* can be "joined"; meaning that pilgrim only performs one set of *Tawaaf* with the *Niyah* for *Tawaaful-Ifadah*. Some people insist that it should be *Niyah* for both. This is no major issue as the *Niyah* is in the heart and the pilgrim will automatically intend to do both. However, it is of the utmost importance that the niyah is for *Ifadah* (as this cannot be left out). One set (7 circuits) only, and don't forget to perform *Sa'ee* if you are performing the *Tamattu* method or for the *Qaarin* or *Mufrid* if you did not perform *Sa'ee* with the welcome *Tawaaf*. There is no *Sa'ee* for *Tawaaful-Wadaa'*.

Tawaaful-Wadaa' is a *Wajib* act of *Hajj*. Any pilgrim that plans to leave the *Haram* area (to go to *Jeddah* and return to Makkah, or those that reside in *Jeddah*), MUST perform this *Tawaaf* first, prior to leaving for *Jeddah*. There are different opinions on this issue, and so many pilgrims seem to opt for the easy way out, by not performing it. Ask yourself: "Is it worth the risk that I should cut corners on the last rite of *Hajj*, after having spent so much time, effort and money for this trip?"

«عَنِ ابنِ عَبَّاسٍ رَضِيَ اللهُ عَنْهُما قالَ: أُمِرَ النَّاسُ أَنْ يَكُونَ آخِرُ عَهْدِهِمْ بالبَيْتِ إلَّا أنَّهُ خُفِّفَ عَنِ الحائِضِ»

Narrated by Ibn Abbas (ﷺ): "The people were ordered to perform the Tawaaf of the Ka'bah (Tawaaful-Wadaa') as the lastly thing, before leaving (Makkah), except the menstruating women who were excused."

(Bukhari:1755)

For those pilgrims who stay for a few days longer in Makkah, they only perform *Tawaaful-Wadaa'* prior to leaving Makkah. In between this time, they resume normal activities as they did prior to the 8th of Dhul-Hijjah.

Use this time to make *Dua'* for yourself, your parents, family and friends and also for Muslims in general.

Do not forget to ask Allah to grant you another opportunity to

return to Makkah Al-Mukarramah.

Hajj is now complete, may Allah accept it!

Departure from Makkah

Going to Madinah

Many pilgrims who did not visit Madinah before *Hajj*

normally do so after *Hajj*.

If it is included in your package then the accommodation will be arranged by your group organiser.

The transportation is already paid for as part of the *Hajj* bus coupons.

There are some groups that have very strange arrangements. I have witnessed, one year during a visit to Madinah (yes I was not on *Hajj* that year), buses full of pilgrims arriving in Madinah at about 2.00pm on the 12th of Dhul-Hijjah. Don't lose sight of your priorities.

Think about it for a moment:

o Firstly they are supposed to *Ramy* the *Jamr'at* after midday. To be in Madinah at 2.00pm, meant that they had to stone before it's time.

o Secondly, they had to perform *Tawaaful-Wadaa'*, and the trip to Madinah is at least 6-8 hours.

o It is wrong on the part of the organisers to force pilgrims to perform *Hajj* rites, either before it's time or in a rush or to omit it altogether, in order to reach Madinah early. (Visiting Madinah is not a part of the *Hajj* rites.)

You need to take all your belongings with you, as you will not be returning to Makkah after Madinah.

For details about Madinah, see chapter 12, in this book.

You need to make arrangements for the bus and to collect your passport, at least 24 hours prior to your departure, from the *Mutawwifs* office in Makkah (see chapter 7).

If you are a small group you may wish to hire a private taxi to take you to Madinah, to avoid waiting until the *Mutawwifs* bus is full. This will be at your cost though. Either way, your passport will be given to the driver as he will in turn hand it in to the *Mutawwifs* office in Madinah.

If you do not have pre-arranged accommodation in Madinah, then you may have trouble finding a place to stay as Madinah is extremely crowded for a few weeks after *Hajj*, with pilgrims.

Ensure that all your luggage is securely packed. Do not place fragile items in your luggage, and remember to take your *Zamzam* water with you.

Going Home

"Cash in" that last bag of patience, you will need it.

The following points apply for both, leaving for home from Makkah or Madinah.

Bookings/flights

Many pilgrims are very anxious to get home after *Hajj*. There departure dates may be a week or two later and they now wish to leave immediately. They end up spending so much time and aggravation trying to change their flights, with no success. Believe me it is virtually impossible to get an earlier departure. Avoid the stress and enjoy your last few days in Makkah.

This is why you need to reconfirm your return bookings very early. Some airlines charge a fee (up to $30.00 per ticket) just to change your departure date.

Some airlines will not reconfirm your booking by phone. Their method of reconfirmation is that you are at the airport to check in at least 12 hours before the actual departure time.

Some airlines will issue you with your boarding pass in Makkah. In this case you need to make 100% sure you make it for this flight. If you fail to make it for this flight, you will have to buy new tickets in order to get home, and that is expensive.

This is the time when your travel agent will show his or her true worth!

Which Terminal?

Make sure you know which terminal you will be departing from: *Hajj*, South (Saudi Arabian Airlines), or North (other airlines) terminal. If you are not sure, DO NOT go to the *Hajj* terminal first. You may not be able to leave the Hajj Terminal, once you have entered. Hence it is better to go to the other terminal first. I don't know how many times I have advised pilgrims about this, but every year the same thing happens, as there is always some 'smarty' on the bus.

Once you are at the terminal make sure that your flight is leaving from there. Check it by flight number, and not by destination, as there are flights to the same destination from all three terminals. Don't only ask one person, check the boards or ask at least three people. Do I sound paranoid? Well, if you experience the agony of helping or watching pilgrims that have missed their flights year after year, you will know why I am emphasising this so much.

Many pilgrims have been stranded for days as they missed their flight due to being at the wrong terminal or for turning up on the wrong day. Remember to check your departure times very carefully (i.e. 0230 on the 15th, means morning of the 15th and not the 16th). I once met a lady at the North Terminal who was in tears. Her husband left for the Hajj Terminal 24 hours earlier just to check if that was the right Terminal. He obviously could not leave from there, so I advised her to go to the Hajj Terminal. I guess another piece of advice would be, not to separate from your partner or group. Sounds ridiculous, but it happens!

Money

If you happen to have any Saudi riyals left (which you should), do not spend them, as you may need money at the airport to buy food, in the event of any delays or for excess baggage (overweight) charges. Also you can always use it when you come again. Alternatively you can keep it and give it as a gift to future pilgrims.

With exception of the Hajj Terminal, food is very expensive at the other two terminals. Recently I was buying some coffee at the shop inside the terminal and I overheard a lady telling the man behind the counter, after he told her the cost of her order: "I only ordered a coffee and piece of cake I did not buy the restaurant."

On the odd chance, your flight may get cancelled and you could be delayed for a number of days. On many occasions pilgrims have been delayed for up to a week at the terminal. Other pilgrims had to return to Makkah to wait for the next available flight, which was a week later. So keep that spare money.

Luggage

Show me a pilgrim that did not do any shopping...!

Ensure that you have all your luggage and it is securely packed and marked.

So, if your bags are overweight, then it might be better to check in as a group. On the other hand if your bags are not overweight, I suggest you do not check in with the group. From experience, you may end up paying a lot, as the group as a whole may have excess baggage, and they will collect money from everybody.

All *Zamzam* will have to be checked in. All airlines do not allow *Zamzam* as carry-on (hand) luggage anymore. Some airlines count this as part of your luggage weight allowance. Hence check all these things before you travel.

Do not put the *Zamzam* water containers inside your suitcase.

Getting your passport

This can be a very easy or a very daunting task. It varies from year to year. If your agent is taking care of this then let him do it.

You need to make an appointment 24 hours prior to your departure with the *Mutawwifs* office in Makkah (or Madinah) - see chapter 7. If you are not a big group then the office will recommend that you arrange your own transport. You can use any taxi, but it must be a Saudi driver, as he will have to collect and sign for your passports. You will have to pay for this. However if you wish to use the assigned buses (which is paid for), then you may have to wait until the bus is full.

The general rule is that if you are departing from the *Hajj*

Terminal, you need to be there 12 hours before your flight departure and only 6 hours if you are departing from the other terminals.

You need to give yourself plenty of time, as there can be delays at the *Mutawwifs* office. During the *Hajj* of 1419 (1999), two buses full of pilgrims missed their flight due to the delays at this office, and needed to stay in Jeddah for another week. And these are only the ones I know about. On the other hand, I have collected passports from this office and it took me all of fifteen minutes.

So if you wish to get home, I suggest you start "moving" from Makkah at least 24 hours before your flight. You may think this is a long time, but let us quickly review the possible delay points: *Tawaaful-Wadaa'* (crowd); passport office; waiting for the bus; journey to the airport (traffic); checkpoints; possibly at the wrong terminal; flight check-in delays; booking problems; luggage; immigration. Convinced?

Once you get to the airport the taxi driver will hand in your passports to the *Hajj* office, where he will have a paper stamped and then you will be given your passports back. The *Hajj* office at the North terminal is at entrance number 3. Finally you will have your passport in your hand again. Now you are free to check in and obtain refunds for unused coupons. There is normally a desk outside the *Hajj* office where you need to complete some forms and in turn collect your money from the bank at the airport.

The Journey

Do not neglect your *Salah* on your way home, even if it means performing it on the aeroplane. Most airlines are obliging, if you request a small space to pray. Normally by the entry door is a good place.

Upon your arrival home, avoid providing misleading information to the local customs about the items (jewelry,

electronic equipment, etc.) you purchased on your trip. Some
pilgrims do this to minimise the duties they may have to pay.
Apart from lying, it also leaves a very bad impression about
Muslims. It is not worth it; you have just completed *Hajj*.

Supplication for the return journey

«اللهُ أَكْبَرُ، اللهُ أَكْبَرُ، اللهُ أَكْبَرُ، سُبْحَانَ الَّذِي سَخَّرَ لَنَا هَذَا وَمَا
كُنَّا لَهُ مُقْرِنِينَ، وَإِنَّا إِلَىٰ رَبِّنَا لَمُنْقَلِبُونَ، اللَّهُمَّ! [إِنَّا] نَسْأَلُكَ
فِي سَفَرِنَا هَذَا الْبِرَّ وَالتَّقْوَىٰ، وَمِنَ الْعَمَلِ مَا تَرْضَىٰ، اللَّهُمَّ!
هَوِّنْ عَلَيْنَا سَفَرَنَا هَذَا، وَاطْوِ عَنَّا بُعْدَهُ، اللَّهُمَّ أَنْتَ الصَّاحِبُ
فِي السَّفَرِ، وَالْخَلِيفَةُ فِي الْأَهْلِ، اللَّهُمَّ! إِنِّي أَعُوذُ بِكَ مِنْ
وَعْثَاءِ السَّفَرِ، وَكَآبَةِ الْمَنْظَرِ، وَسُوءِ الْمُنْقَلَبِ فِي الْمَالِ
وَالْأَهْلِ»، وَإِذَا رَجَعَ قَالَهُنَّ، وَزَادَ فِيهِنَّ: «آيِبُونَ، تَائِبُونَ،
عَابِدُونَ، لِرَبِّنَا حَامِدُونَ»

"Allahu Akbar Allahu Akbar Allahu Akbar. Subhanaladhee
sakh-khar-ra-lana hadhaa wamaa kunnaa lahu muqrineen wa
innaa ilaa rabbinaa lamunqaliboon; Allahumma innaa
nasaluka fee safarinaa hadhal-bir wa-taqwaa wa minal
a'malimaa tarthaa; Allahumma howwin a'laynaa safaranaa
hadhaa wat-wi'annaa bu'dahu; Allahumma anta ssaahibu
fissafari walkhalifatu fil-ahli; Allahumma inni a'uoodhubika
min wa'thaa'issafari wa kaabatil-manthari wa
soo'ilmunqalabi filmaali wal ahli; Ayiboona taa'iboona
'aabidoona lirabbinaa haamidoona."

(Allah is the Greatest, Allah is the Greatest, Allah is the
Greatest. How perfect He is, The One Who has placed
this (transport) at our service, and we ourselves would
not have been capable of that, and to our Lord is our
final destiny. Oh Allah we ask You for *Birr** and *Taqwaa*
in this journey of ours, and we ask You for deeds which
please You. Oh Allah, make easy for us this journey of
ours and fold up (i.e. shorten) for us its distance. Oh

Allah, You are the companion in travel and the caretaker of the family. Oh Allah, I seek refuge in You from the hardship of travel and from (finding) a distressing sight or an unhappy return in regard to (my) property and family. We return, repent, worship and praise our Lord.)

(Muslim:1342)

(*Birr* & *Taqwaa* = two comprehensive terms which individually, refer to all good actions and obedience.)

Home Sweet Home

Do not forget to complete any fasting that you are obliged to do for *Hady* (7 days) or for *Fidyah*, if you were unable to afford the sacrifice.

Once you are back at home and you receive visitors try to talk only about the positive points of the *Hajj*, in order to encourage others to go.

Hajj is not a normal trip, so people (and you) should expect that many difficulties will arise during the trip.

Let me repeat a *Hadith*:

'Aishah (鮮) reported:

«اسْتَأْذَنْتُ النَّبِيَّ ﷺ في الجِهادِ فَقالَ : «جِهادُكُنَّ الحَجُّ»

"Once I asked the Prophet (ﷺ) for permission to take part in Jihad, and he said,'The Jihad of women is Hajj.'"

(Bukhari: 2875 & Ibn Majah: 2901)

If one goes for *Jihad* one has in one's mind either that one will die or be injured. Similarly when one goes for *Hajj*, one must be prepared for many difficult things; hence one should pay one's debts (or make arrangements) and make a will as there is a chance that one may not return. *Hajj* is certainly not an easy assignment. So people should not be surprised when the pilgrims talk about their difficulties.

However, as a pilgrim it is also important to know one's

audience when relating *Hajj* experiences in order not to frighten those that haven't been. Stick to the positive points and relay any negative points you may have only when speaking to those that have been on *Hajj* before and can relate to your experiences.

We must be patient at all times and also when talking to people we must try to remember the privilege that Allah has bestowed upon us and say *"Alhamdulillah"*, instead of constantly complaining.

I believe that any negative feelings some pilgrims may feel are not actually about the *Hajj* rites itself, but more about the treatment and delays they experienced. If you ask the same person a few months later to tell you about their *Hajj* you will find that they will relate a totally different story. As a matter of fact those same pilgrims are ready to go again.

I was told that only about 50 years ago the *Hajj* was even more treacherous. People were actually surprised when you returned home, as they did not expect to see you again. Hence the title of *Hajji* was very important as it was certainly earned. Today we are too used to modern comforts, so we have so much more to complain about.

Many pilgrims become very arrogant after returning from *Hajj* as they believe that they are "better" than others. One should be a better Muslim instead. As a learned man once told me:

"Your behaviour and the way you live your life after returning from *Hajj* is an indication of the acceptance of your *Hajj* from Allah."

Chapter 11
Supplications from the Qur'an and *Sunnah*

This chapter contains a selection of *Dua's* that our beloved Prophet (ﷺ) used and recommended us to use. In some books there are many long *Dua's* for every round of *Tawaaf* and *Sa'ee*, most of which have no basis in the *Sunnah*. I urge you to use the following *Dua's*, especially in Arafat. Also review the manner of supplication in chapter 8. If you wish to keep these *Dua's* with you to use all the time, keep in mind that I have published a pocket guide with these *Dua's*.

﴿رَبَّنَا ظَلَمْنَا أَنفُسَنَا وَإِن لَّمْ تَغْفِرْ لَنَا وَتَرْحَمْنَا لَنَكُونَنَّ مِنَ ٱلْخَٰسِرِينَ﴾

"Our Lord, we have wronged our souls, so if You do not forgive us and have mercy upon us, (then) we will surely be among the losers."

Surah Al-A'raf (7: 23)

﴿أَن لَّآ إِلَٰهَ إِلَّآ أَنتَ سُبْحَٰنَكَ إِنِّي كُنتُ مِنَ ٱلظَّٰلِمِينَ﴾

"There is no god except You. Glory unto You. Truly was I among the wrongdoers."

Surah Al-Anbiya (21:87)

﴿وَتُبْ عَلَيْنَآ إِنَّكَ أَنتَ ٱلتَّوَّابُ ٱلرَّحِيمُ﴾

"And accept our repentance. Truly, You are the One who (continually) accepts repentance, the Most Merciful."

Surah Al-Baqarah (2:128)

﴿رَبَّنَا لَا تُؤَاخِذْنَآ إِن نَّسِينَآ أَوْ أَخْطَأْنَا رَبَّنَا وَلَا تَحْمِلْ عَلَيْنَآ إِصْرًا كَمَا حَمَلْتَهُۥ عَلَى ٱلَّذِينَ مِن قَبْلِنَا رَبَّنَا وَلَا تُحَمِّلْنَا مَا لَا طَاقَةَ لَنَا بِهِۦ وَٱعْفُ عَنَّا وَٱغْفِرْ لَنَا وَٱرْحَمْنَآ أَنتَ مَوْلَىٰنَا فَٱنصُرْنَا عَلَى ٱلْقَوْمِ ٱلْكَٰفِرِينَ﴾

*"Our Lord, blame us not if we forget or fall into error. Our
Lord, lay not upon us a burden like that which You placed
upon those before us. Our Lord, lay not upon us a burden
greater than we can bear. And pardon us and forgive us and
have mercy upon us. You are our protector, so give us victory
over the disbelieving people."*

Surah Al-Baqarah (2:286)

﴿رَبَّنَا لَا تُزِغْ قُلُوبَنَا بَعْدَ إِذْ هَدَيْتَنَا وَهَبْ لَنَا مِن لَّدُنكَ رَحْمَةً إِنَّكَ أَنتَ ٱلْوَهَّابُ﴾

*"Our Lord, do not let our hearts deviate after You have
guided us and give us from Yourself mercy. Indeed, it is You
who is the Giver (of all things)."*

Surah Al-Imran (3:8)

﴿رَّبِّ ٱغْفِرْ لِي وَلِوَٰلِدَيَّ وَلِمَن دَخَلَ بَيْتِيَ مُؤْمِنًا وَلِلْمُؤْمِنِينَ
وَٱلْمُؤْمِنَٰتِ وَلَا تَزِدِ ٱلظَّٰلِمِينَ إِلَّا تَبَارًا﴾

*"My Lord, forgive me and my parents and whoever enters my
house a believer and the believing men and believing women.
And increase not the wrongdoers except in ruin."*

Surah Nuh (71:28)

﴿رَبَّنَآ ءَاتِنَا فِي ٱلدُّنْيَا حَسَنَةً وَفِي ٱلْأَخِرَةِ حَسَنَةً وَقِنَا عَذَابَ
ٱلنَّارِ﴾

*"Our Lord, give us in this world that which is good and in
the Hereafter that which is good and protect us from the
torment of the Fire."*

Surah Al-Baqarah (2:201)

﴿رَبِّ أَوْزِعْنِيٓ أَنْ أَشْكُرَ نِعْمَتَكَ ٱلَّتِيٓ أَنْعَمْتَ عَلَيَّ وَعَلَىٰ وَٰلِدَيَّ وَأَنْ أَعْمَلَ
صَٰلِحًا تَرْضَىٰهُ وَأَصْلِحْ لِي فِي ذُرِّيَّتِيٓ إِنِّي تُبْتُ إِلَيْكَ وَإِنِّي مِنَ ٱلْمُسْلِمِينَ﴾

*"O my Lord, grant me power and ability to be grateful for
Your favour which You have bestowed upon me and upon my
parents, and that I may work righteousness such as will*

please You; and make my offspring righteous. Truly have I repented to You, and truly do I submit (to You) in Islam."

Surah Al-Ahqaf (46:15)

﴿رَبَّنَا تَقَبَّلْ مِنَّاۤ إِنَّكَ أَنتَ ٱلسَّمِيعُ ٱلْعَلِيمُ﴾

"Our Lord, accept this from us. Truly, You are the most Hearing, Knowing."

Surah Al-Baqarah (2:127)

«اللَّهُمَّ أَنْتَ رَبِّي، لا إِلَهَ إِلَّا أَنْتَ، خَلَقْتَنِي وأنا عَبْدُكَ، وأنا عَلىٰ عَهْدِكَ وَوَعْدِكَ ما اسْتَطَعْتُ، أَبوءُ لك بِنِعْمَتِكَ، وأبوءُ لك بِذَنْبِي فاغْفِر لي، فإنَّهُ لا يَغْفِرُ الذُّنوبَ إلَّا أَنْتَ»

"O Allah, You are my Lord. There is no god but You. You created me and I am Your servant, and I uphold Your covenant and (my) promise to You as much as I am able. I seek refuge in You from the evil I have done. I acknowledge before You Your favour upon me, and I acknowledge my sin; so forgive me. Indeed, there is none who can forgive sins except You."

(Bukhari and Ibn Majah: 6323:5070)

«رَبِّ اغْفِرْ لي خَطِيئَتِي وَجَهْلِي وَإِسْرَافِي في أَمْرِي كُلِّهِ، وَما أَنْتَ أَعلمُ بِهِ مِنّي. اللَّهُمَّ اغْفِرْ لي خَطايايَ وعَمْدِي وجَهْلِي وَجِدِّي، وكُلُّ ذلكَ عِندي. اللهُمَّ اغْفِرْ لي ما قَدَّمْتُ وَما أَخَّرْتُ، وَما أَسْرَرْتُ وَما أَعْلَنْتُ، أَنْتَ الْمُقَدِّمُ وَأَنْتَ المؤَخِّرُ، وَأَنْتَ عَلى كُلّ شَيْءٍ قَديرٌ»

"O Allah, forgive me my sins, my ignorance and my excesses, and that which You know more than I. O Allah, forgive me for that committed by me in jest or seriousness, in error or deliberation, and all of that is with (in) me. O Allah, forgive me my past and present (sins) and that committed secretly and openly and that which You know more than I. You are

the Advancer, the Postponer and You have the ability over all things."

(Bukhari and Muslim: 6398:2719)

«أَسْتَغْفِرُ الله الَّذِي لَا إِلَهَ إِلَّا هُوَ الْحَيُّ الْقَيُّومُ وَأَتُوبُ إِلَيْهِ»

"I seek forgiveness from Allah, other than whom there is no god, the Living, the Self-sustaining, and I repent to Him."

(Abu Dawud & Tirmidhi: 1517:3397)

«اللَّهُمَّ إِنَّكَ عَفُوٌّ [كَرِيمٌ] تُحِبُّ العَفْوَ فاعْفُ عَنِّي»

"O Allah, You are forgiving. You love forgiveness, so forgive me."

(Ahmad and Tirmidhi: 25384:3513)

«اللَّهُمَّ إِنِّي أَعُوذُ بكَ مِنَ الهَمِّ والحَزَنِ، والعَجْزِ والكَسَلِ، والجُبنِ والبُخلِ، وَضَلَعِ الدَّينِ، وَغَلَبَةِ الرِّجالِ»

"O Allah, I seek refuge in You from anxiety and grief, from inability and laziness and cowardice and stinginess, and I seek refuge in You from the burden of debt and the coercion of people."

(Bukhari:6369)

«اللّهُمَّ! إِنِّي أَعُوذُ بكَ مِنْ عِلمٍ لَا يَنْفَعُ، وَمِنْ قَلْبٍ لَا يَخْشَعُ، وَمِنْ نَفْسٍ لَا تَشْبَعُ، وَمِنْ دَعْوَةٍ لَا يُسْتَجَابُ لَهَا»

"O Allah, I seek refuge in You from knowledge that does not benefit me, from a heart that is not subdued, from a soul that is not satisfied, and from a supplication that is not answered."

(Muslim:2722)

«اللّهُمَّ! إِنِّي أَعُوذُ بكَ مِنْ زَوَالِ نِعْمَتِكَ، وَتَحَوُّلِ عَافِيَتِكَ، وَفُجَاءَةِ نِقْمَتِكَ، وَجَمِيعِ سَخَطِكَ»

"O Allah, I seek refuge in You from the cessation of Your

favours, from a change in the well-being You have given me, from the unexpectedness of Your vengeance, and from all that angers You."

(Muslim:2739)

«اللّٰهُمَّ! إِنِّي أَعُوذُ بِكَ مِنْ شَرِّ مَا عَمِلْتُ، وَمِنْ شَرِّ مَا لَمْ أَعْمَلْ»

"O Allah, I seek refuge in You from the evil of what I have done and the evil of what I have not done."

(Muslim:2716)

«اللّٰهُمَّ! إِنِّي أَعُوذُ بِكَ مِنْ عَذَابِ جَهَنَّمَ، وَمِنْ عَذَابِ الْقَبْرِ، وَمِنْ فِتْنَةِ الْمَحْيَا وَالْمَمَاتِ، وَمِنْ شَرِّ فِتْنَةِ الْمَسِيحِ الدَّجَّالِ»

"O Allah, I seek refuge in You from the punishment of the Fire and from the punishment of the grave and from the trial of life and death and from the evil of the trial of the false Messiah."

(Muslim:588)

«اللّٰهُمَّ! إِنِّي أَعُوذُ بِرِضَاكَ مِنْ سَخَطِكَ، وَبِمُعَافَاتِكَ مِنْ عُقُوبَتِكَ، وَأَعُوذُ بِكَ مِنْكَ، لَا أُحْصِي ثَنَاءً عَلَيْكَ، أَنْتَ كَمَا أَثْنَيْتَ عَلَىٰ نَفْسِكَ»

"O Allah I seek refuge in Your acceptance from Your anger and in Your forgiveness from Your retribution. I seek refuge in You from You. I cannot enumerate (all of) the praises of You. You are as You have praised Yourself."

(Muslim, Abu Dawud and Tirmidhi: 486:879:3493)

«اللَّهُمَّ إِنِّي أَعُوذُ بِكَ مِنْ مُنْكَرَاتِ الأَخْلَاقِ وَالأَعْمَالِ وَالأَهْوَاءِ»

"O Allah, I seek refuge in You from undesirable morals and deeds, and from desires and diseases."

(Tirmidhi:3591)

«كَانَ رَسُولُ اللهِ ﷺ يَتَعَوَّذُ مِنْ جَهْدِ البَلَاءِ، وَدَرَكِ الشَّقَاءِ، وَسُوءِ القَضَاءِ وَشَمَاتَةِ الأَعْدَاءِ»

"O Allah, I seek refuge in You from the distress of trial, from the lowest level of misery, from the perversity of fate, and from the malicious rejoicing of enemies."

(Bukhari and Muslim: 6347:2707)

«اللّٰهُمَّ! اغْفِرْ لِي وَارْحَمْنِي وَاهْدِنِي وَعَافِنِي وَارْزُقْنِي»

"O Allah, forgive me, have mercy upon me, guide me, give me health, and provide me with sustenance."

(Muslim:2697)

«اللّٰهُمَّ! أَصْلِحْ لِي دِينِيَ الَّذِي هُوَ عِصْمَةُ أَمْرِي، وَأَصْلِحْ لِي دُنْيَايَ الَّتِي فِيهَا مَعَاشِي، وَأَصْلِحْ لِي آخِرَتِي الَّتِي فِيهَا مَعَادِي، وَاجْعَلِ الْحَيَاةَ زِيَادَةً لِي فِي كُلِّ خَيْرٍ، وَاجْعَلِ الْمَوْتَ رَاحَةً لِي مِنْ كُلِّ شَرٍّ»

"O Allah, set right my religion, which is the safeguard of my affairs; and set right my world, wherein is my living; and set right my next life, to which is my return. And make life for me an increase in all good and make death a relief for me from every evil."

(Muslim:2720)

«اللّٰهُمَّ اسْتُرْ عَوْرَتِي وَآمِنْ رَوْعَتِي»

"O Allah, conceal my faults and remove my fears."

(Tabarani:10/180)

«اللّٰهُمَّ اكْفِنِي بِحَلَالِكَ عَنْ حَرَامِكَ، وَأَغْنِنِي بِفَضْلِكَ عَمَّنْ سِوَاكَ»

"O Allah, make sufficient for me what You have made lawful

so that I may avoid what You have made unlawful. And make me self-sufficient by Your favour, (free) from (need of) anyone but You."

(Tirmidhi:3563)

«اللَّهم إني أَسأَلُكَ الْعَفْوَ وَالعَافِيَةَ في دِينِي وَدُنْيَايَ وأَهْلِي وَمَالِي »

"O Allah I ask You for forgiveness and for freedom from evil in (the matters of) my religion and worldly life, my family and property."

(Al-Bazzar:2160)

«اللَّهُمَّ صَلِّ على مُحَمَّدٍ، وَعَلى آلِ مُحَمَّدٍ، كما صَلَّيْتَ على آلِ إبراهيمَ، إِنَّكَ حَمِيدٌ مَجِيدٌ. اللَّهُمَّ بارِكْ عَلى مُحَمَّدٍ، وَعَلى آلِ مُحَمَّدٍ، كما بارَكْتَ عَلى آلِ إبراهيمَ إِنَّكَ حميدٌ مَجيدٌ»

"O Allah confer blessings upon Muhammad and upon the family of Muhammad as You conferred blessings upon Ibraheem and upon the family of Ibraheem. Indeed, You are Praiseworthy and Honourable. O Allah, and continue to bless Muhammad and the family of Muhammad as You have blessed Ibraheem and the family of Ibraheem. Indeed, You are Praiseworthy and Honourable."

(Bukhari and Muslim: 6357:406)

Aameeen! When not supplicating, try to keep busy with *Dhikr.*

﴿ فَٱذْكُرُونِيٓ أَذْكُرْكُمْ ﴾

"Therefore remember Me, I will remember you."

Surah Al-Baqarah (2:152)

Chapter 12
Madinah Al-Munawarah

Narrated Anas (ﷺ): The Prophet (ﷺ) said:

«المَدِينَةُ حَرَمٌ مِنْ كَذَا إِلى كَذَا، لا يُقْطَعُ شَجَرُها، ولا يُحْدَثُ فِيها حَدَثٌ، مَنْ أَحْدَثَ فِيهَا حَدَثًا فَعَلَيْهِ لَعْنَةُ اللهِ والمَلائِكَةِ والنَّاسِ أَجْمَعِينَ».

"Al-Madinah is a sanctuary from that place to that. Its trees should not be cut and no heresy should be innovated nor any sin should be committed in it, and whoever innovates in it heresy or commits sins (bad deeds), then he will incur the curse of Allah, the angels, and all the people."

(Bukhari: 1867 & Muslim: 1366)

The importance of Madinah

Abdullah bin Zaid bin Asim (ﷺ) reported: Allah's Messenger (ﷺ) as saying:

«إِنَّ إِبْرَاهِيمَ حَرَّمَ مَكَّةَ وَدَعَا لِأَهْلِهَا، وَإِنِّي حَرَّمْتُ الْمَدِينَةَ كَمَا حَرَّمَ إِبْرَاهِيمُ مَكَّةَ، وَإِنِّي دَعَوْتُ فِي صَاعِهَا وَمُدِّهَا بِمِثْلَي مَا دَعَا بِهِ إِبْرَاهِيمُ لِأَهْلِ مَكَّةَ».

"Verily Ibraheem declared Makkah sacred and supplicated (for blessings to be showered) upon its inhabitants, and I declare Madinah to be sacred as Ibraheem declared Makkah to be sacred. I have supplicated (Allah for His blessings to be showered) in its Sa' and its Mudd (two standards of weight and measurement) twice as did Ibraheem for the inhabitants of Makkah."

(Muslim:1360)

The rewards of praying in the *Haram* in Madinah

Abu Hurrairah (ﷺ) reported: Allah's Messenger (ﷺ) said:

«صَلَاةٌ فِي مَسْجِدِ رَسُولِ اللهِ ﷺ أَفْضَلُ مِنْ أَلْفِ صَلَاةٍ فِيمَا سِوَاهُ مِنَ الْمَسَاجِدِ، إِلَّا الْمَسْجِدَ الْحَرَامَ».

"A prayer in my mosque is a thousand times more excellent than a prayer in any other mosque, except Masjid-al-Haram (Makkah)."

(Muslim:1394)

About the people of Madinah

Narrated Sa'd ﷺ that he heard the Prophet (ﷺ) saying:

«لا يَكِيدُ أَهْلَ الْمَدِينَةِ أَحَدٌ إِلَّا انْمَاعَ، كَمَا يَنْمَاعُ الْمِلْحُ فِي الْمَاءِ».

"None plots against the people of Al-Madinah but that he will be dissolved (destroyed) like the salt is dissolved in water."

(Bukhari:1877 and Muslim:3361)

Other names of Madinah

As narrated in various *Ahadith* in Bukhari, Madinah was also referred to as Yathrib and Taba by the Prophet (ﷺ).

Visiting the Prophet's (ﷺ) Mosque

Visiting the city of Madinah is not a devotional rite of *Hajj* and has nothing to do with *Hajj*. However it is highly commendable to visit the Prophet's (ﷺ) mosque.

Your intention must not be to visit the grave of the Prophet (ﷺ), but it should be to visit the mosque.

Many books quote various *Ahadith* about visiting the grave after or before *Hajj*. This causes undue stress on those who are unable to do so. These references have no authentic source. Below are some of these statements, which are **INCORRECT**:

- ✗ One who performs *Hajj* and does not visit me, wrongs me.
- ✗ One who visits me after my death is as if he visited me during my life.
- ✗ One who visits me and my ancestor Ibraheem within a year, I guarantee for him *Jannah* with Allah.
- ✗ One who visits my grave, my intercession for him is certainly due.

Salutations

Send salutations on the Messenger (ﷺ) as often possible. This should be done at all times and not only while you are in Madinah.

The Prophet (ﷺ) said:

«مَنْ صَلَّىٰ عَلَيَّ وَاحِدَةً، صَلَّى اللهُ عَلَيْهِ عَشْرًا».

"Whoever asks Allah to bless me once, Allah will bless him for that ten times."

(Muslim:408)

Extending greetings on behalf of other people (this is a very common practice) has no basis in the *Sunnah*.

Abu Hurairah (ﷺ) relates that the Prophet (ﷺ) said:

«لَا تَجْعَلُوا بُيُوتَكُمْ قُبُوراً، وَلَا تَجْعَلُوا قَبْرِي عِيداً، وَصَلُّوا عَلَيَّ فإِنَّ صَلَاتَكُمْ تَبْلُغُنِي حَيْثُ كُنْتُمْ».

"Do not make your houses graves and do not make my grave a place of festivity and merry-making (but) invoke blessings upon me for your blessings will reach me, wherever you may be."

(Abu Dawud:2042)

Etiquette for visiting the graves

As with any other mosque, enter with your right foot and recite the supplication (see chapter 8 for the *Dua'*).

Perform two *Rak'at* (*Tahiyatul-Masjid*) *Salah*.

Proceed to the front of the mosque to visit the graves of Allah's Messenger (ﷺ) and his two Companions, Abu Bakr and Umar (ﷺ), if possible.

Do not push and walk over fellow Muslims inside the mosque.

Following is a picture of the front (gates) of the graves inside the mosque.

Visit the grave of our beloved Prophet (ﷺ) if you can, and extend your greetings while facing his grave (if possible). It is the center gate. Say:

السَّلامُ عَلَيْكَ يَا رَسُولَ اللهِ وَرَحْمَةُ اللهِ وَبَرَكَاتُهُ

"Assalaamu 'alayka yaa Rasullulah wa rahmatullahi wa barakaatuhu."

(Peace be upon you, O Messenger of Allah, and Allah's mercy and blessings.)

Move about two steps to the right and extend your greetings to Abu-Bakr (رضي الله عنه).

السَّلَامُ عَلَيْكَ يَاأَبَابَكْرٍ

"Assalaamu 'alayka yaa Abu-Bakr."

(Peace be upon you, O Abu Bakr.)

Move another step or two to the right and extend greetings to Umar (رضي الله عنه).

السَّلَامُ عَلَيْكَ يَا عُمَرُ

"Assalaamu 'alayka yaa Umar."

(Peace be upon you, O 'Umar.)

If it is crowded, it is quite acceptable just to walk past the graves (or from anywhere in the mosque) and pronounce the greetings as above.

There is no need to pass the graves after every *Salah*. Also the long *Dua's* and greetings as many books teach have no authentic evidence in the *Sunnah*.

Sending greetings on behalf of someone also has no evidence in the *Sunnah*. The *Hadith* related earlier in the chapter, indicates that one can send greetings upon the Prophet (ﷺ) from wherever one is in the world.

$$\text{«وَصَلُّوا عَلَيَّ فإِنَّ صَلَاتَكُمْ تَبْلُغُنِي حَيْثُ كُنْتُمْ»}$$

"...invoke blessings upon me for your blessings will reach me, wherever you may be."

(Abu Dawud:2042)

It is improper (even sinful) for a visitor to the Prophet's (ﷺ) mosque to stand before the graves and indulge in the following:

× Crying, beseeching from the Prophet (ﷺ), and supplicating to the Prophet (ﷺ);

× Supplicating long *Dua's* and seeking the Prophet's (ﷺ) intercession;

× Touching and kissing the lattice and walls.

The Prophet (ﷺ) said:

$$\text{«لا تُطْرُونِي كما أَطْرَتِ النَّصَارَى ابنَ مَرْيَمَ»}$$

"Do not praise me as the Christians did Eesa bin Maryam (Jesus)."

(Bukhari:3445)

Walking backwards away from the tombs to leave the *Masjid* is an innovation.

Raudah-tul-Jannah

Try to perform *Salah* in the area called '*Raudah-tul-Jannah*. This area is marked by white pillars and different coloured carpet, close to the front of the mosque.

«مَا بَيْنَ مِنْبَرِي وَبَيْتِي رَوْضَةٌ مِنْ رِيَاضِ الْجَنَّةِ» .

"Between my house and my pulpit is a garden from the gardens of Paradise."

(Muslim:1390)

There is no requirement to make *Salah* or *Dua'* at every pillar in this area as many books teach.

Avoid performing *Salah* in the forbidden times. Do not contravene a law with an action that is not part of the *Sunnah*.

If you are fortunate to get a chance to perform *Salah* here, and you wish to make *Dua'*, do it while you are in *Sujood*, as the guards will move you as soon as you sit down to make *Dua'*.

There are special times for ladies to enter the *Raudah-tul-Jannah* area. Normally at about 7.00am and after *Zuhr Salah*. These times vary from year to year, so ask one of the guards at the door for the appropriate times.

You have to go very early, as it is sometimes impossible, due to the crowds, to get a chance to perform *Salah* in this area.

On Fridays people sit in this area from after *Salatul-Fajr* until after *Jumuah*.

Salah in General

All the aspects of *Salah* (*Sutrah*, *Sunnah*, *Nafl*, *Janazah*, where to sit) mentioned for Makkah are applicable to Madinah as well. Also as with Makkah, going very early for *Jumuah Salah* is essential.

As there is no *Tawaaf*, try to spend your time with all the other aspects of *Ibadah* as mentioned for Makkah.

There are no special rewards to make *Salah* in the 'old *Mihrab*'.

You will notice many people queuing and pushing to make *Salah* in the small *Mimbar* located next to the *Raudah*. Some people even go to the extent of performing *Salah* in the forbidden times in this area. Once again do not contravene a law with an action that is not part of the *Sunnah*.

The *Haram* is locked every day about one hour after *'Eshaa* until *Tahajjud* (about 3.00am, depending on the season).

The *Haram* gets very full even by 4.00am. So be early for your prayers, in order to get a place inside the mosque. The mosque has been extended and is now quite large and has two levels (ground and roof level). Keep in mind that there are thousands and thousands of people in Madinah, before and after *Hajj*. The new section is air-conditioned.

Personal Behaviour

You are in Madinah. The city of our beloved Prophet (ﷺ). All the aspects regarding personal behaviour in the previous chapters apply to Madinah also.

Let the two opening *Ahadith* in this chapter guide your behaviour.

Once again, apply patience. If you are pushed or poked in the back in the crowds, gently remove the offender's hand and try to maintain that smile of yours.

Staying 8 days in Madinah

There is no authentic evidence from the Qur'an or the *Sunnah* about any additional benefit in staying 8 days (40 prayers) in Madinah. The reason many people insist on this is based on a *Da'eef* (weak) *Hadith* about performing 40 prayers in the Prophet's (ﷺ) mosque. This *Hadith* is weak or a distortion of the *Sahih Hadith* which says, 40 days in any mosque with *Takbir-Tahrimah* (first *Takbir*), and not 40 prayers in Madinah.

Question:

Let me relate the answer given by a renowned scholar when asked the following question:

"Is the offering of 40 consecutive prayers in the Prophet's (ﷺ) mosque a must?"

Answer:

"Many people tend to think that offering 40 prayers with the congregation in the Prophet's (ﷺ) mosque has a special significance. Well, if it did, then there should be something associated with this number which should make it preferable to an even larger number. The fact is that there is none. If you offer 41 prayers in the Prophet's (ﷺ) mosque, whether consecutive or not, you are better off than offering 40 prayers. The reason is that Allah gives us for every prayer we offer there the reward of 1000 prayers anywhere else (except Makkah). Hence the more prayers we offer the greater the reward."

Let us look at the mathematical calculation.

One *Salah* in Madinah = 1000 rewards, hence 40 prayers in Madinah = 40,000 (40 x 1000). One *Salah* in Makkah = 100,000 rewards; meaning that 8 days in Madinah equates to less than half of the reward for ONE *Salah* in Makkah. Shouldn't this encourage any person to get to Makkah as soon as possible or stay longer in Makkah?

Don't get me wrong. If time and finances permit, it is good to stay as long as possible. Stay 20 days if you want.

I personally love Madinah very much. However, do not let your stay in Madinah "affect" the time you should spend in Makkah. Many people insist on spending 8 days in Madinah and only arrive in Makkah about one or two days before *Hajj*. Your time for *Hajj* is better spent in Makkah.

Arriving a few days just before the actual *Hajj* also means that Makkah will be very crowded and you will not be able to enjoy the *Haram* as much as you would when it is less crowded. Even *Nafl Tawaaf* becomes extremely difficult to perform, due to the crowds. Pilgrims are performing their prayers in the streets as they are unable to enter the *Haram*.

Believe me, the lines for *Salah* stretches for kilometres in all directions outside the mosque.

Many people will fight and argue no end over this issue of staying 8 days in Madinah, but ask them about staying 3 days in Mina (or staying in Mina at all). They have all sorts of excuses for not being able to stay in Mina until the 13th. Keep in mind, the days in Mina are part of *Hajj*, and Madinah is not.

Let me relate two stories to highlight how we sometimes lose sight of our priorities:

During the *Hajj* year of 1409 (1989) we ascribed to the same view about the 40 prayers in Madinah. There were four of us (two couples) that were "counting" together. One of the ladies started menstruating (even after taking pills to ensure this wouldn't happen, in order to make the 40) after the count was at 30. She was devastated and needed special counselling. At *Salah* number 36, my wife developed a severe bout of the flu. In order for her not to miss the 40 prayers in the *Masjid* we virtually forced her to the *Masjid*. We made our life very difficult due to ignorance! (My wife still reminds me of it.)

During the *Hajj* year of 1416 (1996) a group of pilgrims insisted on spending 8 days in Madinah. They arrived in Makkah two days before the 8th of Dhul-Hijjah. They went to Mina on the 8th (which was on a Friday). After Arafat they returned to Mina for *Ramy* and proceeded to Makkah where they spent the rest of the days. They went to Mina every day for *Ramy*, but spent most of their time in Makkah. They then departed for home the following Thursday. Now this group did not stay in Mina (*Wajib* act); did not perform any *Jumu'ah* (not a requirement though) in Makkah; spent most of their time in Madinah. This is a classical example of bad planning and lack of priorities on the part of the organisers.

Visiting other sites around Madinah

Madinah is full of Islamic history and there are plenty of places to visit. However there is no religious merit in visiting other mosques or historical sites except for Quba Mosque and the gravesites.

As in Makkah, if the visit to any place means missing *Salah* in the *Haram*, avoid it.

As mentioned before, people save for a lifetime to come to *Hajj* and to Madinah and wish to visit some of the historical places. It is acceptable to do so merely out of interest without considering it an act of worship.

It is *Sunnah* to visit the graveyards:

The Prophet (ﷺ) said:

«زُورُوا الْقُبُورَ . فَإِنَّهَا تُذَكِّرُكُمُ الآخِرَةَ» .

"Visit graves in that these remind you of the Hereafter."

(Ibn Majah:1569 and Abu Dawud:3235)

Al-Baqee Cemetery

Many of the Companions and family members of the Prophet (ﷺ) are buried in Al-Baqee cemetery. There are no marked gravestones to indicate specific graves. It is not necessary to concern oneself or to dwell over any particular gravesite.

The *Sunnah Dua'* one should recite at any graveyard:

«السَّلَامُ عَلَيْكُمْ دَارَ قَوْمٍ مُؤْمِنِينَ، وَأَتَاكُمْ مَاتُوعَدُونَ غَدًا، مُؤَجَّلُونَ، وَإِنَّا – إِنْ شَاءَ اللهُ – بِكُمْ لَاحِقُونَ»

"Assalaamu alaykum daara qawmin mu'minin, wa atakum ma Tū'adun ghadan, mu'ajjalūn, wa innaa in sha-allahu bikum laahiqoon."

(Peace be upon the Muslim people of these dwellings. That which was promised to you for the tomorrow has reached you. You were given respite. And we will be joining you soon, if Allah wills.)

(Muslim:974)

Women are not allowed to enter the graveyard. You will

notice at the entrance a big sign warning women against the visiting of the graves. Most women stand outside at the fence and supplicate the preceding *dua*.

The cemetery gates are locked and are open only at certain times. Normally it is open after *Salatul-Fajr* and *'Asr*.

If you wish to enter the cemetery and see how a burial is performed in Madinah, I suggest you follow (help carry) the bier (*Janazah*) from the mosque. As in Makkah there are many burials in Madinah during the *Hajj* period. Word of caution though; be ready to carry the bier all the way.

Many groups also visit the gravesite of Hamzah who was martyred at the battle of Uhud, and the other Companions (🙏), and make various supplications there. If you do visit this site, refrain from facing the graves and making the wrong supplications. The only supplication to make is the one mentioned before.

With regards to women visiting the gravesites, including that of the Prophet (ﷺ); the issue is addressed in chapter 3 ("About Women"). I would like to remind my readers that the *Fiqh* views expressed in this book are not my own opinions. These are the rulings of the *Imams* and scholars I have used as my reference. Needless to say they are also the views to which I ascribe.

Yes, there are opposing views on this subject. I had to either omit this issue from the book or abide by my general approach on the *Fiqh* issues in this book. If you disagree with this view, no problem, but as I mentioned before, at least take a moment to review the basis upon which it is established.

Quba Mosque

There is no specific supplication for the Quba Mosque, but it is one of the few places recommended to visit, while you are in Madinah:

Sahl bin Haneef (🙏) reported that the Prophet (ﷺ) said:

«مَنْ تَطَهَّرَ فِي بَيْتِهِ، ثُمَّ أَتَىٰ مَسْجِدَ قُبَاءٍ، فَصَلَّىٰ فِيهِ صَلَاةً، كَانَ لَهُ كَأَجْرِ عُمْرَةٍ» .

"One who does Wudu' at home, then offers prayers in Quba Mosque is entitled to the reward of an Umrah."

(Ahmad:3/487, Nasa'i:700, Ibn Majah:1412 and Hakim:3/12)

Other

Many groups visit the "Seven Mosques" and people push and fight to perform *Salah* inside these small mosques. There is no need.

If you have a good guide he will show you the area where the battle of the trench happened. The location of the actual trench is now a road, so there is not much to see, but merely standing in places of such historical significance is a great feeling. Also at Uhud let him show you and take you on the hill where the archers stood.

You may ask about Badr. Well it is not as close to Madinah as you may have thought. It is actually about 150km from Madinah and there are generally no trips to it.

A place of interest to visit is the King Fahd Qur'an printing press where they print the Qur'ans you find inside the mosques. You need to make an appointment to visit this facility. Most agents know the procedures to follow in order to obtain permission for a visit.

Doors of the *Haram*

As in Makkah the doors of the *Haram* have names and can be used as a means of identifying your location.

Some of the door names are:

- Baabus-Salaam;
- Baabur-Rahmah;
- Baabuj-Jibreel;
- Baabun-Nisaa;
- Baabus-Siddiq;
- Baabul-Malik Abdul Aziz.

Follow the "procedure" below as it will help you to achieve, praying in *Raudah, Fard Salah* in the front row and passing the graves:

> In relation to the diagram below: ❶ Be early and enter from the appropriate door nearest to your location. Proceed to the *Raudah* area❷ and perform your *Tahiyatul-Masjid* and *Sunnah Salah* here. Move towards the first row❸ and perform your *Fard Salah* here. After *Salah* wait for the crowd to lessen while you perform *Dhikr, Tasbih*, reciting Qur'an, etc. Proceed towards the door while passing by the graves❹ and extending your greetings.

If you exit from this door ❺ you will be in the general area of Al-Baqee cemetery.

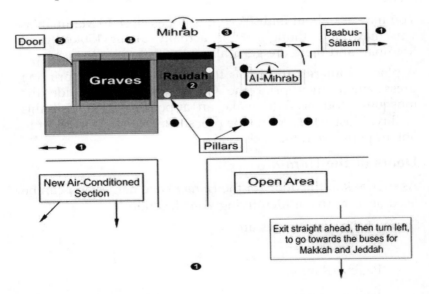

Access to the *Haram*

The doors are all numbered and, unlike Makkah, there are specific doors for men and women to enter. There is no need to memorise the door numbers, as the entrances are rather obvious.

Some door numbers that are worth remembering:

- The graves are near door no. 41;
- Door no. 29 is where the ladies enter to go to *Raudah-tul-Jannah*;
- Access to roof area (men only) is via doors 6, 10, 15, 27, 31.

All the larger doors have wheelchair ramps for easy access.

Medical Facilities

There are specialist hospitals in and around Madinah.

There used to be a large clinic in Madinah very near to the *Haram*, but it has since been removed. The best place to ask about new medical facilities is at any pharmacy (chemist).

If you have a 'simple' complaint such as a common cold, or muscle cramps, the pharmacists are normally pretty good at prescribing the required medicine (without a prescription).

Toilets

There are lots and lots of toilets and *Wudu* facilities around the *Haram* area, both for men and women.

The women's toilet locations are:

- Near doors 12, 13, 21, 23, 24, 25, 26, 29.
- These doors are also the entrances to the *Masjid* for the women.

The men's toilet locations are:

- Near doors 1, 5, 6, 7, 8, 14, 16, 17, 18, 19, 20, 21, 32, 38.

Shopping

Madinah has one of the best fresh date markets.

As with Makkah there are plenty of shopping opportunities. Once again, try not to spend too much time shopping as it can be better spent in *Ibadah*.

Many pilgrims wonder whether it is better (or cheaper) to buy in Makkah or Madinah. A simple rule: If you like the item and the price, buy it! You may not find it again, let alone the shop.

Zamzam

The water contained in the grey containers inside the *Haram* is *Zamzam* water.

As in Makkah, some of the containers contain room temperature *Zamzam*. It has blue writing on it: *"Zamzam* water, not cold".

If you did not get a chance to get *Zamzam* to take home in Makkah, there is a *Zamzam* filling 'station' outside the mosque near door number eight (8).

Transport

The trip to and from Madinah airport by taxi takes about 30 to 45 minutes, and could cost up to 50 Saudi riyals. The *Mutawwif's* office will arrange a bus for you, but you may need a taxi when going home.

As a pilgrim you will be using the *Mutawwif* assigned buses for all your transport needs.

Leaving Madinah

Do not walk backwards out of the *Haram*.

There are no specified supplications, but one should read the supplication when departing from any mosque (see the last page of chapter 8).

Ensure that all your luggage is secure and marked (labelled) correctly.

Collect your passport from the *Mutawwif's* office.

To Makkah

You need to prepare yourself for *Ihraam* conditions (i.e. *Ghusl*, trim nails).

You will stop at the *Meqaat* Dhul-Hulaifah where you will adopt *Ihraam* (you may put on your *Ihraam* clothes at your hotel prior to leaving) and make your *Niyah* at the *Meqaat*.

The bus journey could take up to 12 hours, so keep some water with you. The bus will stop on the way for *Salah* and food and also at certain checkpoints.

For Home

Do not spend all your riyals, as you may need these for food or excess baggage charges.

See chapter 10, under "Going Home" for important information regarding obtaining your passport and coupon refunds, and many aspects about going home.

Chapter 13
A Touch of History

This chapter deals briefly with some of the more historical aspects of certain landmarks that the pilgrim will come across during *Hajj*. It is not very comprehensive it is merely to wet your appetite.

Makkah:

$$﴿وَإِذْ جَعَلْنَا ٱلْبَيْتَ مَثَابَةً لِّلنَّاسِ وَأَمْنًا﴾$$

"And (remember) when We made the House a place of resort for mankind and a place of safety..."

Surah Al-Baqarah (2:125)

$$﴿وَإِذْ قَالَ إِبْرَٰهِـۧمُ رَبِّ ٱجْعَلْ هَـٰذَا بَلَدًا ءَامِنًا وَٱرْزُقْ أَهْلَهُ مِنَ ٱلثَّمَرَٰتِ مَنْ ءَامَنَ مِنْهُم بِٱللَّهِ وَٱلْيَوْمِ ٱلْءَاخِرِ﴾$$

"And (remember) when Ibraheem said, 'My Lord make this city (Makkah) a place of sanctuary and provide its people with fruits, such of them as believe in Allah and the Last Day'..."

Surah Al-Baqarah (2:126)

$$﴿إِنَّ أَوَّلَ بَيْتٍ وُضِعَ لِلنَّاسِ لَلَّذِى بِبَكَّةَ مُبَارَكًا وَهُدًى لِّلْعَٰلَمِينَ﴾$$

"Verily, the first house (of worship) appointed for mankind was that at Bakkah (Makkah), full of blessing, and guidance for Al-Alamin (mankind and jinns)."

Surah Al-Imran (3:96)

Allah commanded Prophet Ibraheem (ﷺ) to leave his second wife Hagar and their newly born son Ismail alone in the uninhabited valley of Bakkah.

Narrated Ibn Abbas (ﷺ):

$$«أَوَّلَ مَا اتَّخَذَ النِّسَاءُ المِنْطَقَ مِنْ قِبَلِ أُمِّ إِسْمَاعِيلَ، اتَّخَذَتْ$$

مِنْطَقًا لِتُعَفِّيَ أَثَرَها على سارَةَ، ثُمَّ جاءَ بها إِبْرَاهِيمُ وبابِنِها
إِسْمَاعِيلَ وهيَ تُرْضِعُهُ حتَّى وضَعَهُما عِنْدَ البَيْتِ عنْدَ دَوْحَةٍ
فَوْقَ الزَّمزم في أعْلى المَسْجِدِ ولَيْسَ بِمَكَّةَ يَوْمَئِذٍ أَحَدٌ، ولَيْسَ
بها ماءٌ فَوَضَعَهُما هُنالكَ، ووَضَعَ عِنْدَهُما جِرَابًا فِيهِ تَمْرٌ
وسِقاءً فِيهِ ماءٌ ثُمَّ قَفَّى إِبْرَاهِيمُ مُنْطَلِقًا، فَتَبِعَتْهُ أُمُّ إِسْمَاعِيلَ
فَقالَتْ: ياإِبْرَاهِيمُ، أَيْنَ تَذْهَبُ وتَتْرُكُنا فِي هَذا الوَادِي الذِي
لَيْسَ فِيهِ أَنِيسٌ ولا شَيْءٌ؟ فَقالَتْ لَهُ ذٰلكَ مِرَارًا، وجَعَلَ لا
يَلْتَفِتُ إِلَيها فَقالَتْ لَهُ: آللَّهُ أَمَرَكَ بهذا؟ قالَ: نَعَمْ، قالَتْ:
إِذَنْ لا يُضَيِّعُنا، ثُمَّ رَجَعَتْ، فانْطَلَقَ إِبْرَاهِيمُ حتَّى إِذَا كانَ عِنْدَ
الثَّنِيَّةِ حَيْثُ لا يَرَوْنَهُ اسْتَقْبَلَ بِوَجْهِهِ البَيْتَ ثُمَّ دَعا بِهٰؤُلاءِ
الدَّعواتِ ورَفَعَ يَدَيْهِ فَقالَ:))

"The first lady to use a girdle was the mother of Ismail. She used a girdle so that she might hide her tracks from Sarah. Ibraheem brought her and her son Ismail while she was suckling him, to a place near the Ka'bah under a tree on the spot of Zamzam, at the highest place in the mosque. During those days there was nobody in Makkah, nor was there any water. So he made them sit over there and placed near them a leather bag containing some dates, and a small water-skin containing some water, and set out homeward. Ismail's mother followed him saying, 'O Ibraheem! Where are you going, leaving us in this valley where there is no person whose company we may enjoy, nor is there anything (to enjoy)?' She repeated that to him many times, but he did not look back at her. Then she asked him, 'Has Allah ordered you to do so?' He said, 'Yes.' She said, 'Then He will not neglect us', and returned while Ibraheem proceeded onwards, and on reaching the Thaniya where they could not see him, he faced the Ka'bah, and raising both hands, invoked Allah saying the following prayers:

(Bukhari:3364)

﴿رَّبَّنَا إِنِّي أَسْكَنتُ مِن ذُرِّيَّتِي بِوَادٍ غَيْرِ ذِى زَرْعٍ عِندَ بَيْتِكَ ٱلْمُحَرَّمِ رَبَّنَا لِيُقِيمُوا ٱلصَّلَوٰةَ فَٱجْعَلْ أَفْـِٔدَةً مِّنَ ٱلنَّاسِ تَهْوِىٓ إِلَيْهِمْ وَٱرْزُقْهُم مِّنَ ٱلثَّمَرَٰتِ لَعَلَّهُمْ يَشْكُرُونَ﴾

'O our Lord! I have made some of my offspring to dwell in a valley with no cultivation, by your Sacred House (the Ka'bah at Makkah); in order, O our Lord, that they may offer prayers perfectly, so fill some hearts among men with love towards them, and (O Allah) provide them with fruits so that they may give thanks.'

Surah Ibraheem (14:37)

Running during *Sa'ee*

«وَجَعَلَتْ أُمُّ إِسْمَاعِيلَ تُرْضِعُ إِسْمَاعِيلَ وتَشْرَبُ مِن ذٰلكَ المَاءِ حَتَّى إِذَا نَفِدَ ما في السِّقَاءِ عَطِشَتْ وعَطِشَ ابْنُها فَجَعَلَتْ تَنْظُرُ إِلَيْهِ يَتَلَوَّى - أَوْ قَالَ: يَتَلَبَّط - فَانْطَلَقَتْ كَرَاهِيَةَ أَنْ تَنْظُرَ إِلَيْهِ، فَوَجَدَتِ الصَّفا أَقْرَبَ جَبَلٍ في الأرْضِ يَلِيها، فَقَامَتْ عَلَيْهِ ثُمَّ اسْتَقْبَلَتِ الوَادِيَ تَنْظُرُ هَلْ تَرَى أَحَدًا فَلَمْ تَرَ أَحَدًا، فَهَبَطَتْ مِنَ الصَّفا حَتَّى إِذَا بَلَغَت الوَادِيَ رَفَعَتْ طَرَفَ دِرْعِها ثُمَّ سَعَتْ سَعْيَ الإِنْسَانِ المجهُودِ حتَّى جَاوَزَتِ الوَادِيَ، ثُمَّ أَتَتِ المَرْوَةَ فَقَامَتْ عَلَيها فَنَظَرتْ هَلْ تَرَى أَحَدًا فَلَمْ تَر أَحَدًا، فَفَعَلَتْ ذٰلكَ سَبْعَ مَرَّاتٍ. قَالَ ابنُ عَبَّاسٍ: قَالَ النَّبِيُّ ﷺ: «فَذٰلكَ سَعْيُ النَّاسِ بَيْنَهُما»، فَلَمَّا أَشْرَفَتْ عَلى المَرْوَةِ سَمِعَتْ صَوْتًا فَقَالَتْ: صَهٍ، تُرِيدُ نَفْسَها، ثُمَّ تَسَمَّعَتْ فَسَمِعَتْ أَيْضًا، فَقَالَتْ: قَدْ أَسْمَعْتَ إِنْ كَانَ عِنْدَكَ غُوَاثٌ»

"...Ismail's mother went on suckling Ismail and drinking from the water (she had). When the water in the water-skin had all been used up, she became thirsty and her child also

became thirsty. She started looking at him (i.e. Ismail) tossing in agony. She left him, for she could not endure looking at him, and found that the mountain of Safaa was the nearest mountain to her on that land. She stood on it and started looking at the valley keenly so that she might see somebody, but she could not see anybody. Then she descended from Safaa and when she reached the valley, she tucked up her robe and ran in the valley like a person in distress and trouble, till she crossed the valley and reached the Marwah mountain where she stood and started looking, expecting to see somebody, but she could not see anybody. She repeated that (running between Safaa and Marwah) seven times.

The Prophet (ﷺ) said, 'This is the source of the tradition of the walking of people between them (i.e. Safaa and Marwah). When she reached the Marwah (for the last time) she heard a voice and she asked herself to be quiet and listened attentively. She heard the voice again and said, 'O, (whoever you may be)! You have made me hear your voice; have you got something to help me?'...''

Zamzam Well

«فَإِذَا هِيَ بِالمَلَكِ عِنْدَ مَوْضِع زَمْزَمَ فَبَحَثَ بِعَقِبِهِ – أَوْ قَالَ: بِجَنَاحِهِ – حَتَّى ظَهَرَ المَاءُ فَجَعَلَتْ تُحَوِّضُهُ وتقُولُ بِيدِها هكَذَا، وجَعَلَتْ تَغْرِفُ مِنَ المَاءِ فِي سِقائِها وهُوَ يَفُورُ بَعْدَما تَغْرِفُ. قالَ ابنُ عَبَّاسٍ: قالَ النَّبِيّ ﷺ: «يَرْحَمُ اللهُ أُمَّ إسمَاعِيلَ لَوْ تَرَكَتْ زمزم – أَوْ قالَ: لَوْ لَمْ تَغْرِفْ مِنْ زَمْزَمَ – لَكانَتْ زَمْزَمُ عَيْنًا مَعِينًا»، قالَ: فَشَرِبَتْ وأَرْضَعَتْ ولَدَها»

"...And behold! She saw an angel at the place of Zamzam, digging the earth with his heel (or his wing), till water flowed from that place. She started to make something like a basin around it, using her hand in this way, and started filling her water-skin with water with her hands, and the water was flowing out after she had scooped some of it."

"The Prophet (ﷺ) added, 'May Allah bestow Mercy on Ismail's mother! Had she let the Zamzam (flow without trying to control it) (or had she not scooped from that water) (to fill her water-skin), Zamzam would have been a stream flowing on the surface of the earth.' The Prophet (ﷺ) further added, 'Then she drank (water) and suckled her child...'"

(Bukhari:3364)

This was the start of the Zamzam water well, and it is still producing water today for the pilgrims and visitors to Makkah. This well was closed for a while during its history. The Prophet's (ﷺ) uncle, Abu Talib received a dream about digging for the Zamzam well, which he did, and the well was reopened.

Ka'bah

«فَقَالَ لَهَا المَلَكُ: لا تخافُوا الضَّيْعَةَ، فإنَّ هَذَا بَيْتُ اللهِ يَبْنِي هَذَا الغُلامُ وأبُوهِ، وإنَّ اللهَ لا يُضِيعُ أَهْلَهُ»

"...The angel said to her, 'don't be afraid of being neglected, for this is the House of Allah which will be built by this boy and his father, and Allah never neglects His people...'"

«ثُمَّ لَبِثَ عَنْهُمْ ما شاءَ اللهُ ثُمَّ جاءَ بَعْدَ ذلِكَ وإسماعِيلُ يَبري نَبْلًا له تَحْتَ دَوْحَةٍ قَرِيبًا مِنْ زَمْزَمَ، فَلَمَّا رَآهُ قامَ إِلَيْهِ فَصَنَعا كما يَصْنَعُ الوَالِدُ بالوَلَدِ والوَلَدُ بالوَالِدِ، ثُمَّ قالَ: يا إسْماعِيلُ، إنَّ اللهَ أَمَرَني بأمْرٍ، قالَ: فاصْنَعْ ما أَمَرَكَ رَبُّكَ، قالَ: وَتُعِينُني؟ قالَ: وأُعِينُكَ، قالَ: فإنَّ اللهَ أَمَرَني أَنْ أَبْنِيَ هاهُنا بَيْتًا - وأشارَ إلى أكَمَةٍ مُرْتَفِعَةٍ عَلى ما حَوْلَها - قالَ: فَعِنْدَ ذلِكَ رَفَعا القَوَاعِدَ مِنَ البَيْتِ، فَجَعَلَ إسْماعِيلُ يأتي بالحِجارَةِ وإبْراهِيمُ يَبْني حتَّى إذا ارْتَفَعَ البِناءُ جاءَ بهذا الحَجَرِ فَوَضَعَهُ لَهُ فَقامَ عَلَيْهِ وهُوَ يَبْني وإسْماعِيلُ يُناوِلُهُ الحِجارَةَ وهما يَقُولانِ: ﴿رَبَّنَا تَقَبَّلْ مِنَّا إِنَّكَ أَنتَ السَّمِيعُ الْعَلِيمُ﴾

"Then Ibraheem stayed away from them for a period as long as Allah wished, and called on them afterwards. He saw Ismail under a tree near Zamzam, sharpening his arrows. When he saw Ibraheem, he rose up to welcome him (and they greeted each other as a father does with his son or a son does with his father). Ibraheem said, 'Oh Ismail! Allah has given me an order.' Ismail said, 'Do what your Lord has ordered you to do.' Ibraheem asked, 'Will you help me?' Ismail said, 'I will help you.' Ibraheem said, 'Allah has ordered me to build a house here,' pointing to a hillock higher than the land surrounding it. The Prophet (ﷺ) added, 'Then they raised the foundations of the House (i.e. the Ka'bah). Ismail brought the stones and Ibraheem was building, and when the walls became high, Ismail brought this stone and put it for Ibraheem who stood over it and carried on building, while Ismail was handing him the stones, and both of them were saying, 'O our Lord! Accept (this service) from us, Verily, You are the All-Hearing, the All-Knowing'. "

(Bukhari:3364)

﴿وَإِذْ بَوَّأْنَا لِإِبْرَهِيمَ مَكَانَ ٱلْبَيْتِ﴾

"And (remember) when We showed Ibraheem the site of the (Sacred) House..."

Surah Al-Hajj (22:26)

Hajrul-Aswad (Black Stone)

A special stone was placed in its eastern corner to mark the starting point for the circling of the Ka'bah. This stone according to the Prophet's (ﷺ) explanation, was originally shining white in colour when it was brought down from Paradise. However, due to the sins of man it changed to its present colour of black, hence the name *Hajrul-Aswad* (the Black Stone).

Narrated Ibn Abbas (﵁), Allah's Messenger (ﷺ) said:

«نَزَلَ الْحَجَرُ الْأَسْوَدُ مِنَ الْجَنَّةِ وَهُوَ أَشَدُّ بَيَاضًا مِنَ اللَّبَنِ

فَسَوَّدَتْهُ خَطَايَا بَنِي آدَمَ»

*"The black stone descended from Paradise whiter than milk,
but the sins of the descendants of Adam made it black."*

(Tirmidhi:877)

Tawaaf

Circling of the Ka'bah has been performed since the building
of the Ka'bah. In the days of ignorance the polytheists used to
circle it while naked. The Prophet (ﷺ) Muhammad stopped
this practice.

Abu Hurraira (ﷺ) reported:

«بَعَثَنِي أَبُو بَكْرٍ الصِّدِّيقُ فِي الْحَجَّةِ الَّتِي أَمَّرَهُ عَلَيْهَا رَسُولُ
اللهِ ﷺ، قَبْلَ حَجَّةِ الْوَدَاعِ، فِي رَهْطٍ، يُؤَذِّنُونَ فِي النَّاسِ يَوْمَ
النَّحْرِ: لَا يَحُجُّ بَعْدَ الْعَامِ مُشْرِكٌ، وَلَا يَطُوفُ بِالْبَيْتِ عُرْيَانٌ»

*"Abu Bakr Siddiq (ﷺ) sent me during Hajj before the
Farewell Pilgrimage for which Allah's Messenger (ﷺ) had
appointed him an Amir, among a group of people whom he
had ordered to make announcement to the people on the day of
Nahr: 'After this year no polytheist may perform the
Pilgrimage and no naked person may circumambulate the
House'."*

(Muslim:1347)

Maqaam Ibraheem

During the building of the Ka'bah, Prophet Ibraheem (عليه السلام)
stood on a large stone block in order to complete the upper
part of its walls. He used to move the block around the Ka'bah
as it was built and, on completion of the building, it was left
outside the Ka'bah near the eastern wall and became known
in later years as the *Maqaam Ibraheem* (the standing place of
Ibraheem). Allah refers to it in the Qur'an:

﴿فِيهِ ءَايَٰتٌ بَيِّنَٰتٌ مَّقَامُ إِبْرَٰهِيمَ﴾

"In it are Manifest signs (for example), the Maqaam (place) of Ibraheem..."

Surah Al-Imran (3:97)

Area known as the *Hijr*

During its history the Ka'bah was destroyed and rebuilt a few times.

«عَنْ عَائِشَةَ قَالَتْ: سَأَلْتُ رَسُولَ اللهِ ﷺ، عَنِ الْجَدْرِ؟ أَمِنَ الْبَيْتِ هُوَ؟ قَالَ: «نَعَمْ» قُلْتُ: فَلِمَ لَمْ يُدْخِلُوهُ الْبَيْتَ؟ قَالَ: «إِنَّ قَوْمَكِ قَصَّرَتْ بِهِمُ النَّفَقَةُ» قُلْتُ: فَمَا شَأْنُ بَابِهِ مُرْتَفِعٌ؟ قَالَ: «فَعَلَ ذٰلِكِ قَوْمُكِ لِيُدْخِلُوا مَنْ شَآءُوْا وَيَمْنَعُوا مَنْ شَآءُوْا، وَلَوْلَا أَنَّ قَوْمَكِ حَدِيثٌ عَهْدُهُمْ فِي الْجَاهِلِيَّةِ، فَأَخَافُ أَنْ تُنْكِرَ قُلُوبُهُمْ، لَنَظَرْتُ أَنْ أُدْخِلَ الْجَدْرَ فِي الْبَيْتِ، وَأَنْ أُلْزِقَ بَابَهُ بِالْأَرْضِ»

"Aishah (🙏) reported: 'I asked Allah's Messenger (ﷺ) about the wall, circumpassing the House (i.e. whether the wall on the side of Hijr was included in the Ka'bah). He said: 'Yes'. 'I said: Then why did they not include it in the house?'

He said: 'Your people ran short of the means (to do so).' I said: 'Why is it that the level of its door is raised high?' He said:

'Your people did it so that they should admit one whom they liked, and forbid him whom they disliked, and if your people were not converts to faith, and I did not apprehend that their hearts would feel agitated at this, I would have definitely included (the area of) this wall in the House and would have brought the door to the level of the ground'."

(Muslim:1333)

Many books refer to this area as the Hijr-Ismail. Some go as far as to say that Prophet Ismail and his mother Hagar (🙏) are buried here, hence the name. There is no authentic proof for this or the name. The fact that we are allowed to make

Salah in this area is proof enough that this cannot be true, as we are not allowed to make *Salah* on graves. Also the Prophet (ﷺ) referred to this area as Al-Hijr.

Mina

Allah commanded Ibraheem (in a dream) to sacrifice his son Ismail. In order to fulfil his command Ibraheem took Ismail and went to the area (Mina).

﴿فَلَمَّا بَلَغَ مَعَهُ ٱلسَّعْىَ قَالَ يَٰبُنَىَّ إِنِّى أَرَىٰ فِى ٱلْمَنَامِ أَنِّىٓ أَذْبَحُكَ فَٱنظُرْ مَاذَا تَرَىٰ ۚ قَالَ يَٰٓأَبَتِ ٱفْعَلْ مَا تُؤْمَرُ ۖ سَتَجِدُنِىٓ إِن شَآءَ ٱللَّهُ مِنَ ٱلصَّٰبِرِينَ﴾

"And, when he (his son) was old enough to walk with him, he said: 'O my son! I have seen in a dream that I am slaughtering you (offering you in sacrifice to Allah), so look what you think!' He said: 'O my father! Do that which you are commanded, Insha Allah, you shall find me of As-Sabirin' (the patient ones, etc.)..."

Surah As-Saffat (37:102)

Jamr'at and Stoning

On his way to Mina the *Shaytaan* tempted him three times to disobey the order. Ibraheem threw seven stones at the *Shaytaan* each time. (Some narrations of this story say the *Shaytaan* tempted Ismail the first time; and the second time the *Shaytaan* tried to persuade Ismail's mother to try and make her persuade her husband; and the third time he tempted Ibraheem.)

These are the positions where the 3 *Jamr'at* are located today.

This is also the reason for the pilgrim stoning 7 pebbles at the *Jamr'at*.

Jamrah Al-Aqabah (the big one) is on the left side inside Mina; the *Jamrah Al-Wusta* (the middle *Jamrah*) is in the middle as the name implies and the last one is *Jamrah Al-Sughra* (the smallest *Jamrah*).

The Sacrifice

Just as Ibraheem was about to sacrifice Ismail, Allah put a ram there for him to sacrifice instead.

﴿فَلَمَّآ أَسْلَمَا وَتَلَّهُ لِلْجَبِينِ ۞ وَنَدَيْنَهُ أَن يَـٰٓإِبْرَٰهِيمُ ۞ قَدْ صَدَّقْتَ ٱلرُّءْيَآ إِنَّا كَذَٰلِكَ نَجْزِى ٱلْمُحْسِنِينَ ۞ إِنَّ هَـٰذَا لَهُوَ ٱلْبَلَـٰٓؤُا۟ ٱلْمُبِينُ ۞ وَفَدَيْنَهُ بِذِبْحٍ عَظِيمٍ ۞﴾

"Then, when they had both submitted themselves (to the Will of Allah), and he had laid him prostrate on his forehead (or on the side of his forehead for slaughtering). And We called out to him: 'O Ibraheem! You have fulfilled the dream (vision)!' Verily! Thus do We reward the Muhsinin (good-doers). Verily, that indeed was a manifest trial. And We ransomed him with a great sacrifice (i.e. a ram)."

Surah As-Saffat (37:103-107)

Arafat

It is stated that when Ibraheem came to Arafat he said: *"Ariftu"*, meaning "I know this place", and this where the name comes from. Arafat is also mentioned by name in the Qur'an. (See the ayah on the next page).

Allah also instructed Ibraheem (عليه السلام) to proclaim to mankind to perform the pilgrimage.

﴿وَأَذِّن فِى ٱلنَّاسِ بِٱلْحَجِّ يَأْتُوكَ رِجَالًا وَعَلَىٰ كُلِّ ضَامِرٍ يَأْتِينَ مِن كُلِّ فَجٍّ عَمِيقٍ﴾

"And proclaim to mankind the Hajj (pilgrimage). They will come to you on foot and on every lean camel, they will come from every deep and distant (wide) mountain highway (to perform Hajj)."

Surah Al-Hajj (22:27)

The Prophet (ﷺ) said:

«الْحَجُّ عَرَفَاتٌ»

"Hajj is Arafat."

(Tirmidhi:2975)

Since that time the *Hajj* has been performed. These pilgrims also spent the day in Arafat. Over the years that followed some of the rites and actions of Ibraheem became distorted and changed until the advent of the final Messenger (ﷺ).

Muzdalifah

The *Hajj* rites were now put back in their proper sequence and place, including the stay at Muzdalifah:

﴿لَيْسَ عَلَيْكُمْ جُنَاحٌ أَن تَبْتَغُوا فَضْلًا مِّن رَّبِّكُمْ فَإِذَآ أَفَضْتُم مِّنْ عَرَفَاتٍ فَاذْكُرُوا اللَّهَ عِندَ الْمَشْعَرِ الْحَرَامِ وَاذْكُرُوهُ كَمَا هَدَىٰكُمْ وَإِن كُنتُم مِّن قَبْلِهِۦ لَمِنَ الضَّآلِّينَ﴾

"There is no sin on you if you seek Bounty of your Lord. Then when you leave Arafat, remember Allah at the Mash'ar-il-Haram. And remember Him as He has guided you, and verily, you were before, of those who were astray."

Surah Al-Baqarah (2:198)

Chapter 14
Revision

Following is a list of questions to test yourself. The questions are not in any particular order. You can find the answers in the next section, but they are given without any explanation. Further details about a particular answer (issue) can be found in the appropriate section of this book.

1. Is it acceptable for me to smoke when I am in the state of *Ihraam*?

2. Which *Hajj* method is recommended to be performed, *Tamattu*, *Qiran* or *Ifrad*?

3. When should my right shoulder be covered and when must it be uncovered, while I am in *Ihraam* (men)?

4. Can I apply perfume while I am preparing for the state of *Ihraam* (men)?

5. Do I put the perfume on my body or my *Ihraam* (men)?

6. Do I put the perfume on before or after I am in the state of *Ihraam* (men)?

7. Can a woman cover her face and hands while in the state of *Ihraam*?

8. Can a woman wear make-up or perfume while in the state of *Ihraam*?

9. Can a pilgrim in *Ihraam* change his or her Ihraam clothes?

10. Can a woman's *Ihraam* clothes be any colour or must it be white?

11. Is it necessary for me to shave my hair (under arms, etc.) and to trim my nails before entering into the state of *Ihraam*?

12. What time does the 'day of *Wuqoof* (Arafat)' start?

13.   What time do I leave Arafat?

14.   Must I be on the Mountain of Mercy (*Jabal Rahma*) in Arafat?

15.   Arafat: Can I join my *Zuhr* and *'Asr Salah* if I am in a tent?

16.   Do I shorten my prayers in Arafat (*Zuhr* & *'Asr* - 2 instead of 4 each)?

17.   When do I pray *Maghrib Salah* on the 9th (Arafat)?

18.   Should I stop in Muzdalifah?

19.   Is it a must to collect my stones in Muzdalifah or can I take them from Mina?

20.   Which *Jamrah* do I stone on the first day (10th) and from what time?

21.   Which is better, to shave my head or cut my hair (men), and why?

22.   How much hair does a women cut?

23.   When I shave my hair, should I shave my beard as well?

24.   What is the 10th day of Dhul-Hijjah called? Is it counted as one of the 3 days of *Tashreek*?

25.   Do I shorten my prayers during my stay in Mina (*Zuhr*, *'Asr* & *'Eshaa*)?

26.   Do I join my prayers during my stay in Mina?

27.   What are the next three days called (11th, 12th & 13th of Dhul-Hijjah)?

28.   In which order and at what time do I throw the *Jamr'at* on the 11th -13th?

29.   Should women run between the green lights during *Sa'ee*?

30.   Which day is the preferred day to go to Makkah to perform *Tawaaful-Ifadah*?

31.   What are the actions to be performed on the 10th of

Dhul-Hijjah?

32. On the 10th of Dhul-Hijjah, can I perform these rites in any order?

33. When I stone the *Jamr'at*, must I hit the target or is it acceptable if it falls into the circle without hitting the target?

34. Can I stone (*Ramy*) for somebody else, and how?

35. Is it acceptable to get somebody to throw for me if I am afraid of the crowds?

36. Can I pay somebody to throw for me?

37. Must I face *Qiblah* when I stone the *Jamr'at*?

38. If I perform *Tamattu Hajj* and I do not have sufficient funds for the sacrifice, what is my alternative?

39. When and by what time must I leave Mina if I wish to stay only for 2 days of *Tashreek*?

40. What happens if I do not leave Mina by sunset?

41. What do I do if I omit one of the obligatory acts?

42. Can Jeddah be regarded as a *Meqaat*?

43. Can I enter the *Haram* (Makkah) from any door for *Umrah* or *Hajj* or must I enter from the door named Baabus-Salaam?

44. Is it acceptable to read aloud during *Tawaaf*?

45. Is it acceptable to pass in front of a person making *Salah* in the *Haram*?

46. Is it preferable to perform *Tawaaf* in a big group?

47. Can I perform the *Hajj* on behalf of a deceased relative or friend?

48. How many *Umrahs* did the Prophet (ﷺ) perform in his lifetime?

49. How many animals did the Prophet (ﷺ) offer for sacrifice during his farewell pilgrimage?

50. How many of the animals did he sacrifice himself?

51. What is the significance of this number (Quest. 50)?

52. Who sacrificed the rest of the animals?

53. How many rounds (circuits) are there in *Tawaaf*?

54. How many laps are there in *Sa'ee*?

55. How many pebbles do I throw at the *Jamrah*?

56. What are the major rites of *Umrah*?

57. What are the compulsory (pillars) of *Hajj*?

58. What are the obligatory (*Wajib*) rites of *Hajj*?

59. What are the three methods of *Hajj* called?

60. What are the major differences between the three methods?

61. What are the three types of sacrifices?

62. How many sacrifices does the *Mutamatti* and *Qaarin* perform and what is it called?

63. Where in the Qur'an is the reference for this (Quest.62)?

Answers to the Questions about *Hajj*:

1. No.

2. *Tamattu.*

3. It should be covered all of the time except while performing *Tawaaf* (for *Umrah* or *Qudoom*).

4. Yes.

5. On your body.

6. Before entering into the state of *Ihraam*.

7. Yes, while she is in the presence of strange (non-*Mahram*) men, but not with a *Niqaab* or gloves (for her hands).

8. No.

9. Yes.

10.   It can be of any colour.

11.   It is *Sunnah* to do so, at least every 40 days.

12.   After the performance of the *Salatul Zuhr* and *'Asr*, joined at *Zuhr* time.

13.   After sunset.

14.   No.

15.   Yes.

16.   Yes.

17.   With *'Eshaa* in Muzdalifah (*Maghrib* = 3 *Rak'at* and *'Eshaa* = 2 *Rak'at*).

18.   Yes.

19.   No, they can be collected in Mina.

20.   Only the big *Jamrah* (*Aqaba*), from after sunrise.

21.   Shave. The Prophet (ﷺ) made *Dua'* three times for those who shaved and only once for those who cut their hair.

22.   Approximately one inch of hair only (from one place).

23.   No.

24.   *Yaumun-Nahr* (*Yaumul-'Eid* or *Yaumul-Hajjil-Akbar*). No.

25.   Yes.

26.   No.

27.   *Ayaamut-Tashreek*.

28.   The small *Jamrah* first, followed by the middle one and finishing at the big one. After midday (*Zawaal*).

29.   No.

30.   On the 10th of Dhul-Hijjah.

31.   *Ramy* of the big *Jamrah*; sacrificing of the animal for the *Muttamatti* and the *Qaarin*; shaving of your head or cutting your hair; performing *Tawaaful-Ifadah* and *Sa'ee* for *Hajj*.

32. It is acceptable if it falls into the circle without hitting the target.

33. Yes.

34. Yes. First throw your 7 pebbles, followed by the 7 for the other person; proceed to the next *Jamrah* and do the same.

35. No.

36. No.

37. No.

38. To fast for 10 days: 3 days during *Hajj* and 7 upon your return home.

39. On the 12th of Dhul-Hijjah, before sunset.

40. You should stay until the next day (13th), unless it is beyond your control (i.e. you are stuck in the traffic; delayed by the organisers). Basically it means you cannot decide to leave after sunset.

41. Offer a sacrifice (one sheep or goat) and the meat is to be distributed amongst the needy in Makkah.

42. No.

43. You can enter from any door.

44. No.

45. No.

46. No.

47. Yes. (If you have already performed your *Fard Hajj*.)

48. 4.

49. 100 camels.

50. 63.

51. One for each year of his life.

52. Ali bin Talib (ﷺ).

53. 7.

54.   7.

55.   7.

56.   *Ihraam* at the *Meqaat* (with *Niyah*); *Tawaaf* and *Sa'ee*; shaving the head or cutting the hair.

57.   Pillars of *Hajj* (4):

  1. *Ihraam* (with *Niyah*);

  2. Standing at Arafat;

  3. *Tawaaful-Ifadah*;

  4. *Sa'ee* for *Hajj*.

58.   Obligatory rites of *Hajj* (7):

  1. *Ihraam* at the *Meqaat*;

  2. Staying in Arafat until sunset;

  3. Staying in Muzdalifah;

  4. Stoning the *Jamr'at*;

  5. Shaving or cutting of the hair;

  6. Staying in Mina;

  7. Performing *Tawaaful-Wadaa'*.

59.   *Tamattu, Qiran* and *Ifrad*.

60.   *Tamattu: Umrah* and *Hajj* with two separate *Ihraams* (*Niy'at*); sacrifice is compulsory. *Qiran: Umrah* and *Hajj* with one *Ihraam* (*Niyah*); sacrifice is compulsory. *Ifrad*: *Hajj* only; sacrifice is optional.

61.   *Hady, Udhiyah* and *Fidyah*.

62.   1, *Hady*.

63.   *Surah Al-Baqarah, Ayah* 196.

Suggested Supplications to Memorise

Following is a list of *Dua's* which I suggest you try to memorise. This way you will not need to take any books with you when going to the *Haram* for *Umrah*, *Tawaaf* or *Salah*. The transliterations and meanings can be found in the appropriate chapters.

→ *Talbiyah:*

«لَبَّيْكَ اللَّهُمَّ لَبَّيْكَ، لَبَّيْكَ لَا شَرِيكَ لَكَ لَبَّيْكَ، إِنَّ الْحَمْدَ وَالنِّعْمَةَ لَكَ وَالمُلْكَ، لَا شَرِيكَ لَكَ»

→ **Entering the Mosque:**

«بِسْمِ اللهِ وَالصَّلاةُ وَالسَّلامُ عَلَى رسُولِ الله، اللَّهُمَّ افتَحْ لِي أبوابَ رَحْمَتِكَ»

→ **Drinking Zamzam water:**

«اللَّهُمَّ إِنِّي أَسْأَلُكَ عِلْمًا نَافِعًا وَرِزْقًا وَاسِعًا وَشِفَاءً مِنْ كُلِّ دَاءٍ»

→ *Tawaaf:*

بِسْمِ الله وَاللهُ أَكْبَرُ

﴿رَبَّنَا ءَاتِنَا فِي ٱلدُّنْيَا حَسَنَةً وَفِي ٱلْأَخِرَةِ حَسَنَةً وَقِنَا عَذَابَ ٱلنَّارِ﴾

﴿وَٱتَّخِذُوا مِن مَّقَامِ إِبْرَهِمَ مُصَلًّى﴾

→ *Sa'ee:*

﴿إِنَّ ٱلصَّفَا وَٱلْمَرْوَةَ مِن شَعَآئِرِ ٱللَّهِ﴾

«أَبْدَأُ بِمَا بَدَأَ اللهُ بِهِ»

«الْحَمْدُ لله وَلَا إِلَهَ إِلَّا اللهُ وَاللهُ أَكْبَرُ، لَا إِلَهَ إِلَّا اللهُ وَحْدَهُ لَا شَرِيكَ لَهُ، لَهُ الْمُلْكُ وَلَهُ الْحَمْدُ يُحْيِي وَيُمِيتُ وَهُوَ عَلَى كُلِّ شَيْءٍ قَدِيرٌ، لَا إِلَهَ إِلَّا اللهُ وَحْدَهُ، صَدَقَ وَعْدَهُ، وَنَصَرَ عَبْدَهُ، وَهَزَمَ الأَحْزَابَ وَحْدَهُ».

«رَبِّ اغْفِرْ وَارْحَمْ إِنَّك أَنْتَ الأَعَزُّ الأَكْرَمُ»

→ **Leaving the Mosque:**

«بِسْمِ الله والصَّلاةُ وَالسَّلامُ على رسُولِ الله، اللَّهُمَّ إِنِّي أَسأَلُكَ مِنْ فضلِكَ وَرَحْمِتِكَ»

→ **On Arafat:**

The Prophet (ﷺ) faced *Qiblah*, and raising his hands up to the level of his chest, he supplicated earnestly until sunset. He informed the people that the best supplication is that of the day of Arafat and the best which I and the other Prophets before me have said (is):

«لَا إِلَهَ إِلَّا اللهُ وَحْدَهُ لَا شَرِيكَ لَهُ ، لَهُ الْمُلْكُ وَلَهُ الْحَمْدُ وَهُوَ عَلَى كُلِّ شَيْءٍ قَدِيرٌ»

Summary of the Six Days of Hajj

8th Dhul-Hijjah (*Yaum-at-Tarweya*)

This day the pilgrims adopt Ihraam with niyah for Hajj and proceed from Makkah to Mina where they pray 5 salawaat (*Dhuhr-Fajr*).

9th Dhul-Hijjah (*Yaum-ul-Arafat*)

This day the pilgrims go to Arafat where they spend the day in supplication, after combining Dhuhr and Asr Salawaat, until sunset.

Mabeet-fi-Muzdalifah:

After sunset the pilgrims leave for Muzdalifah where they pray Maghrib and *Eshaa* joined. They spend the night or part of it here, and depart for Mina just before sunrise.

10th Dhul-Hijjah (*Yaumul-Hajjil-Akbar*):

This day the pilgrims return to Mina and *Ramy* (throw 7 pebbles) at the big *Jamrah*; perform their sacrifice; cut their hair; go to Makkah to perform *Tawaaful-Ifadah* and *Sa'ee* for *Hajj*; and then return to Mina.

11th - 13th Dhul-Hijjah (*Ayaamat-Tashreek*):

The pilgrims spend the next 2 or 3 days in Mina, *Ramy* all three *Jamr'at* on all three days. They may leave for Makkah before sunset on the 12th or stay until the 13th.

Makkah:

The pilgrims return to Makkah and perform *Tawaaful-Wadaa'* (farewell *Tawaaf*) as the last rite before departing for home. *Hajj* is complete!

The Diary of *Hajj Tamattu*

8th Dhul-Hijjah (Yaum-at-Tarweya):

ɕ Ihraam with appropriate Niyah (if not already in Ihraam).

ɕ Complete Umrah or Tawaaf-ul-Qudoom as appropriate.

ɕ Proceed to Mina and spend the night.

ɕ Perform 5 salawaat in Mina if possible (Dhuhr*, Asr*, Maghrib, Eshaa* and Fajr). {* = shortened to 2 rak'at each, but not joined}.

ɕ Prepare/reflect for Arafat and recite the Talbiyah as often as possible.

ɕ Leave for Arafat after sunrise on the 9th.

This day is not obligatory to spend in Mina. The pilgrim may proceed directly to Arafat on the 9th, and omit this day in Mina without incurring a fidyah (expiation).

Day 1

9th Dhul-Hijjah (Yaum-ul-Arafat):

ɕ Listen to the Khutbah in Namira mosque if possible.

ɕ Perform Salatul-Dhuhr and Asr {shortened to 2 rak'at each and joined at Dhuhr time. One adhaan and two iqaama't}.

ɕ Wuqoof (standing) has now started and ends at sunset, so

ɕ Supplicate, Supplicate, Supplicate!

ɕ Leave for Muzdalifah after sunset (nafarah).

ɕ Continue to recite the Talbiyah as often as possible.

"Hajj is Arafat"
(Tirmidhi)

The Prophet (ﷺ) said: "I stand here, but the whole of Arafat is a standing place" (Muslim)

Day 2

Night 2 - (Mabeet-fi-Muzdalifah):

ɕ Perform Salatul-Maghrib and Eshaa (joined) as soon as you reach Muzdalifah or where you are if it is close to midnight {Eshaa shortened to 2 units. One adhaan and two iqaama't} + Witr.

ɕ Spend the night (the weak, women and children may leave after midnight).

ɕ Rest and sleep.

ɕ Perform Salatul-Fajr (including the sunnah salah).

ɕ Supplicate.

ɕ Proceed to Mina before sunrise.

ɕ Continue to recite the Talbiyah as often as possible.

"...Then when you leave Arafat, remember Allah at the Mash'ar-al-Haram" (2:198)

The Prophet (ﷺ) said: "I am standing here, but the whole of Muzdalifah is a place of standing." (Muslim)

10th Dhul-Hijjah (Yaum-ul-Hajj il-Akbar):

☾ Day also known as Yaum-un-Nahr (day of sacrifice) or Yaum-ul-Eid

☾ Collect 7 pebbles on your way to Mina.

☾ Proceed to Jamarah Aqaba (big - the one closest to Makkah) and cast 7 pebbles , one at a time, saying: الله اكبر (Allah is Greater).

☾ Stop reciting the Talbiyah and recite the Takbir as often as possible.

☾ Perform your sacrifice (Hady). {Tamattu and Qiran}.

☾ Men: Perform Halq (shaving of the head) or Taqseer (haircut) ; Women: Gather her hair and cut approx. 1inch from one place only.

☾ Above 3 actions can be done in any order, though this is the preferred order.

☾ Ihraam restrictions partially lifted (still no marital relations allowed).

☾ Shower, perfume (men) and adopt normal clothes.

☾ Proceed to Makkah if convenient to perform Tawaaf-al-Ifadah, also Sa'ee for Hajj (for Tamattu, and for Qiran and Ifrad if it was not done before). This can be delayed until after the days in Mina if required.

☾ All Ihraam restrictions are lifted once the Tawaaf and Sa'ee are done.

☾ Return to Mina where you should spend the next 2 or 3 nights.

11th - 13th Dhul-Hijjah (Ayaam-at-Tashreek):

☾ Continue to recite the Takbir as often as possible (until Asr of day 3)

☾ Casting of pebbles procedure for all 3 days:

1. Collect 21 pebbles and proceed to the Jamrah.
2. Start time is after Zawaal until sunset (and later if required).
3. Pebbles should fall within the circled area.
4. Do not use stones that have already been casted.
5. Start at the small Jamrah and cast 7 pebbles, one at a time, saying: الله اكبر.
6. Move to the side, face Qiblah and supplicate.
7. Proceed to the middle Jamrah and repeat as above.
8. Proceed to the big Jamrah and ramy as above, but there is no supplication at the end.

☾ You may proceed to Makkah if convenient to perform Tawaaf-al-Ifadah & Sa'ee for Hajj, if it was not done before.

☾ If you wish to leave Mina on the 12th, then you should do so before sunset (but after Zawaal and Ramy).

☾ On the 13th proceed to Makkah after Zawaal and Ramy.

☾ Perform Tawaaf-al-Wadaa as the last rite prior to departing home.

☾ Hajj is complete. May Allah accept it! Aameen.

And a declaration from Allah and His Messenger to mankind on the greatest day (the 10th of Dhul-Hijjah) that Allah is free from (all) obligations to the Mushrikin and so is His Messenger."
(9:3)

Day 3
So on that day, when the Prophet (ﷺ) was asked about anything (as regards the ceremonies) of Hajj performed before or after its due time, his reply was: "Do it (now) and there is no harm."
(Bukhari)

Days 4, 5, 6
"And remember Allah during the appointed days. But whosoever hastens to leave in two days, there is no sin on him and whosoever stays on, there is no sin on him, if his aim is to do good and obey Allah (fear Him)"
(2:203)

The people were ordered to perform the Tawaaf of the Ka'bah as the lastly thing, before leaving (Makkah), except menstruating women who were excused.
(Bukhari)

Surat Al-Hajj (The Pilgrimage) XXII

Interpretation of the Meanings. By: Dr.Muhammad Taqiud-Din & Dr. Muhammad Muhsin Khan

بِسْمِ اللهِ الرَّحْمَنِ الرَّحِيمِ

In the Name of Allâh the Most Gracious, the Most Merciful.

﴿يَٰٓأَيُّهَا ٱلنَّاسُ ٱتَّقُوا۟ رَبَّكُمْ إِنَّ زَلْزَلَةَ ٱلسَّاعَةِ شَىْءٌ عَظِيمٌ﴾

"O mankind! Fear your Lord and be dutiful to Him! Verily, the earthquake of the Hour (of Judgement) is a terrible thing."

﴿يَوْمَ تَرَوْنَهَا تَذْهَلُ كُلُّ مُرْضِعَةٍ عَمَّآ أَرْضَعَتْ وَتَضَعُ كُلُّ ذَاتِ حَمْلٍ حَمْلَهَا وَتَرَى ٱلنَّاسَ سُكَٰرَىٰ وَمَا هُم بِسُكَٰرَىٰ وَلَٰكِنَّ عَذَابَ ٱللَّهِ شَدِيدٌ﴾

"The Day you shall see it, every nursing mother will forget her nursling, and every pregnant one will drop her load, and you shall see mankind as in a drunken state, yet they will not be drunken, but severe will be the Torment of Allâh."

﴿وَمِنَ ٱلنَّاسِ مَن يُجَٰدِلُ فِى ٱللَّهِ بِغَيْرِ عِلْمٍ وَيَتَّبِعُ كُلَّ شَيْطَٰنٍ مَّرِيدٍ﴾

"And among mankind is he who disputes concerning Allâh, without knowledge, and follows every rebellious (disobedient to Allâh) Shaitân (devil) (devoid of each and every kind of good)."

﴿كُتِبَ عَلَيْهِ أَنَّهُ مَن تَوَلَّاهُ فَأَنَّهُ يُضِلُّهُ وَيَهْدِيهِ إِلَىٰ عَذَابِ ٱلسَّعِيرِ﴾

"For him (the devil) it is decreed that whosoever follows him, he will mislead him, and will drive him to the torment of the Fire."

﴿يَٰٓأَيُّهَا ٱلنَّاسُ إِن كُنتُمْ فِى رَيْبٍ مِّنَ ٱلْبَعْثِ فَإِنَّا خَلَقْنَٰكُم مِّن تُرَابٍ﴾

ثُمَّ مِن نُّطْفَةٍ ثُمَّ مِنْ عَلَقَةٍ ثُمَّ مِن مُّضْغَةٍ مُّخَلَّقَةٍ وَغَيْرِ مُخَلَّقَةٍ
لِّنُبَيِّنَ لَكُمْ وَنُقِرُّ فِى ٱلْأَرْحَامِ مَا نَشَاءُ إِلَىٰ أَجَلٍ مُّسَمًّى ثُمَّ
نُخْرِجُكُمْ طِفْلًا ثُمَّ لِتَبْلُغُوٓا۟ أَشُدَّكُمْ وَمِنكُم مَّن يُتَوَفَّىٰ
وَمِنكُم مَّن يُرَدُّ إِلَىٰٓ أَرْذَلِ ٱلْعُمُرِ لِكَيْلَا يَعْلَمَ مِنۢ بَعْدِ عِلْمٍ
شَيْئًا وَتَرَى ٱلْأَرْضَ هَامِدَةً فَإِذَآ أَنزَلْنَا عَلَيْهَا ٱلْمَآءَ ٱهْتَزَّتْ وَرَبَتْ
وَأَنۢبَتَتْ مِن كُلِّ زَوْجٍ بَهِيجٍ ﴾

"O mankind! If you are in doubt about the Resurrection, then
verily We have created you (i.e. Adam) from dust, then from a
Nutfah (mixed drops of male and female sexual discharge i.e.
offspring of Adam), then from a clot (a piece of thick
coagulated blood) then from a little lump of flesh - some
formed and some unformed (as in the case of miscarriage) -
that We may make (it) clear to you (i.e. to show you Our
Power and Ability to do what We will). And We cause whom
We will to remain in the wombs for an appointed term, then
We bring you out as infants, then (give you growth) that you
may reach your age of full strength. And among you there is
he who dies (young), and among you there is he who is
brought back to the miserable old age, so that he knows
nothing after having known. And you see the earth barren,
but when We send down water (rain) on it, it is stirred (to
life), and it swells and puts forth every lovely kind (of
growth)."

﴿ذَٰلِكَ بِأَنَّ ٱللَّهَ هُوَ ٱلْحَقُّ وَأَنَّهُ يُحْىِ ٱلْمَوْتَىٰ وَأَنَّهُ عَلَىٰ كُلِّ شَىْءٍ قَدِيرٌ﴾

"That is because Allâh: He is the Truth, and it is He Who
gives life to the dead, and it is He Who is Able to do all
things."

﴿وَأَنَّ ٱلسَّاعَةَ ءَاتِيَةٌ لَّا رَيْبَ فِيهَا وَأَنَّ ٱللَّهَ يَبْعَثُ مَن فِى ٱلْقُبُورِ﴾

"And surely, the Hour is coming, there is no doubt about it;
and certainly, Allâh will resurrect those who are in the

graves."

﴿وَمِنَ ٱلنَّاسِ مَن يُجَٰدِلُ فِى ٱللَّهِ بِغَيْرِ عِلْمٍ وَلَا هُدًى وَلَا كِتَٰبٍ مُّنِيرٍ﴾

"And among men is he who disputes about Allâh, without knowledge or guidance, or a Book giving light (from Allah),"

﴿ثَانِىَ عِطْفِهِۦ لِيُضِلَّ عَن سَبِيلِ ٱللَّهِ لَهُۥ فِى ٱلدُّنْيَا خِزْىٌ وَنُذِيقُهُۥ يَوْمَ ٱلْقِيَٰمَةِ عَذَابَ ٱلْحَرِيقِ﴾

"Bending his neck in pride (far astray from the Path of Allâh), and leading (others) too (far) astray from the Path of Allâh. For him there is disgrace in this worldly life, and on the Day of Resurrection We shall make him taste the torment of burning (Fire)."

﴿ذَٰلِكَ بِمَا قَدَّمَتْ يَدَاكَ وَأَنَّ ٱللَّهَ لَيْسَ بِظَلَّٰمٍ لِّلْعَبِيدِ﴾

"That is because of what your hands have sent forth, and verily, Allâh is not unjust to (His) slaves."

﴿وَمِنَ ٱلنَّاسِ مَن يَعْبُدُ ٱللَّهَ عَلَىٰ حَرْفٍ فَإِنْ أَصَابَهُۥ خَيْرٌ ٱطْمَأَنَّ بِهِۦ وَإِنْ أَصَابَتْهُ فِتْنَةٌ ٱنقَلَبَ عَلَىٰ وَجْهِهِۦ خَسِرَ ٱلدُّنْيَا وَٱلْءَاخِرَةَ ذَٰلِكَ هُوَ ٱلْخُسْرَانُ ٱلْمُبِينُ﴾

"And among mankind is he who worships Allâh as it were, upon the edge (i.e. in doubt): if good befalls him, he is content therewith; but if a trial befalls him, he turns back on his face (i.e. reverts back to disbelief after embracing Islâm). He loses both this world and the Hereafter. That is the evident loss."

﴿يَدْعُواْ مِن دُونِ ٱللَّهِ مَا لَا يَضُرُّهُۥ وَمَا لَا يَنفَعُهُۥ ذَٰلِكَ هُوَ ٱلضَّلَٰلُ ٱلْبَعِيدُ﴾

"He calls besides Allâh unto that which hurts him not, nor profits him. That is a straying far away."

﴿يَدْعُواْ لَمَن ضَرُّهُۥٓ أَقْرَبُ مِن نَّفْعِهِۦ لَبِئْسَ ٱلْمَوْلَىٰ وَلَبِئْسَ ٱلْعَشِيرُ﴾

*"He calls unto him whose harm is nearer than his profit:
certainly, an evil Maulâ (patron) and certainly an evil
friend!"*

﴿إِنَّ ٱللَّهَ يُدْخِلُ ٱلَّذِينَ ءَامَنُواْ وَعَمِلُواْ ٱلصَّٰلِحَٰتِ جَنَّٰتٍ تَجْرِى مِن
تَحْتِهَا ٱلْأَنْهَٰرُ إِنَّ ٱللَّهَ يَفْعَلُ مَا يُرِيدُ﴾

*"Truly, Allâh will admit those who believe (in Islâmic
Monotheism) and do righteous good deeds (according to the
Qur'ân and the sunnah) to Gardens underneath which rivers
flow (in Paradise). Verily, Allâh does what He wills."*

﴿مَن كَانَ يَظُنُّ أَن لَّن يَنصُرَهُ ٱللَّهُ فِى ٱلدُّنْيَا وَٱلْأَخِرَةِ فَلْيَمْدُدْ بِسَبَبٍ
إِلَى ٱلسَّمَاءِ ثُمَّ لِيَقْطَعْ فَلْيَنظُرْ هَلْ يُذْهِبَنَّ كَيْدُهُ مَا يَغِيظُ﴾

*"Whoever thinks that Allâh will not help him (Muhammad
(peace be upon him)) in this world and in the Hereafter, let
him stretch out a rope to the ceiling and let him strangle
himself. Then let him see whether his plan will remove that
whereat he rages!"*

﴿وَكَذَٰلِكَ أَنزَلْنَٰهُ ءَايَٰتٍ بَيِّنَٰتٍ وَأَنَّ ٱللَّهَ يَهْدِى مَن يُرِيدُ﴾

*"Thus have We sent it (this Qur'ân) down (to Muhammad
(peace be upon him)) as clear signs, evidences and proofs, and
surely, Allâh guides whom He wills."*

﴿إِنَّ ٱلَّذِينَ ءَامَنُواْ وَٱلَّذِينَ هَادُواْ وَٱلصَّٰبِئِينَ وَٱلنَّصَٰرَىٰ وَٱلْمَجُوسَ وَٱلَّذِينَ
أَشْرَكُواْ إِنَّ ٱللَّهَ يَفْصِلُ بَيْنَهُمْ يَوْمَ ٱلْقِيَٰمَةِ إِنَّ ٱللَّهَ عَلَىٰ كُلِّ
شَىْءٍ شَهِيدٌ﴾

*"Verily, those who believe (in Allâh and in His Messenger
Muhammad (ﷺ)) and thse who are Jews, and the Sabians,
and the Christians, and the Majûs, and those who worship
others besides Allâh, truly, Allâh will judge between them on
the Day of Resurrection. Verily! Allâh is over all things a
Witness."*

﴿أَلَمْ تَرَ أَنَّ اللَّهَ يَسْجُدُ لَهُۥ مَن فِى السَّمَٰوَٰتِ وَمَن فِى الْأَرْضِ وَالشَّمْسُ وَالْقَمَرُ وَالنُّجُومُ وَالْجِبَالُ وَالشَّجَرُ وَالدَّوَابُّ وَكَثِيرٌ مِّنَ النَّاسِ وَكَثِيرٌ حَقَّ عَلَيْهِ الْعَذَابُ وَمَن يُهِنِ اللَّهُ فَمَا لَهُۥ مِن مُّكْرِمٍ إِنَّ اللَّهَ يَفْعَلُ مَا يَشَاءُ﴾

"See you not that whoever is in the heavens and whoever is on the earth, and the sun, and the moon, and the stars, and the mountains, and the trees, and Ad-Dawab (moving (living) creatures, beasts), and many of mankind prostrate themselves to Allâh. But there are many (men) on whom the punishment is justified. And whomsoever Allâh disgraces, none can honor him. Verily! Allah does what He wills."

﴿هَٰذَانِ خَصْمَانِ اخْتَصَمُوا فِى رَبِّهِمْ فَالَّذِينَ كَفَرُوا قُطِّعَتْ لَهُمْ ثِيَابٌ مِّن نَّارٍ يُصَبُّ مِن فَوْقِ رُءُوسِهِمُ الْحَمِيمُ﴾

"These two opponents (believers and disbelievers) dispute with each other about their Lord: then as for those who disbelieved, garments of fire will be cut out for them, boiling water will be poured down over their heads."

﴿يُصْهَرُ بِهِۦ مَا فِى بُطُونِهِمْ وَالْجُلُودُ﴾

"With it will melt (or vanish away) what is within their bellies, as well as (their) skins."

﴿وَلَهُم مَّقَٰمِعُ مِنْ حَدِيدٍ﴾

"And for them are hooked rods of iron (to punish them)."

﴿كُلَّمَا أَرَادُوا أَن يَخْرُجُوا مِنْهَا مِنْ غَمٍّ أُعِيدُوا فِيهَا وَذُوقُوا عَذَابَ الْحَرِيقِ﴾

"Every time they seek to get away therefrom, from anguish, they will be driven back therein, and (it will be) said to them: 'Taste the torment of burning!'

﴿إِنَّ ٱللَّهَ يُدْخِلُ ٱلَّذِينَ ءَامَنُوا۟ وَعَمِلُوا۟ ٱلصَّٰلِحَٰتِ جَنَّٰتٍ تَجْرِى مِن تَحْتِهَا ٱلْأَنْهَٰرُ يُحَلَّوْنَ فِيهَا مِنْ أَسَاوِرَ مِن ذَهَبٍ وَلُؤْلُؤًا وَلِبَاسُهُمْ فِيهَا حَرِيرٌ﴾

"Truly, Allâh will admit those who believe (in the Oneness of Allâh - Islâmic Monotheism) and do righteous good deeds, to Gardens underneath which rivers flow (in Paradise), wherein they will be adorned with bracelets of gold and pearls and their garments therein will be of silk."

﴿وَهُدُوا۟ إِلَى ٱلطَّيِّبِ مِنَ ٱلْقَوْلِ وَهُدُوا۟ إِلَىٰ صِرَٰطِ ٱلْحَمِيدِ﴾

"And they are guided (in this world) unto goodly speech (i.e. Lâ ilâha illallâh, Alhamdu lillâh, recitation of the Qur'ân, etc.) and they are guided to the Path of Him (i.e. Allâh's religion of Islâmic Monotheism). Who is Worthy of all praises."

﴿إِنَّ ٱلَّذِينَ كَفَرُوا۟ وَيَصُدُّونَ عَن سَبِيلِ ٱللَّهِ وَٱلْمَسْجِدِ ٱلْحَرَامِ ٱلَّذِى جَعَلْنَٰهُ لِلنَّاسِ سَوَآءً ٱلْعَٰكِفُ فِيهِ وَٱلْبَادِ وَمَن يُرِدْ فِيهِ بِإِلْحَادٍ بِظُلْمٍ نُذِقْهُ مِنْ عَذَابٍ أَلِيمٍ﴾

"Verily, those who disbelieved and hinder (men) from the Path of Allâh, and from Al-Masjid-al-Harâm (at Makkah) which We have made (open) to (all) men, the dweller in it and the visitor from the country are equal there (as regards its sanctity and pilgrimage (Hajj and 'Umrah)) - and whoever inclines to evil actions therein or to do wrong (i.e. practice polytheism and leave Islâmic Monotheism), him We shall cause to taste a painful torment."

﴿وَإِذْ بَوَّأْنَا لِإِبْرَٰهِيمَ مَكَانَ ٱلْبَيْتِ أَن لَّا تُشْرِكْ بِى شَيْئًا وَطَهِّرْ بَيْتِيَ لِلطَّآئِفِينَ وَٱلْقَآئِمِينَ وَٱلرُّكَّعِ ٱلسُّجُودِ﴾

"And (remember) when We showed Ibrâhim (Abraham) the site of the (Sacred) House (the Ka'bah at Makkah) (saying):

"Associate not anything (in worship) with Me, (Lâ ilahâ illâllâh (none has the right to be worshipped but Allah) - Islâmic Monotheism), and sanctify My House for those who circumambulate it, and those who stand up (for prayer), and those who bow (submit themselves with humility and obedience to Allâh), and make prostration (in prayer)."

﴿وَأَذِّن فِى ٱلنَّاسِ بِٱلْحَجِّ يَأْتُوكَ رِجَالًا وَعَلَىٰ كُلِّ ضَامِرٍ يَأْتِينَ مِن كُلِّ فَجٍّ عَمِيقٍ﴾

"And proclaim to mankind the Hajj (pilgrimage). They will come to you on foot and on every lean camel, they will come from every deep and distant (wide) mountain highway (to perform Hajj)."

﴿لِّيَشْهَدُوا۟ مَنَٰفِعَ لَهُمْ وَيَذْكُرُوا۟ ٱسْمَ ٱللَّهِ فِىٓ أَيَّامٍ مَّعْلُومَٰتٍ عَلَىٰ مَا رَزَقَهُم مِّنۢ بَهِيمَةِ ٱلْأَنْعَٰمِ فَكُلُوا۟ مِنْهَا وَأَطْعِمُوا۟ ٱلْبَآئِسَ ٱلْفَقِيرَ﴾

"That they may witness things that are of benefit to them (i.e. reward of Hajj in the Hereafter, and also some worldly gain from trade), and mention the Name of Allâh on appointed days (i.e. 10th, 11th, 12th, and 13th day of Dhul-Hijjah), over the beast of cattle that He has provided for them (for sacrifice) (at the time of their slaughtering by saying: Bismillah, Wallâu-Akbar Allâhumma Minka wa Ilaik). Then eat thereof and feed therewith the poor who have a very hard time."

﴿ثُمَّ لْيَقْضُوا۟ تَفَثَهُمْ وَلْيُوفُوا۟ نُذُورَهُمْ وَلْيَطَّوَّفُوا۟ بِٱلْبَيْتِ ٱلْعَتِيقِ﴾

"Then let them complete the prescribed duties (Manâsik of Hajj) and perform their vows, and circumambulate the Ancient House (the Ka'bah at Makkah)."

﴿ذَٰلِكَ وَمَن يُعَظِّمْ حُرُمَٰتِ ٱللَّهِ فَهُوَ خَيْرٌ لَّهُۥ عِندَ رَبِّهِۦٓ

$$\text{وَأُحِلَّتْ لَكُمُ ٱلْأَنْعَمُ إِلَّا مَا يُتْلَىٰ عَلَيْكُمْ فَٱجْتَنِبُوا۟}$$
$$\text{ٱلرِّجْسَ مِنَ ٱلْأَوْثَنِ وَٱجْتَنِبُوا۟ قَوْلَ ٱلزُّورِ}$$

"That (Manâsik - prescribed duties of Hajj is the obligation that mankind owes to Allâh), and whoever honors the sacred things of Allâh, then that is better for him with his Lord. The cattle are lawful to you, except those (that will be) mentioned to you (as exceptions). So shun the abomination (worshipping) of idol, and shun lying speech (false statements) -"

$$\text{حُنَفَآءَ لِلَّهِ غَيْرَ مُشْرِكِينَ بِهِۦ وَمَن يُشْرِكْ بِٱللَّهِ فَكَأَنَّمَا خَرَّ مِنَ ٱلسَّمَآءِ}$$
$$\text{فَتَخْطَفُهُ ٱلطَّيْرُ أَوْ تَهْوِى بِهِ ٱلرِّيحُ فِى مَكَانٍ سَحِيقٍ}$$

"Hunafâ' Lillâh (i.e. worshiping none but Allâh), not associating partners (in worship) unto Him; and whoever assigns partners to Allâh, it is as if he had fallen from the sky, and the birds had snatched him, or the wind had thrown him to a far off place."

$$\text{ذَٰلِكَ وَمَن يُعَظِّمْ شَعَٰٓئِرَ ٱللَّهِ فَإِنَّهَا مِن تَقْوَى ٱلْقُلُوبِ}$$

"Thus it is (what has been mentioned in the above said Verses (28, 29, 30, 31) is an obligation that mankind owes to Allah) and whosoever honors the Symbols of Allâh, then it is truly from the piety of the hearts."

$$\text{لَكُمْ فِيهَا مَنَٰفِعُ إِلَىٰٓ أَجَلٍ مُّسَمًّى ثُمَّ مَحِلُّهَآ إِلَى ٱلْبَيْتِ ٱلْعَتِيقِ}$$

"In them (cattle offered for sacrifice) are benefits for you for an appointed term, and afterwards they are brought for sacrifice unto the ancient House (the Haram – sacred territory of Makkah)."

$$\text{وَلِكُلِّ أُمَّةٍ جَعَلْنَا مَنسَكًا لِّيَذْكُرُوا۟ ٱسْمَ ٱللَّهِ عَلَىٰ مَا رَزَقَهُم مِّنۢ}$$
$$\text{بَهِيمَةِ ٱلْأَنْعَٰمِ فَإِلَٰهُكُمْ إِلَٰهٌ وَٰحِدٌ فَلَهُۥٓ أَسْلِمُوا۟ وَبَشِّرِ ٱلْمُخْبِتِينَ}$$

"And for every nation We have appointed religious ceremonies, that they may mention the Name of Allâh over the beast of cattle that He has given them for food. And your Ilâh (God) is One Ilah (God – Allâh), so you must submit to Him Alone (in Islâm). And (O Muhammad (peace be upon him)) give glad tidings to the Mukhbitûn (those who obey Allâh with humility and are humble from among the true believers of Islâmic Monotheism),"

﴿ٱلَّذِينَ إِذَا ذُكِرَ ٱللَّهُ وَجِلَتْ قُلُوبُهُمْ وَٱلصَّٰبِرِينَ عَلَىٰ مَآ أَصَابَهُمْ وَٱلْمُقِيمِى ٱلصَّلَوٰةِ وَمِمَّا رَزَقْنَٰهُمْ يُنفِقُونَ﴾

"Whose hearts are filled with fear when Allah is mentioned and As-Sabirūn (who patiently bear whatever may befall them (of calamities)) and who perform As-Salât (Iqamat-as-Salât), and who spend (in Allâh's Cause) out of what We have provided them".

﴿وَٱلْبُدْنَ جَعَلْنَٰهَا لَكُم مِّن شَعَٰٓئِرِ ٱللَّهِ لَكُمْ فِيهَا خَيْرٌ فَٱذْكُرُوا۟ ٱسْمَ ٱللَّهِ عَلَيْهَا صَوَآفَّ فَإِذَا وَجَبَتْ جُنُوبُهَا فَكُلُوا۟ مِنْهَا وَأَطْعِمُوا۟ ٱلْقَانِعَ وَٱلْمُعْتَرَّ كَذَٰلِكَ سَخَّرْنَٰهَا لَكُمْ لَعَلَّكُمْ تَشْكُرُونَ﴾

"And the Budn (cows, oxen, or camels driven to be offered as sacrifices by the pilgrims at the sanctuary of Makkah) We have made for you as among the Symbols of Allâh, wherein you have much good. So mention the Name of Allâh over them when they are drawn up in lines (for sacrifice). Then, when they are down on their sides (after slaughter), eat thereof, and feed the poor who does not ask (men), and the beggar who asks (men). Thus have We made them subject to you that you may be grateful."

﴿لَن يَنَالَ ٱللَّهَ لُحُومُهَا وَلَا دِمَآؤُهَا وَلَٰكِن يَنَالُهُ ٱلتَّقْوَىٰ مِنكُمْ كَذَٰلِكَ سَخَّرَهَا لَكُمْ لِتُكَبِّرُوا۟ ٱللَّهَ عَلَىٰ مَا هَدَىٰكُمْ وَبَشِّرِ ٱلْمُحْسِنِينَ﴾

"It is neither their meat nor their blood that reaches Allâh, but it is piety from you that reaches Him. Thus have We made

*them subject to you that you may magnify Allâh for His
Guidance to you. And give glad tidings (O Muhammad
(peace be upon him)) to the Muhsinūn (doers of good)."*

﴿إِنَّ ٱللَّهَ يُدَٰفِعُ عَنِ ٱلَّذِينَ ءَامَنُوٓاْ إِنَّ ٱللَّهَ لَا يُحِبُّ كُلَّ خَوَّانٍ
كَفُورٍ﴾

*"Truly, Allâh defends those who believe. Verily! Allâh likes
not any treacherous ingrate to Allâh [those who disobey Allah
but obey Shaitān (Satan)]."*

﴿أُذِنَ لِلَّذِينَ يُقَٰتَلُونَ بِأَنَّهُمْ ظُلِمُواْ وَإِنَّ ٱللَّهَ عَلَىٰ نَصْرِهِمْ لَقَدِيرٌ﴾

*"Permission to fight (against disbelievers) is given to those
(believers) who are fought against, because they have been
wronged; and surely, Allâh is Able to give them (believers)
victory -"*

﴿ٱلَّذِينَ أُخْرِجُواْ مِن دِيَٰرِهِم بِغَيْرِ حَقٍّ إِلَّآ أَن يَقُولُواْ رَبُّنَا ٱللَّهُ
وَلَوْلَا دَفْعُ ٱللَّهِ ٱلنَّاسَ بَعْضَهُم بِبَعْضٍ لَّهُدِّمَتْ صَوَٰمِعُ وَبِيَعٌ وَصَلَوَٰتٌ
وَمَسَٰجِدُ يُذْكَرُ فِيهَا ٱسْمُ ٱللَّهِ كَثِيرًا وَلَيَنصُرَنَّ ٱللَّهُ مَن يَنصُرُهُۥٓ
إِنَّ ٱللَّهَ لَقَوِيٌّ عَزِيزٌ﴾

*"Those who have been expelled from their homes unjustly
only because they said: "Our Lord is Allâh." For had it not
been that Allâh checks one set of people by means of another,
monasteries, churches, synagogues, and mosques, wherein the
Name of Allâh is mentioned much would surely have been
pulled down. Verily, Allâh will help those who help His
(Cause). Truly, Allâh is All-Strong, All-Mighty."*

﴿ٱلَّذِينَ إِن مَّكَّنَّٰهُمْ فِي ٱلْأَرْضِ أَقَامُواْ ٱلصَّلَوٰةَ وَءَاتَوُاْ ٱلزَّكَوٰةَ
وَأَمَرُواْ بِٱلْمَعْرُوفِ وَنَهَوْاْ عَنِ ٱلْمُنكَرِ وَلِلَّهِ عَٰقِبَةُ ٱلْأُمُورِ﴾

*"Those (Muslim rulers) who, if We give them power in the
land, (they) enjoin Iqamat-as-Salât. (i.e. to perform the five
compulsory congregational Salât (prayers) (the males in*

mosques)) to pay the Zakât and they enjoin Al-Ma'rûf (i.e.
Islamic Monotheism and all that Islâm orders one to do), and
forbid Al-Munkar (i.e. disbelief, polytheism and all that Islâm
has forbidden) (i.e. they make the Qur'ân as the law of their
country in all the spheres of life). And with Allâh rests the
end of (all) matters (of creatures)."

$$﴿وَإِن يُكَذِّبُوكَ فَقَدْ كَذَّبَتْ قَبْلَهُمْ قَوْمُ نُوحٍ وَعَادٌ وَثَمُودُ﴾$$

"And if they belie you (O Muhammad (peace be upon him))
so did belie before them, the people of Nuh (Noah), 'Ad and
Thamūd,"

$$﴿وَقَوْمُ إِبْرَٰهِيمَ وَقَوْمُ لُوطٍ﴾$$

"And the people of Ibrâhim (Abraham) and the people of Lūt
(Lot)."

$$﴿وَأَصْحَٰبُ مَدْيَنَ وَكُذِّبَ مُوسَىٰ فَأَمْلَيْتُ لِلْكَٰفِرِينَ ثُمَّ أَخَذْتُهُمْ فَكَيْفَ كَانَ نَكِيرِ﴾$$

"And the dwellers of Madyan (Midian); and belied was Mūsa
(Moses), but I granted respite to the disbelievers for a while,
then I seized them, and how (terrible) was My punishment
(against their wrong-doing)."

$$﴿فَكَأَيِّن مِّن قَرْيَةٍ أَهْلَكْنَٰهَا وَهِيَ ظَالِمَةٌ فَهِيَ خَاوِيَةٌ عَلَىٰ عُرُوشِهَا وَبِئْرٍ مُّعَطَّلَةٍ وَقَصْرٍ مَّشِيدٍ﴾$$

"And many a township did We destroy while it was given to
wrong-doing, so that it lies in ruins (up to this day), and
(many) a deserted well and lofty castle!"

$$﴿أَفَلَمْ يَسِيرُوا۟ فِى ٱلْأَرْضِ فَتَكُونَ لَهُمْ قُلُوبٌ يَعْقِلُونَ بِهَآ أَوْ ءَاذَانٌ يَسْمَعُونَ بِهَا فَإِنَّهَا لَا تَعْمَى ٱلْأَبْصَٰرُ وَلَٰكِن تَعْمَى ٱلْقُلُوبُ ٱلَّتِى فِى ٱلصُّدُورِ﴾$$

"Have they not traveled through the land, and have they

hearts wherewith to understand and ears wherewith to hear?
Verily, it is not the eyes that grow blind, but it is the hearts
which are in the breasts that grow blind.''

﴿وَيَسْتَعْجِلُونَكَ بِالْعَذَابِ وَلَن يُخْلِفَ ٱللَّهُ وَعْدَهُ وَإِنَّ يَوْمًا عِندَ رَبِّكَ كَأَلْفِ سَنَةٍ مِّمَّا تَعُدُّونَ﴾

"And they ask you to hasten on the torment! And Allâh fails
not His Promise. And verily, a day with your Lord is as a
thousand years of what you reckon.''

﴿وَكَأَيِّن مِّن قَرْيَةٍ أَمْلَيْتُ لَهَا وَهِىَ ظَالِمَةٌ ثُمَّ أَخَذْتُهَا وَإِلَىَّ ٱلْمَصِيرُ﴾

"And many a township did I give respite while it was given to
wrong-doing. Then (in the end) I seized it (with punishment).
And to Me is the (final) return (of all).''

﴿قُلْ يَـٰٓأَيُّهَا ٱلنَّاسُ إِنَّمَآ أَنَا۠ لَكُمْ نَذِيرٌ مُّبِينٌ﴾

"Say (O Muhammad (peace be upon him)) 'O mankind! I am
(sent) to you only as a plain warner.'''

﴿فَٱلَّذِينَ ءَامَنُوا۟ وَعَمِلُوا۟ ٱلصَّـٰلِحَـٰتِ لَهُم مَّغْفِرَةٌ وَرِزْقٌ كَرِيمٌ﴾

"So those who believe (in the Oneness of Allâh - Islamic
Monotheism) and do righteous good deeds, for them is
forgiveness and Rizquân Karîm (generous provision, i.e.
Paradise).''

﴿وَٱلَّذِينَ سَعَوْا۟ فِىٓ ءَايَـٰتِنَا مُعَـٰجِزِينَ أُو۟لَـٰٓئِكَ أَصْحَـٰبُ ٱلْجَحِيمِ﴾

"But those who strive against Our Ayât (proofs, evidences,
verses, lessons, signs, revelations, etc.), to frustrate them,
they will be dwellers of the Hell-fire.''

﴿وَمَآ أَرْسَلْنَا مِن قَبْلِكَ مِن رَّسُولٍ وَلَا نَبِىٍّ إِلَّآ إِذَا تَمَنَّىٰٓ أَلْقَى ٱلشَّيْطَـٰنُ فِىٓ أُمْنِيَّتِهِۦ فَيَنسَخُ ٱللَّهُ مَا يُلْقِى ٱلشَّيْطَـٰنُ ثُمَّ يُحْكِمُ

ٱللَّهُ ءَايَـٰتِهِۦ وَٱللَّهُ عَلِيمٌ حَكِيمٌ ﴾

"Never did We send a Messenger or a Prophet before you but when he did recite the revelation or narrated or spoke, Shaitân (Satan) threw (some falsehood) in it. But Allâh abolishes that which Shaitân (Satan) throws in. Then Allâh establishes His Revelations. And Allâh is All-Knower, All-Wise:"

﴿ لِّيَجْعَلَ مَا يُلْقِى ٱلشَّيْطَـٰنُ فِتْنَةً لِّلَّذِينَ فِى قُلُوبِهِم مَّرَضٌ وَٱلْقَاسِيَةِ قُلُوبُهُمْ وَإِنَّ ٱلظَّـٰلِمِينَ لَفِى شِقَاقٍ بَعِيدٍ ﴾

"That He (Allâh) may make what is thrown in by Shaitân (Satan) a trial for those in whose hearts is a disease (of hypocrisy and disbelief) and whose hearts are hardened. And certainly, the Zalimûn (polytheists and wrong-doers) are in an opposition far-off (from the truth against Allâh's Messenger and the believers)."

﴿ وَلِيَعْلَمَ ٱلَّذِينَ أُوتُوا۟ ٱلْعِلْمَ أَنَّهُ ٱلْحَقُّ مِن رَّبِّكَ فَيُؤْمِنُوا۟ بِهِۦ فَتُخْبِتَ لَهُۥ قُلُوبُهُمْ وَإِنَّ ٱللَّهَ لَهَادِ ٱلَّذِينَ ءَامَنُوٓا۟ إِلَىٰ صِرَٰطٍ مُّسْتَقِيمٍ ﴾

"And that those who have been given knowledge may know that it (this Qur'ân) is the truth from your Lord, so that they may believe therein, and their hearts may submit to it with humility. And verily, Allâh is the Guide of those who believe, to the Straight Path."

﴿ وَلَا يَزَالُ ٱلَّذِينَ كَفَرُوا۟ فِى مِرْيَةٍ مِّنْهُ حَتَّىٰ تَأْتِيَهُمُ ٱلسَّاعَةُ بَغْتَةً أَوْ يَأْتِيَهُمْ عَذَابُ يَوْمٍ عَقِيمٍ ﴾

"And those who disbelieved will not cease to be in doubt about it (this Qur'ân) until the Hour comes suddenly upon them, or there comes to them the torment of the Day after which there will be no night (i.e. the Day of Resurrection)."

﴿ ٱلْمُلْكُ يَوْمَئِذٍ لِّلَّهِ يَحْكُمُ بَيْنَهُمْ فَٱلَّذِينَ ءَامَنُوا۟ وَعَمِلُوا۟ ٱلصَّـٰلِحَـٰتِ فِى جَنَّـٰتِ ٱلنَّعِيمِ ﴾

"The sovereignty on that Day will be that of Allâh (the One Who has no partners). He will judge between them. So those who believed (in the Oneness of Allâh - Islâmic Monotheism) and did righteous good deeds will be in Gardens of delight (Paradise)."

﴿وَٱلَّذِينَ كَفَرُواْ وَكَذَّبُواْ بِـَٔايَٰتِنَا فَأُوْلَٰٓئِكَ لَهُمْ عَذَابٌ مُّهِينٌ﴾

"And those who disbelieved and belied Our Verses (of this Qur'ân), for them will be a humiliating torment (in Hell)."

﴿وَٱلَّذِينَ هَاجَرُواْ فِى سَبِيلِ ٱللَّهِ ثُمَّ قُتِلُوٓاْ أَوْ مَاتُواْ لَيَرْزُقَنَّهُمُ ٱللَّهُ رِزْقًا حَسَنًا وَإِنَّ ٱللَّهَ لَهُوَ خَيْرُ ٱلرَّٰزِقِينَ﴾

"Those who emigrated in the Cause of Allâh and after that were killed or died, surely, Allah will provide a good provision for them. And verily, it is Allâh Who indeed is the Best of those who make provision."

﴿لَيُدْخِلَنَّهُم مُّدْخَلًا يَرْضَوْنَهُۥ وَإِنَّ ٱللَّهَ لَعَلِيمٌ حَلِيمٌ﴾

"Truly, He will make them enter an entrance with which they shall be well-pleased, and verily, Allâh indeed is All-Knowing, Most Forbearing."

﴿ذَٰلِكَ وَمَنْ عَاقَبَ بِمِثْلِ مَا عُوقِبَ بِهِۦ ثُمَّ بُغِىَ عَلَيْهِ لَيَنصُرَنَّهُ ٱللَّهُ إِنَّ ٱللَّهَ لَعَفُوٌّ غَفُورٌ﴾

"That is so. And whoever has retaliated with the like of that which he was made to suffer, and then has again been wronged, Allâh will surely help him. Verily Allâh indeed is Oft-Pardoning, Oft-Forgiving."

﴿ذَٰلِكَ بِأَنَّ ٱللَّهَ يُولِجُ ٱلَّيْلَ فِى ٱلنَّهَارِ وَيُولِجُ ٱلنَّهَارَ فِى ٱلَّيْلِ وَأَنَّ ٱللَّهَ سَمِيعٌ بَصِيرٌ﴾

"That is because Allâh merges the night into the day, and He merges the day into the night. And verily, Allâh is All-

Hearer, All-Seer.''

$$\text{﴿ذَٰلِكَ بِأَنَّ ٱللَّهَ هُوَ ٱلْحَقُّ وَأَنَّ مَا يَدْعُونَ مِن دُونِهِ هُوَ ٱلْبَٰطِلُ وَأَنَّ ٱللَّهَ هُوَ ٱلْعَلِيُّ ٱلْكَبِيرُ﴾}$$

"That is because Allâh - He is the Truth (the only True God of all that exists, Who has no partners or rivals with Him), and what they (the polytheists) invoke besides Him, it is Batil (falsehood). And verily, Allâh - He is the Most High, the Most Great.''

$$\text{﴿أَلَمْ تَرَ أَنَّ ٱللَّهَ أَنزَلَ مِنَ ٱلسَّمَآءِ مَآءً فَتُصْبِحُ ٱلْأَرْضُ مُخْضَرَّةً إِنَّ ٱللَّهَ لَطِيفٌ خَبِيرٌ﴾}$$

"See you not that Allâh sends down water (rain) from the sky, and then the earth becomes green? Verily, Allâh is the Most Kind and Courteous, Well-Acquainted with all things.''

$$\text{﴿لَّهُ مَا فِي ٱلسَّمَٰوَٰتِ وَمَا فِي ٱلْأَرْضِ وَإِنَّ ٱللَّهَ لَهُوَ ٱلْغَنِيُّ ٱلْحَمِيدُ﴾}$$

"To Him belongs all that is in the heavens and all that is on the earth. And verily, Allâh - He is Rich (Free of all needs), Worthy of all praise.''

$$\text{﴿أَلَمْ تَرَ أَنَّ ٱللَّهَ سَخَّرَ لَكُم مَّا فِي ٱلْأَرْضِ وَٱلْفُلْكَ تَجْرِي فِي ٱلْبَحْرِ بِأَمْرِهِ وَيُمْسِكُ ٱلسَّمَآءَ أَن تَقَعَ عَلَى ٱلْأَرْضِ إِلَّا بِإِذْنِهِ إِنَّ ٱللَّهَ بِٱلنَّاسِ لَرَءُوفٌ رَّحِيمٌ﴾}$$

"See you not that Allâh has subjected to you (mankind) all that is on the earth, and the ships that sail through the sea by His Command? He withholds the heaven from falling on the earth except by His Leave. Verily, Allâh is, for mankind, full of Kindness, Most Merciful.''

$$\text{﴿وَهُوَ ٱلَّذِي أَحْيَاكُمْ ثُمَّ يُمِيتُكُمْ ثُمَّ يُحْيِيكُمْ إِنَّ ٱلْإِنسَٰنَ}$$

$$\text{لَكَفُورٌ}$$

"It is He, Who gave you life, and then will cause you to die, and will again give you life (on the Day of Resurrection). Verily man is indeed an ingrate."

$$\text{لِّكُلِّ أُمَّةٍ جَعَلْنَا مَنسَكًا هُمْ نَاسِكُوهُ فَلَا يُنَازِعُنَّكَ فِى ٱلْأَمْرِ وَٱدْعُ إِلَىٰ رَبِّكَ إِنَّكَ لَعَلَىٰ هُدًى مُّسْتَقِيمٍ}$$

"For every nation We have ordained religious ceremonies (e.g. slaughtering of the beast of cattle during the three days of stay at Mina (Makkah) during the Hajj (pilgrimage)) which they must follow; so let them (the pagans) not dispute with you on the matter (i.e. to eat of the cattle which you slaughter, and not to eat of cattle which Allâh kills by its natural death), but invite them to your Lord. Verily you (O Muhammad (peace be upon him)) indeed are on the (true) straight guidance (i.e. the true religion of Islamic Monotheism)."

$$\text{وَإِن جَٰدَلُوكَ فَقُلِ ٱللَّهُ أَعْلَمُ بِمَا تَعْمَلُونَ}$$

"And if they argue with you (as regards the slaughtering of the sacrifices), say 'Allâh knows best of what you do.'"

$$\text{ٱللَّهُ يَحْكُمُ بَيْنَكُمْ يَوْمَ ٱلْقِيَٰمَةِ فِيمَا كُنتُمْ فِيهِ تَخْتَلِفُونَ}$$

"Allâh will judge between you on the Day of Resurrection about that wherein you used to differ."

$$\text{أَلَمْ تَعْلَمْ أَنَّ ٱللَّهَ يَعْلَمُ مَا فِى ٱلسَّمَآءِ وَٱلْأَرْضِ إِنَّ ذَٰلِكَ فِى كِتَٰبٍ إِنَّ ذَٰلِكَ عَلَى ٱللَّهِ يَسِيرٌ}$$

"Know you not that Allâh knows all that is in heaven and on the earth? Verily, it is (all) in the Book (Al-Lauh Al-Mahfûz). Verily that is easy for Allâh."

$$\text{وَيَعْبُدُونَ مِن دُونِ ٱللَّهِ مَا لَمْ يُنَزِّلْ بِهِۦ سُلْطَٰنًا وَمَا لَيْسَ لَهُم بِهِۦ عِلْمٌ وَمَا لِلظَّٰلِمِينَ مِن نَّصِيرٍ}$$

"And they worship besides Allâh others for which He has sent down no authority, and of which they have no knowledge; and for the Zâlimûn (wrongdoers, polytheists and disbelievers in the Oneness of Allâh) there is no helper."

﴿وَإِذَا تُتْلَىٰ عَلَيْهِمْ ءَايَٰتُنَا بَيِّنَٰتٍ تَعْرِفُ فِى وُجُوهِ ٱلَّذِينَ كَفَرُواْ ٱلْمُنكَرَّ يَكَادُونَ يَسْطُونَ بِٱلَّذِينَ يَتْلُونَ عَلَيْهِمْ ءَايَٰتِنَا قُلْ أَفَأُنَبِّئُكُم بِشَرٍّ مِّن ذَٰلِكُمُ ٱلنَّارُ وَعَدَهَا ٱللَّهُ ٱلَّذِينَ كَفَرُواْ وَبِئْسَ ٱلْمَصِيرُ﴾

"And when Our Clear Verses are recited to them, you will notice a denial on the faces of the disbelievers! They are nearly ready to attack with violence those who recite Our Verses to them. Say: 'Shall I tell you of something worse than that? The Fire (of Hell) which Allâh has promised to those who disbelieved, and worst indeed is that destination!"

﴿يَٰٓأَيُّهَا ٱلنَّاسُ ضُرِبَ مَثَلٌ فَٱسْتَمِعُواْ لَهُۥٓ إِنَّ ٱلَّذِينَ تَدْعُونَ مِن دُونِ ٱللَّهِ لَن يَخْلُقُواْ ذُبَابًا وَلَوِ ٱجْتَمَعُواْ لَهُۥ وَإِن يَسْلُبْهُمُ ٱلذُّبَابُ شَيْـًٔا لَّا يَسْتَنقِذُوهُ مِنْهُ ضَعُفَ ٱلطَّالِبُ وَٱلْمَطْلُوبُ﴾

"O mankind! A similitude has been coined, so listen to it (carefully): Verily those on whom you call besides Allâh, cannot create (even) a fly, even though they combine together for the purpose. And if the fly snatches away a thing from them, they will have no power to release it from the fly. So weak are (both) the seeker and the sought."

﴿مَا قَدَرُواْ ٱللَّهَ حَقَّ قَدْرِهِۦٓ إِنَّ ٱللَّهَ لَقَوِىٌّ عَزِيزٌ﴾

"They have not estimated Allâh His Rightful Estimate. Verily, Allâh is All-Strong, All-Mighty."

﴿ٱللَّهُ يَصْطَفِى مِنَ ٱلْمَلَٰٓئِكَةِ رُسُلًا وَمِنَ ٱلنَّاسِ إِنَّ ٱللَّهَ سَمِيعٌ بَصِيرٌ﴾

"Allâh chooses Messengers from angels and from men. Verily, Allâh is All-Hearer, All-Seer."

﴿يَعْلَمُ مَا بَيْنَ أَيْدِيهِمْ وَمَا خَلْفَهُمْ وَإِلَى ٱللَّهِ تُرْجَعُ ٱلْأُمُورُ﴾

"He knows what is before them, and what is behind them. And to Allâh return all matters (for decision)."

﴿يَـٰٓأَيُّهَا ٱلَّذِينَ ءَامَنُوا ٱرْكَعُوا وَٱسْجُدُوا وَٱعْبُدُوا رَبَّكُمْ وَٱفْعَلُوا ٱلْخَيْرَ لَعَلَّكُمْ تُفْلِحُونَ﴾

"O you who have believed! Bow down, and prostrate yourselves, and worship your Lord and do good that you may be successful."

﴿وَجَـٰهِدُوا فِي ٱللَّهِ حَقَّ جِهَادِهِۦ هُوَ ٱجْتَبَىٰكُمْ وَمَا جَعَلَ عَلَيْكُمْ فِي ٱلدِّينِ مِنْ حَرَجٍ مِّلَّةَ أَبِيكُمْ إِبْرَٰهِيمَ هُوَ سَمَّىٰكُمُ ٱلْمُسْلِمِينَ مِن قَبْلُ وَفِي هَـٰذَا لِيَكُونَ ٱلرَّسُولُ شَهِيدًا عَلَيْكُمْ وَتَكُونُوا شُهَدَاءَ عَلَى ٱلنَّاسِ فَأَقِيمُوا ٱلصَّلَوٰةَ وَءَاتُوا ٱلزَّكَوٰةَ وَٱعْتَصِمُوا بِٱللَّهِ هُوَ مَوْلَىٰكُمْ فَنِعْمَ ٱلْمَوْلَىٰ وَنِعْمَ ٱلنَّصِيرُ﴾

"And strive hard in Allâh's Cause as you ought to strive (with sincerity and with all your efforts that His Name should be superior). He has chosen you (to convey His Message of Islâmic Monotheism to mankind by inviting them to His religion of Islâm), and has not laid upon you in religion any hardship: it is the religion of your father Ibraheem (Abraham) (Islâmic Monotheism). It is He (Allâh) Who has named you Muslims both before and in this (the Qur'ân), that the Messenger (Muhammad (peace be upon him)) may be a witness over you and you be witnesses over mankind! So perform As-Salât (Iqamat-as-Salât), give Zakât and hold fast to Allâh (i.e. have confidence in Allâh, and depend upon Him in all your affairs). He is your Maulâ (Patron, Lord), what an Excellent Maulâ (Patron, Lord) and what an Excellent Helper!"

Chapter 15
Checklists

This chapter contains a series of checklists to help you prepare and plan for your trip as well as a useful *Hajj* package evaluation table. There is also an action list for the *Hajj* rites and for noting down useful information. Below is a list of all the checklists:

1. To do List for vacations, bookings, vaccinations, etc.
2. Questions related to the *Hajj* package.
3. *Hajj* package evaluation table.
4. Items to buy and pack for the trip.
5. Traveller's cheques and bank drafts.
6. What to study.
7. Parcels to deliver; things to buy; messages.
8. Important points to remember.
9. Memorable moments.
10. People I met.
11. Gift list.
12. What to take to Mina and Arafat.
13. *Umrah* actions.
14. *Hajj Tamattu* actions.
15. Rites missed/violations - *Fidyah*.
16. Important contact numbers.
17. Notes.
18. Passport details.
19. Emergency details.
20. Makkah, Madinah hotel and agent details.

➢ Planning and Preparing:

Action	Details	Done?
Determine *Hajj* dates		
Arrange vacation		
Evaluate packages		
Make Bookings		
Vaccinations:	Meningitis, Cholera	
Finances		
Visa applications	Letter from Islamic society, application	
Traveller's Cheques		
Bank Drafts		
Passports		
Suitcases		
Doctor	Letter for special medicines; Vaccinations Certificates	
Visas photos	Obtain photos for visas	
Visa	Obtain all required visas	
Extra photos	Obtain some extra photos for the trip	

➤ Questions related to the *Hajj* Package:

Question	Answer	Comments
How far is the hotel from the mosque (by time)?		
Are there any hills or hilly streets on the way?		
Are there any stairs to climb to get to the building?		
How many persons will share a room?		
Are the men and women separate?		
How many bathrooms are there per room?		
How many elevators are there?		
On which floor will you be and how many rooms per floor are there?		
Is the hotel located in a busy(cars)/main street?		
Do the rooms have telephones, fridges, air-conditioning etc.?		
Do the people who manage the hotel speak English (receptionist)?		
Do they provide room cleaning service?		
Do they provide laundry facilities?		
Is food included? If yes, what type of food is provided (If I choose not to take the food option, is food provided for the *Hajj* days)?		
Are there kitchen/cooking facilities in the rooms?		
Who will represent the agent during the trip?		
What type of accommodation is provided in Mina, Arafat and Muzdalifah?		
What facilities are provided (i.e. food, toilets, air-conditioning)?		
Are the buses air-conditioned?		
How far are you from the Namira Mosque in Arafat?		
How far are you from 'Jabal-Rahmah' (Mountain of Mercy) in Arafat?		
How far are you from the *Jamrah* in Mina?		
Will the group spend the night in Muzdalifah?		
On which day will the group return to Makkah to perform *Tawaaful-Ifadah*? Is transport provided?		
What is the format of the actual *Hajj* package: 6 days - 8th to Mina until the 13th?		
5 days - 8th to Mina until the 12th?		
5 days - 9th to Arafat until the 13th in Mina?		
4 Days - 9th to Arafat until the 12th in Mina?		

➢ **Package Evaluation Table:** *(see example in chapter 2)*

		Package				
Importance ranking:						
Overall Total:	↓					
Total for High:	H					
Total for Medium:	M					
Total for Low:	L					
Criteria:	❖	Score:				
Agent Reputation						
Agent - other factors						
Cost:						
Airfare						
Accommodation						
Other						
Accommodation:						
Location (Makkah)						
Type						
Couple-room						
En-suite						
Facilities						
Other						
Mina						
Arafat						
Madinah						
Food						
Madinah						
Flight schedules						
Transport						
No. of days in Makkah						
Move to Aziziah						
Company (sharing with)						

➤ Things to Buy and Pack:

Item	Details	Bought	Packed
Ihraam	At least one set, if you going to Makkah first (otherwise it can be purchased in Madinah)		
Medicine:	● Tablets for Pain & Fever		
	● Salt Tablets		
	● Muscle Cream		
	● Antibiotics		
	● Cough Medicine		
	● Diarrhoea Tablets		
	● Throat Lozenges		
	●		
	●		
	●		
	●		
	●		
	●		
Toiletries:	* Shampoo		
	* Toothpaste		
	* Scent free soap		
	* Moisturising Cream		
	* Pocket Tissues		
	* Liquid soap (shower hair & body wash)		
	* Underarm deodorant		
	* *Miswak*		
	* Sanitary pads		
Money belt			
Umbrella			
Neck Pillow			
Mattress	Inflatable mattress for Mina		
Radio	Small radio for Arafat		
Towels	Not all hotels provide towels		

➢ Travellers cheques:

Number	Cashed at	Date	Amount

➢ Bank drafts:

Cheque Number	Bank	Made to?	Amount

➢ What to Study:

Topic	Done?	Revised?	Remarks
Salah			
Travelling *Salah*			
Janazah Salah			
Talbiyah			
Ihraam requirements/ restrictions			
Umrah			
Different types of *Hajj*			
History of *Hajj*			
Hajj flow			
6 Days of *Hajj*			
Sunnah Dua's			
Hajj for women			
Sacrifices			HUF
Special attention items			Listed in this book

➤ Important points to Remember:

Item	When	Priority/Remarks
Stoning of *Jamr'at* time	Mina	After *Zawaal*
Shortening of *Salah*	Travel / Mina	*Zuhr*, *'Asr*, *'Eshaa*
Change Money to Riyals	Bank / Airport	High Priority
Reconfirm Bookings		

> ➤ **Parcels to deliver; things to buy; messages; for others:**

Action:	For Whom?	From Whom?	Done?

> ➤ **Memorable Moments:**

Event	Date	Place

➤ People I met:

Name	Tel. No	Address/E-Mail

➤ Things (Gifts) to buy:

Person	Item	Budget	Bought?	Actual Cost
TOTAL COST:				

➤ Suggested list of what to take with you to Mina and Arafat:

Items (All for Mina)	Bought?	Packed?	Arafat	Packed?
A small pocket size Qur'an			Yes	
Hajj books			Yes	
Pain and Fever tablets			Yes	
Salt tablets, (especially if you sweat a lot)			Yes	
Muscle cramp ointment				
Vitamin C tablets (take one of these daily)				
Throat lozenges			Yes	
Cough syrup				
Cream for skin irritation				
Plasters				
Any special medicine				
Diarrhoea tablets			Yes	
Non-perfumed soap				
Hair & Body Wash (soap)				
Toothpaste (non flavoured) or Miswak			Yes	
Perfume (men only, for when you are out of Ihraam)				
Shaver (+batteries), hair trimmer or scissors				
Small mirror				
Toothbrush			Yes	
Hairbrush				
Clothes for at least 2 days				
Underwear				
'Spare Ihraam' (if you are going to Mina on the 8th)				
Joggers/Shoes				
Socks (to wear with your shoes/ joggers)				

A hat/cap/*Koefia* or head-scarf			
A towel (dark colour)			
A straw *Hajji* mat (for Muzdalifah also)		Yes	
Prayer mat (for Muzdalifah also)		Yes	
Shoe bag			
Small stone bag		Yes	
Small water spray bottle		Yes	
A small pocket knife		Yes	
Some string. (This is useful to hang clothes)			
Pocket Tissues (none perfumed). Handy as toilet paper		Yes	
Water flask		Yes	
Umbrella		Yes	
Alarm Clock			
Neck (travelling) Pillow			
Dates		Yes	
Biscuits		Yes	
Sweets		Yes	
Pen and a small notepad			
2 person flip-open tent		Yes	

➢ *Umrah:*

No.	Action	√	Remarks
01	Trim nails, if required		
02	Shave under arms, if required		
03	Shave pubic hair, if required		
04	*Ghusl*		
05	Apply Perfume (men only)		
06	*Meqaat* reached		
07	Adopt *Ihraam*		
08	Niyah for *Umrah*		
09	Recite *Talbiyah*		
10	Read *Dua* when entering *Haram*		
11	Expose right shoulder (Men)		
12	Start at the *Hajrul-Aswad* and say "*Bismillahi Allahu Akbar*"		
13	Kiss/Touch/Gesture to Black Stone		
14	Men *Raml* (slow running) in first 3 rounds		
15	Touch the *Rukn-Yamani* Corner if possible		
16	Read "*Rabanaa Aatina...*"		
17	Kiss/touch or gesture and Say "*Allahu Akbar*" as you pass the Black Stone		
18	Complete 7 rounds (circuits)		
19	Cover the right shoulder (Men)		
20	Perform 2 *Rak'at* near *Maqaam Ibraheem*		
21	Read *Surah Al-Kafirun* (109) in 1st *Rakah* after *Suratul-Fatiha*		
22	Read *Surah Al-Ikhlaas* (112) in 2nd *Rakah* after *Suratul-Fatiha*		
23	Drink *Zamzam* water		
24	Kiss/Touch Black Stone if possible		
25	Proceed to *Safaa*		
26	Read "*Inaa Safaa......*"		
27	Read "*Allahu Akbar....*" x 3, with *Dua'* in between		

28	Start *Sa'ee* from Safaa		
29	Men *Raml* (slow running) between the green lights		
30	Stop at Marwah and do the same as at Safaa		
31	Complete 7 laps (Safaa to Marwah = 1)		
32	Cut Hair		
33	Remove *Ihraam*, adopt normal clothes		
34	*Ihraam* restrictions lifted		

➢ *Hajj Tamattu*:

No.	Action	√	Remarks
Day 1	**8th of Dhul Hijjah: *At-Tarweya***		
1.	*Ghusl*		
2.	Apply perfume (men only)		
3.	Adopt *Ihraam* from where you are		
4.	Make *Niyah* for *Hajj*		
5.	Recite *Talbiyah*		
6.	Proceed to Mina		
7.	Perform *Zuhr, 'Asr, Maghrib* & *'Eshaa* in Mina		
8.	Shorten *Zuhr, 'Asr, 'Eshaa* to 2 *Rak'at* each in Mina (Perform *Witr* and the *Sunnah* for *Fajr*)		
Day 2	**9th of Dhul Hijjah: *Wuqoof-bil-Arafat***		
9.	Perform *Salatul-Fajr* in Mina		
10.	Proceed to Arafat		
11.	Listen to *Khutbah*, if possible		
12.	Join & shorten (2 *Rak'at* each) *Zuhr* and *'Asr* Salah at *Zuhr* time		
13.	Wuqoof has now 'started' - Supplication		
14.	After sunset, leave Arafat		
15.	Muzdalifah before 12.00pm?		
16.	Yes, Perform *Maghrib* & *'Eshaa* (2) Joined upon your arrival in Muzdalifah		
17.	No, Perform *Maghrib* & *'Eshaa* where you are		
18.	One *Adhaan* & two *Iqaam'at*		
19.	Collect 7 pebbles in Muzdalifah if you wish		Not a requirement
20.	Sleep		
21.	Perform *Salatul-Fajr* in Muzdalifah		
22.	Supplication		
Day 3	**10th of Dhul-Hijjah: *Yaumun-Nahr***		
23.	Depart for Mina shortly before sunrise		

24.	Collect pebbles in Mina if you did not get them in Muzdalifah		
25.	Stone the big *Jamrah* (*Aqaba*)		
26.	Perform sacrifices (*Hady*)		
27.	Shave hair (men only)		
28.	Women cut hair (approx. 1 inch)		
29.	*Tawaaful-Ifadah*: *Tawaaf* (same as for *Umrah*)		
30.	*Sa'ee* for *Hajj*: *Sa'ee* (same as for *Umrah*)		
31.	Return to Mina		
32.	Shorten (*Zuhr*, *'Asr*, *'Eshaa*) *Salah* (Do not join), while in Mina. (*Witr* & *Fajr Sunnah*)		
Day 4	**11th of Dhul-Hijjah: Day one of *Tashreek*:**		
33.	Collect pebbles (7 x 3 = 21, at least)		
34.	After *Zawaal* (midday)		
35.	Stone the Small *Jamrah*		
36.	Make dua facing *Qiblah*		
37.	Stone the Middle *Jamrah*		
38.	Make dua facing *Qiblah*		
39.	Stone the Big *Jamrah*		
Day 5	**12th of Dhul-Hijjah: Day two of *Tashreek***		
40.	Collect pebbles (7 x 3 = 21, at least)		
41.	After *Zawaal*		
42.	Stone the Small *Jamrah*		
43.	Make dua facing *Qiblah*		
44.	Stone the Middle *Jamrah*		
45.	Make dua facing *Qiblah*		
46.	Stone the Big *Jamrah*		
47.	Leave for Makkah?		
48.	Yes, Before sunset		
49.	No, Stay until 13th		
Day 6	**13th of Dhul-Hijjah: Day three of *Tashreek***		
50.	Collect pebbles (7 x 3 = 21, at least)		
51.	After *Zawaal*		

52.	Stone the Small *Jamrah*		
53.	Make *Dua'* facing *Qiblah*		
54.	Stone the Middle *Jamrah*		
55.	Make *Dua'* facing *Qiblah*		
56.	Stone the Big *Jamrah*		
57.	Return to Makkah		
58.	*Tawaaful-Ifadah* and *Sa'ee* for *Hajj*		If not done earlier
Home	**Ready to leave for Home?**		
59.	Last rite = *Tawaaful-Wadaa'* (no *Sa'ee*)		
60.	Leave for Home		

➤ Rites missed that require payment of *Fidyah* (expiation/*Dumm*):

Rite:	Expiation?	Done?
Violating the *Ihraam* restrictions (i.e., cutting your hair or nails, applying perfume, men wearing fitted clothes or covering their head):	Fast for 3 days or Feed 6 poor persons or 1 x Sheep or goat	
Hunting	See chapter 6	
Sexual Relations	See chapter 6	
Passing the *Meqaat* without *Ihraam*	1 x Sheep or goat*	
Not staying in Arafat until sunset	1 x Sheep or goat*	
Not staying/stopping in Muzdalifah	1 x Sheep or goat*	
Not spending the nights in Mina	1 x Sheep or goat*	
Not pelting the *Jamr'at*	1 x Sheep or goat*	
Not shaving or cutting your hair	1 x Sheep or goat*	
Omitting *Tawaaful-Wadaa'* (Menstruating women exempted)	1 x Sheep or goat*	
	* Option = Share with 6 others in a camel or a cow	
Number of days to fast during *Hajj*		
Number of days to fast at home		
Number of poor persons to feed		
Number of sacrifices to perform		

➢ Important Contact Numbers:

Name	Tel. No	Fax. No	E-mail address

➢ Notes:

Remarks	Related to

➤ **Passport & Emergency Details:**
(Keep a photocopy of this page)

Passport Details

Name: ....

Passport Number: ....

Nationality: ....

Place of Issue: ....

Date of Issue: ....

Expiry Date: ....

Emergency Details

Blood Type: .... **Allergies** ....

In case of an emergency please contact:

Name: ....

....

Relationship: ....

Address: ....

....

Country code: .... **City Code:** ....

Home: .... **Office:** ....

Mobile: .... **Fax:** ....

Internet Address: ....

➤**Agent and Hotel Details:**
(Make a photocopy of this page and leave it with a relative at home)

Local Agent Details

Company Name:...

Contact Name:..

Contact Number:..

Internet Address:...

Saudi Agent Details

Company Name:...

Contact Name:..

Contact Number: 966 + city code....................................

Internet Address:...

Makkah Hotel Details

Hotel Name:..

Contact Number: 9662...

Internet Address:...

Madinah Hotel Details

Hotel Name:..

Contact Number: 9664...

Internet Address:...

In Closing

I sincerely hope that this second edition will be as useful as the first edition was for so many pilgrims. If it is all correct then it is from Allah and if there are any mistakes then it is from me. As the objective of this book is to provide accurate, realistic and useful information, I would once again appreciate any comments, suggestions and constructive criticism, in order to improve any future editions.

The Prophet (ﷺ) said:

«مَثَلُ ما بَعَثَني اللهُ مِنَ الهُدَى وَالعِلْمِ كَمَثَلِ الغَيثِ الكَثيرِ أَصَابَ أَرْضًا، فَكَانَ مِنها نَقِيَّةٌ، قَبِلَتِ المَاءَ، فَأَنْبَتَتِ الكَلأَ وَالعُشْبَ الكَثيرَ، وَكانَتْ مِنها أجادِبُ، أَمْسَكَتِ الماءَ، فَنَفَعَ اللهُ بِها النَّاسَ فَشَرِبُوا وَسَقَوْا وَزَرَعُوا، وَأَصَابَ مِنها طائِفَةً أُخْرَى، إِنَّما هِيَ قِيعانٌ لا تُمْسِكُ ماءً وَلا تُنْبِتُ كَلأً، فَذلِكَ مَثَلُ مَنْ فَقُهَ في دِينِ اللهِ وَنَفَعَهُ ما بَعَثَني اللهُ بِهِ فَعَلِمَ وَعَلَّمَ، وَمَثَلُ مَنْ لَمْ يَرْفَعْ بِذلِكَ رَأْسًا وَلَمْ يَقْبَلْ هُدَى اللهِ الَّذي أُرْسِلْتُ بِهِ».

"The example of guidance and knowledge with which Allah has sent me is like abundant rain falling on the earth. Some of which was fertile soil that absorbed rain-water and brought forth vegetation and grass in abundance. Another portion of it was hard and held the rain water and Allah benefited the people with it and they utilized it for drinking, (making their animals drink from it) and to irrigate the land for cultivation. (And) a portion of it was barren which could neither hold water nor bring forth vegetation (then that land gave no benefits). The first is the example of the person who comprehends Allah's Religion (Islam) and gets benefit (from the knowledge) which Allah has revealed through me (the Prophet) and learns and then teaches it to others. The (last

example is that of a) person who does not care for it and does not take Allah's Guidance revealed through me (He is like the barren land)."

We all know that the shortest distance between two points is a straight line. So, the best way to ensure that we obtain the highest reward for our *Hajj* is to follow a straight line. The straight line being, to perform it the way our Prophet (ﷺ) performed it.

Salah is a "spiritual injection" we obtain five times a day. Fasting in Ramadan is our yearly "spiritual injection". The "spiritual injection" of *Hajj* is one most of us will receive only once in our lifetime. Let us ensure that the dose we obtain is strong enough to vaccinate us for the rest of our life!

And don't forget, stay focused on the PRIZE...

"I bear witness that there is none worthy of worship except Allah and I bear witness that Muhammad is His Messenger."

Abu Hurrairah (ﷺ) says that the Prophet (ﷺ) was once asked:

«أَيُّ الْعَمَلِ أَفْضَلُ؟ قَالَ: «إِيمَانٌ بِاللهِ وَرَسُولِهِ» قِيلَ: ثُمَّ مَاذَا؟ قَالَ: «الْجِهَادُ فِي سَبِيلِ اللهِ» قِيلَ: ثُمَّ مَاذَا؟ قَالَ: «حَجٌّ مَبْرُورٌ»

"Which action is the best of all?' He said: 'To believe in Allah and His Messengers.' He was further asked: 'And what next?' He said: 'Jihad (striving) in the cause of Allah'. He was asked again: 'And what after that?' He answered:

'The Pilgrimage, free from vices and defects.'"

(Bukhari:26 & Muslim:83)

Glossary

Ahadith	-	Plural for *Hadith*.
Arafat	-	Name of the area located 11km from Mina, where the pilgrims spend the 9th of Dhul-Hijjah. Sometimes spelt Arafah.
Aswad	-	Black.
Aurah	-	Parts of the body that must be covered.
Ay'at	-	Plural for *Ayah* (Verse from the Qur'an).
Ayaam	-	Days.
Barakah	-	Blessings of Allah.
Dhikr	-	Mentioning Allah's name and attributes (in *Ibadah*).
Dua'	-	Supplication, invocation.
Dumm	-	Blood. The sacrifice of a goat, sheep, etc., in order to compensate for failing to perform a *Wajib* act of *Hajj*.
Dhul-Hijjah	-	The 12th month of the Muslim (*Hijrah*) calendar.
Dhul-Qadah	-	The 11th month of the Muslim (*Hijrah*) calendar.
Eidul-Adhah	-	The 10th of Dhu-Hijjah. The day of celebration after the day of Arafat.
Fidyah	-	Expiation for a missed rite (normally by sacrificing a sheep or a goat).
Ghusl	-	Taking a bath in a special ceremonial way.
Hady	-	The sacrifice (sheep, goat, etc.) for the *Tamattu* & *Qiran* pilgrims.
Hajrul-Aswad	-	The Black Stone implanted in the corner of the Ka'bah.
Halq	-	Shaving one's hair.
Haraam	-	Forbidden, prohibited.
Haram	-	The mosques in Makkah and in Madinah are referred to as the *Haram*; also the areas around them.
Idtiba	-	Uncovering the right shoulder (men) while in *Ihraam*.
Ifrad	-	*Hajj-Ifrad* is *Hajj* only, without *Umrah*.
Ihraam	-	The state of ritual consecration. The ceremonial state of making *Umrah* or *Hajj* or the garments themselves.

Istilam	-	Touching the Black Stone or *Rukn–Yamani* Corner.
Jabal-Rahma	-	The Mountain of Mercy in Arafat.
Jamrah	-	The pillars in Mina for stoning, is signifying the places where the *Shaytaan* tempted Prophet Ibraheem.
Jamr'at	-	Plural for *Jamrah*.
Janazah	-	The dead.
Jannah	-	Paradise.
Ka'bah	-	The cube structure in the mosque in *Masjid-al-Haram* in Makkah.
Khutbah	-	Lecture, sermon.
Kiswat	-	The cloth that covers the Ka'bah.
Manasik	-	Rites (rules).
Maqaam-Ibraheem	-	The station where Prophet Ibraheem stood while building the Ka'bah. (It was moved from its original place, which was next to the Ka'bah.)
Marwah	-	The hill where the *Sa'ee* ends.
Meqaat	-	Boundary of the area around Makkah, which a pilgrim should not pass without being in *Ihraam*.
Mihrab	-	The place where the *Imam* stands during congregation *Salah*.
Mimbar	-	The place where the *Imam* stands while delivering a *Khutbah* (sermon).
Mina (Muna)	-	One of the *Hajj* ceremonial sites, 8km from Makkah.
Muakkadah	-	Strongly recommended.
Muhrim	-	A person in *Ihraam*.
Mutamatti	-	A pilgrim performing *Hajj-Tamattu*.
Muzdalifah	-	One of the *Hajj* ceremonial sites, between Mina and Arafat.
Namirah	-	The Mosque in Arafat.
Nafl	-	Optional (voluntary).
Nafarah	-	Process of pilgrims departing from Arafat on the 9th.
Nahr	-	10th of Dhul-Hijjah.

Niqaab	-	Face covering for women.
Niyah	-	Intention.
Niy'at	-	Plural for *Niyah*.
Qasr	-	Cutting of one's hair.
Qaswaa	-	The name of the camel of the Prophet (ﷺ)
Qiblah	-	The direction of prayer for Muslims.
Qiran	-	*Hajj* with *Umrah* without coming out of *Ihraam* after *Umrah*.
Quba	-	The name of a mosque in Madinah.
Rakah	-	A unit of prayer.
Rak'at	-	Plural for *Rakah*.
Raml	-	A brisk walking in the first 3 rounds of *Tawaaf* while in *Ihraam*.
Rida	-	The upper cloth of the *Ihraam*.
Ramy	-	Stoning of the *Jamr'at*.
Rukn	-	Important pillar.
Rukn-al-Yamani	-	The corner of the Ka'bah which faces Yemen (South).
Sa'ee	-	The walk made between Safaa and Marwah.
Sadaqa	-	Anything given voluntarily in charity.
Safaa	-	The hill where you start your *Sa'ee*.
Shubriah	-	A stretcher-like chair, used to carry pilgrims for *Tawaaf*.
Sujood	-	Prostration in *Salah*.
Sunnah	-	Way of the Prophet (ﷺ).
Surah	-	A chapter of the Qur'an.
Shawaal	-	The 10th month of the Muslim (*Hijrah*) calendar.
Takbir	-	Saying "Allahu Akbar".
Talbiyah	-	The supplication one recites once in *Ihraam* and having made the intention.
Tamattu	-	*Hajj* performed with *Umrah* preceding it (two *Niy'at*).
Tarweya	-	Quenching (The 8th day of Dhul-Hijjah).
Tashreek	-	Drying of meat (11th, 12th & 13th of Dhul-Hijjah).
Tawaaf	-	Circumambulation of the Ka'bah.
Tawaaful-Ifadah	-	*Tawaaf* for *Hajj* (Pillar of *Hajj*).

Tawaaful- *Qudoom*	-	Welcome *Tawaaf*, done by *Ifrad* and *Qiran* pilgrims.
Tawaaful-Wadaa	-	Farewell *Tawaaf*.
Umrah	-	Minor *Hajj*, the combination of *Tawaaf* & *Sa'ee*.
Udhiya	-	Sacrifice of an animal on the day of *Eidul-Adha*.
Wajib	-	Obligatory, requisite.
Wudu	-	A prescribed method of washing to prepare for *Salah* (prayer). Ablution.
Wuqoof	-	Standing/staying (in Arafat on the 9th of Dhul-Hijjah).
Zamzam	-	The sacred well inside the *Haram* in Makkah. The water from it is commonly known as *Zamzam*.
Zawaal	-	When the sun is at its zenith. Midday.

Bibliography

(Referring to the English Translations/versions, where applicable)

1. Airlines, Saudi Arabian. *How to perform Umrah,* Published by Islamic awareness group in Saudi Arabian Airlines (Jeddah).

2. Al-Albaanee, Shaikh Muhammad Naasir-ud-Deen. *The Prophet's Prayer,* Published by Al-Haneef Publications (Suffolk) - 1993.

3. Al-Albaanee, Shaikh Muhammad Naasir-ud-Deen. *The Rites of Hajj & Umrah from the book of Sunnah and narrations from the pious predecessors,* Published by Jami'at Ihyaa' Minhaj Al-sunnah (U.K.) - 1994.

4. Al-Fouzan, Dr. Saleh bin Fouzan. *Explanation of what a Pilgrim and a Muslim performing Umrah should do,* Published by Al-Imam Mohammad bin Saud Islamic University - 1991.

5. Al-Jehani, Imam Ahmad (Lecturer). *Student Notes from Hajj Classes.* Notes taken: Author (Jeddah) - 1990-2004.

6. Al-Qahtaani, Sa'eed bin Ali bin Wahf. *Fortification of the Muslim through remembrance and supplication from the Qur'an & Sunnah,* Published by Dar-Al-Khair (Jeddah) - 1996.

7. Al-Shoura, Ibraheem. *Opinions of the selected sects about the Pilgrimage, the lesser Pilgrimage and the visit,* Published by Dar Al-Arabia (Lebanon).

8. Al-Uthaimeen, Shaikh Muhammad As-Salih. *How to perform the rituals of Hajj and Umrah,* Published by the Dawah Centre (Jeddah) - 1992.

9. Alli, Haroon Molvi Abdul Kader. *Hajj on your Own,* Published by Alli, Haroon Molvi Abdul Kader (South Africa) - 1992.

10. An-Nawawi, Imam Abu Zakariya Yahya bin Sharif. *Riyadus-Saleheen* Vols. 1 & 2, Published by Dar-al-Arabia (Lebanon).

11. Ash-Shuwaib, Fahd Ibn 'Abdir Rahman. *Sifat Wedoo' in Nabee*, Published by International Islamic Publishing House (Riyadh).

12. Author and fellow Pilgrims. *Actual Hajj experiences, Notes and Interview Material*, Notes taken: Author - 1989-2006.

13. Bin Baz, Shaikh Abdul Aziz Bin Abdullah. *Hajj, Umrah and Ziyarah (in light of the Qur'an and sunnah)*, Published by Maktaba Darussalam (Riyadh) - 1995.

14. Bin Baz, Shaikh Abdul Aziz bin Abdullah. *Important Fatwas regarding the rites of Hajj and Umrah*, Published by the Islamic Ministry (Riyadh) - 1993.

15. Fida, Abbas Abdullah. The Comprehensive Islamic Book Published by Al Haramein Trade Centre (Makkah).

16. Husain, Ibraheem. *Handbook of Hajj*, Published by Islamic Teaching Center (Indianapolis)

17. Kazi, Dr. Mashar U. *A Treasury of Hadith*, Published by Abul Qasim Publishing House (Jeddah) - 1992.

18. Khan, Dr. Muhammad Muhsin. *Summarized Sahih Al-Bukhari*, Published by Darus-Salam Publications (Riyadh) - 1994.

19. Khan, Dr. Muhammad Muhsin. *Sahih Al-Bukhari Volumes 1-9*, Published by Darul-Arabia Publishing (Beirut) - 1985.

20. Khan, Dr. Muhammad Muhsin. *The Noble Qur'an (in the English Language)*, Published by Darus-Salam Publications (Riyadh) - 1996.

21. KSA, Presidency of Islamic Research. *A Guide to Hajj, Umrah and visiting the Prophet's Mosque*,

Published by Presidency of Islamic Research (Riyadh) - 1991.

22. Matthews, Anis Daud. *A Guide for Hajj and Umrah,* Published by Kazi Publications (Pakistan) - 1979.

23. Nadvi, Maulana Mukhtar Ahmed. *Hajj and Umrah according to Sunnah,* Published by Abul Qasim Publishing House (Jeddah) - 1995.

24. Najaar, Sheikh A. *The Pilgrims' Companion, Hajj and Umrah made Easy,* Published by Al-Khaleel Publications (South Africa) - 1992.

25. Natal, Jamiate-Ulema-. 5 Days of *Hajj,* *Published by Islamic Propagation Centre (South Africa).*

26. Philips, Dr. Abu Ameenah Bilal. *Hajj and Umrah.* Published by Abul Qasim Publishing House (Jeddah) - 1993.

27. Philips, Dr. Abu *Ameenah Bilal. Islamic Rules on Menstruation and post-natal bleeding,* Published by Dar-al-Fatah Publications (Sharjah) - 1995.

28. Ra'oof, Moulana Mufti Abdur. *The first ten days of Zil-Hijja and Qurbani,* Published by Moosa Valli Publications (South Africa) - 1991.

29. Sabiq, As-Sayyid. *Fiqhus-Sunnah Volumes 1, 2 & 5,* Published by International Islamic Publishing House (Jeddah) - 1992.

30. Saqib, M.A.K. *A Guide to Prayer in Islam,* Published by Ta-Ha Publishers & Muslim Book Centre (UK) - 1986.

31. Siddiqi, Abdul Hamid. *Sahih Muslim Volumes 1-4,* Published by Darul-Arabia (Lebanon).

32. Zeno, Muhammad bin Jamil. *The Pillars of Islam & Iman,* Published by Darus-Salam Publications (Riyadh) - 1996.